VOLTRON® YEAR ONE

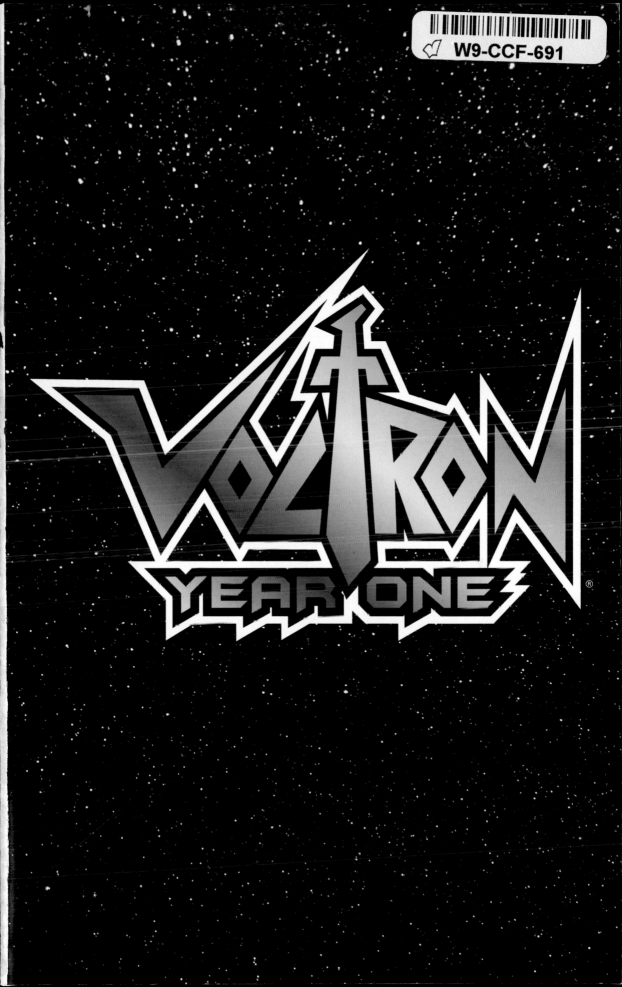

Written by:

BRANDON THOMAS

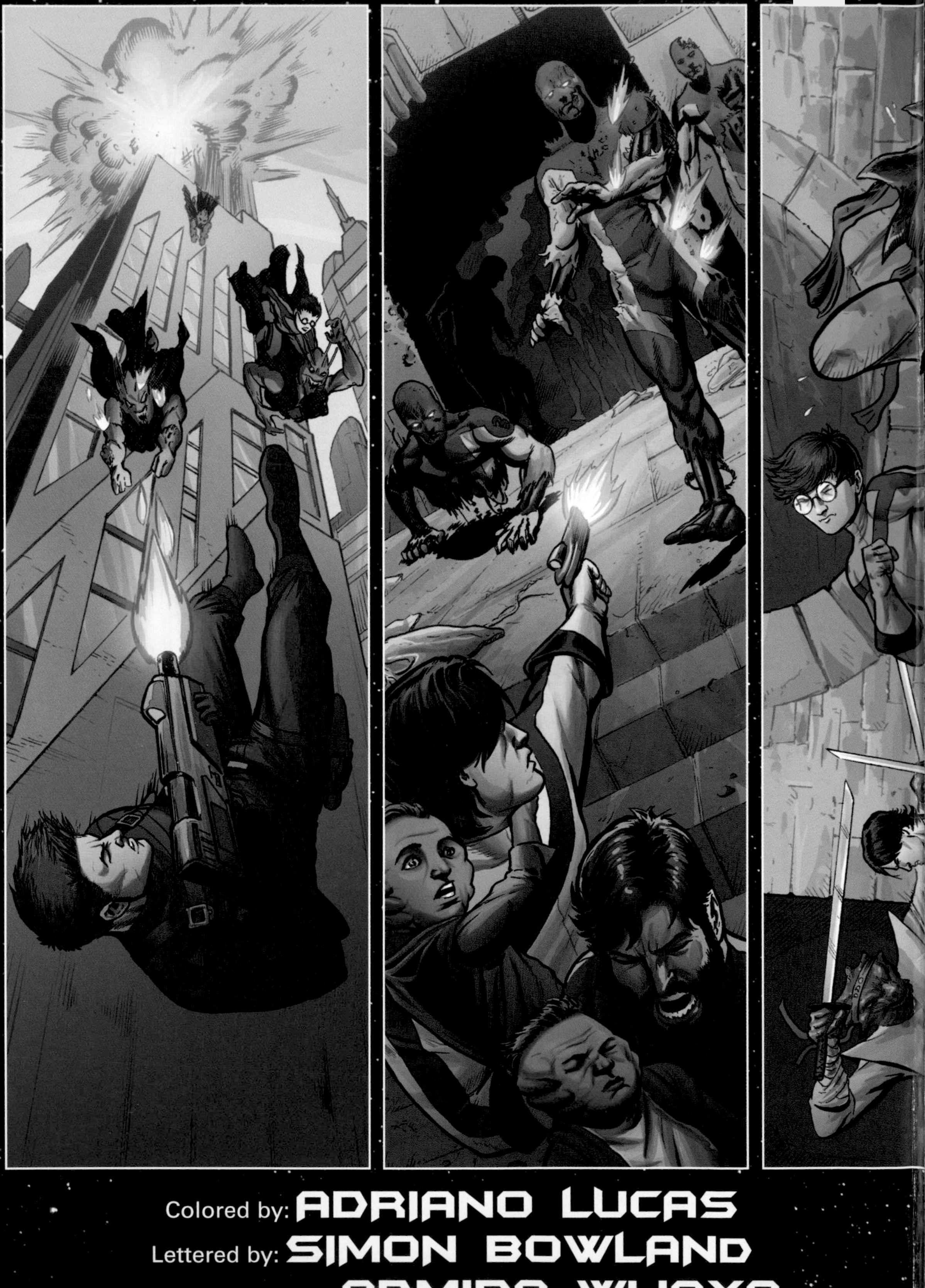

Colored by: **ADRIANO LUCAS**

Lettered by: **SIMON BOWLAND**

Collection cover by: **ADMIRA WIJAYA**

Illustrated by:

CRAIG CERMAK

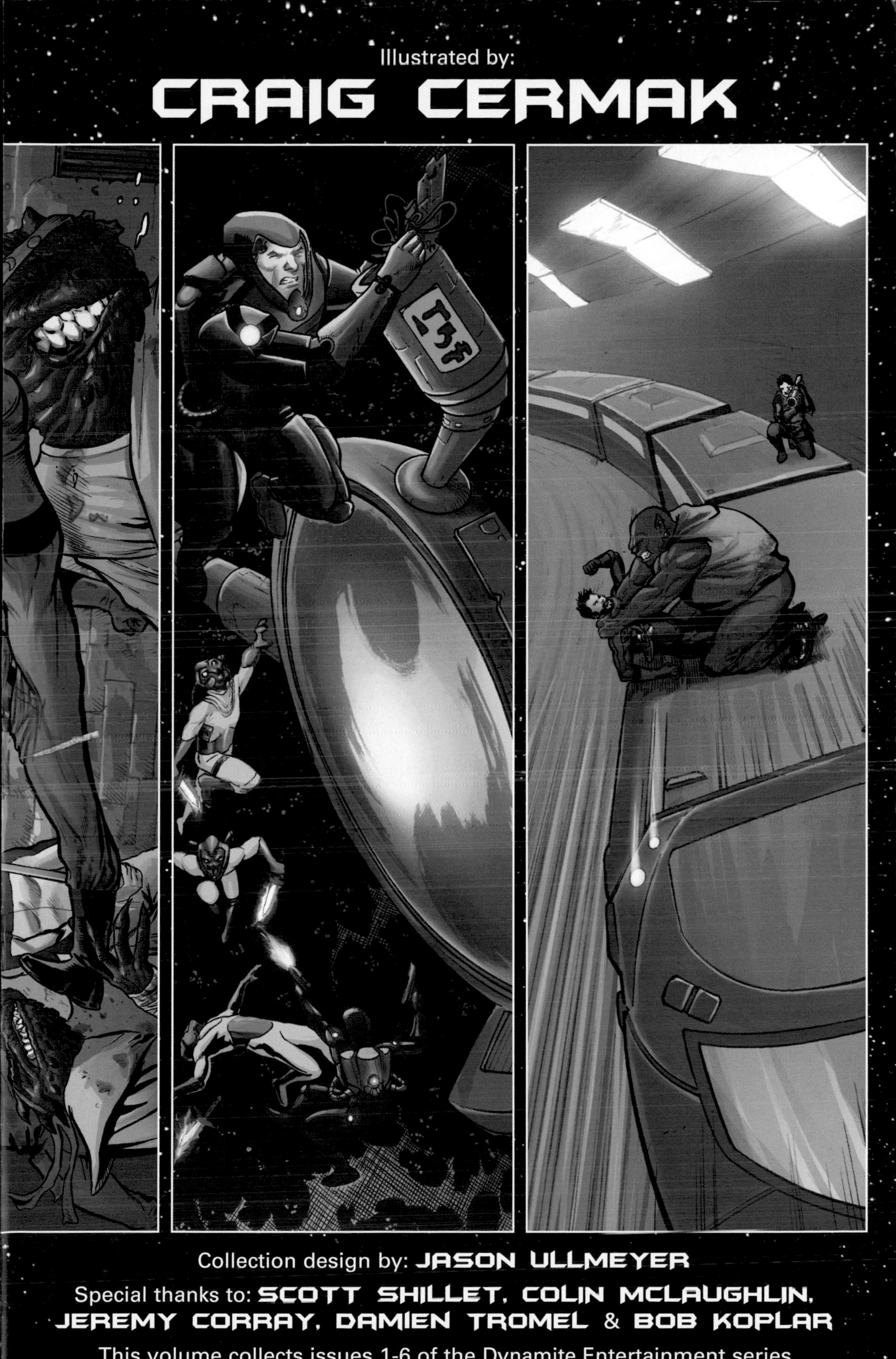

Collection design by: **JASON ULLMEYER**

Special thanks to: **SCOTT SHILLET, COLIN MCLAUGHLIN, JEREMY CORRAY, DAMIEN TROMEL & BOB KOPLAR**

This volume collects issues 1-6 of the Dynamite Entertainment series

BEFORE ARUS

BEFORE VOLTRON

THEY WERE SPACE EXPLORER
SQUADRON #686

DYNAMITE®

Visit us online at **www.DYNAMITE.net**
Follow us on Twitter **@dynamitecomics**
Follow us on Facebook **/DynamiteComics**

Nick Barrucci, President
Juan Collado, Chief Operating Officer
Joe Rybandt, Editor
Josh Johnson, Creative Director
Rich Young, Director Business Development
Jason Ullmeyer, Senior Designer
Josh Green, Traffic Coordinator
Chris Caniano, Production Assistant

wep world events productions

ClassicMedia™

First Printing
ISBN-10: 1-60690-365-9
ISBN-13: 978-1-60690-365-0
10 9 8 7 6 5 4 3 2 1

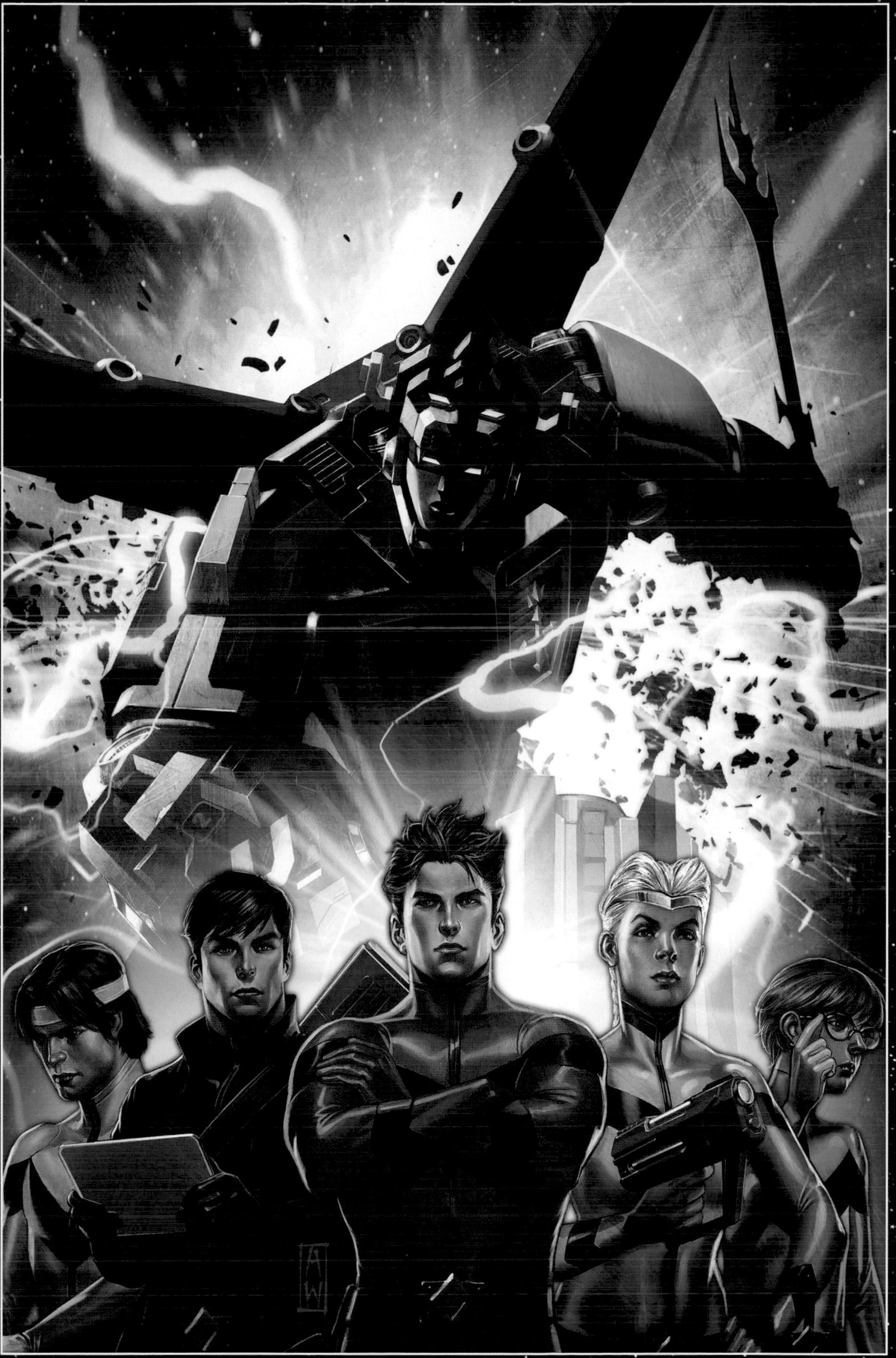
AW

Issue #1 cover by ADMIRA WIJAYA

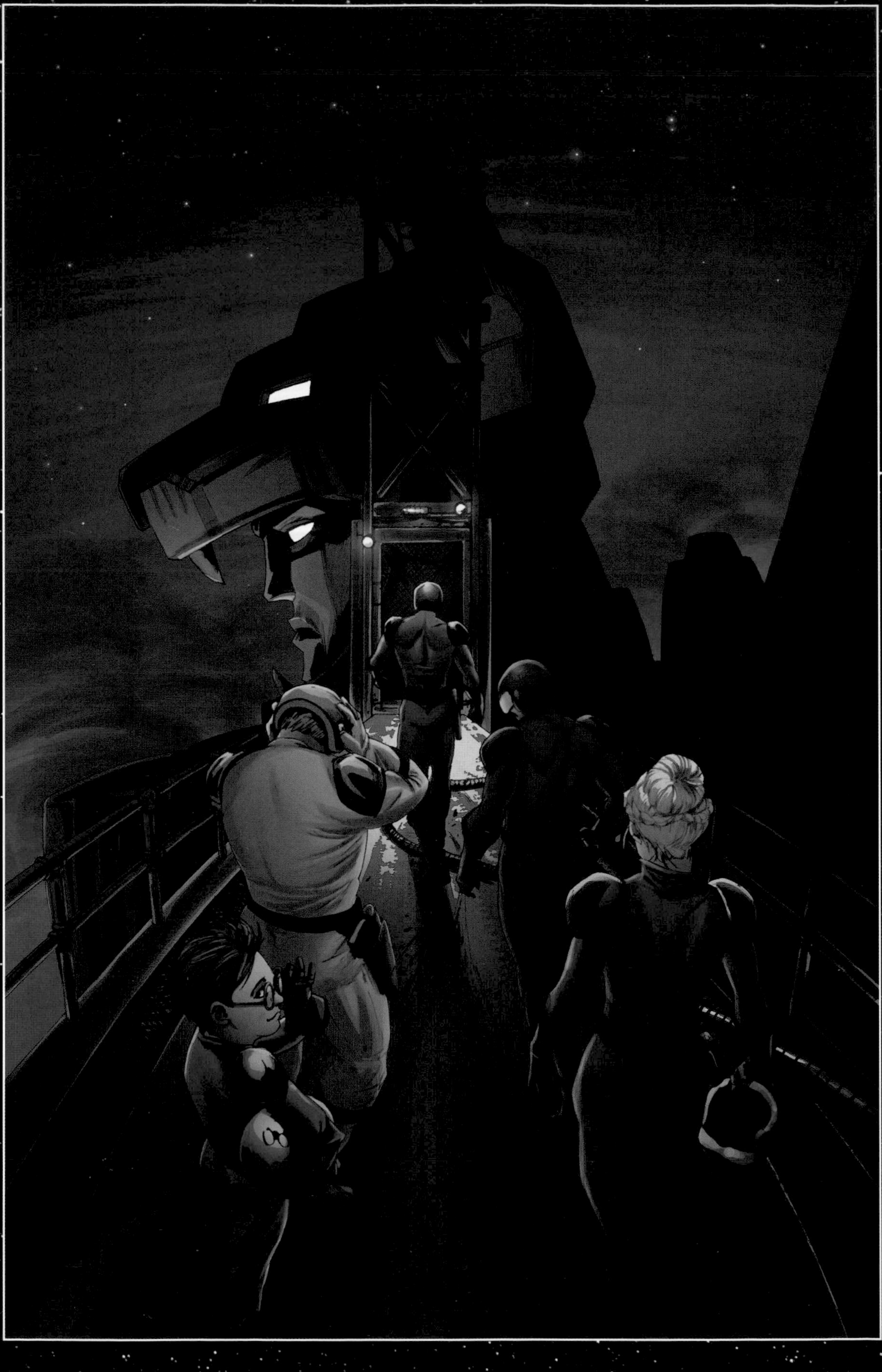

Issue #1 alternate cover by JONATHAN LAU

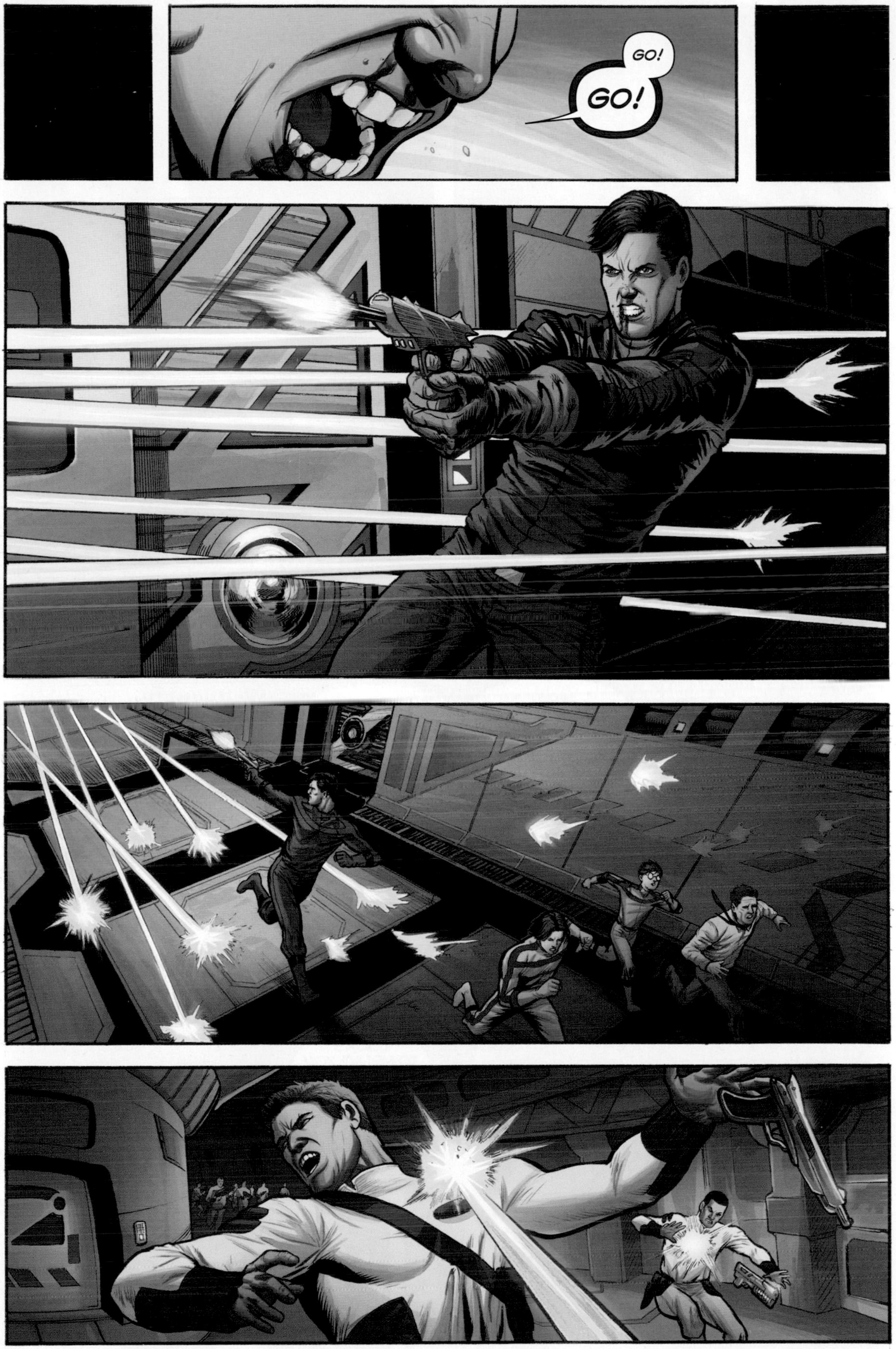
GO!
GO!

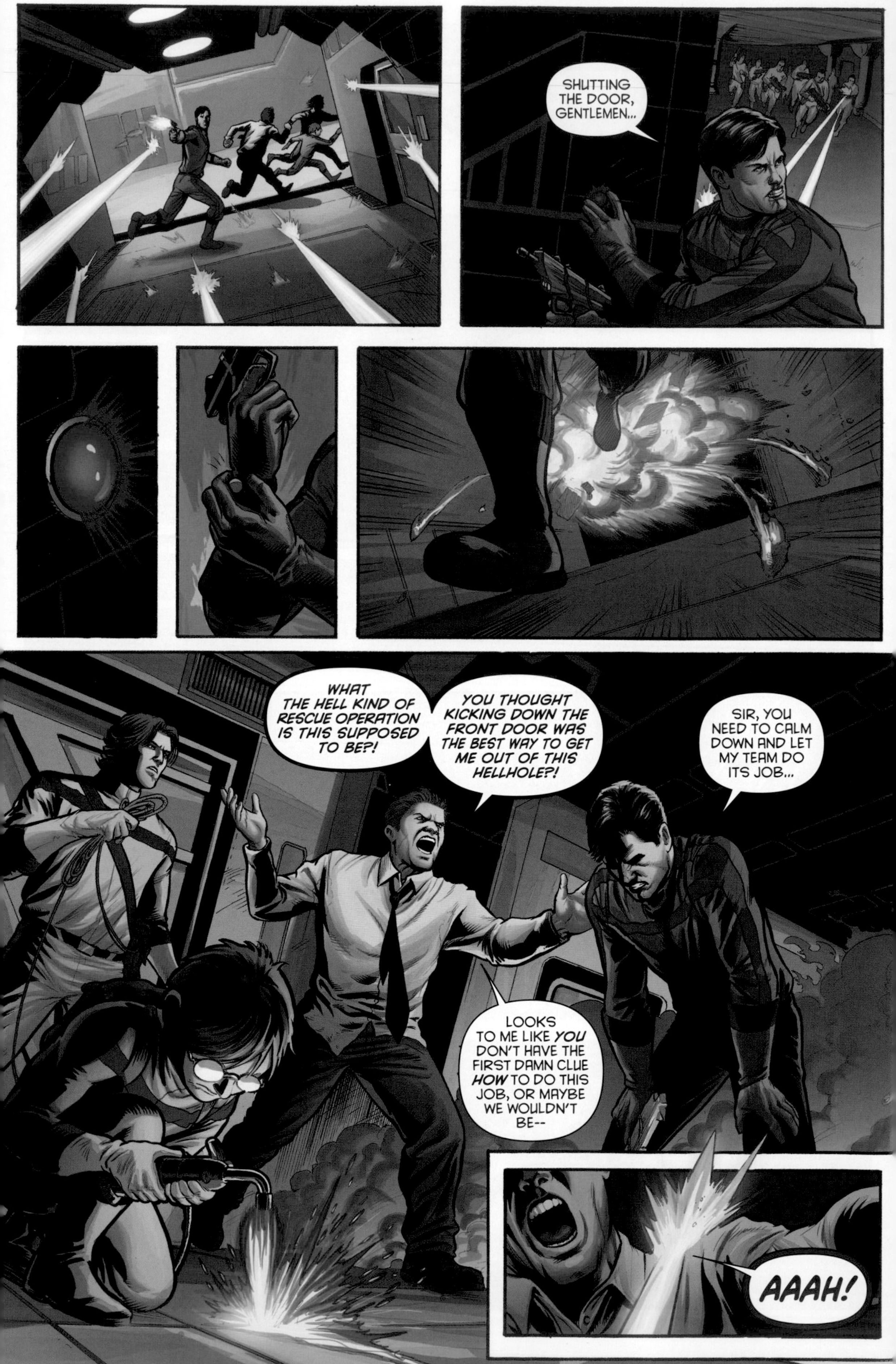
SHUTTING THE DOOR, GENTLEMEN...
WHAT THE HELL KIND OF RESCUE OPERATION IS THIS SUPPOSED TO BE?!
YOU THOUGHT KICKING DOWN THE FRONT DOOR WAS THE BEST WAY TO GET ME OUT OF THIS HELLHOLE?!
SIR, YOU NEED TO CALM DOWN AND LET MY TEAM DO ITS JOB...
LOOKS TO ME LIKE *YOU* DON'T HAVE THE FIRST DAMN CLUE *HOW* TO DO THIS JOB, OR MAYBE WE WOULDN'T BE--
AAAH!

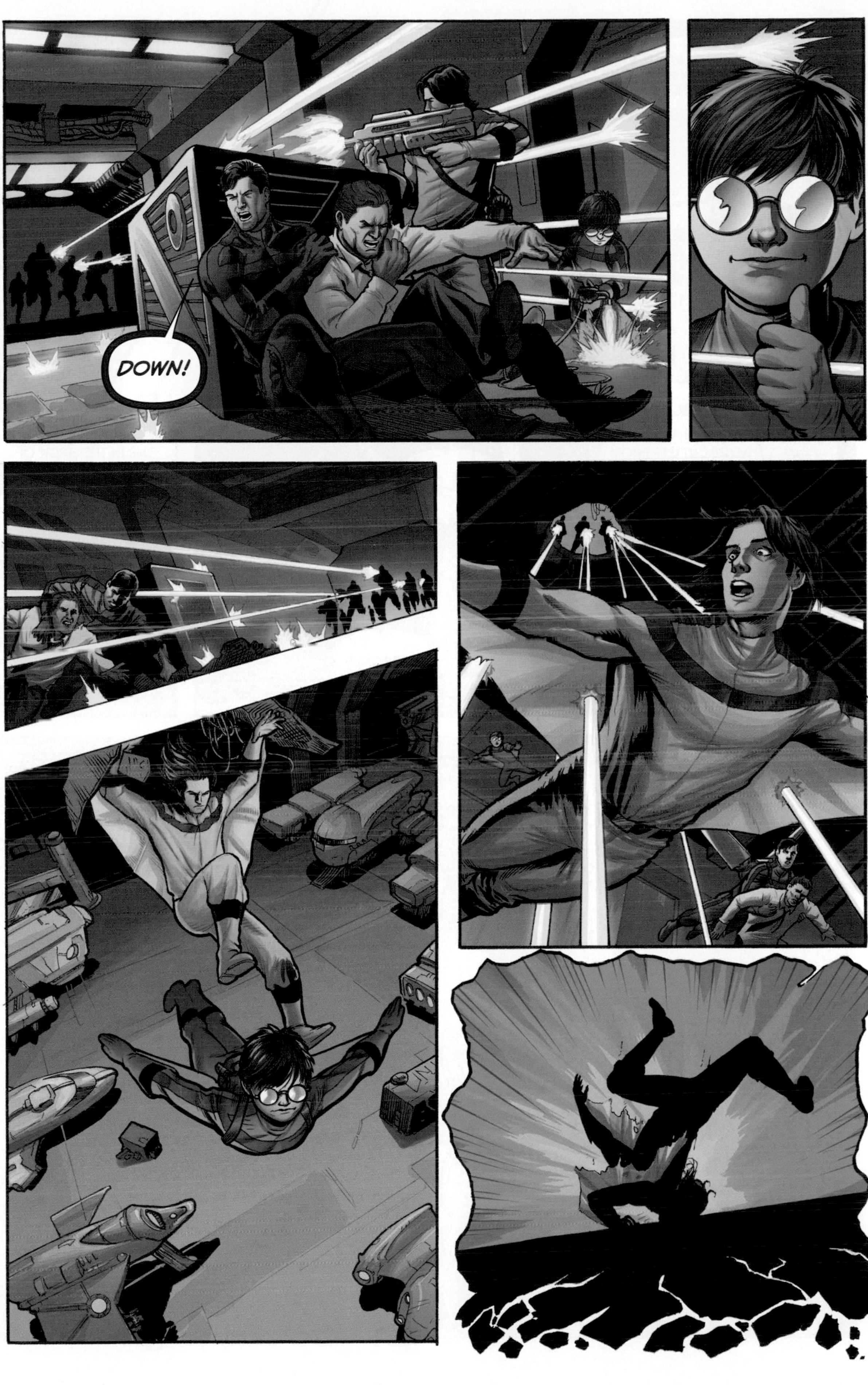
DOWN!

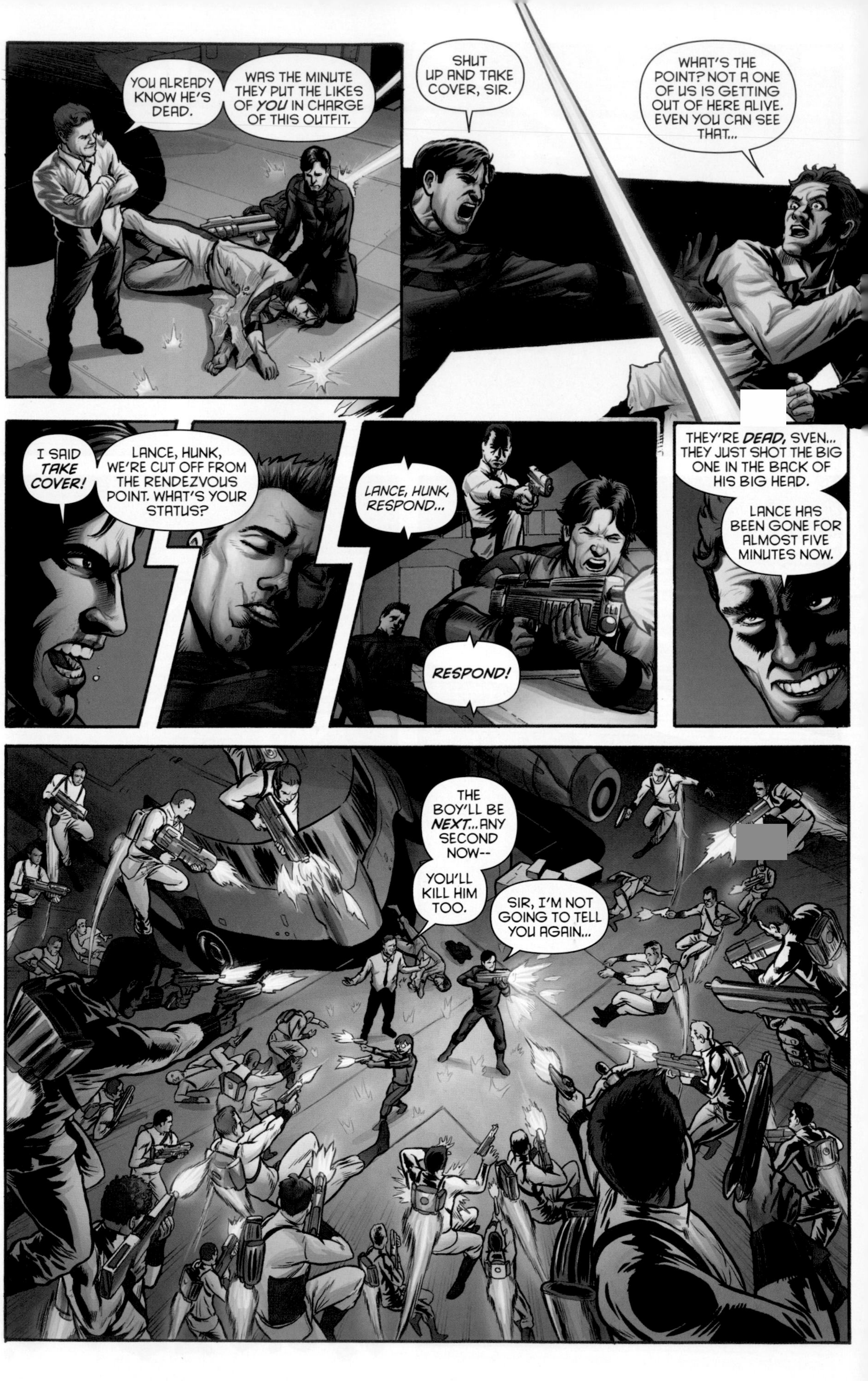
YOU ALREADY KNOW HE'S DEAD.
WAS THE MINUTE THEY PUT THE LIKES OF *YOU* IN CHARGE OF THIS OUTFIT.
SHUT UP AND TAKE COVER, SIR.
WHAT'S THE POINT? NOT A ONE OF US IS GETTING OUT OF HERE ALIVE. EVEN YOU CAN SEE THAT...
I SAID *TAKE COVER!*
LANCE, HUNK, WE'RE CUT OFF FROM THE RENDEZVOUS POINT. WHAT'S YOUR STATUS?
LANCE, HUNK, RESPOND...
RESPOND!
THEY'RE *DEAD,* SVEN... THEY JUST SHOT THE BIG ONE IN THE BACK OF HIS BIG HEAD.
LANCE HAS BEEN GONE FOR ALMOST FIVE MINUTES NOW.
THE BOY'LL BE *NEXT*... ANY SECOND NOW--
YOU'LL KILL HIM TOO.
SIR, I'M NOT GOING TO TELL YOU AGAIN...

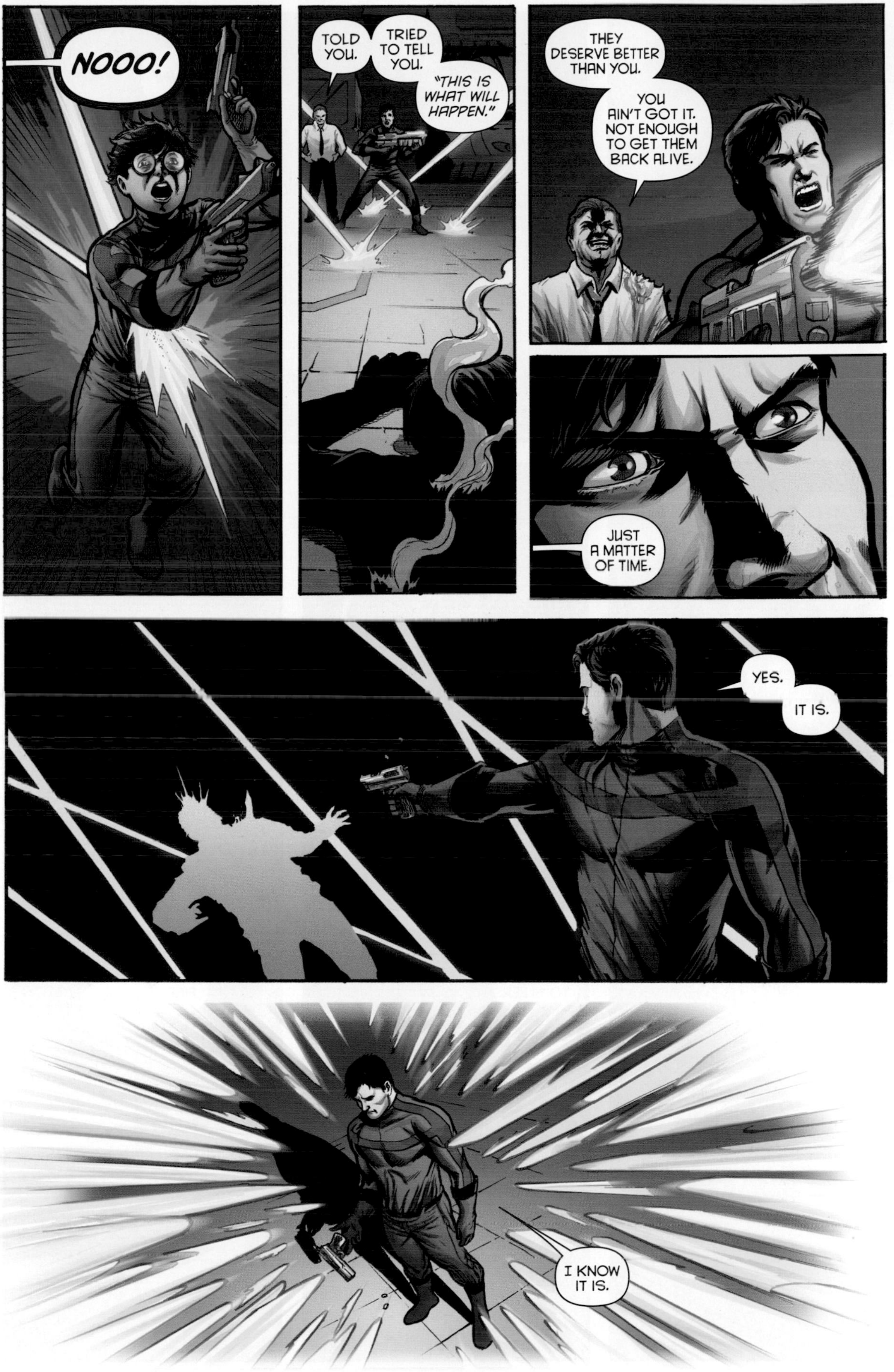
NOOO!
TOLD YOU.
TRIED TO TELL YOU.
"THIS IS WHAT WILL HAPPEN."
THEY DESERVE BETTER THAN YOU.
YOU AIN'T GOT IT. NOT ENOUGH TO GET THEM BACK ALIVE.
JUST A MATTER OF TIME.
YES.
IT IS.
I KNOW IT IS.

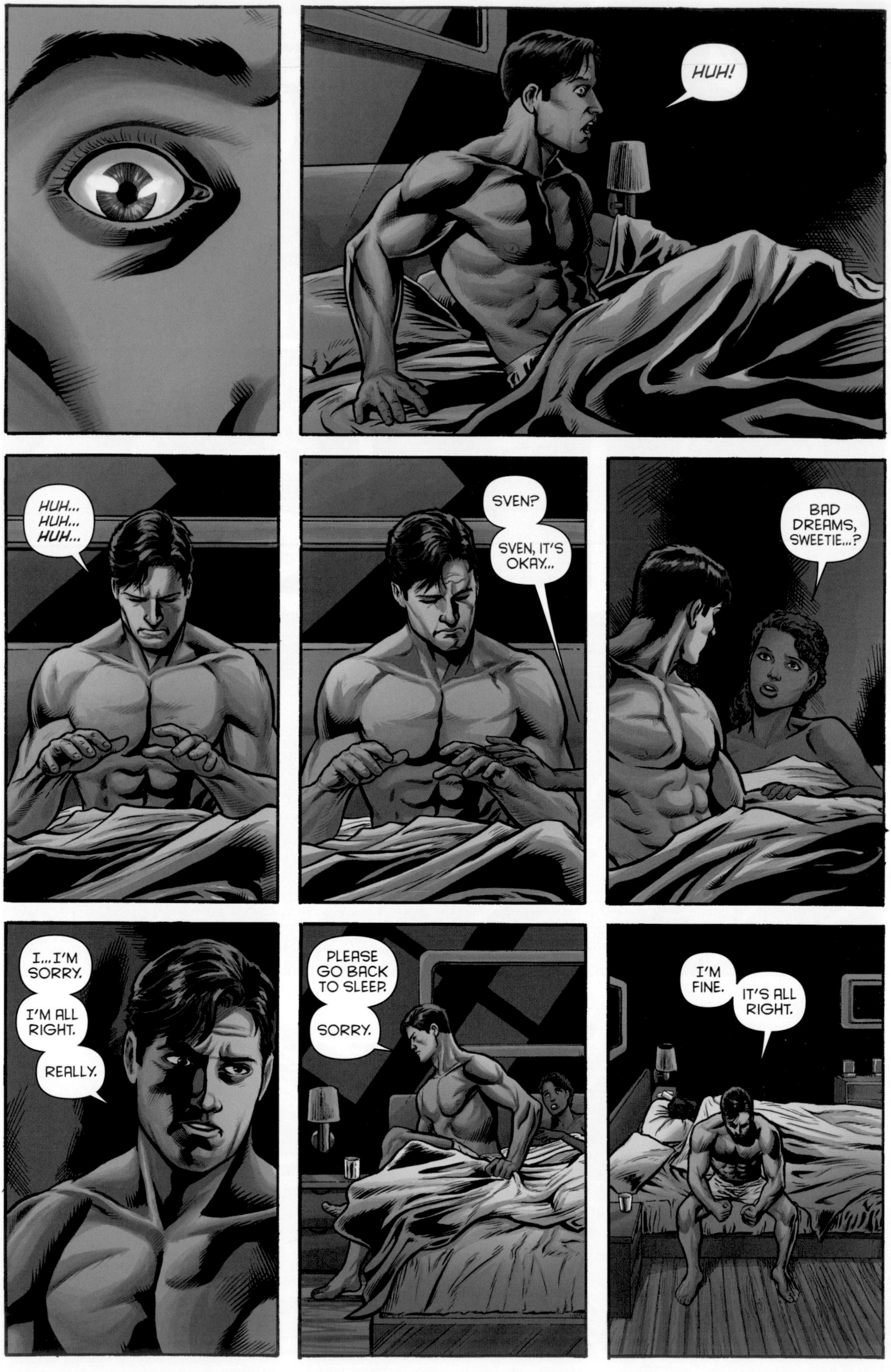
HUH!
HUH... HUH... HUH...
SVEN?
SVEN, IT'S OKAY...
BAD DREAMS, SWEETIE...?
I...I'M SORRY.
I'M ALL RIGHT.
REALLY.
PLEASE GO BACK TO SLEEP.
SORRY.
I'M FINE.
IT'S ALL RIGHT.

VOLTRON YEAR ONE

FEARLESS LEADER

1: THE CROWN

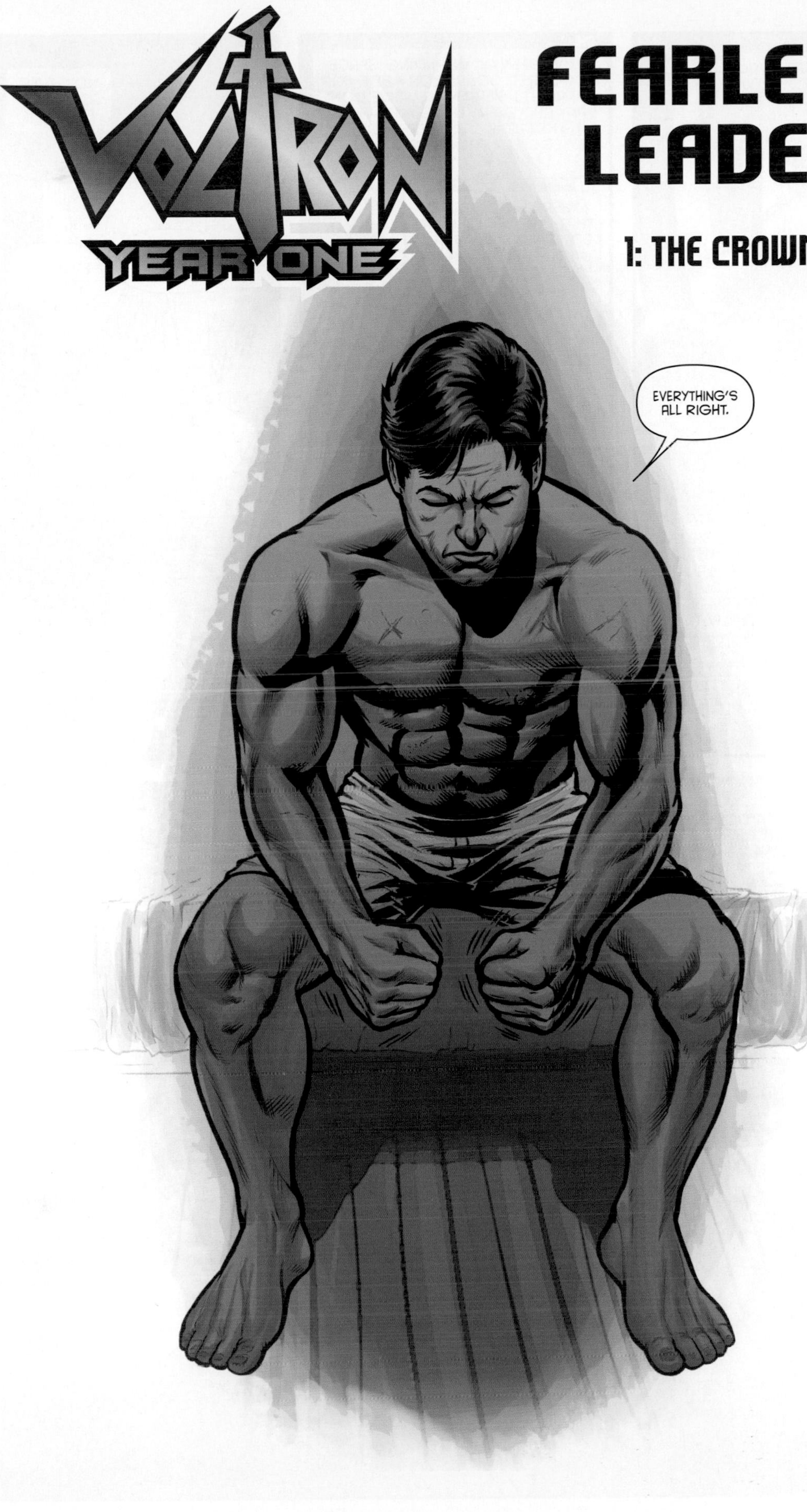
EVERYTHING'S ALL RIGHT.

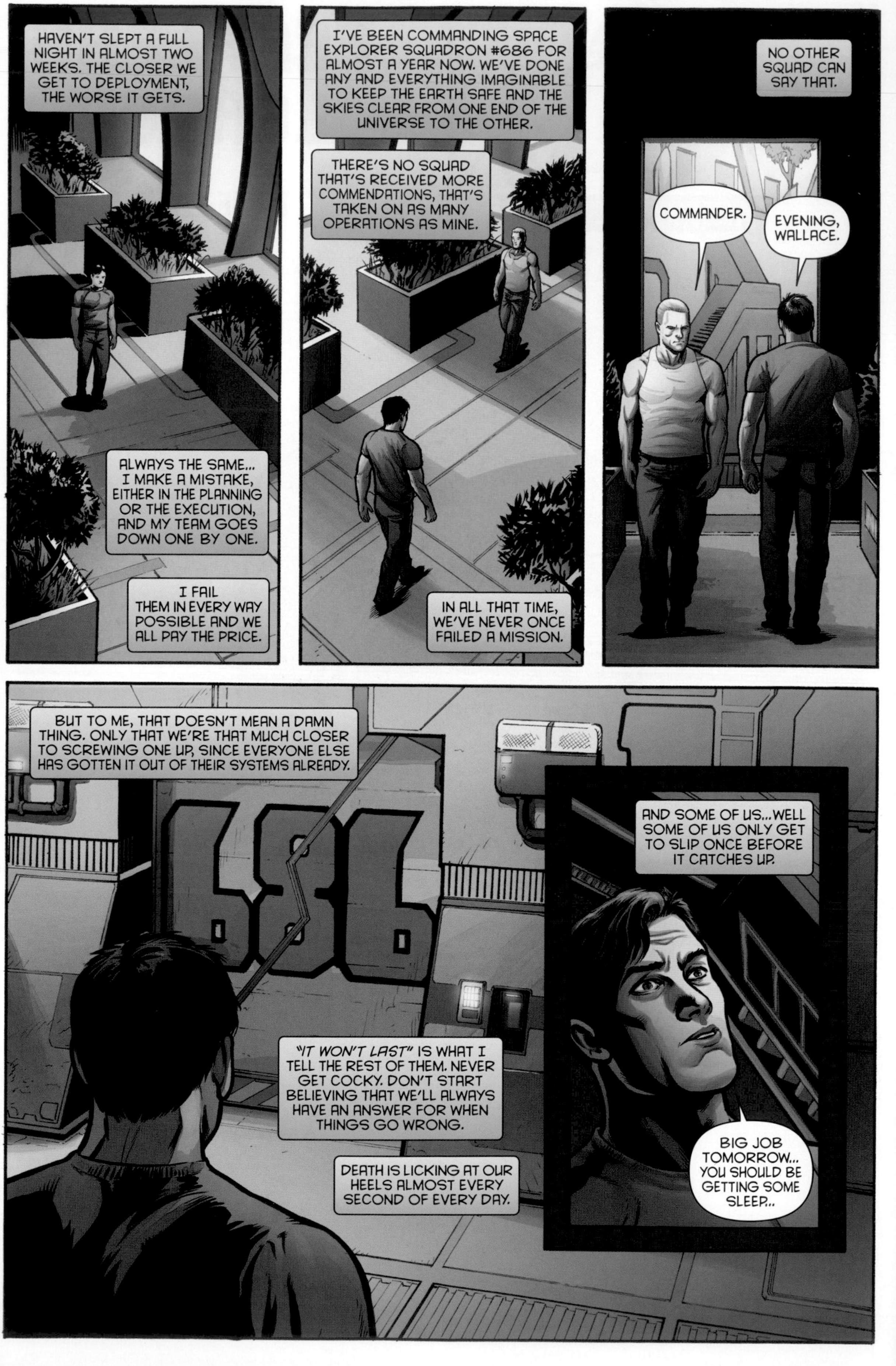
HAVEN'T SLEPT A FULL NIGHT IN ALMOST TWO WEEKS. THE CLOSER WE GET TO DEPLOYMENT, THE WORSE IT GETS.
ALWAYS THE SAME... I MAKE A MISTAKE, EITHER IN THE PLANNING OR THE EXECUTION, AND MY TEAM GOES DOWN ONE BY ONE.
I FAIL THEM IN EVERY WAY POSSIBLE AND WE ALL PAY THE PRICE.
I'VE BEEN COMMANDING SPACE EXPLORER SQUADRON #686 FOR ALMOST A YEAR NOW. WE'VE DONE ANY AND EVERYTHING IMAGINABLE TO KEEP THE EARTH SAFE AND THE SKIES CLEAR FROM ONE END OF THE UNIVERSE TO THE OTHER.
THERE'S NO SQUAD THAT'S RECEIVED MORE COMMENDATIONS, THAT'S TAKEN ON AS MANY OPERATIONS AS MINE.
IN ALL THAT TIME, WE'VE NEVER ONCE FAILED A MISSION.
NO OTHER SQUAD CAN SAY THAT.
COMMANDER.
EVENING, WALLACE.
BUT TO ME, THAT DOESN'T MEAN A DAMN THING. ONLY THAT WE'RE THAT MUCH CLOSER TO SCREWING ONE UP, SINCE EVERYONE ELSE HAS GOTTEN IT OUT OF THEIR SYSTEMS ALREADY.
686
"IT WON'T LAST" IS WHAT I TELL THE REST OF THEM. NEVER GET COCKY. DON'T START BELIEVING THAT WE'LL ALWAYS HAVE AN ANSWER FOR WHEN THINGS GO WRONG.
DEATH IS LICKING AT OUR HEELS ALMOST EVERY SECOND OF EVERY DAY.
AND SOME OF US...WELL SOME OF US ONLY GET TO SLIP ONCE BEFORE IT CATCHES UP.
BIG JOB TOMORROW... YOU SHOULD BE GETTING SOME SLEEP...

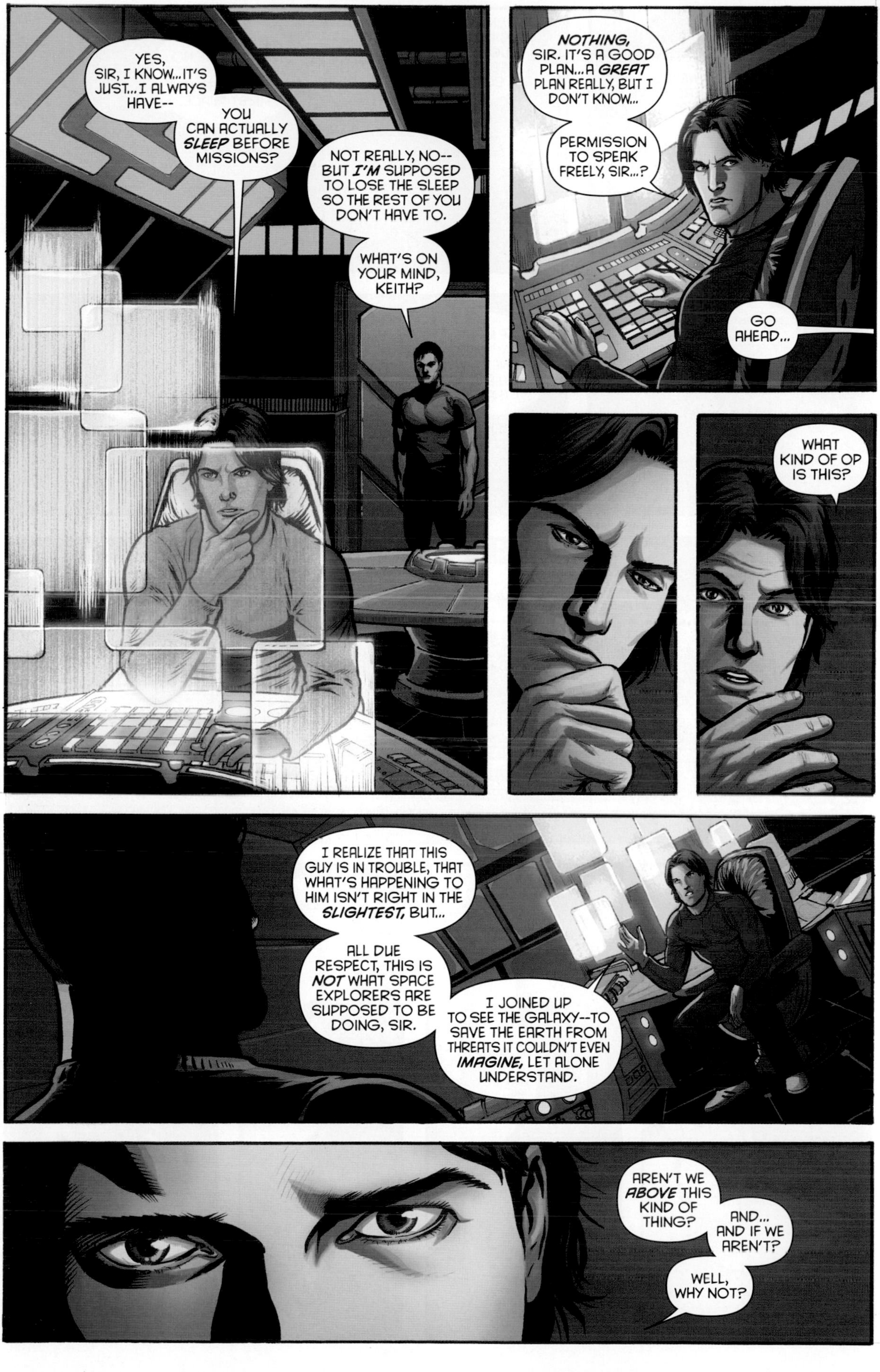
YES, SIR, I KNOW...IT'S JUST...I ALWAYS HAVE--
YOU CAN ACTUALLY SLEEP BEFORE MISSIONS?
NOT REALLY, NO-- BUT I'M SUPPOSED TO LOSE THE SLEEP SO THE REST OF YOU DON'T HAVE TO.
WHAT'S ON YOUR MIND, KEITH?
NOTHING, SIR. IT'S A GOOD PLAN...A GREAT PLAN REALLY, BUT I DON'T KNOW...
PERMISSION TO SPEAK FREELY, SIR...?
GO AHEAD...
WHAT KIND OF OP IS THIS?
I REALIZE THAT THIS GUY IS IN TROUBLE, THAT WHAT'S HAPPENING TO HIM ISN'T RIGHT IN THE SLIGHTEST, BUT...
ALL DUE RESPECT, THIS IS NOT WHAT SPACE EXPLORERS ARE SUPPOSED TO BE DOING, SIR.
I JOINED UP TO SEE THE GALAXY--TO SAVE THE EARTH FROM THREATS IT COULDN'T EVEN IMAGINE, LET ALONE UNDERSTAND.
AREN'T WE ABOVE THIS KIND OF THING?
AND... AND IF WE AREN'T?
WELL, WHY NOT?

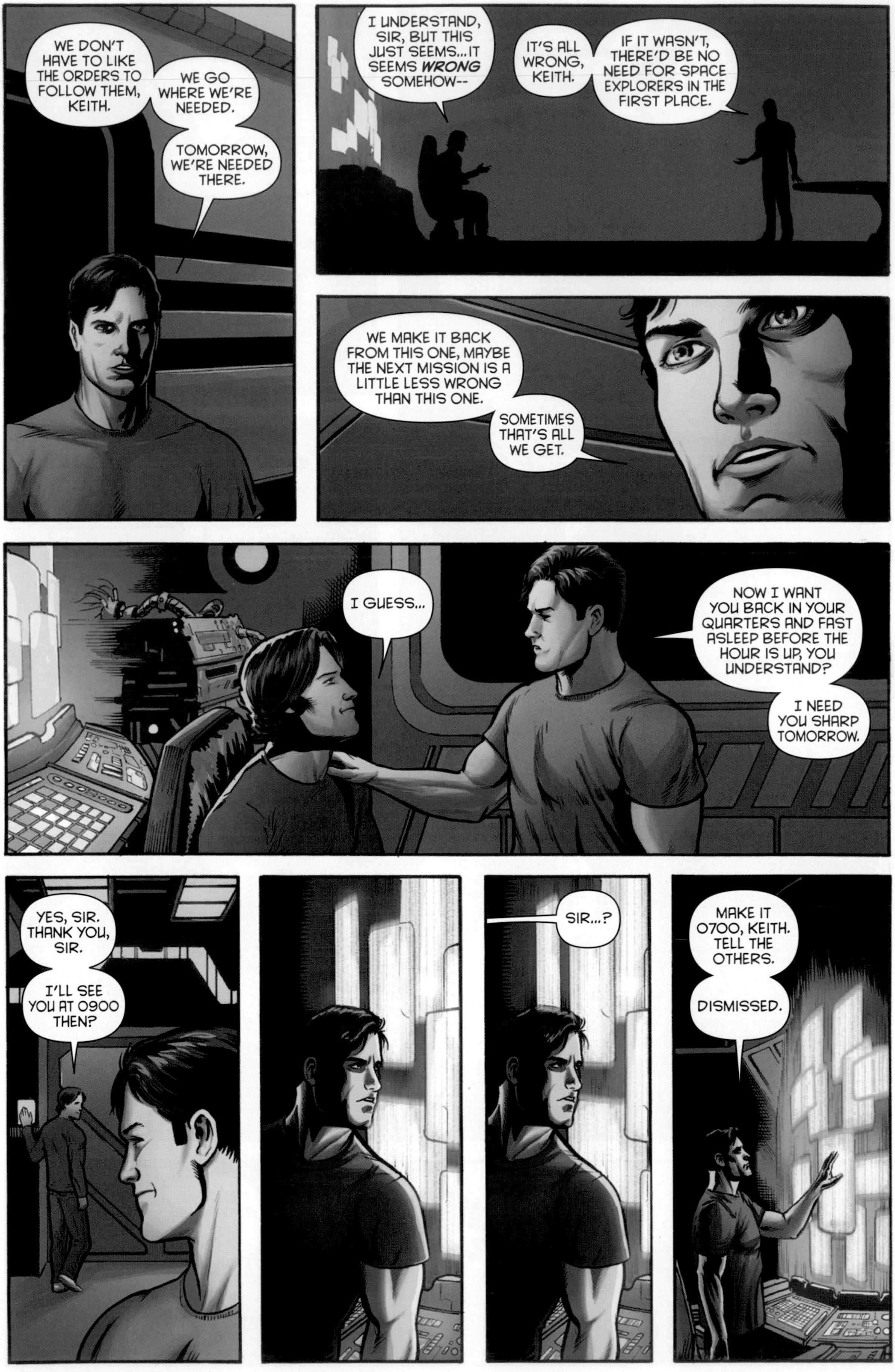
WE DON'T HAVE TO LIKE THE ORDERS TO FOLLOW THEM, KEITH.
WE GO WHERE WE'RE NEEDED.
TOMORROW, WE'RE NEEDED THERE.
I UNDERSTAND, SIR, BUT THIS JUST SEEMS... IT SEEMS **WRONG** SOMEHOW--
IT'S ALL WRONG, KEITH.
IF IT WASN'T, THERE'D BE NO NEED FOR SPACE EXPLORERS IN THE FIRST PLACE.
WE MAKE IT BACK FROM THIS ONE, MAYBE THE NEXT MISSION IS A LITTLE LESS WRONG THAN THIS ONE.
SOMETIMES THAT'S ALL WE GET.
I GUESS...
NOW I WANT YOU BACK IN YOUR QUARTERS AND FAST ASLEEP BEFORE THE HOUR IS UP, YOU UNDERSTAND?
I NEED YOU SHARP TOMORROW.
YES, SIR. THANK YOU, SIR.
I'LL SEE YOU AT 0900 THEN?
SIR...?
MAKE IT 0700, KEITH. TELL THE OTHERS.
DISMISSED.

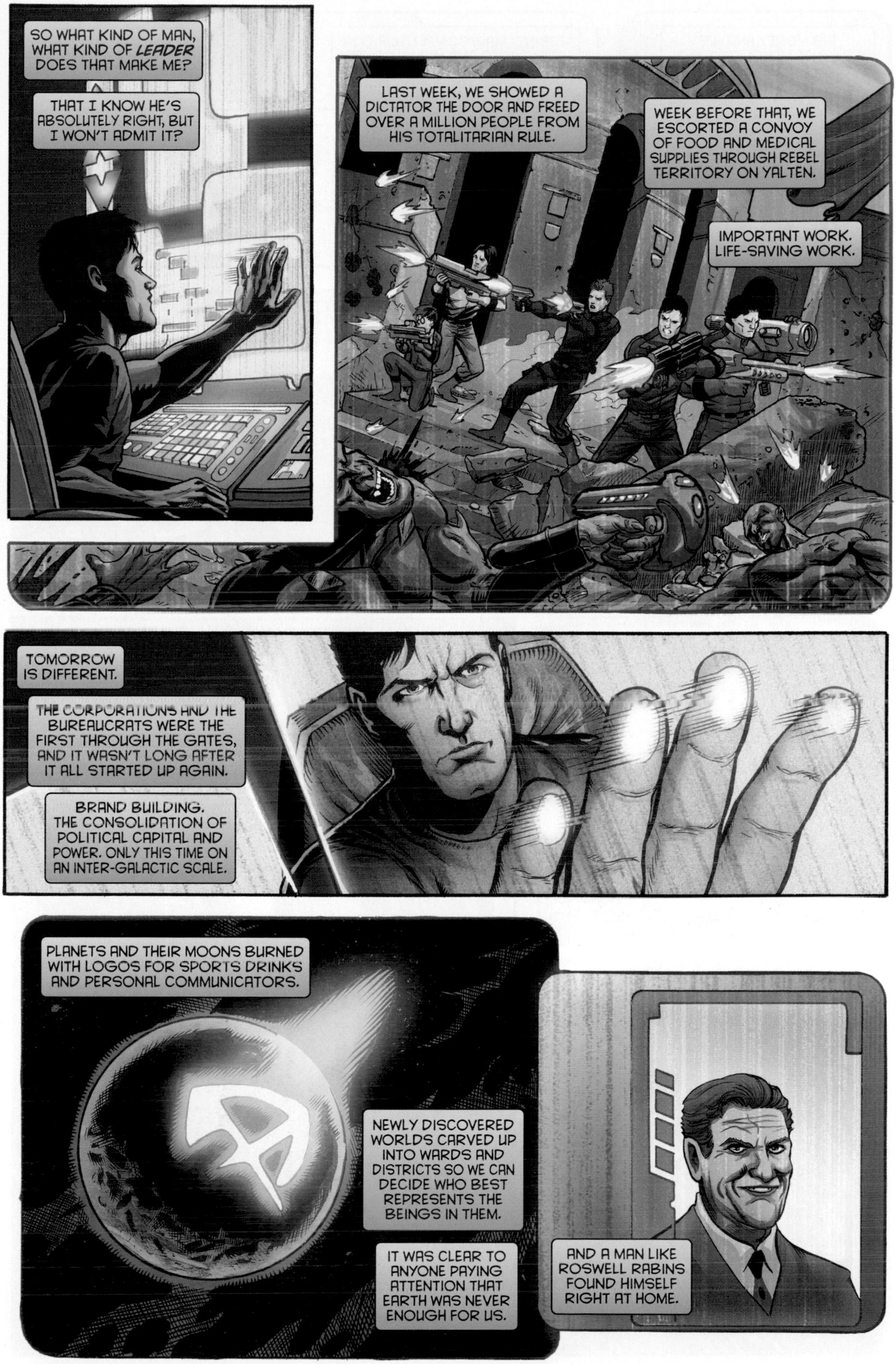
SO WHAT KIND OF MAN, WHAT KIND OF LEADER DOES THAT MAKE ME?
THAT I KNOW HE'S ABSOLUTELY RIGHT, BUT I WON'T ADMIT IT?
LAST WEEK, WE SHOWED A DICTATOR THE DOOR AND FREED OVER A MILLION PEOPLE FROM HIS TOTALITARIAN RULE.
WEEK BEFORE THAT, WE ESCORTED A CONVOY OF FOOD AND MEDICAL SUPPLIES THROUGH REBEL TERRITORY ON YALTEN.
IMPORTANT WORK. LIFE-SAVING WORK.
TOMORROW IS DIFFERENT.
THE CORPORATIONS AND THE BUREAUCRATS WERE THE FIRST THROUGH THE GATES, AND IT WASN'T LONG AFTER IT ALL STARTED UP AGAIN.
BRAND BUILDING. THE CONSOLIDATION OF POLITICAL CAPITAL AND POWER. ONLY THIS TIME ON AN INTER-GALACTIC SCALE.
PLANETS AND THEIR MOONS BURNED WITH LOGOS FOR SPORTS DRINKS AND PERSONAL COMMUNICATORS.
NEWLY DISCOVERED WORLDS CARVED UP INTO WARDS AND DISTRICTS SO WE CAN DECIDE WHO BEST REPRESENTS THE BEINGS IN THEM.
IT WAS CLEAR TO ANYONE PAYING ATTENTION THAT EARTH WAS NEVER ENOUGH FOR US.
AND A MAN LIKE ROSWELL RABINS FOUND HIMSELF RIGHT AT HOME.

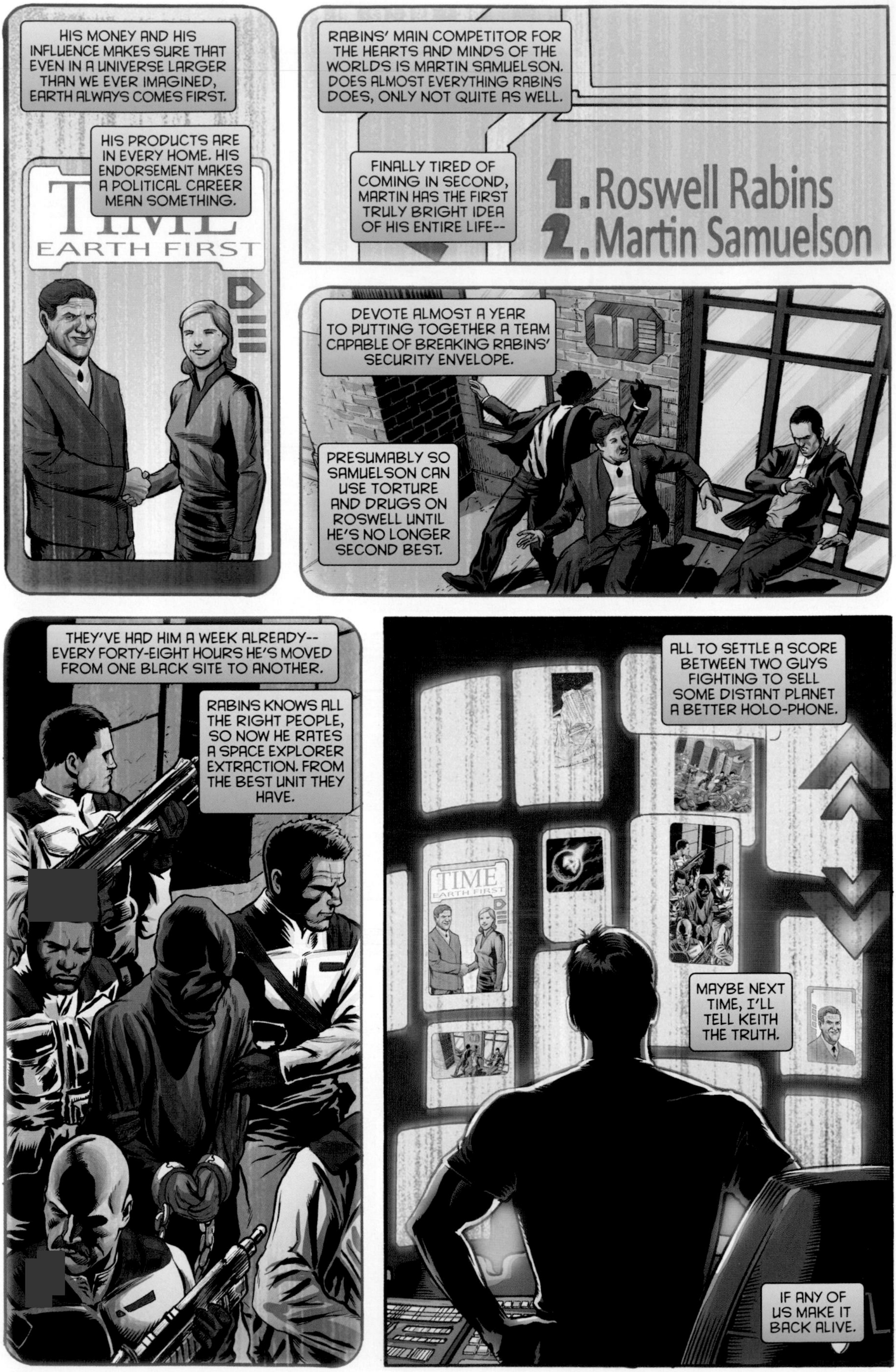
HIS MONEY AND HIS INFLUENCE MAKES SURE THAT EVEN IN A UNIVERSE LARGER THAN WE EVER IMAGINED, EARTH ALWAYS COMES FIRST.
HIS PRODUCTS ARE IN EVERY HOME. HIS ENDORSEMENT MAKES A POLITICAL CAREER MEAN SOMETHING.
TIME
EARTH FIRST
RABINS' MAIN COMPETITOR FOR THE HEARTS AND MINDS OF THE WORLDS IS MARTIN SAMUELSON. DOES ALMOST EVERYTHING RABINS DOES, ONLY NOT QUITE AS WELL.
FINALLY TIRED OF COMING IN SECOND, MARTIN HAS THE FIRST TRULY BRIGHT IDEA OF HIS ENTIRE LIFE--
1. Roswell Rabins
2. Martin Samuelson
DEVOTE ALMOST A YEAR TO PUTTING TOGETHER A TEAM CAPABLE OF BREAKING RABINS' SECURITY ENVELOPE.
PRESUMABLY SO SAMUELSON CAN USE TORTURE AND DRUGS ON ROSWELL UNTIL HE'S NO LONGER SECOND BEST.
THEY'VE HAD HIM A WEEK ALREADY-- EVERY FORTY-EIGHT HOURS HE'S MOVED FROM ONE BLACK SITE TO ANOTHER.
RABINS KNOWS ALL THE RIGHT PEOPLE, SO NOW HE RATES A SPACE EXPLORER EXTRACTION. FROM THE BEST UNIT THEY HAVE.
ALL TO SETTLE A SCORE BETWEEN TWO GUYS FIGHTING TO SELL SOME DISTANT PLANET A BETTER HOLO-PHONE.
TIME
EARTH FIRST
MAYBE NEXT TIME, I'LL TELL KEITH THE TRUTH.
IF ANY OF US MAKE IT BACK ALIVE.

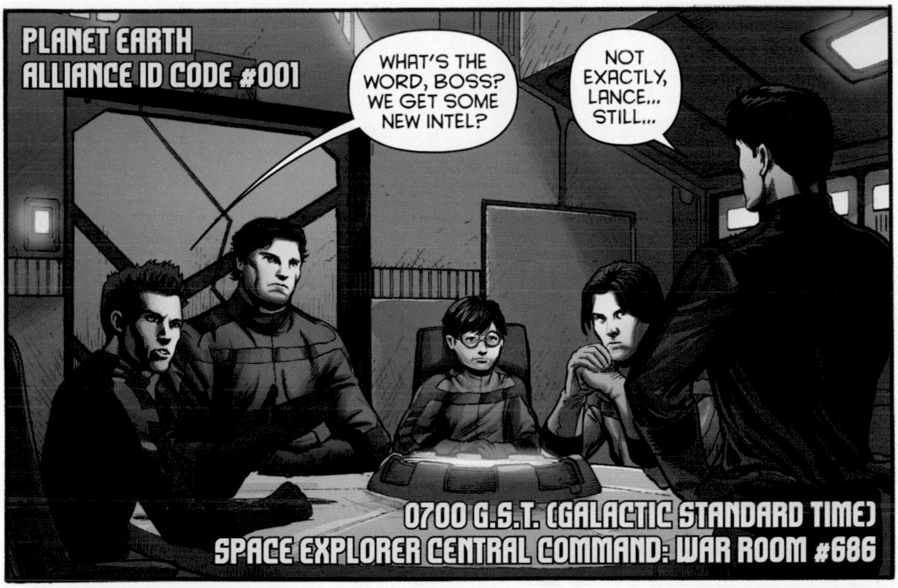
PLANET EARTH
ALLIANCE ID CODE #001
WHAT'S THE WORD, BOSS? WE GET SOME NEW INTEL?
NOT EXACTLY, LANCE... STILL...
0700 G.S.T. (GALACTIC STANDARD TIME)
SPACE EXPLORER CENTRAL COMMAND: WAR ROOM #686

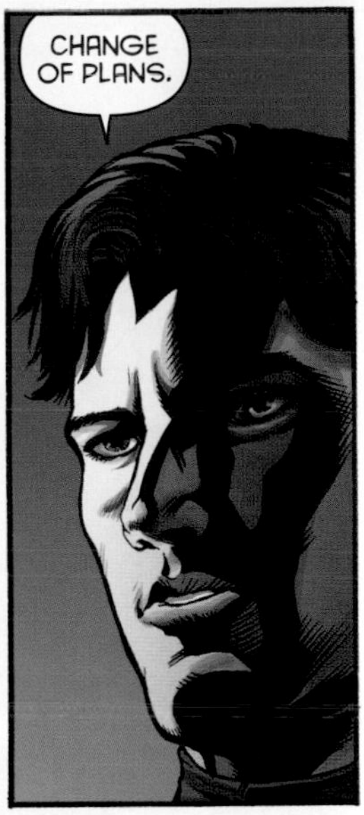
CHANGE OF PLANS.

MISSION PROFILE (REVISED):

OPERATION FIFTY-ONE

OBJECTIVES-

*INTERCEPT "M.T.S. INTERGALACTIC" PRIVATE SECURITY OPERATIVES PRE-DEPLOYMENT [VY1.1.13.14]
*PENETRATE BLACK SITE AND REVIVE COUNTER-INTELLIGENCE OPERATOR [VY1.1.16.17]
*MIRROR INTERNAL SECURITY SYSTEMS TO REMOTE OVERWATCH POST [VY1.1.20]
*LOCATE AND RETRIEVE PACKAGE [VY1.1.21]
*DEACTIVATE EXTERNAL SECURITY MEASURES AND COMMANDEER D-CLASS SHUTTLE [VY1.2.**]
*RENDEZVOUS AT EXTRACTION POINT WITH SUPPORT TEAM [VY1.2.**]

OPERATORS-

FIELD TEAM-
SVEN [COMMANDER].
LANCE [COMMANDER-2ND].
PIDGE [COUNTER-INTELLIGENCE].

SUPPORT TEAM-
KEITH [TACTICAL SUPPORT/OVERWATCH].
HUNK [EXTRACTION].

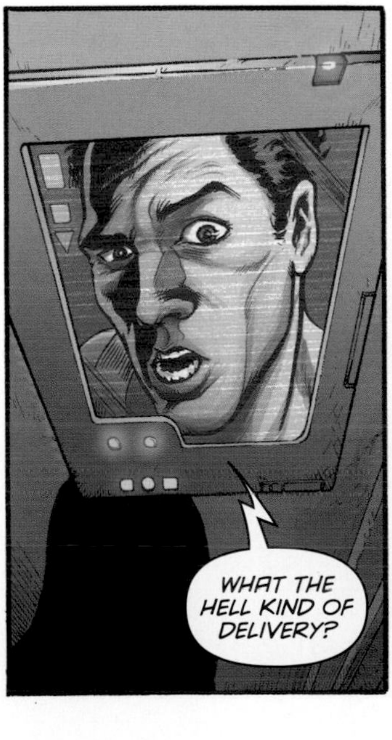
WHAT THE HELL KIND OF DELIVERY?

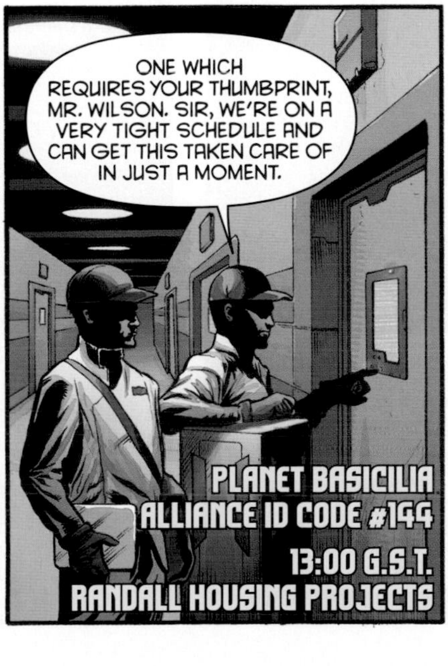
ONE WHICH REQUIRES YOUR THUMBPRINT, MR. WILSON. SIR, WE'RE ON A VERY TIGHT SCHEDULE AND CAN GET THIS TAKEN CARE OF IN JUST A MOMENT.
PLANET BASICILIA
ALLIANCE ID CODE #144
13:00 G.S.T.
RANDALL HOUSING PROJECTS

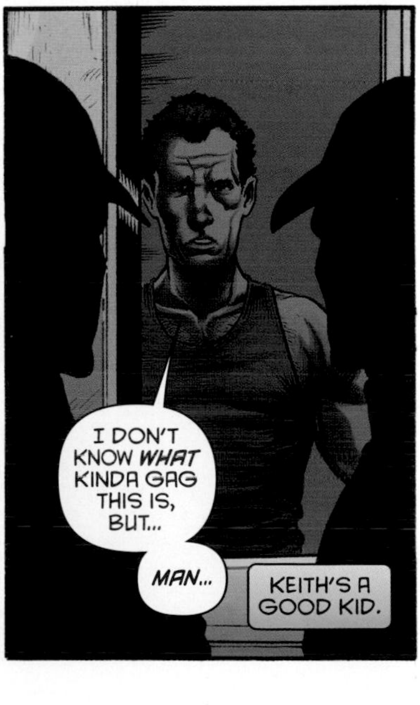
I DON'T KNOW *WHAT* KINDA GAG THIS IS, BUT...
MAN...
KEITH'S A GOOD KID.

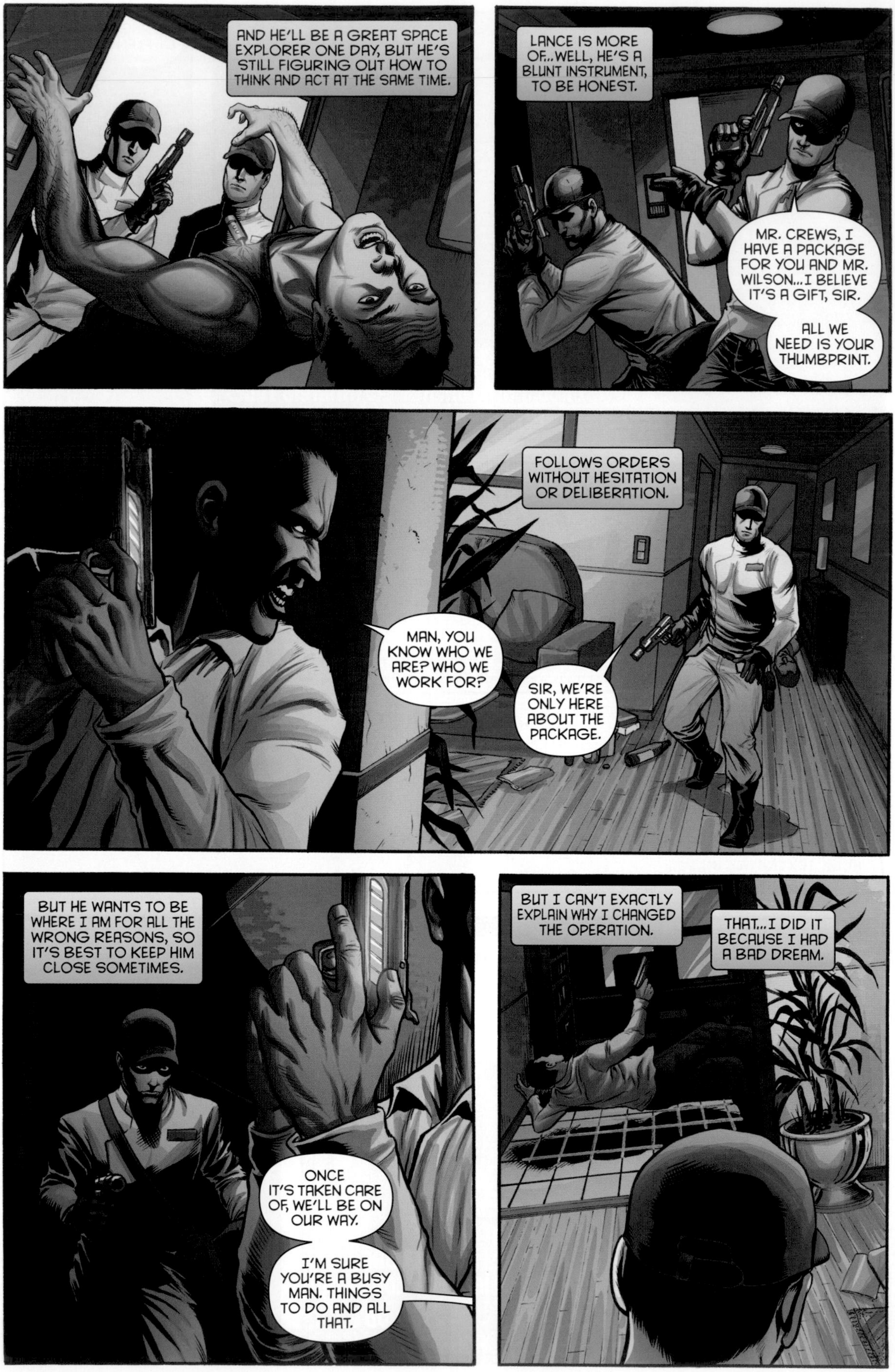
AND HE'LL BE A GREAT SPACE EXPLORER ONE DAY, BUT HE'S STILL FIGURING OUT HOW TO THINK AND ACT AT THE SAME TIME.
LANCE IS MORE OF...WELL, HE'S A BLUNT INSTRUMENT, TO BE HONEST.
MR. CREWS, I HAVE A PACKAGE FOR YOU AND MR. WILSON...I BELIEVE IT'S A GIFT, SIR.
ALL WE NEED IS YOUR THUMBPRINT.
FOLLOWS ORDERS WITHOUT HESITATION OR DELIBERATION.
MAN, YOU KNOW WHO WE ARE? WHO WE WORK FOR?
SIR, WE'RE ONLY HERE ABOUT THE PACKAGE.
BUT HE WANTS TO BE WHERE I AM FOR ALL THE WRONG REASONS, SO IT'S BEST TO KEEP HIM CLOSE SOMETIMES.
ONCE IT'S TAKEN CARE OF, WE'LL BE ON OUR WAY.
I'M SURE YOU'RE A BUSY MAN. THINGS TO DO AND ALL THAT.
BUT I CAN'T EXACTLY EXPLAIN WHY I CHANGED THE OPERATION.
THAT...I DID IT BECAUSE I HAD A BAD DREAM.

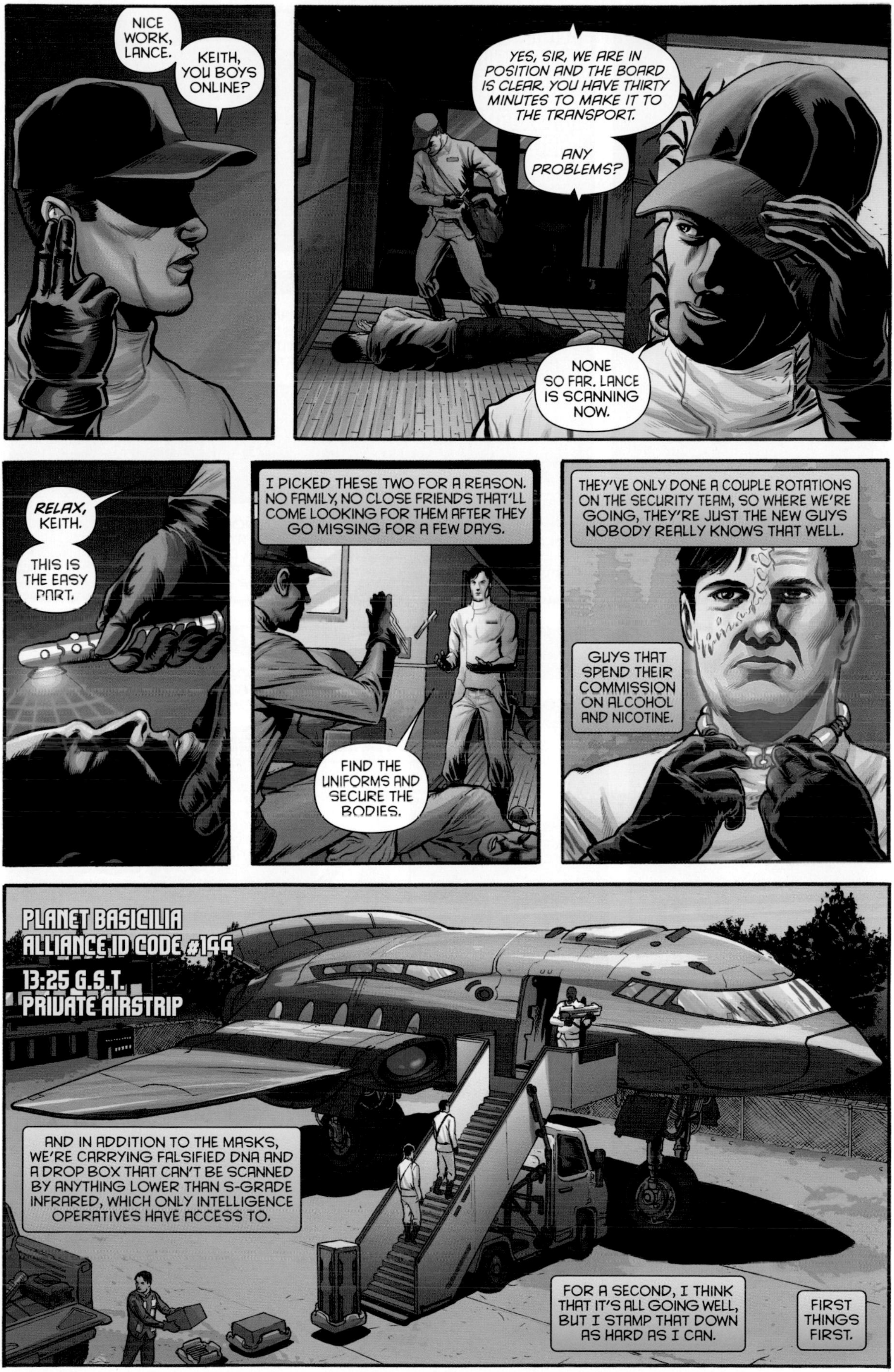
NICE WORK, LANCE.
KEITH, YOU BOYS ONLINE?
YES, SIR, WE ARE IN POSITION AND THE BOARD IS CLEAR. YOU HAVE THIRTY MINUTES TO MAKE IT TO THE TRANSPORT.
ANY PROBLEMS?
NONE SO FAR. LANCE IS SCANNING NOW.
RELAX, KEITH.
THIS IS THE EASY PART.
I PICKED THESE TWO FOR A REASON. NO FAMILY, NO CLOSE FRIENDS THAT'LL COME LOOKING FOR THEM AFTER THEY GO MISSING FOR A FEW DAYS.
FIND THE UNIFORMS AND SECURE THE BODIES.
THEY'VE ONLY DONE A COUPLE ROTATIONS ON THE SECURITY TEAM, SO WHERE WE'RE GOING, THEY'RE JUST THE NEW GUYS NOBODY REALLY KNOWS THAT WELL.
GUYS THAT SPEND THEIR COMMISSION ON ALCOHOL AND NICOTINE.
PLANET BASICILIA
ALLIANCE ID CODE #144
13:25 G.S.T.
PRIVATE AIRSTRIP
AND IN ADDITION TO THE MASKS, WE'RE CARRYING FALSIFIED DNA AND A DROP BOX THAT CAN'T BE SCANNED BY ANYTHING LOWER THAN S-GRADE INFRARED, WHICH ONLY INTELLIGENCE OPERATIVES HAVE ACCESS TO.
FOR A SECOND, I THINK THAT IT'S ALL GOING WELL, BUT I STAMP THAT DOWN AS HARD AS I CAN.
FIRST THINGS FIRST.

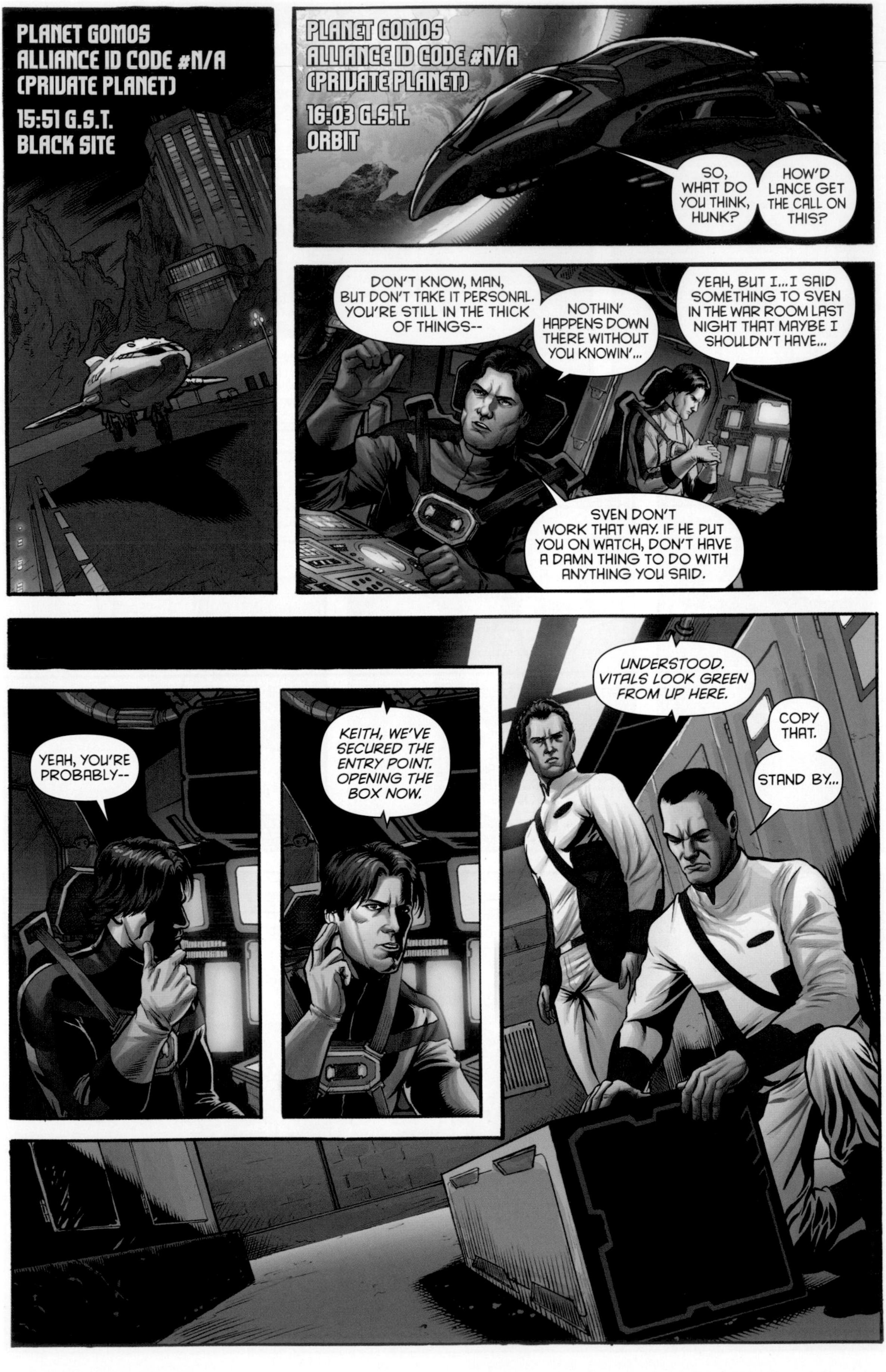
PLANET GOMOS
ALLIANCE ID CODE #N/A
(PRIVATE PLANET)
15:51 G.S.T.
BLACK SITE
PLANET GOMOS
ALLIANCE ID CODE #N/A
(PRIVATE PLANET)
16:03 G.S.T.
ORBIT
SO, WHAT DO YOU THINK, HUNK?
HOW'D LANCE GET THE CALL ON THIS?
DON'T KNOW, MAN, BUT DON'T TAKE IT PERSONAL. YOU'RE STILL IN THE THICK OF THINGS--
NOTHIN' HAPPENS DOWN THERE WITHOUT YOU KNOWIN'...
YEAH, BUT I...I SAID SOMETHING TO SVEN IN THE WAR ROOM LAST NIGHT THAT MAYBE I SHOULDN'T HAVE...
SVEN DON'T WORK THAT WAY. IF HE PUT YOU ON WATCH, DON'T HAVE A DAMN THING TO DO WITH ANYTHING YOU SAID.
YEAH, YOU'RE PROBABLY--
KEITH, WE'VE SECURED THE ENTRY POINT. OPENING THE BOX NOW.
UNDERSTOOD. VITALS LOOK GREEN FROM UP HERE.
COPY THAT.
STAND BY...

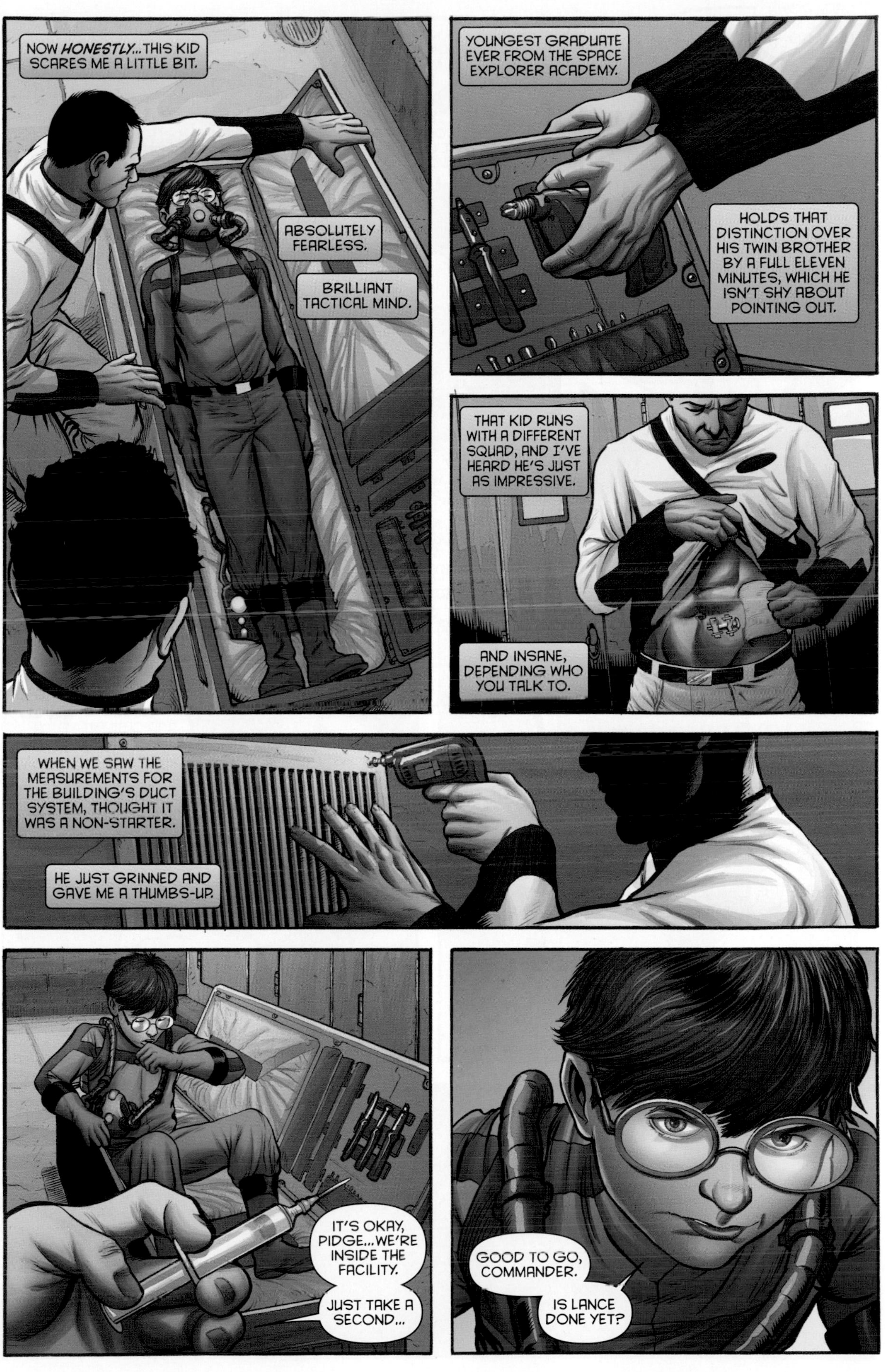
NOW *HONESTLY*... THIS KID SCARES ME A LITTLE BIT.
ABSOLUTELY FEARLESS.
BRILLIANT TACTICAL MIND.
YOUNGEST GRADUATE EVER FROM THE SPACE EXPLORER ACADEMY.
HOLDS THAT DISTINCTION OVER HIS TWIN BROTHER BY A FULL ELEVEN MINUTES, WHICH HE ISN'T SHY ABOUT POINTING OUT.
THAT KID RUNS WITH A DIFFERENT SQUAD, AND I'VE HEARD HE'S JUST AS IMPRESSIVE.
AND INSANE, DEPENDING WHO YOU TALK TO.
WHEN WE SAW THE MEASUREMENTS FOR THE BUILDING'S DUCT SYSTEM, THOUGHT IT WAS A NON-STARTER.
HE JUST GRINNED AND GAVE ME A THUMBS-UP.
IT'S OKAY, PIDGE... WE'RE INSIDE THE FACILITY.
JUST TAKE A SECOND...
GOOD TO GO, COMMANDER.
IS LANCE DONE YET?

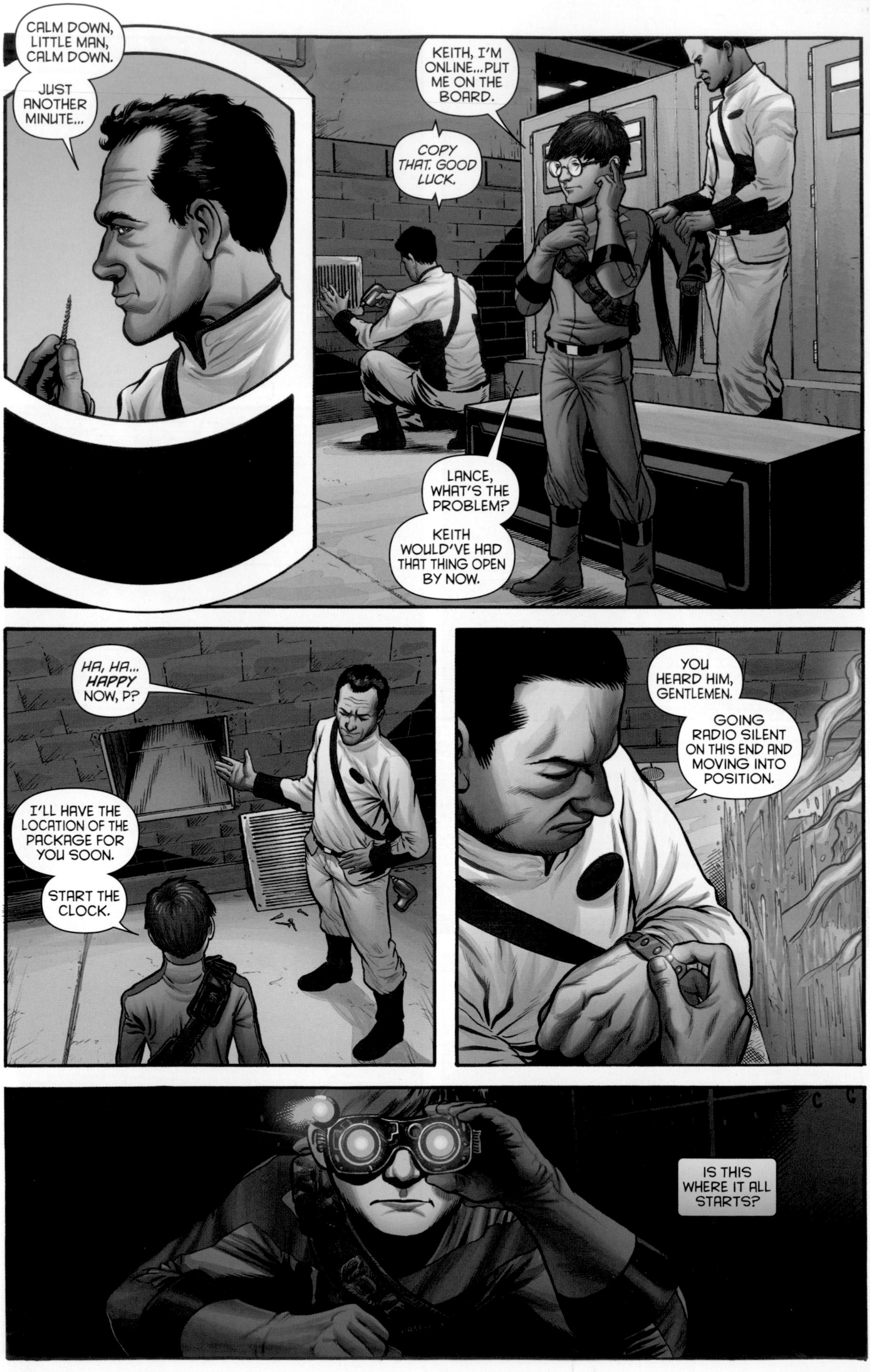
CALM DOWN, LITTLE MAN, CALM DOWN.
JUST ANOTHER MINUTE...
KEITH, I'M ONLINE...PUT ME ON THE BOARD.
COPY THAT. GOOD LUCK.
LANCE, WHAT'S THE PROBLEM?
KEITH WOULD'VE HAD THAT THING OPEN BY NOW.
HA, HA... HAPPY NOW, P?
I'LL HAVE THE LOCATION OF THE PACKAGE FOR YOU SOON.
START THE CLOCK.
YOU HEARD HIM, GENTLEMEN.
GOING RADIO SILENT ON THIS END AND MOVING INTO POSITION.
IS THIS WHERE IT ALL STARTS?

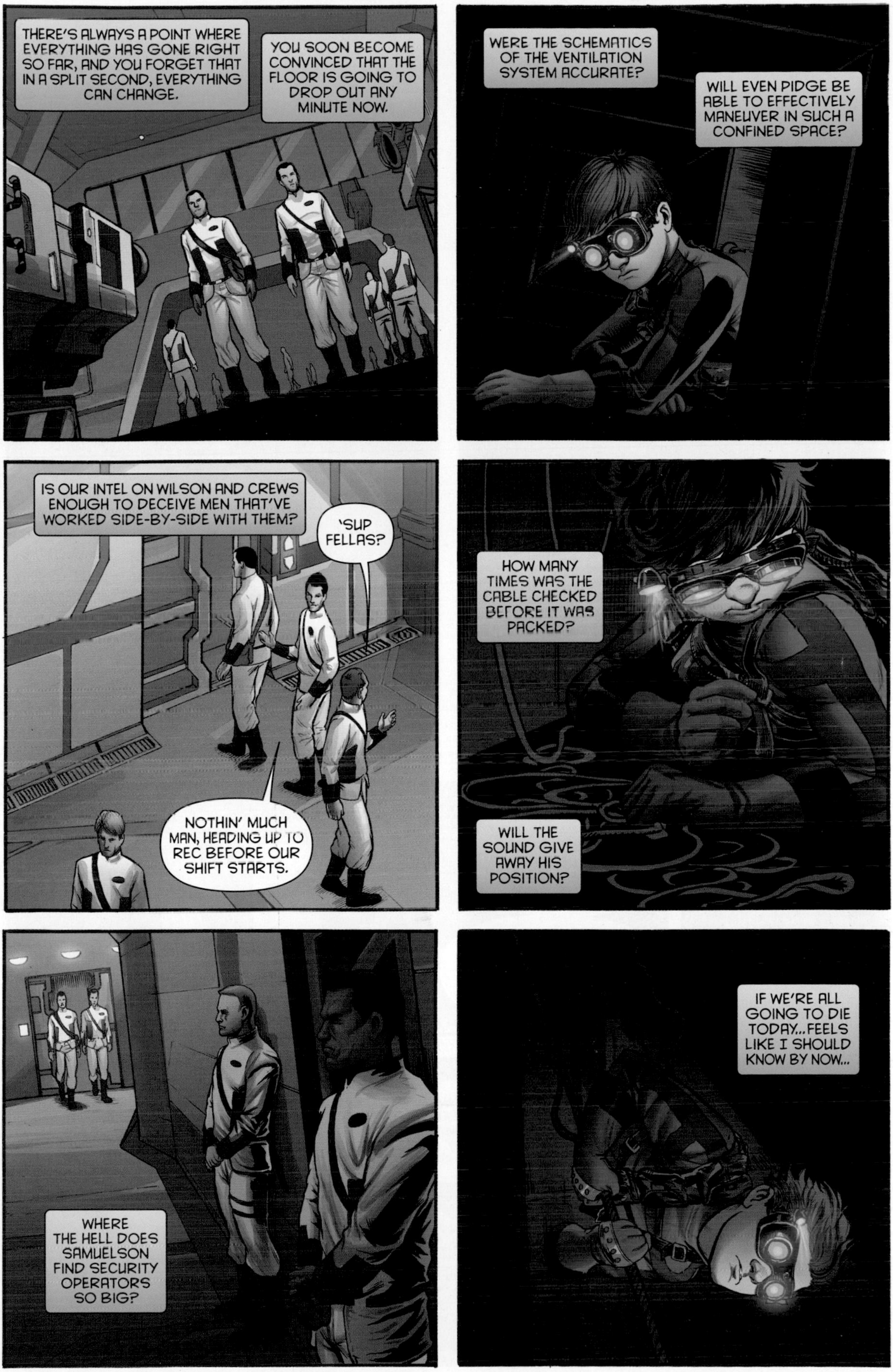
THERE'S ALWAYS A POINT WHERE EVERYTHING HAS GONE RIGHT SO FAR, AND YOU FORGET THAT IN A SPLIT SECOND, EVERYTHING CAN CHANGE.
YOU SOON BECOME CONVINCED THAT THE FLOOR IS GOING TO DROP OUT ANY MINUTE NOW.
WERE THE SCHEMATICS OF THE VENTILATION SYSTEM ACCURATE?
WILL EVEN PIDGE BE ABLE TO EFFECTIVELY MANEUVER IN SUCH A CONFINED SPACE?
IS OUR INTEL ON WILSON AND CREWS ENOUGH TO DECEIVE MEN THAT'VE WORKED SIDE-BY-SIDE WITH THEM?
'SUP FELLAS?
NOTHIN' MUCH MAN, HEADING UP TO REC BEFORE OUR SHIFT STARTS.
HOW MANY TIMES WAS THE CABLE CHECKED BEFORE IT WAS PACKED?
WILL THE SOUND GIVE AWAY HIS POSITION?
WHERE THE HELL DOES SAMUELSON FIND SECURITY OPERATORS SO BIG?
IF WE'RE ALL GOING TO DIE TODAY...FEELS LIKE I SHOULD KNOW BY NOW...

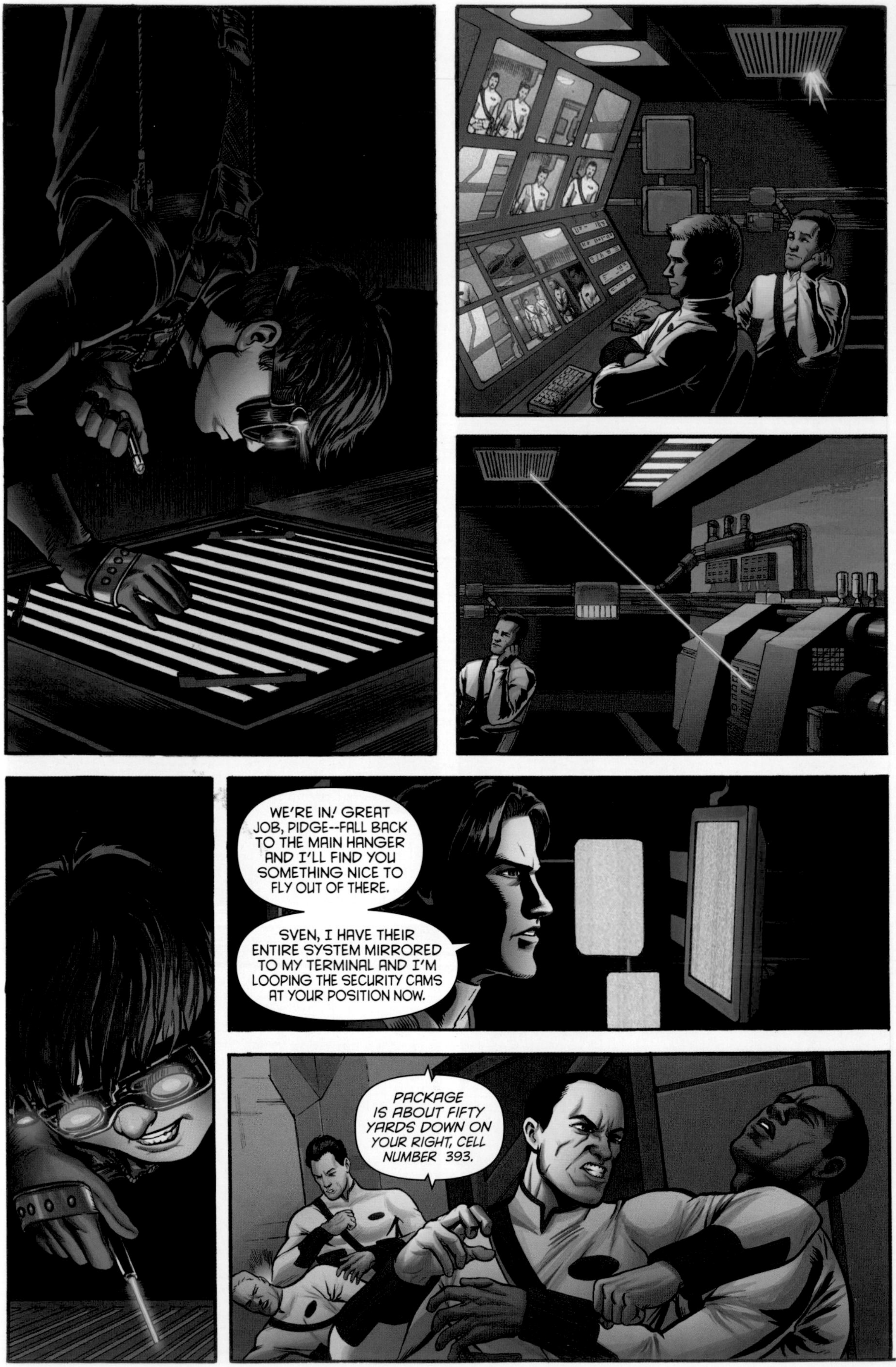
WE'RE IN! GREAT JOB, PIDGE--FALL BACK TO THE MAIN HANGER AND I'LL FIND YOU SOMETHING NICE TO FLY OUT OF THERE.
SVEN, I HAVE THEIR ENTIRE SYSTEM MIRRORED TO MY TERMINAL AND I'M LOOPING THE SECURITY CAMS AT YOUR POSITION NOW.
PACKAGE IS ABOUT FIFTY YARDS DOWN ON YOUR RIGHT, CELL NUMBER 393.

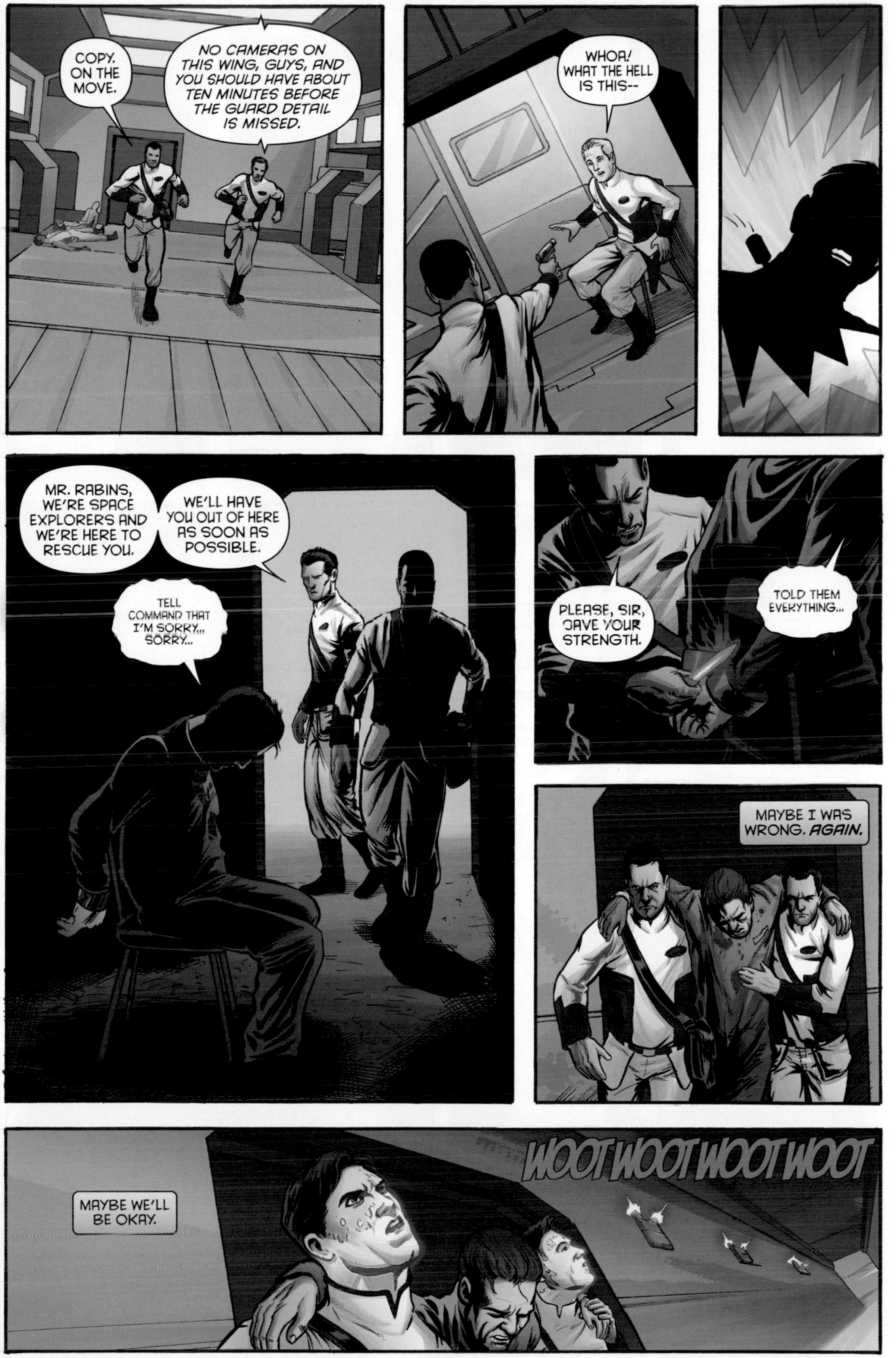
COPY. ON THE MOVE.
NO CAMERAS ON THIS WING, GUYS, AND YOU SHOULD HAVE ABOUT TEN MINUTES BEFORE THE GUARD DETAIL IS MISSED.
WHOA! WHAT THE HELL IS THIS--
MR. RABINS, WE'RE SPACE EXPLORERS AND WE'RE HERE TO RESCUE YOU.
WE'LL HAVE YOU OUT OF HERE AS SOON AS POSSIBLE.
TELL COMMAND THAT I'M SORRY... SORRY...
PLEASE, SIR, SAVE YOUR STRENGTH.
TOLD THEM EVERYTHING...
MAYBE I WAS WRONG. AGAIN.
WOOT WOOT WOOT WOOT
MAYBE WE'LL BE OKAY.

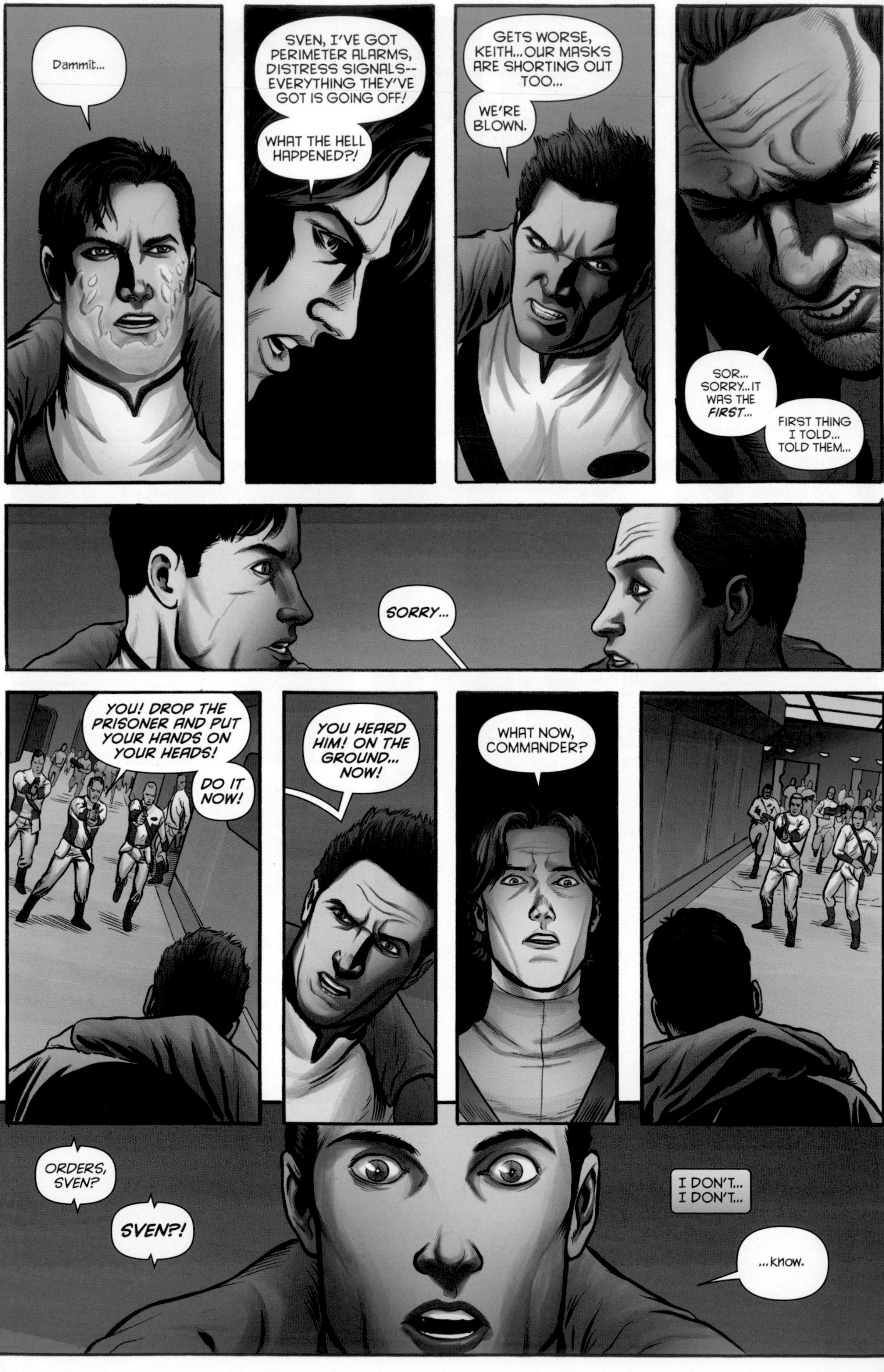

Dammit...
SVEN, I'VE GOT PERIMETER ALARMS, DISTRESS SIGNALS-- EVERYTHING THEY'VE GOT IS GOING OFF!
WHAT THE HELL HAPPENED?!
GETS WORSE, KEITH...OUR MASKS ARE SHORTING OUT TOO...
WE'RE BLOWN.
SOR... SORRY...IT WAS THE FIRST...
FIRST THING I TOLD... TOLD THEM...
SORRY...
YOU! DROP THE PRISONER AND PUT YOUR HANDS ON YOUR HEADS!
DO IT NOW!
YOU HEARD HIM! ON THE GROUND... NOW!
WHAT NOW, COMMANDER?
ORDERS, SVEN?
SVEN?!
I DON'T... I DON'T...
...know.

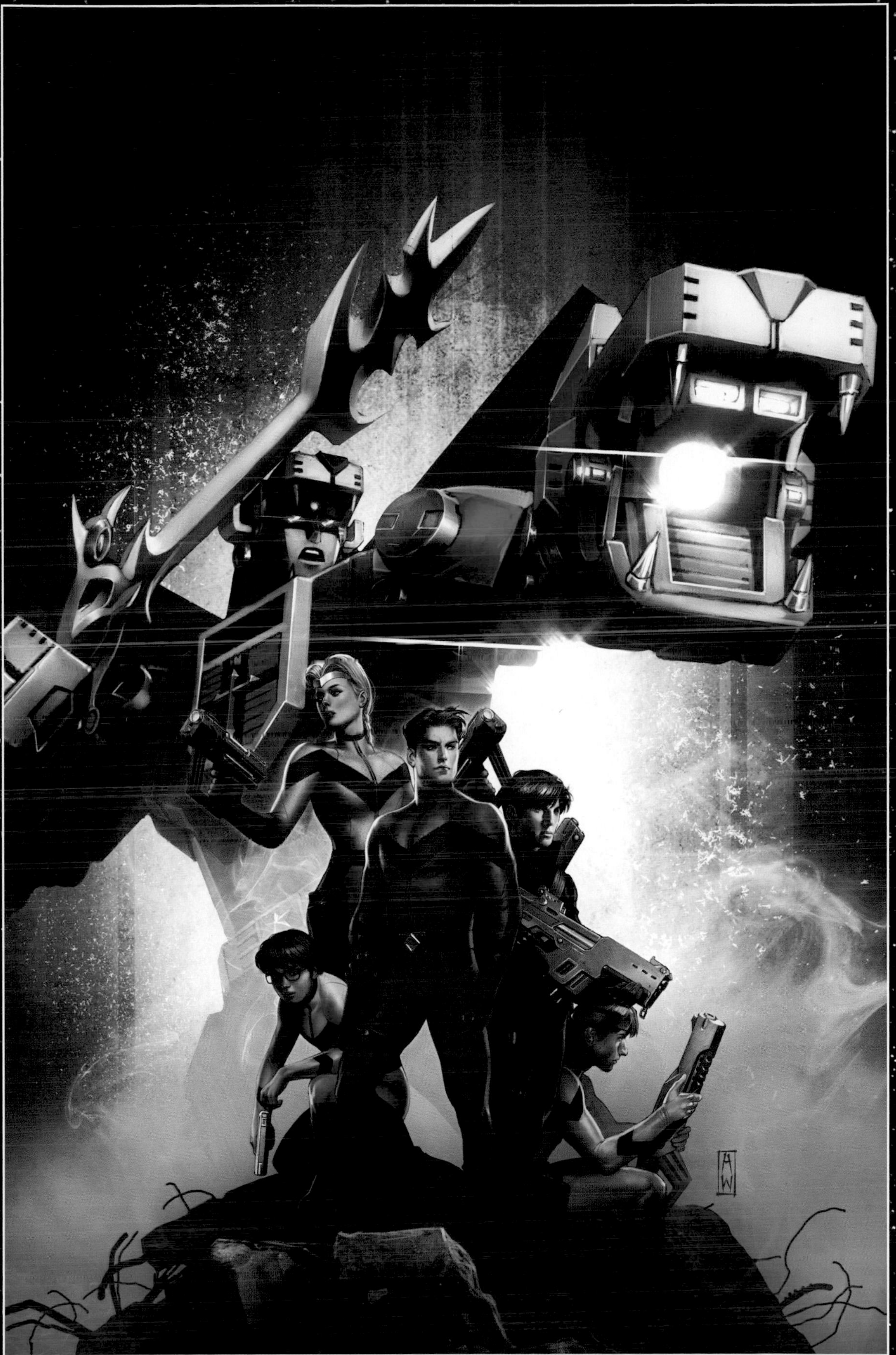

Issue #2 cover by ADMIRA WIJAYA

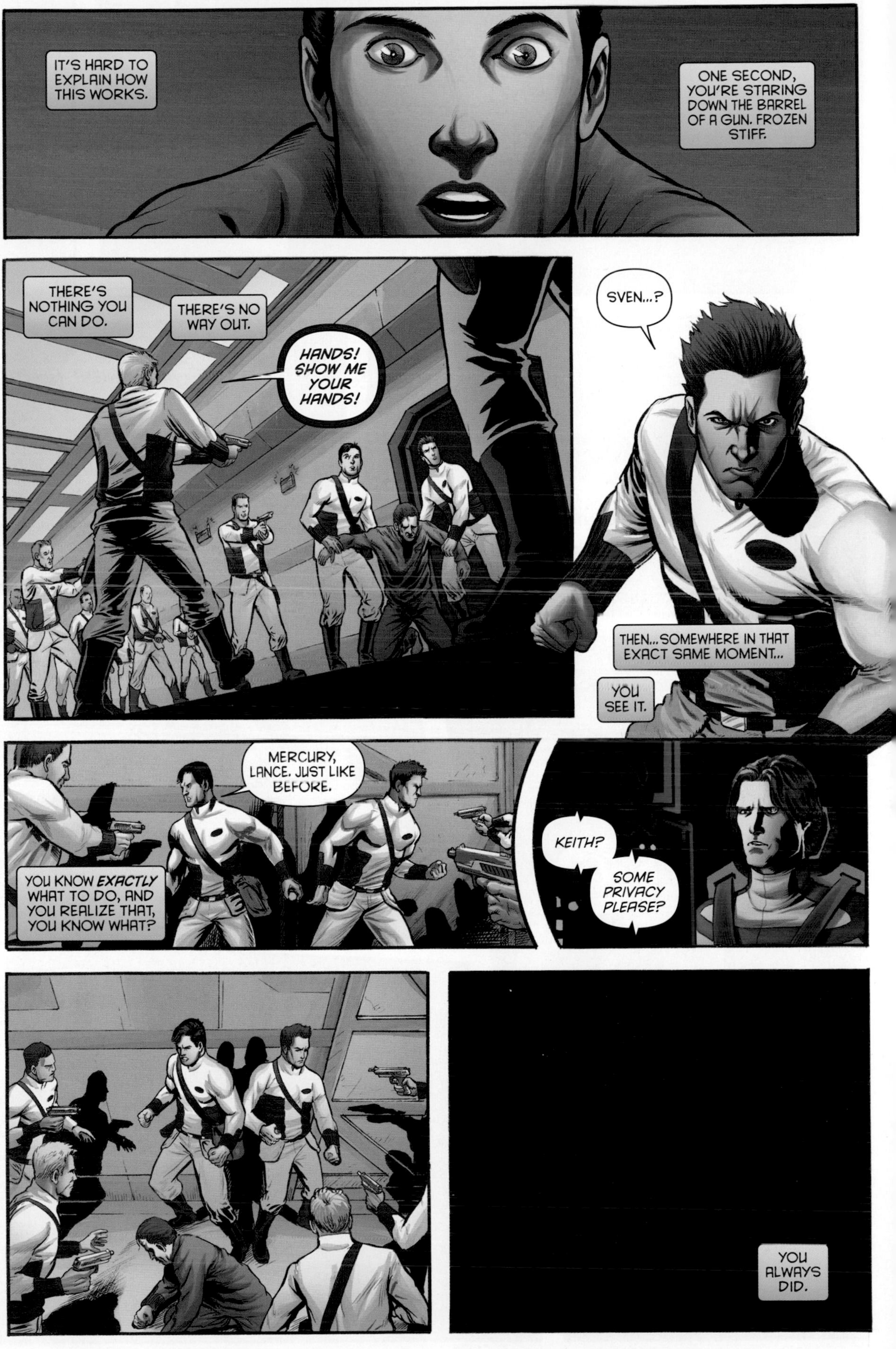
IT'S HARD TO EXPLAIN HOW THIS WORKS.
ONE SECOND, YOU'RE STARING DOWN THE BARREL OF A GUN. FROZEN STIFF.
THERE'S NOTHING YOU CAN DO.
THERE'S NO WAY OUT.
HANDS! SHOW ME YOUR HANDS!
SVEN...?
THEN...SOMEWHERE IN THAT EXACT SAME MOMENT...
YOU SEE IT.
MERCURY, LANCE. JUST LIKE BEFORE.
YOU KNOW *EXACTLY* WHAT TO DO, AND YOU REALIZE THAT, YOU KNOW WHAT?
KEITH?
SOME PRIVACY PLEASE?
YOU ALWAYS DID.

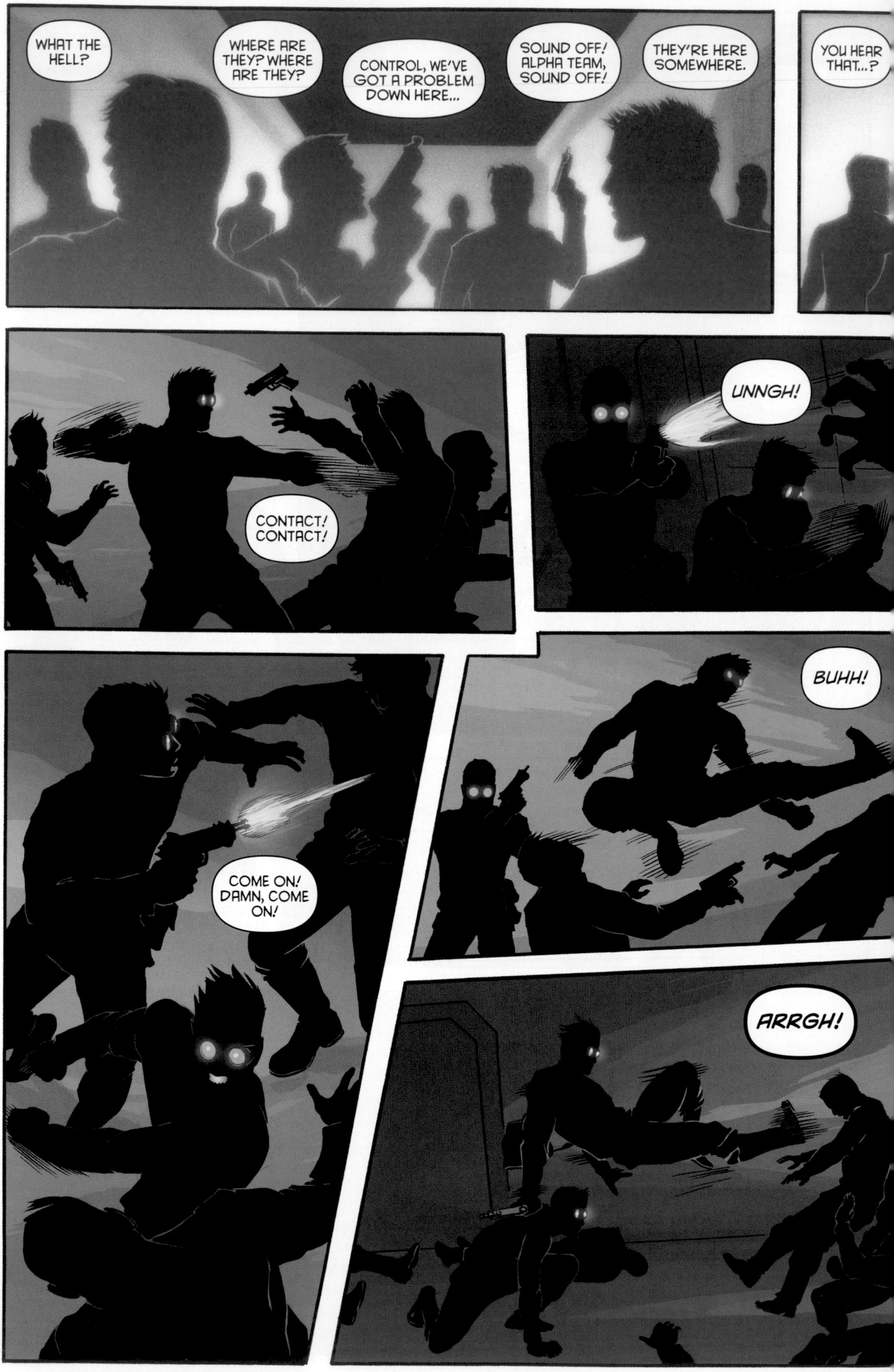
WHAT THE HELL?
WHERE ARE THEY? WHERE ARE THEY?
CONTROL, WE'VE GOT A PROBLEM DOWN HERE...
SOUND OFF! ALPHA TEAM, SOUND OFF!
THEY'RE HERE SOMEWHERE.
YOU HEAR THAT...?
CONTACT! CONTACT!
UNNGH!
COME ON! DAMN, COME ON!
BUHH!
ARRGH!

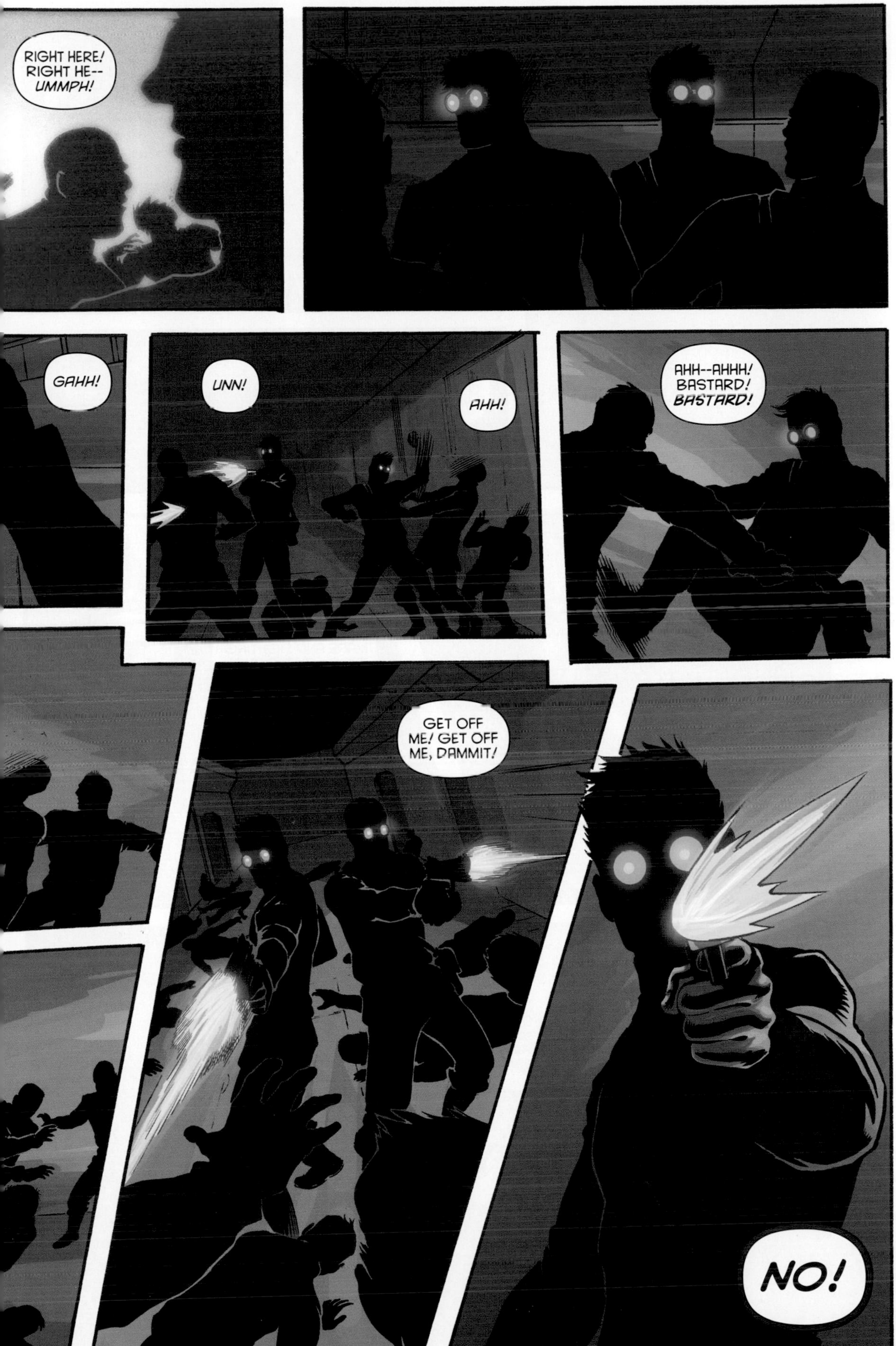
RIGHT HERE! RIGHT HE-- UMMPH!
GAHH!
UNN!
AHH!
AHH--AHHH! BASTARD! BASTARD!
GET OFF ME! GET OFF ME, DAMMIT!
NO!

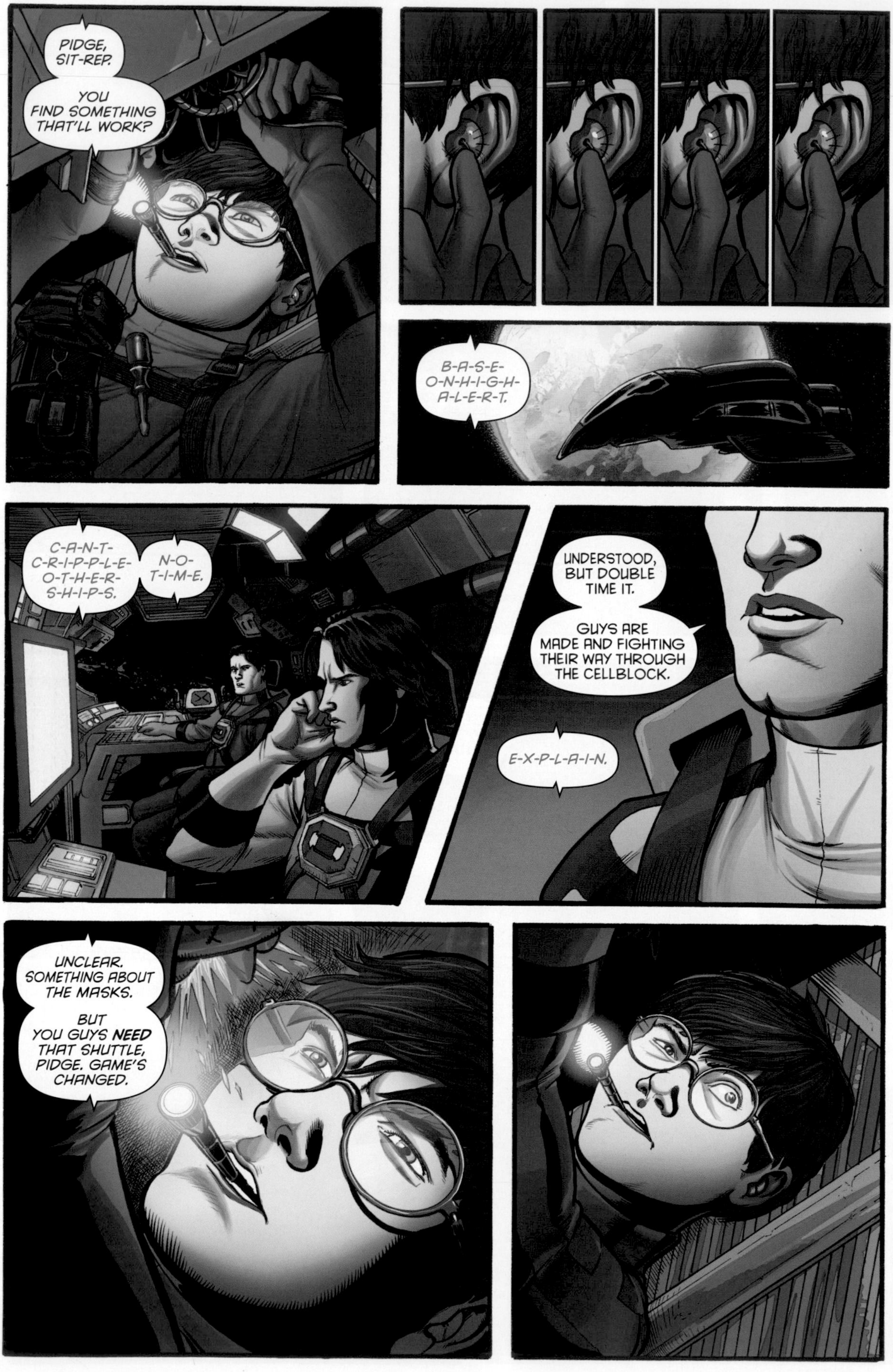
PIDGE, SIT-REP.
YOU FIND SOMETHING THAT'LL WORK?
B-A-S-E- O-N-H-I-G-H- A-L-E-R-T.
C-A-N-T- C-R-I-P-P-L-E- O-T-H-E-R- S-H-I-P-S.
N-O- T-I-M-E.
UNDERSTOOD, BUT DOUBLE TIME IT.
GUYS ARE MADE AND FIGHTING THEIR WAY THROUGH THE CELLBLOCK.
E-X-P-L-A-I-N.
UNCLEAR. SOMETHING ABOUT THE MASKS.
BUT YOU GUYS **NEED** THAT SHUTTLE, PIDGE. GAME'S CHANGED.

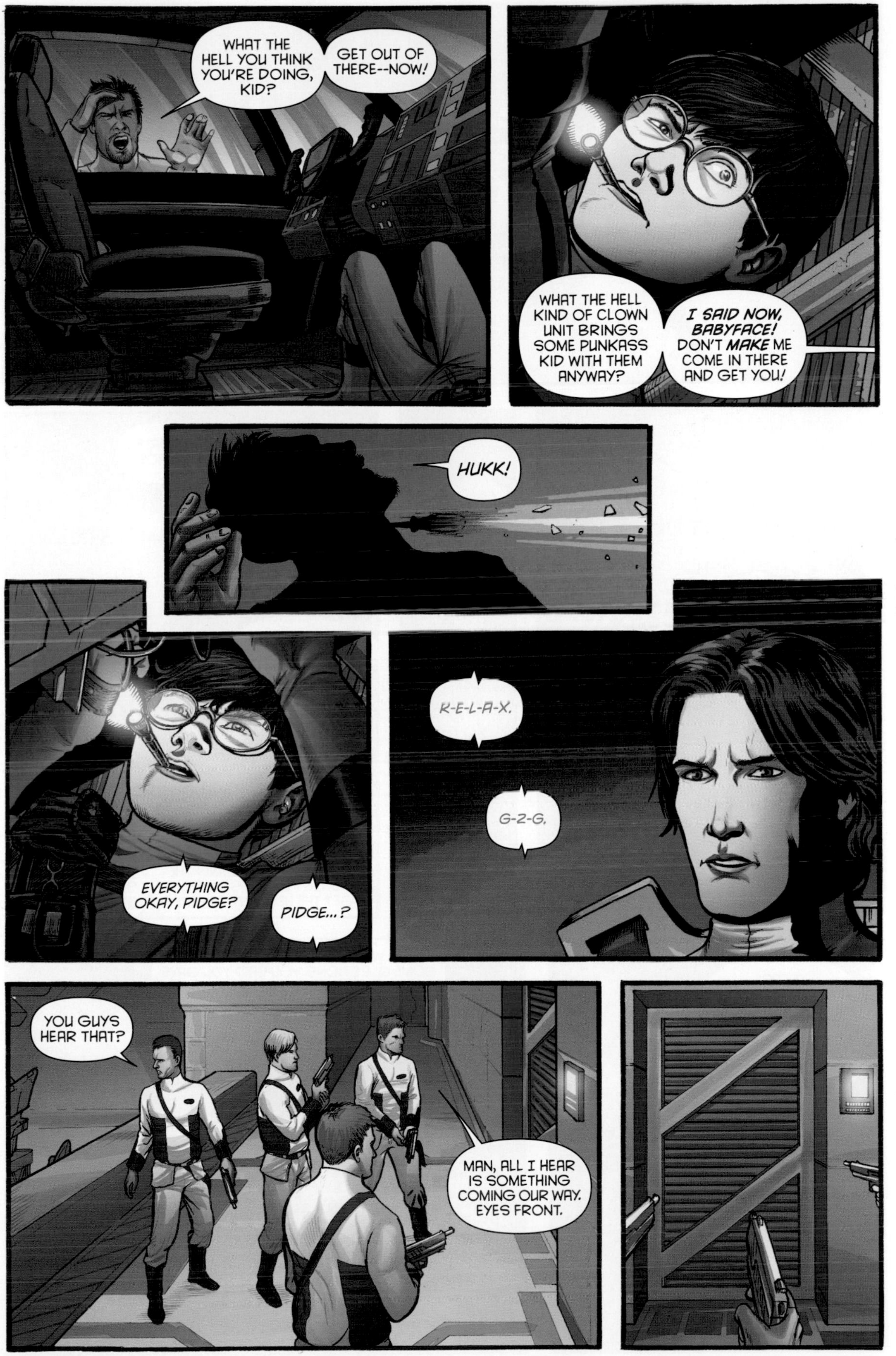

WHAT THE HELL YOU THINK YOU'RE DOING, KID?
GET OUT OF THERE--NOW!
WHAT THE HELL KIND OF CLOWN UNIT BRINGS SOME PUNKASS KID WITH THEM ANYWAY?
I SAID NOW, BABYFACE! DON'T MAKE ME COME IN THERE AND GET YOU!
HUKK!
EVERYTHING OKAY, PIDGE?
PIDGE...?
R-E-L-A-X.
G-2-G.
YOU GUYS HEAR THAT?
MAN, ALL I HEAR IS SOMETHING COMING OUR WAY. EYES FRONT.

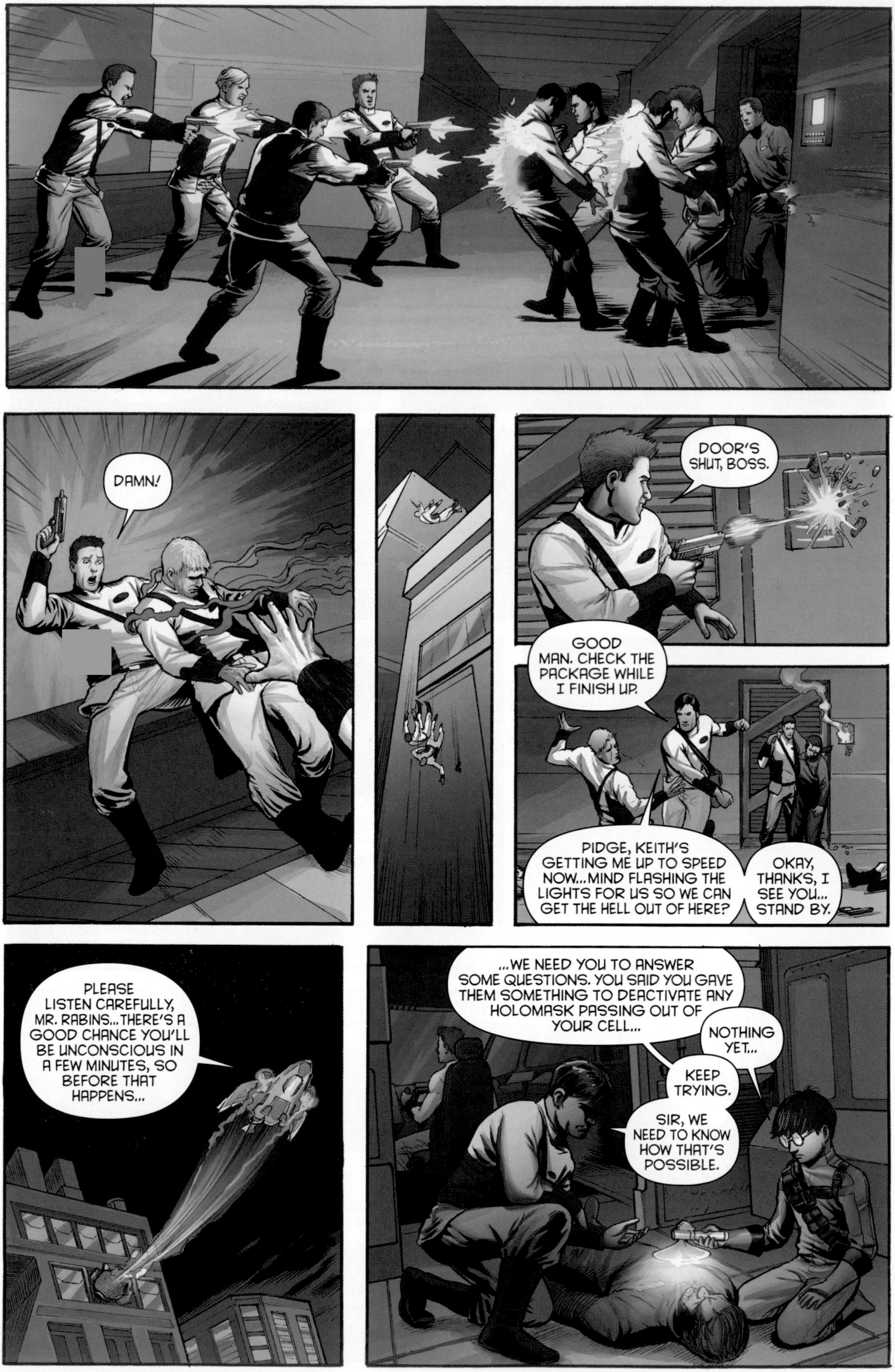
DAMN!
DOOR'S SHUT, BOSS.
GOOD MAN. CHECK THE PACKAGE WHILE I FINISH UP.
PIDGE, KEITH'S GETTING ME UP TO SPEED NOW...MIND FLASHING THE LIGHTS FOR US SO WE CAN GET THE HELL OUT OF HERE?
OKAY, THANKS, I SEE YOU... STAND BY.
PLEASE LISTEN CAREFULLY, MR. RABINS...THERE'S A GOOD CHANCE YOU'LL BE UNCONSCIOUS IN A FEW MINUTES, SO BEFORE THAT HAPPENS...
...WE NEED YOU TO ANSWER SOME QUESTIONS. YOU SAID YOU GAVE THEM SOMETHING TO DEACTIVATE ANY HOLOMASK PASSING OUT OF YOUR CELL...
NOTHING YET...
KEEP TRYING.
SIR, WE NEED TO KNOW HOW THAT'S POSSIBLE.

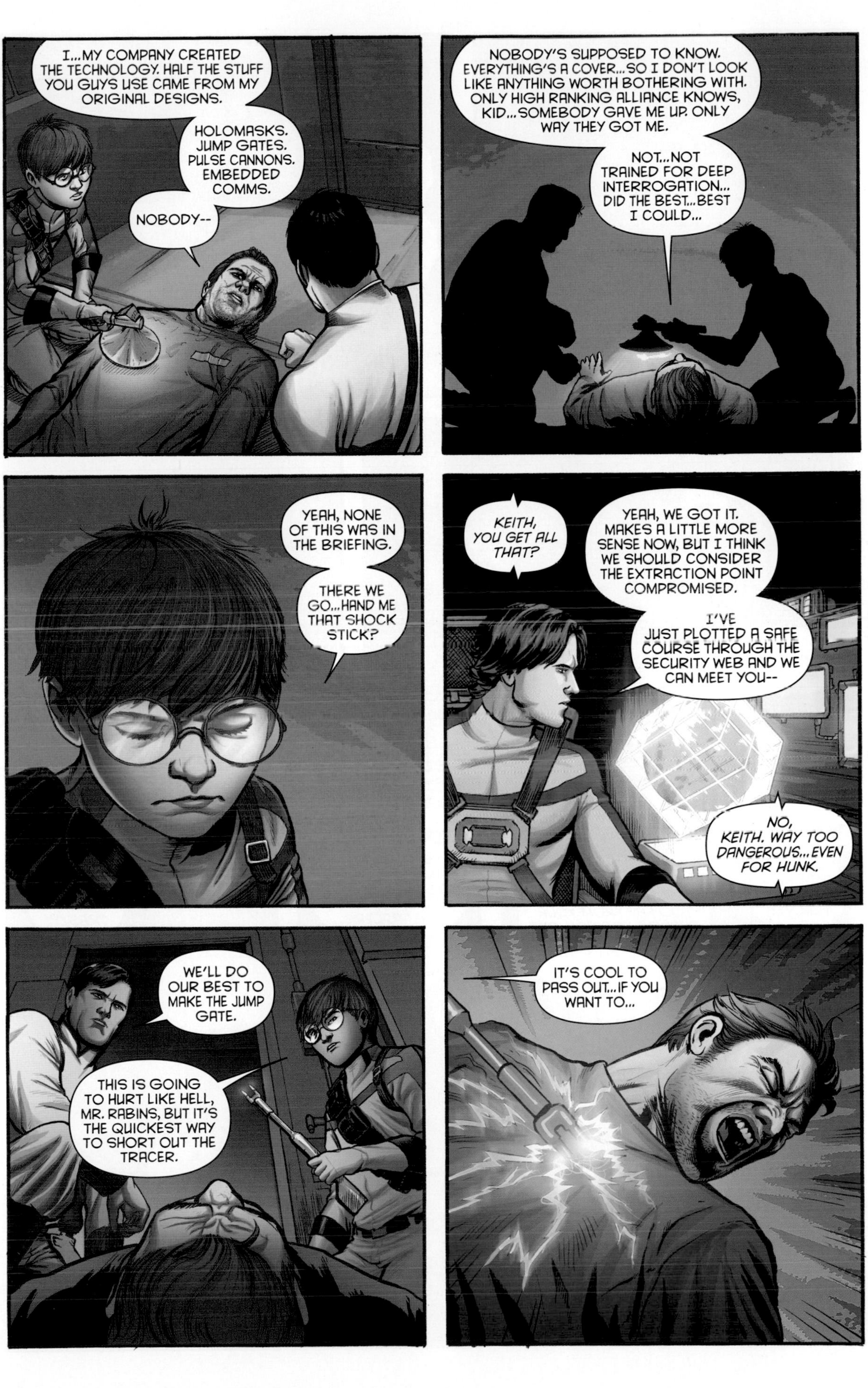
I...MY COMPANY CREATED THE TECHNOLOGY. HALF THE STUFF YOU GUYS USE CAME FROM MY ORIGINAL DESIGNS.
HOLOMASKS. JUMP GATES. PULSE CANNONS. EMBEDDED COMMS.
NOBODY--
NOBODY'S SUPPOSED TO KNOW. EVERYTHING'S A COVER...SO I DON'T LOOK LIKE ANYTHING WORTH BOTHERING WITH. ONLY HIGH RANKING ALLIANCE KNOWS, KID...SOMEBODY GAVE ME UP. ONLY WAY THEY GOT ME.
NOT...NOT TRAINED FOR DEEP INTERROGATION... DID THE BEST...BEST I COULD...
YEAH, NONE OF THIS WAS IN THE BRIEFING.
THERE WE GO...HAND ME THAT SHOCK STICK?
KEITH, YOU GET ALL THAT?
YEAH, WE GOT IT. MAKES A LITTLE MORE SENSE NOW, BUT I THINK WE SHOULD CONSIDER THE EXTRACTION POINT COMPROMISED.
I'VE JUST PLOTTED A SAFE COURSE THROUGH THE SECURITY WEB AND WE CAN MEET YOU--
NO, KEITH. WAY TOO DANGEROUS...EVEN FOR HUNK.
WE'LL DO OUR BEST TO MAKE THE JUMP GATE.
THIS IS GOING TO HURT LIKE HELL, MR. RABINS, BUT IT'S THE QUICKEST WAY TO SHORT OUT THE TRACER.
IT'S COOL TO PASS OUT...IF YOU WANT TO...

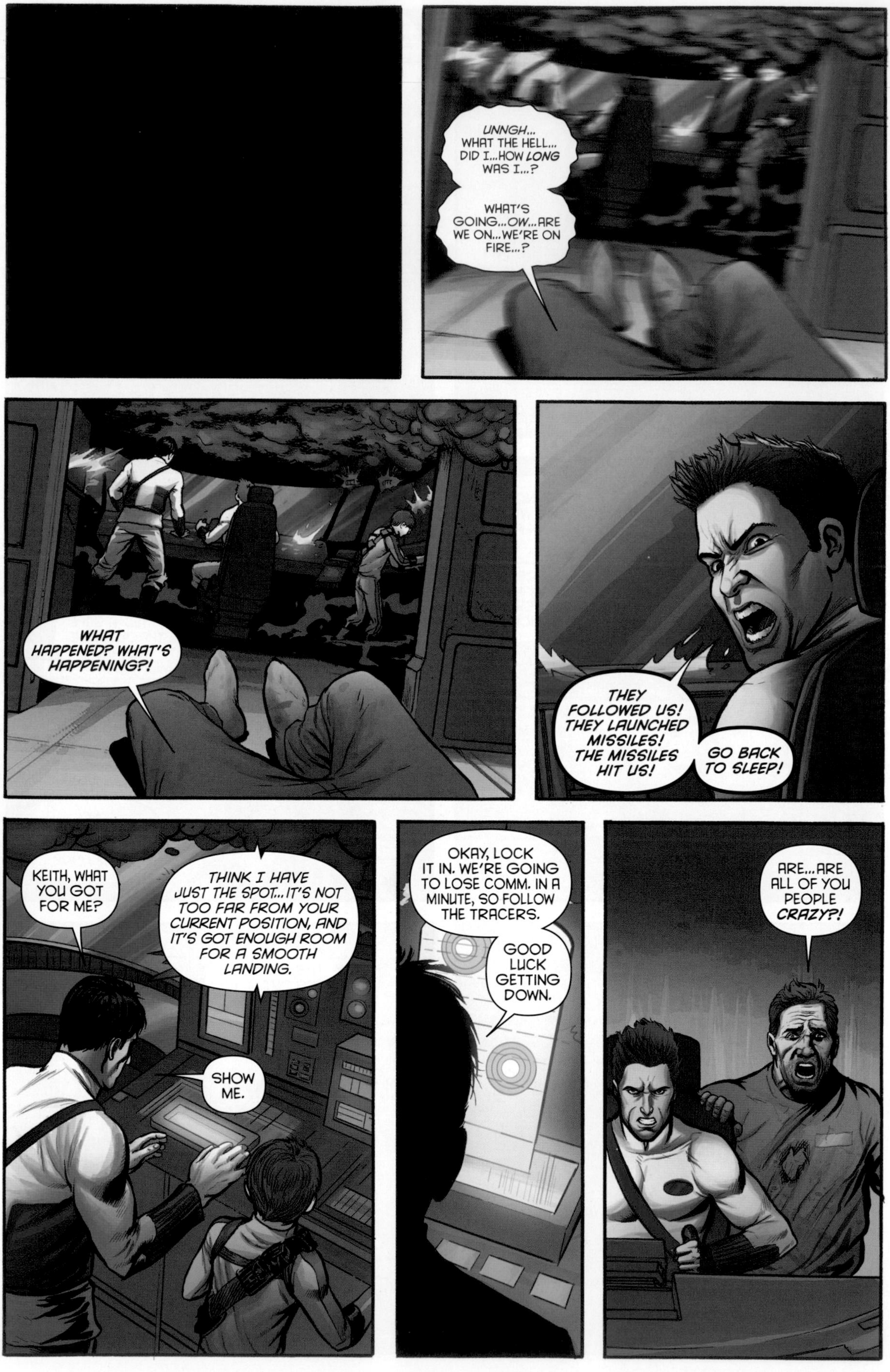
UNNGH... WHAT THE HELL... DID I...HOW LONG WAS I...?
WHAT'S GOING...OW...ARE WE ON...WE'RE ON FIRE...?
WHAT HAPPENED? WHAT'S HAPPENING?!
THEY FOLLOWED US! THEY LAUNCHED MISSILES! THE MISSILES HIT US!
GO BACK TO SLEEP!
KEITH, WHAT YOU GOT FOR ME?
THINK I HAVE JUST THE SPOT...IT'S NOT TOO FAR FROM YOUR CURRENT POSITION, AND IT'S GOT ENOUGH ROOM FOR A SMOOTH LANDING.
SHOW ME.
OKAY, LOCK IT IN. WE'RE GOING TO LOSE COMM. IN A MINUTE, SO FOLLOW THE TRACERS.
GOOD LUCK GETTING DOWN.
ARE...ARE ALL OF YOU PEOPLE CRAZY?!

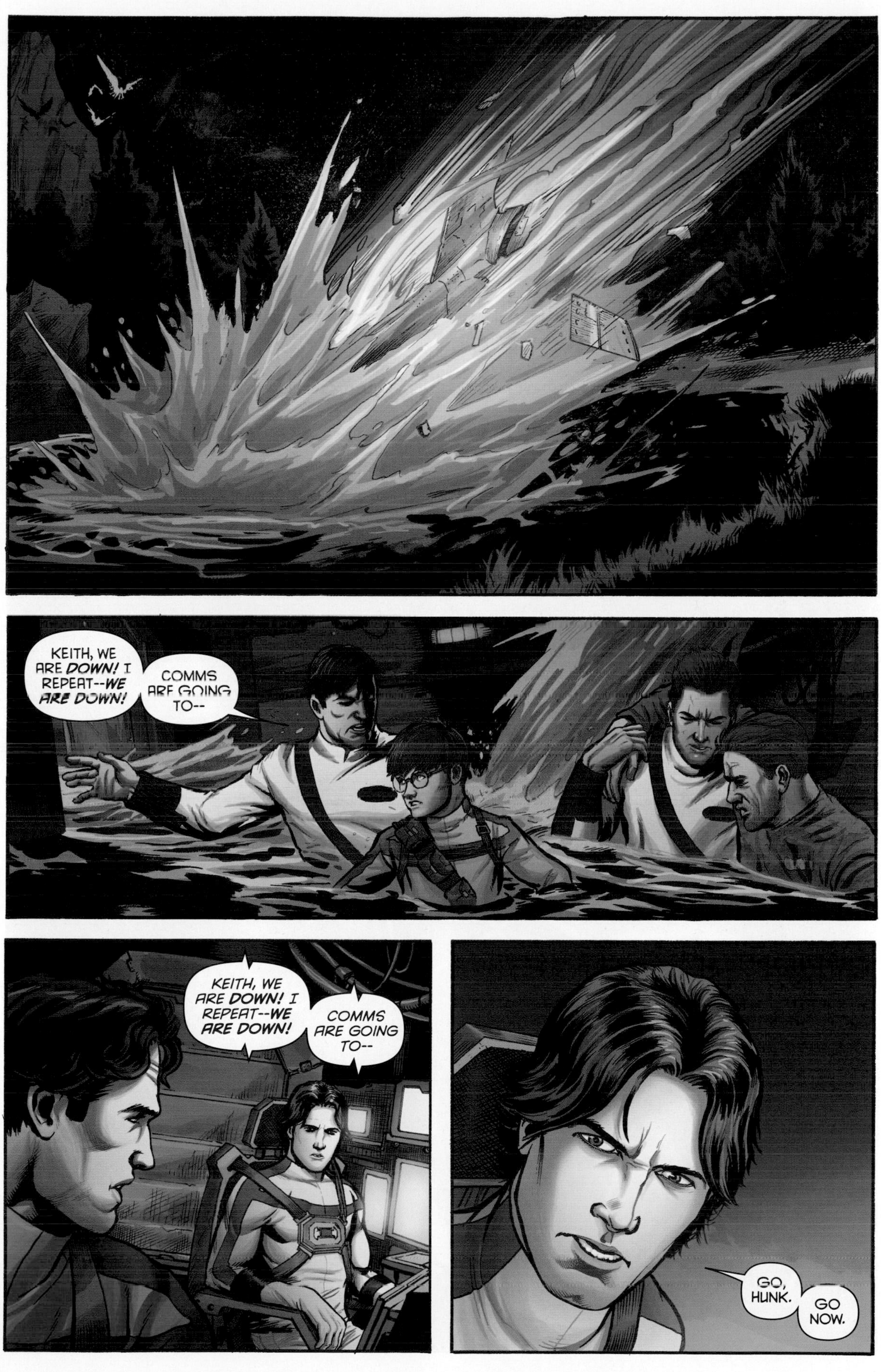
KEITH, WE ARE *DOWN!* I REPEAT--*WE ARE DOWN!*
COMMS ARE GOING TO--
KEITH, WE ARE *DOWN!* I REPEAT--*WE ARE DOWN!*
COMMS ARE GOING TO--
GO, HUNK.
GO NOW.

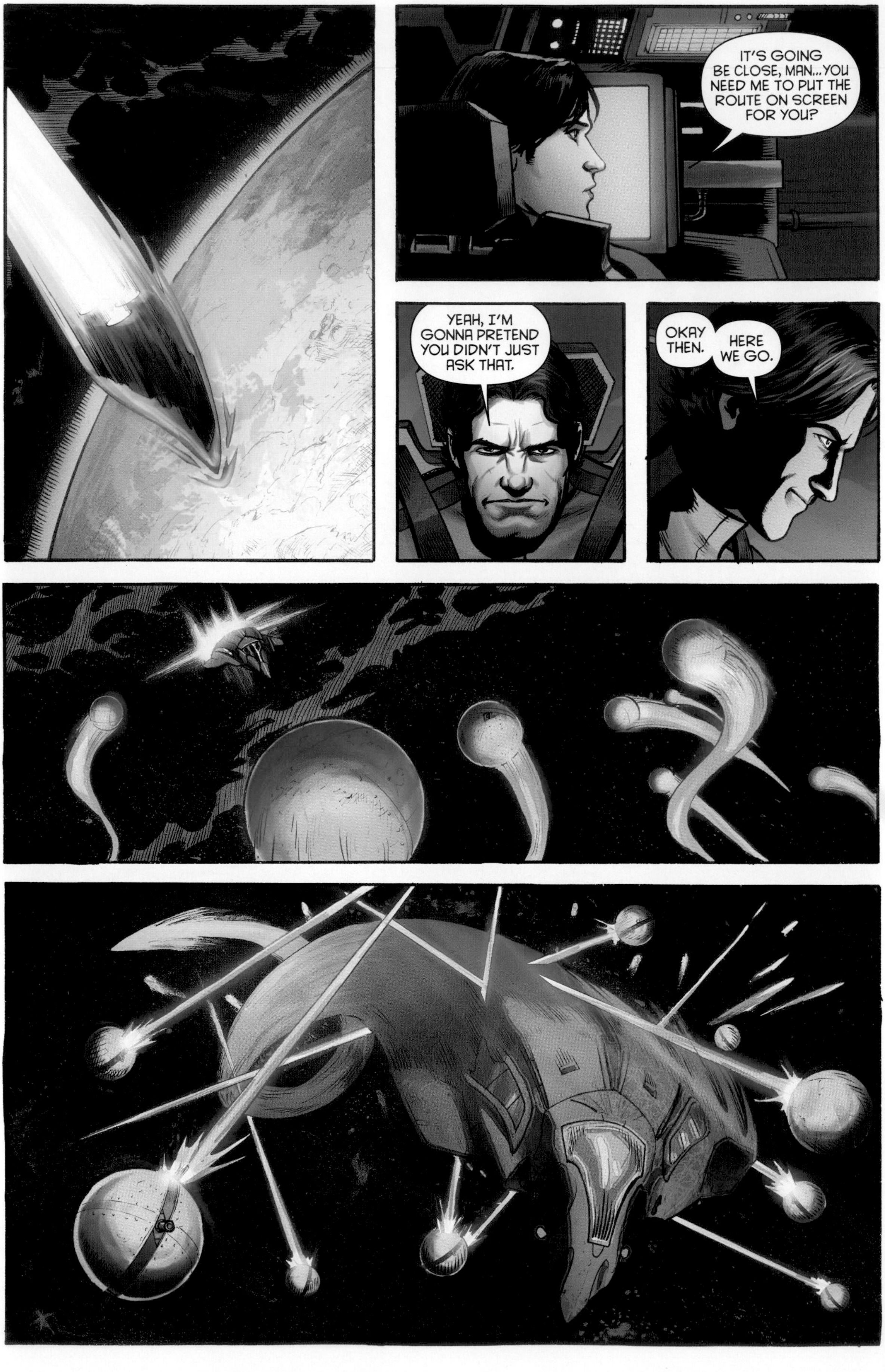
IT'S GOING BE CLOSE, MAN...YOU NEED ME TO PUT THE ROUTE ON SCREEN FOR YOU?
YEAH, I'M GONNA PRETEND YOU DIDN'T JUST ASK THAT.
OKAY THEN.
HERE WE GO.

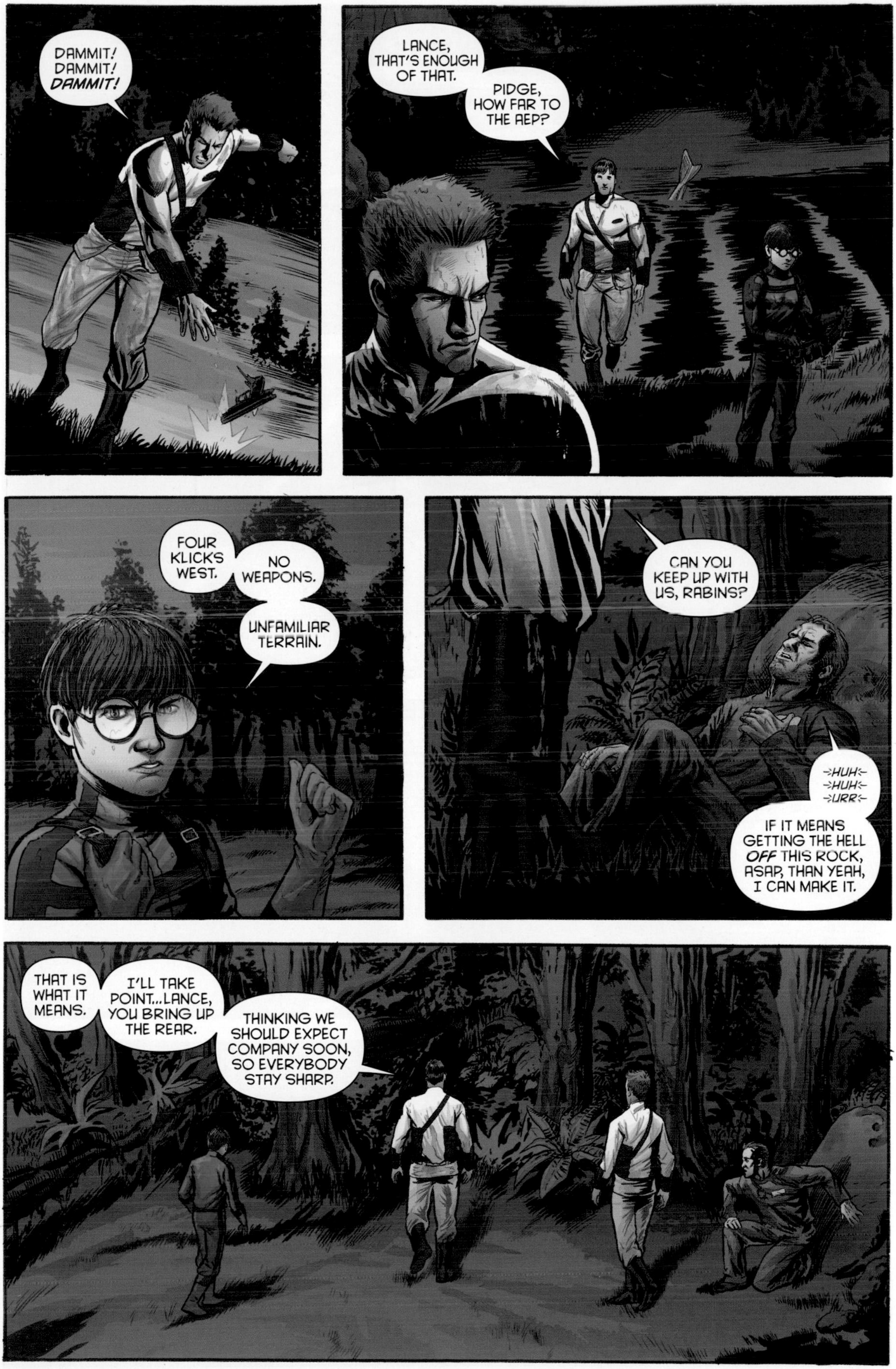
DAMMIT! DAMMIT! DAMMIT!
LANCE, THAT'S ENOUGH OF THAT.
PIDGE, HOW FAR TO THE AEP?
FOUR KLICKS WEST.
NO WEAPONS.
UNFAMILIAR TERRAIN.
CAN YOU KEEP UP WITH US, RABINS?
HUH HUH URR
IF IT MEANS GETTING THE HELL OFF THIS ROCK, ASAP, THAN YEAH, I CAN MAKE IT.
THAT IS WHAT IT MEANS.
I'LL TAKE POINT...LANCE, YOU BRING UP THE REAR.
THINKING WE SHOULD EXPECT COMPANY SOON, SO EVERYBODY STAY SHARP.

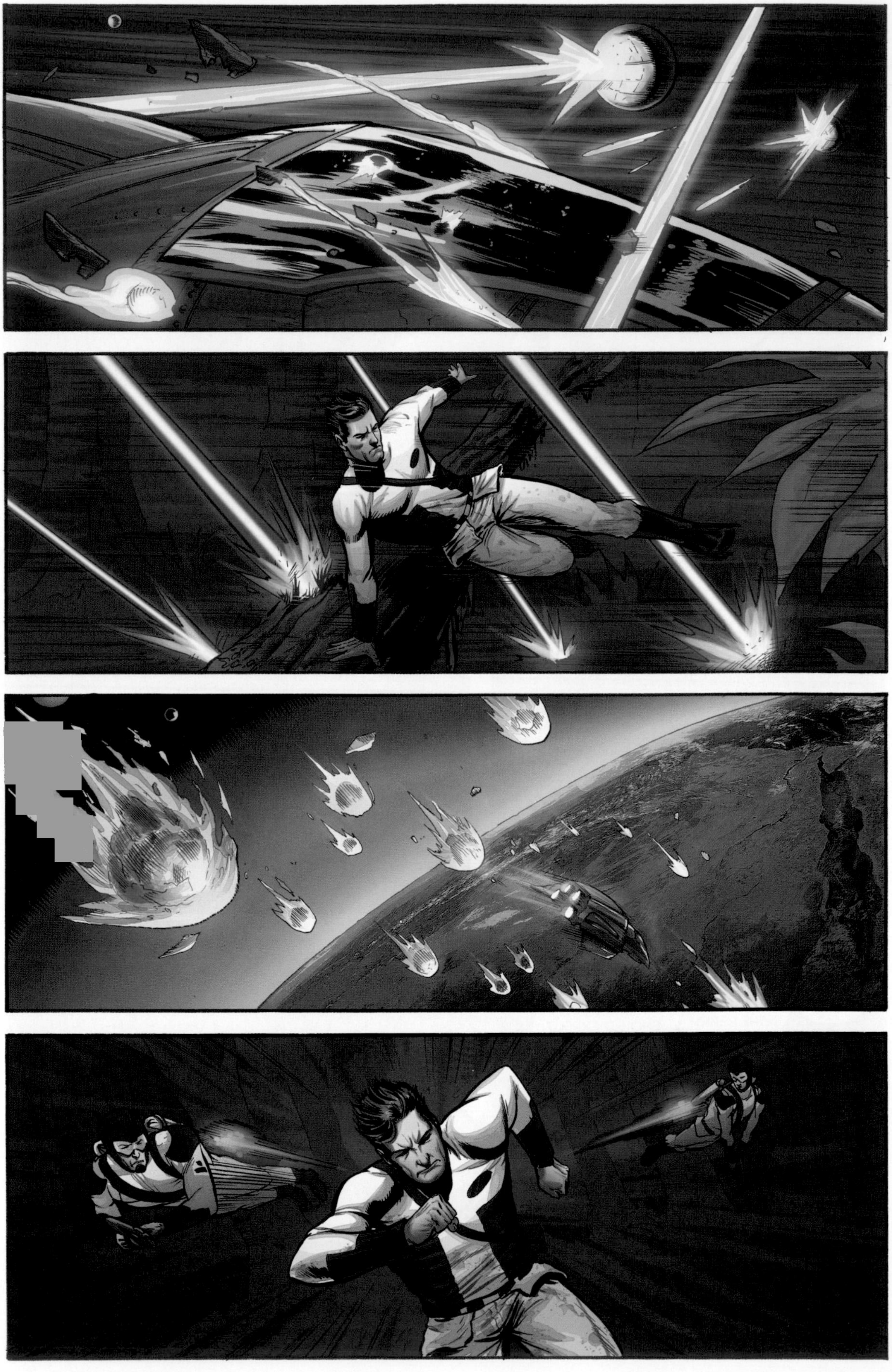

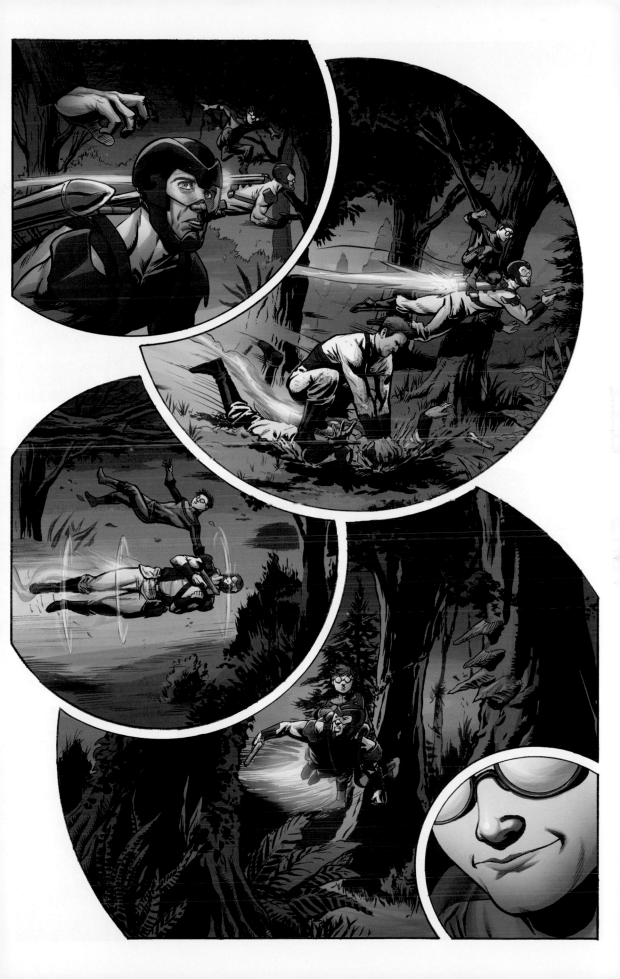

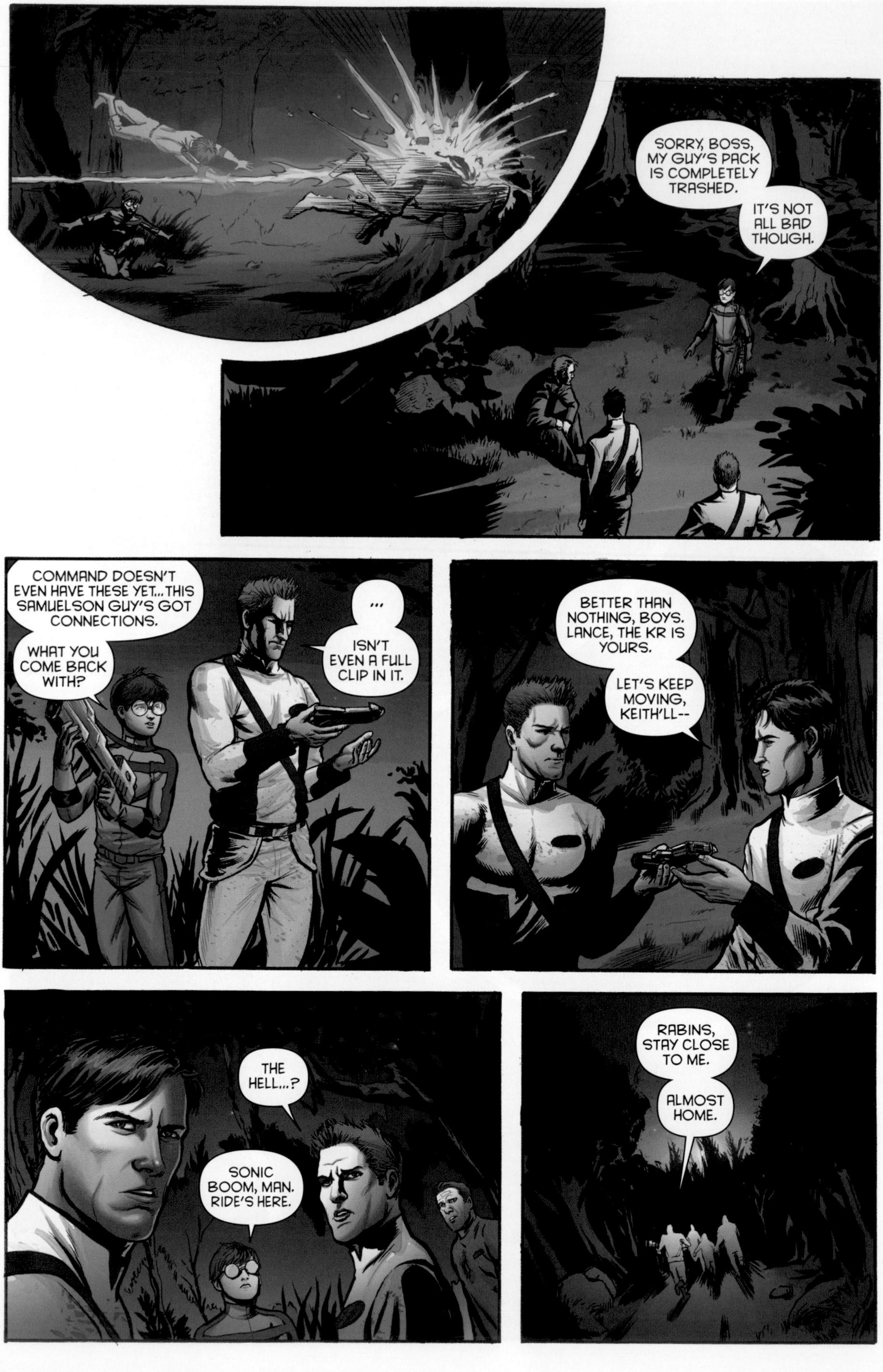
SORRY, BOSS, MY GUY'S PACK IS COMPLETELY TRASHED.
IT'S NOT ALL BAD THOUGH.
COMMAND DOESN'T EVEN HAVE THESE YET... THIS SAMUELSON GUY'S GOT CONNECTIONS.
WHAT YOU COME BACK WITH?
...
ISN'T EVEN A FULL CLIP IN IT.
BETTER THAN NOTHING, BOYS. LANCE, THE KR IS YOURS.
LET'S KEEP MOVING, KEITH'LL--
THE HELL...?
SONIC BOOM, MAN. RIDE'S HERE.
RABINS, STAY CLOSE TO ME.
ALMOST HOME.

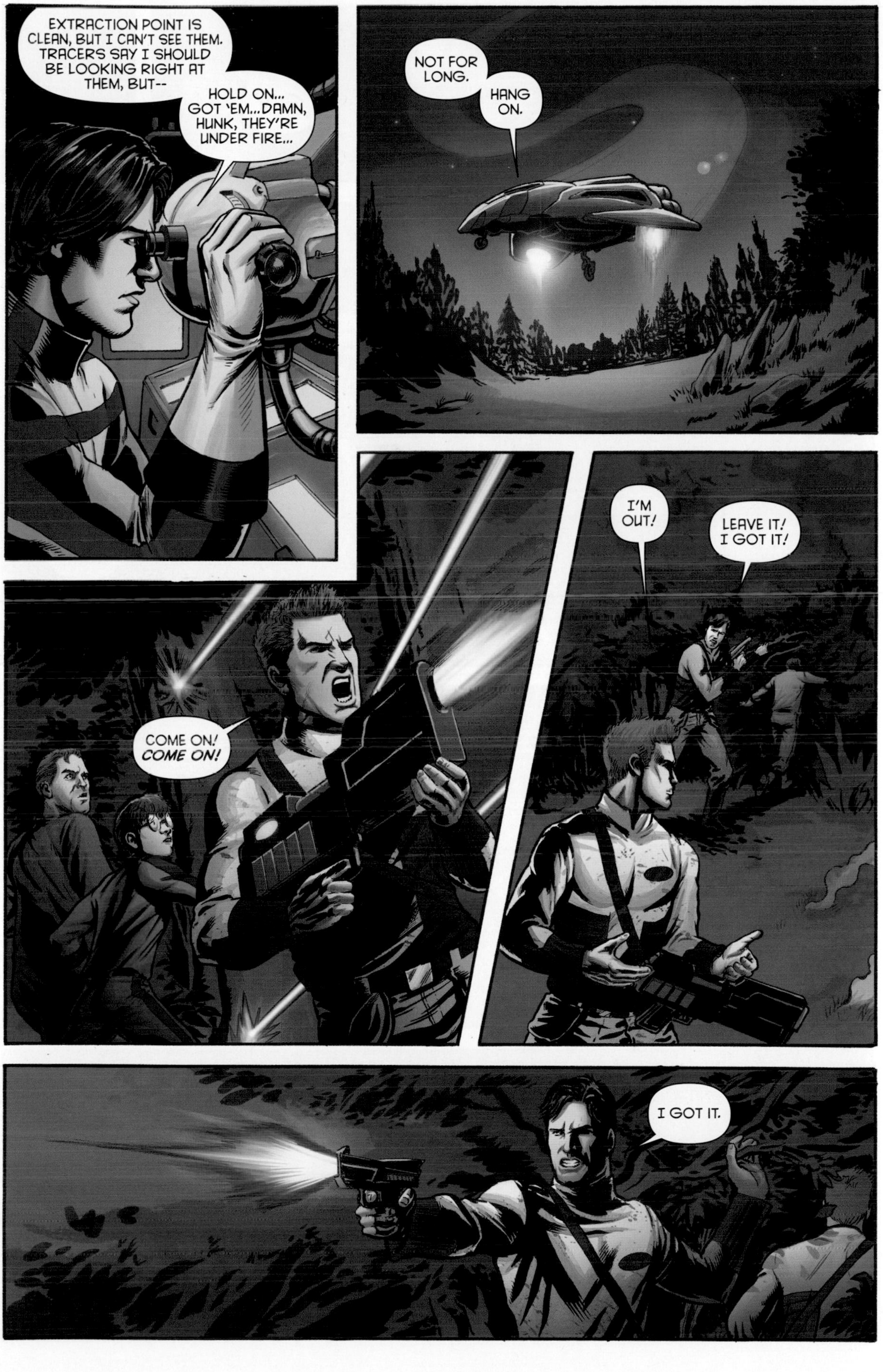
EXTRACTION POINT IS CLEAN, BUT I CAN'T SEE THEM. TRACERS SAY I SHOULD BE LOOKING RIGHT AT THEM, BUT--
HOLD ON... GOT 'EM...DAMN, HUNK, THEY'RE UNDER FIRE...
NOT FOR LONG.
HANG ON.
COME ON! *COME ON!*
I'M OUT!
LEAVE IT! I GOT IT!
I GOT IT.

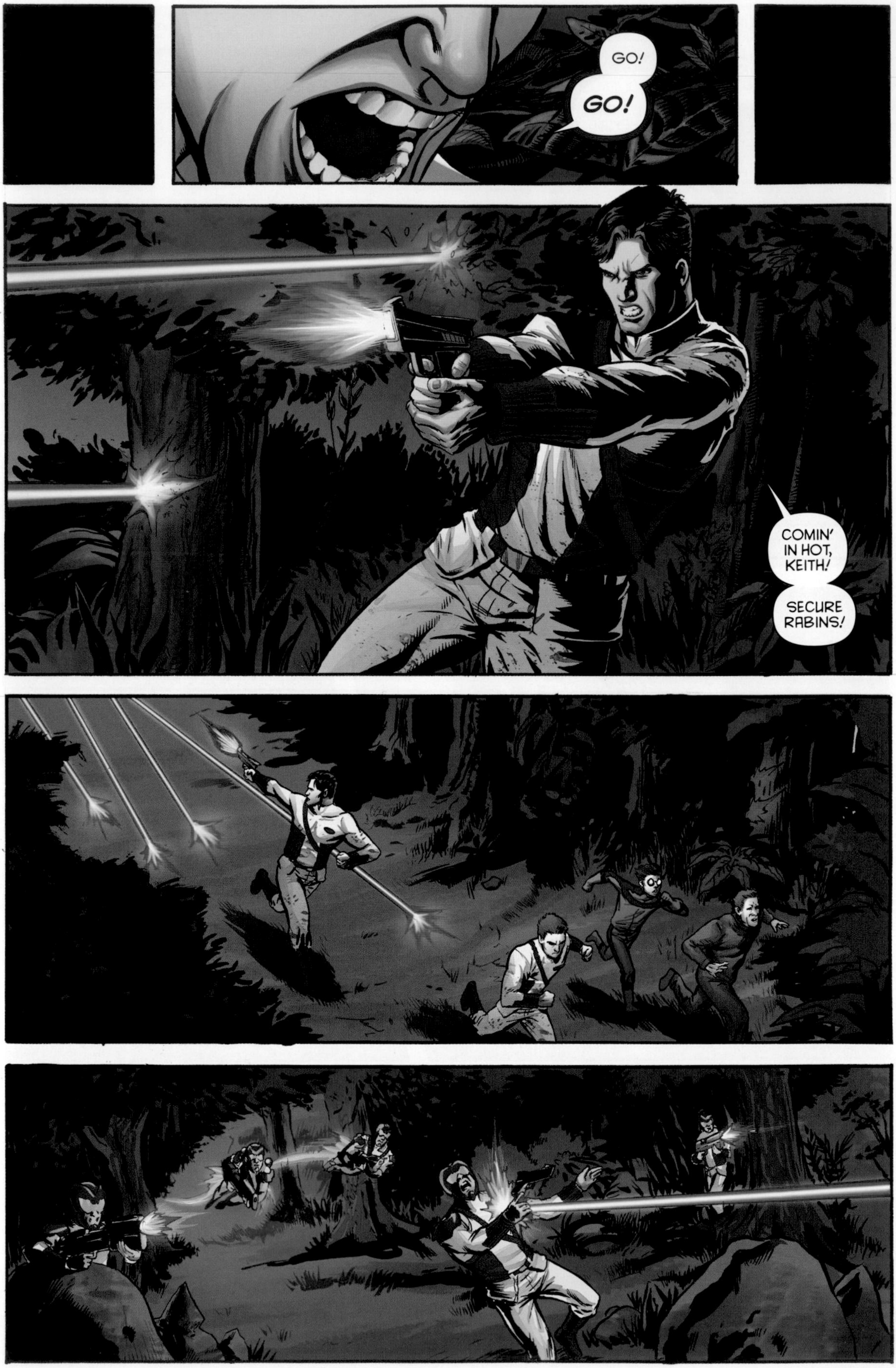
GO!
GO!
COMIN' IN HOT, KEITH!
SECURE RABINS!

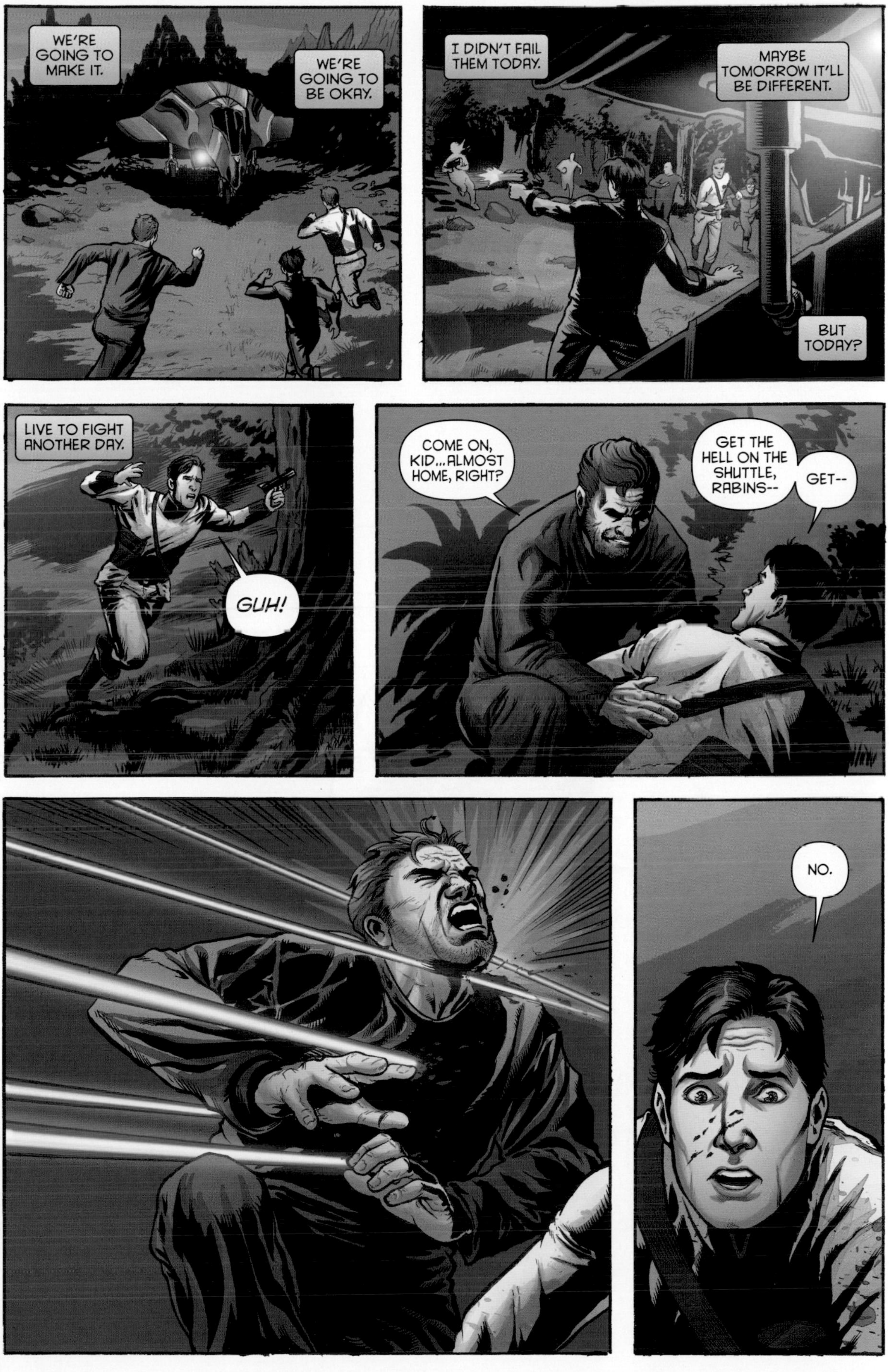
WE'RE GOING TO MAKE IT.
WE'RE GOING TO BE OKAY.
I DIDN'T FAIL THEM TODAY.
MAYBE TOMORROW IT'LL BE DIFFERENT.
BUT TODAY?
LIVE TO FIGHT ANOTHER DAY.
GUH!
COME ON, KID...ALMOST HOME, RIGHT?
GET THE HELL ON THE SHUTTLE, RABINS--
GET--
NO.

VOLTRON
YEAR ONE

FE[illegible]LESS LEADER

2: THE MARK

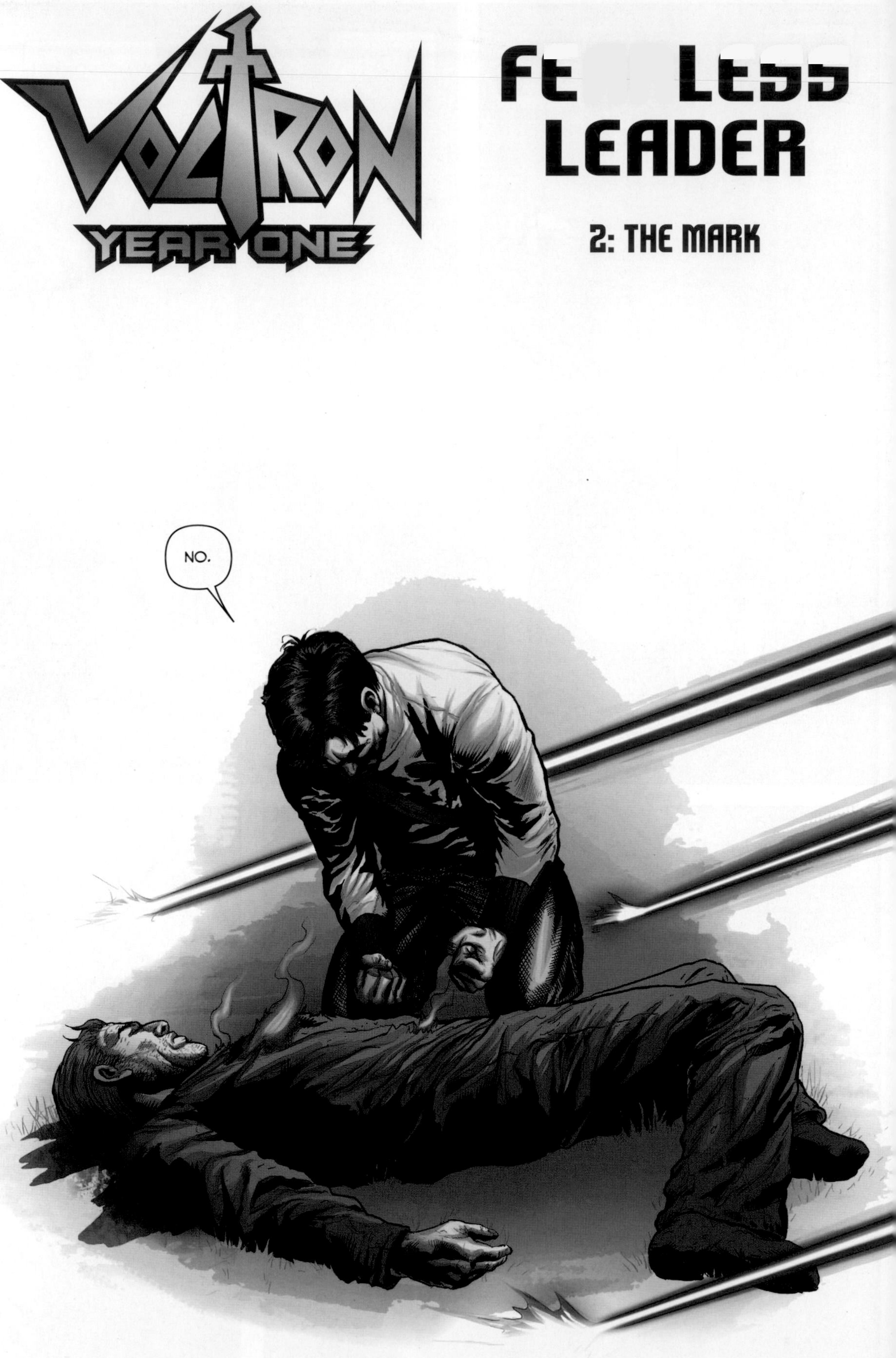
NO.

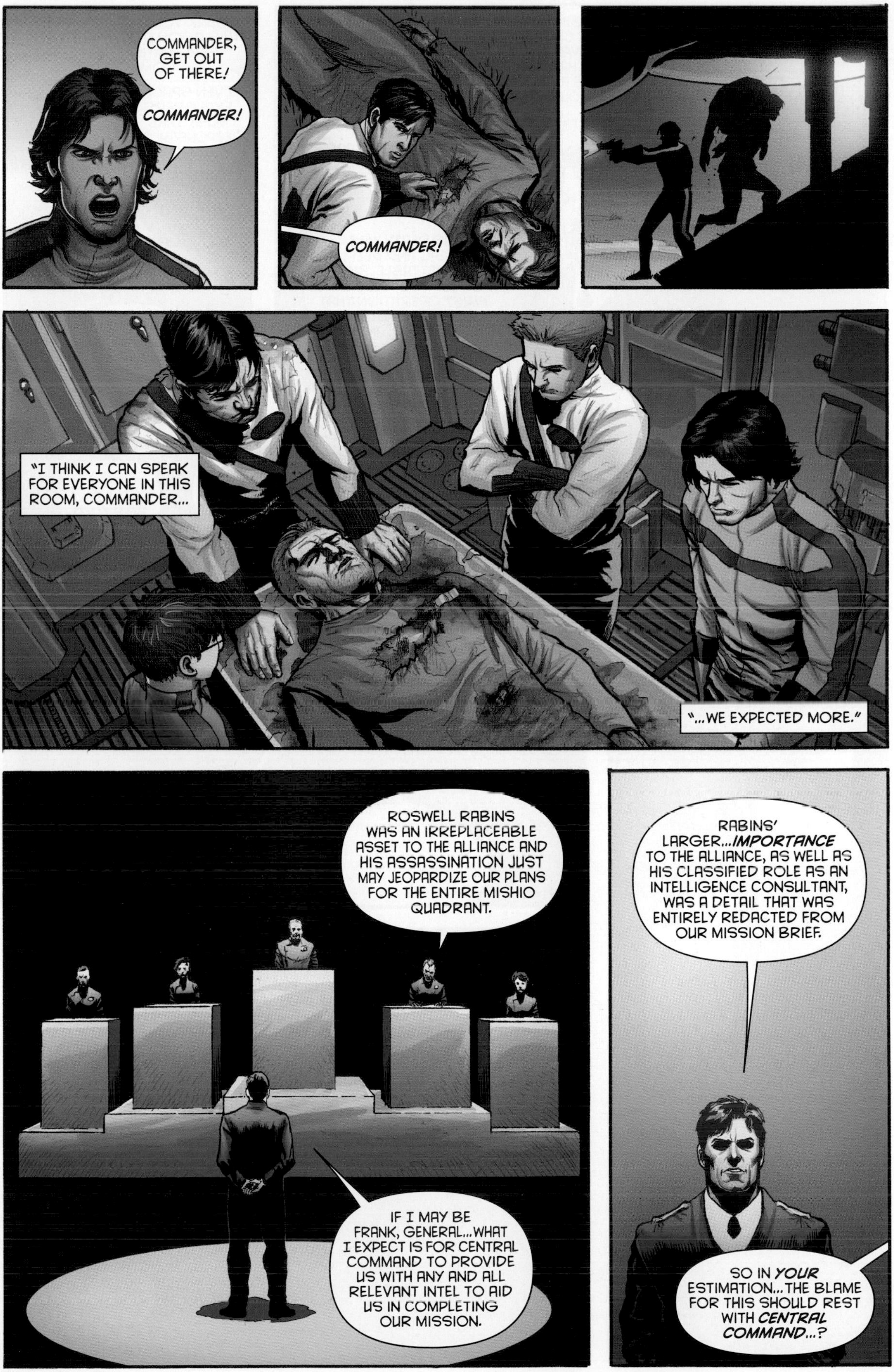
COMMANDER, GET OUT OF THERE!
COMMANDER!
COMMANDER!
"I THINK I CAN SPEAK FOR EVERYONE IN THIS ROOM, COMMANDER...
"...WE EXPECTED MORE."
ROSWELL RABINS WAS AN IRREPLACEABLE ASSET TO THE ALLIANCE AND HIS ASSASSINATION JUST MAY JEOPARDIZE OUR PLANS FOR THE ENTIRE MISHIO QUADRANT.
IF I MAY BE FRANK, GENERAL...WHAT I EXPECT IS FOR CENTRAL COMMAND TO PROVIDE US WITH ANY AND ALL RELEVANT INTEL TO AID US IN COMPLETING OUR MISSION.
RABINS' LARGER...IMPORTANCE TO THE ALLIANCE, AS WELL AS HIS CLASSIFIED ROLE AS AN INTELLIGENCE CONSULTANT, WAS A DETAIL THAT WAS ENTIRELY REDACTED FROM OUR MISSION BRIEF.
SO IN YOUR ESTIMATION...THE BLAME FOR THIS SHOULD REST WITH CENTRAL COMMAND...?

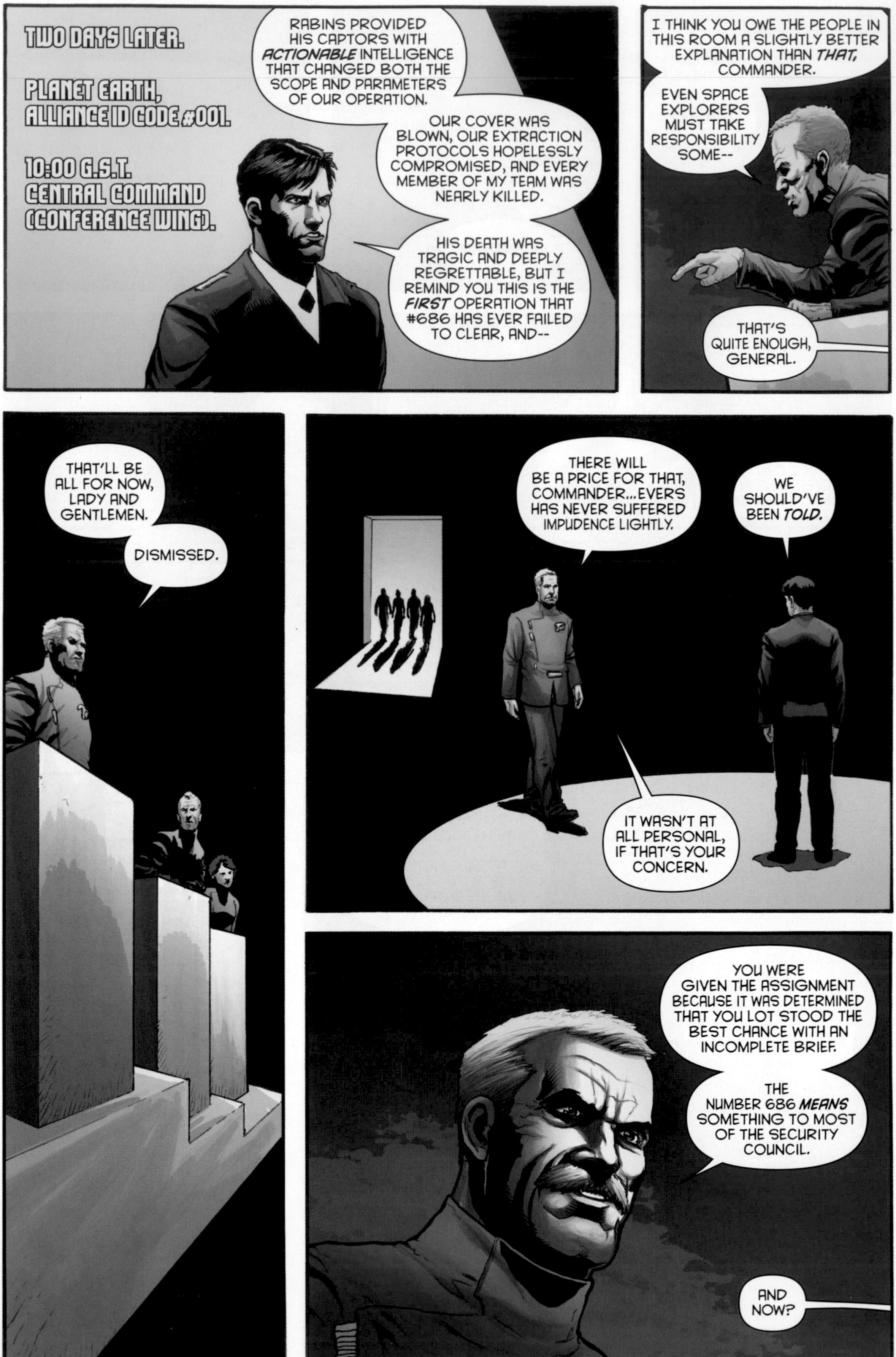
TWO DAYS LATER.
PLANET EARTH, ALLIANCE ID CODE #001.
10:00 G.S.T. CENTRAL COMMAND (CONFERENCE WING).
RABINS PROVIDED HIS CAPTORS WITH ACTIONABLE INTELLIGENCE THAT CHANGED BOTH THE SCOPE AND PARAMETERS OF OUR OPERATION.
OUR COVER WAS BLOWN, OUR EXTRACTION PROTOCOLS HOPELESSLY COMPROMISED, AND EVERY MEMBER OF MY TEAM WAS NEARLY KILLED.
HIS DEATH WAS TRAGIC AND DEEPLY REGRETTABLE, BUT I REMIND YOU THIS IS THE FIRST OPERATION THAT #686 HAS EVER FAILED TO CLEAR, AND--
I THINK YOU OWE THE PEOPLE IN THIS ROOM A SLIGHTLY BETTER EXPLANATION THAN THAT, COMMANDER.
EVEN SPACE EXPLORERS MUST TAKE RESPONSIBILITY SOME--
THAT'S QUITE ENOUGH, GENERAL.
THAT'LL BE ALL FOR NOW, LADY AND GENTLEMEN.
DISMISSED.
THERE WILL BE A PRICE FOR THAT, COMMANDER...EVERS HAS NEVER SUFFERED IMPUDENCE LIGHTLY.
WE SHOULD'VE BEEN TOLD.
IT WASN'T AT ALL PERSONAL, IF THAT'S YOUR CONCERN.
YOU WERE GIVEN THE ASSIGNMENT BECAUSE IT WAS DETERMINED THAT YOU LOT STOOD THE BEST CHANCE WITH AN INCOMPLETE BRIEF.
THE NUMBER 686 MEANS SOMETHING TO MOST OF THE SECURITY COUNCIL.
AND NOW?

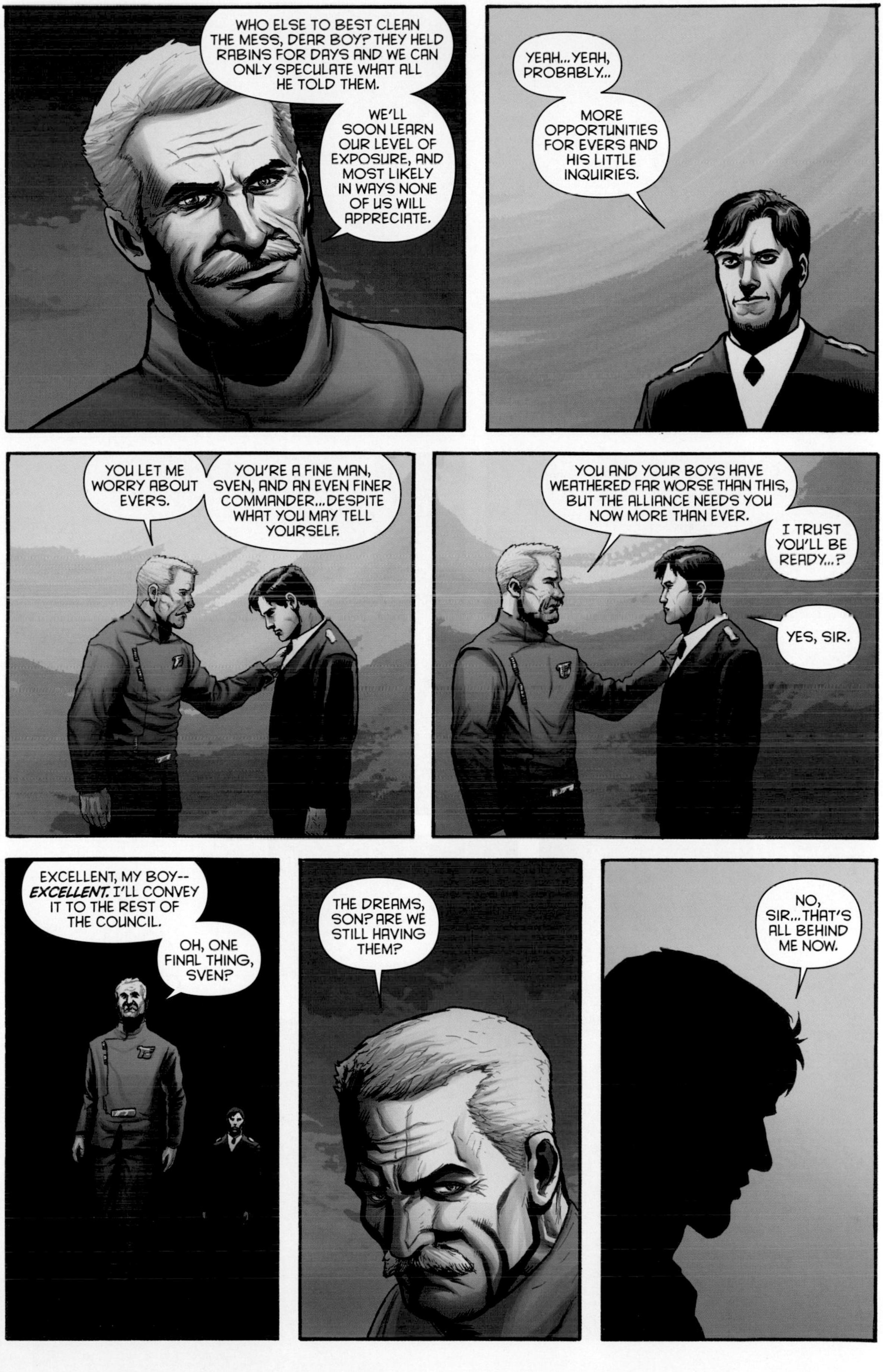
WHO ELSE TO BEST CLEAN THE MESS, DEAR BOY? THEY HELD RABINS FOR DAYS AND WE CAN ONLY SPECULATE WHAT ALL HE TOLD THEM.
WE'LL SOON LEARN OUR LEVEL OF EXPOSURE, AND MOST LIKELY IN WAYS NONE OF US WILL APPRECIATE.
YEAH...YEAH, PROBABLY...
MORE OPPORTUNITIES FOR EVERS AND HIS LITTLE INQUIRIES.
YOU LET ME WORRY ABOUT EVERS.
YOU'RE A FINE MAN, SVEN, AND AN EVEN FINER COMMANDER...DESPITE WHAT YOU MAY TELL YOURSELF.
YOU AND YOUR BOYS HAVE WEATHERED FAR WORSE THAN THIS, BUT THE ALLIANCE NEEDS YOU NOW MORE THAN EVER.
I TRUST YOU'LL BE READY...?
YES, SIR.
EXCELLENT, MY BOY-- *EXCELLENT.* I'LL CONVEY IT TO THE REST OF THE COUNCIL.
OH, ONE FINAL THING, SVEN?
THE DREAMS, SON? ARE WE STILL HAVING THEM?
NO, SIR...THAT'S ALL BEHIND ME NOW.

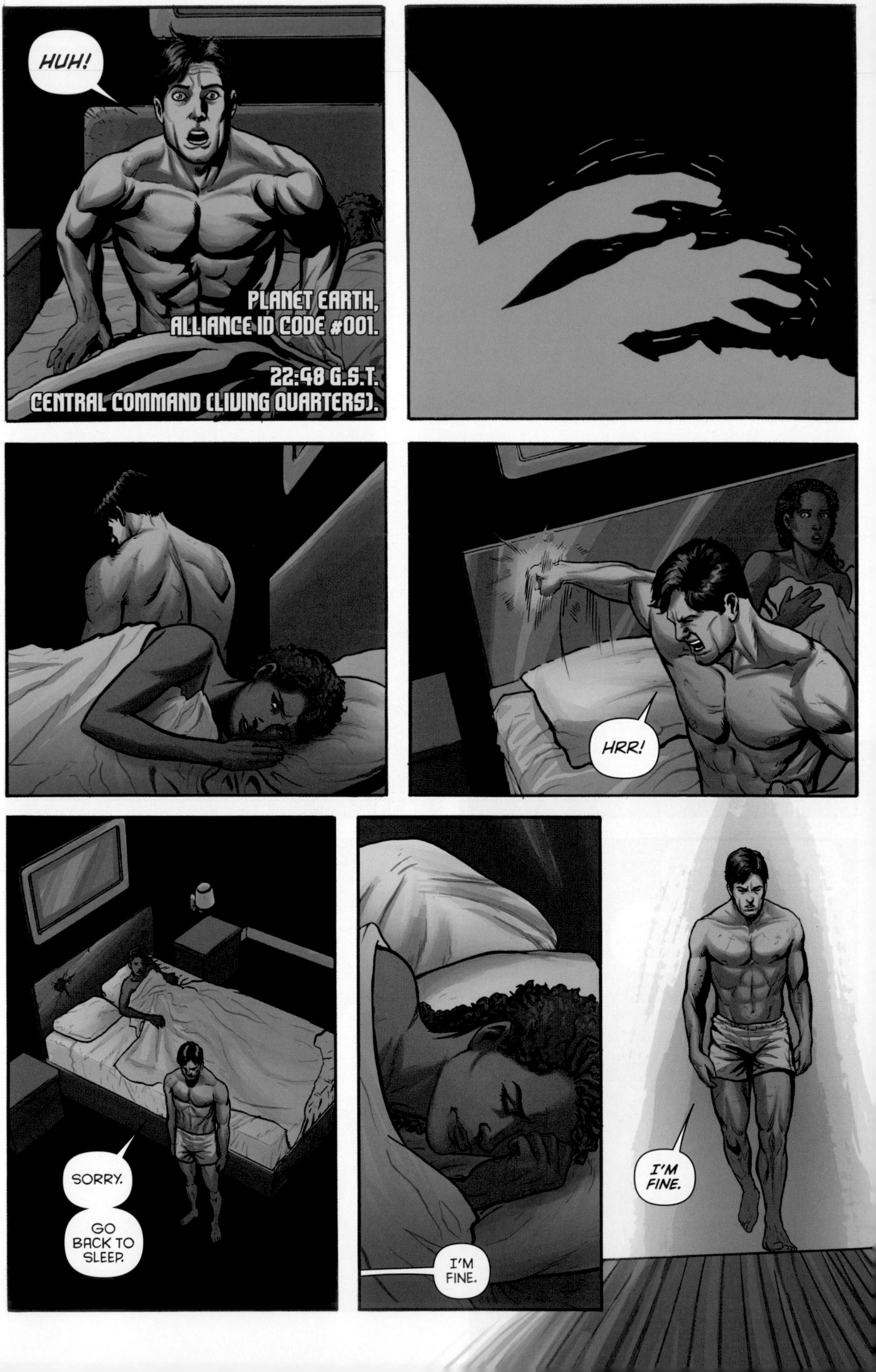
HUH!
PLANET EARTH,
ALLIANCE ID CODE #001.
22:48 G.S.T.
CENTRAL COMMAND (LIVING QUARTERS).
HRR!
SORRY.
GO BACK TO SLEEP.
I'M FINE.
I'M FINE.

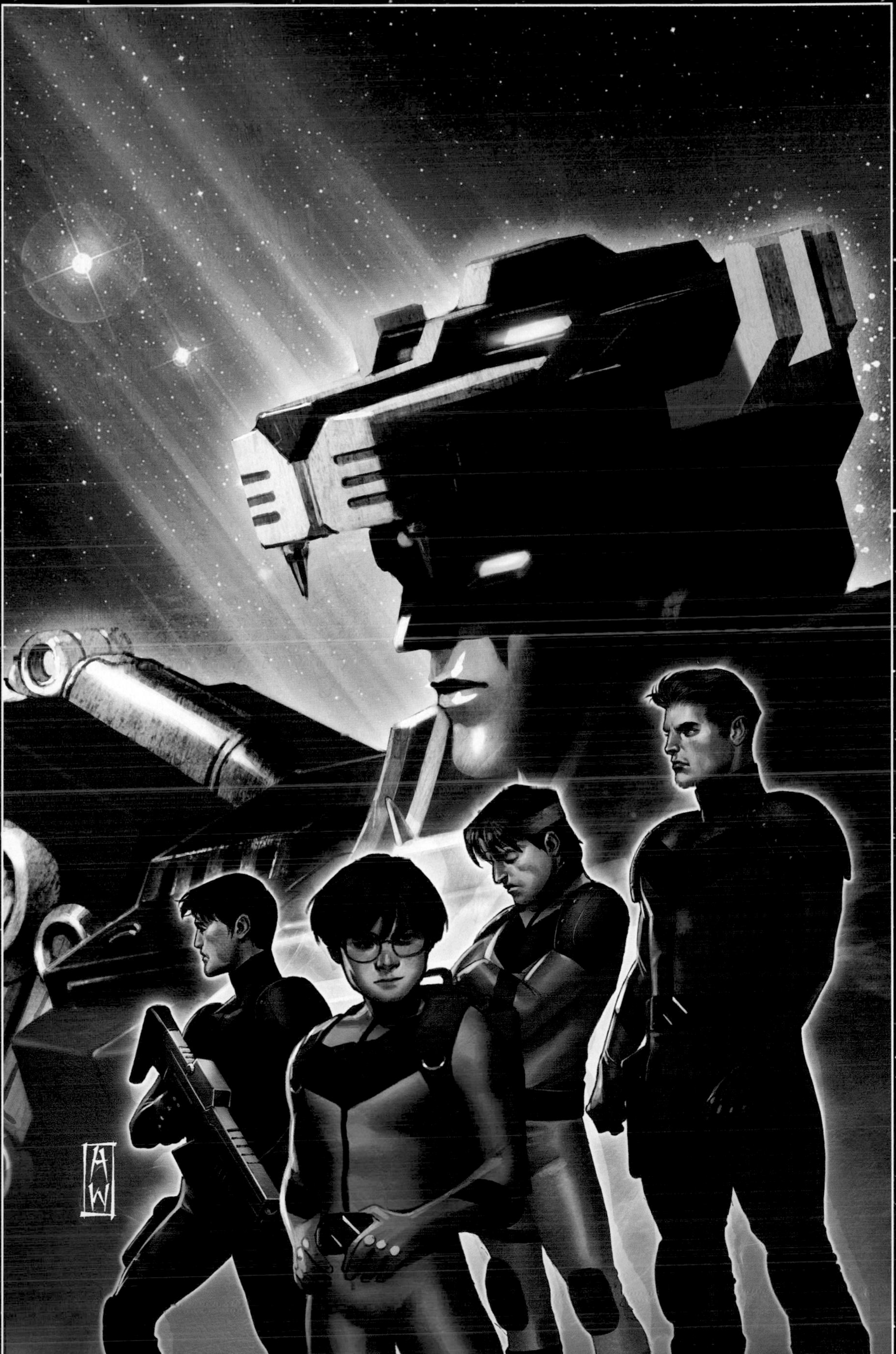
AW

Issue #3 cover by ADMIRA WIJAYA

ALL OF THIS IS MY FAULT.

I KNOW THAT.

EVERYONE IN THIS ROOM KNOWS THAT.

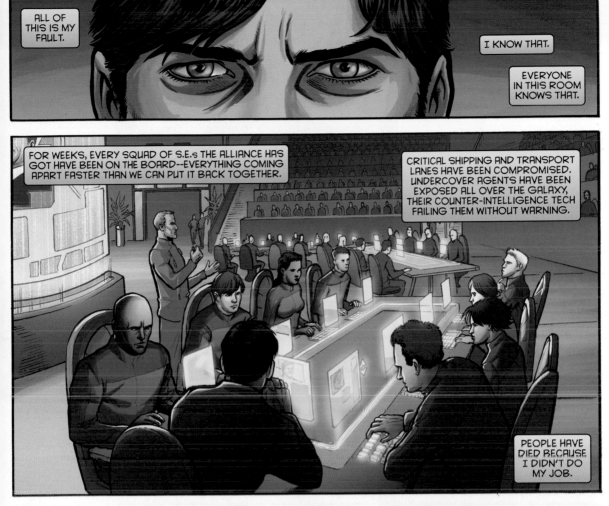

FOR WEEKS, EVERY SQUAD OF S.E.s THE ALLIANCE HAS GOT HAVE BEEN ON THE BOARD--EVERYTHING COMING APART FASTER THAN WE CAN PUT IT BACK TOGETHER.

CRITICAL SHIPPING AND TRANSPORT LANES HAVE BEEN COMPROMISED. UNDERCOVER AGENTS HAVE BEEN EXPOSED ALL OVER THE GALAXY, THEIR COUNTER-INTELLIGENCE TECH FAILING THEM WITHOUT WARNING.

PEOPLE HAVE DIED BECAUSE I DIDN'T DO MY JOB.

AND BY THE TIME THIS BRIEFING IS OVER, MORE PEOPLE WILL LIKELY BE DEAD.

GENERAL EVERS DOESN'T HAVE TO REMIND EVERYONE OF THAT FACT, BUT HE DOES ANYWAY.

MY TEAM FAILS ANOTHER OP AND EVERY SINGLE ONE OF US IS BENCHED UNTIL THE NEXT CYCLE.

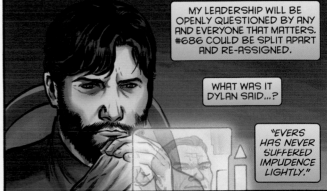

MY LEADERSHIP WILL BE OPENLY QUESTIONED BY ANY AND EVERYONE THAT MATTERS. #686 COULD BE SPLIT APART AND RE-ASSIGNED.

WHAT WAS IT DYLAN SAID...?

"EVERS HAS NEVER SUFFERED IMPUDENCE LIGHTLY."

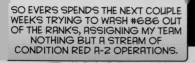
SO EVERS SPENDS THE NEXT COUPLE WEEKS TRYING TO WASH #686 OUT OF THE RANKS, ASSIGNING MY TEAM NOTHING BUT A STREAM OF CONDITION RED A-2 OPERATIONS.

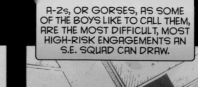
A-2s, OR GORSES, AS SOME OF THE BOYS LIKE TO CALL THEM, ARE THE MOST DIFFICULT, MOST HIGH-RISK ENGAGEMENTS AN S.E. SQUAD CAN DRAW.

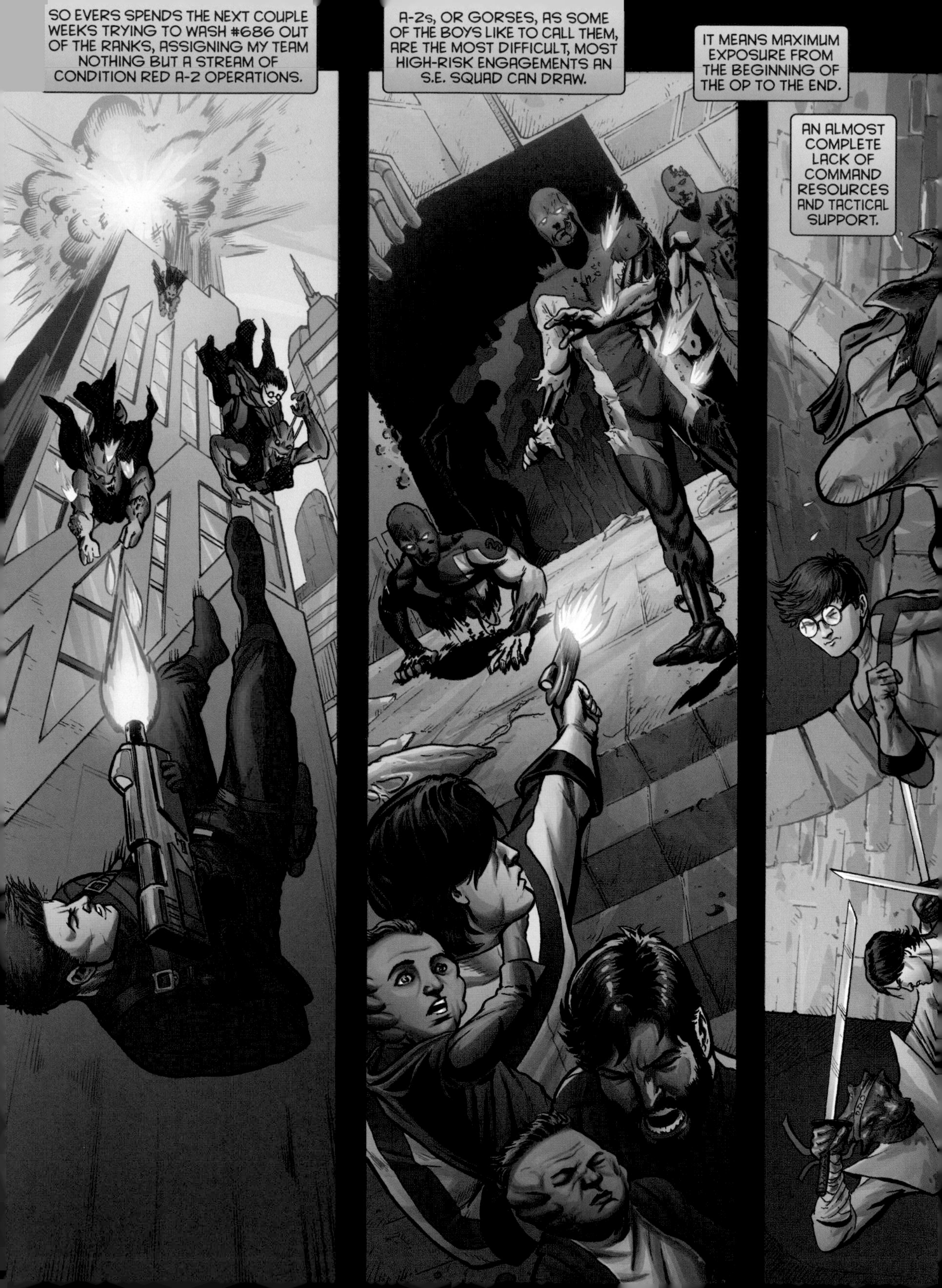

IT MEANS MAXIMUM EXPOSURE FROM THE BEGINNING OF THE OP TO THE END.

AN ALMOST COMPLETE LACK OF COMMAND RESOURCES AND TACTICAL SUPPORT.

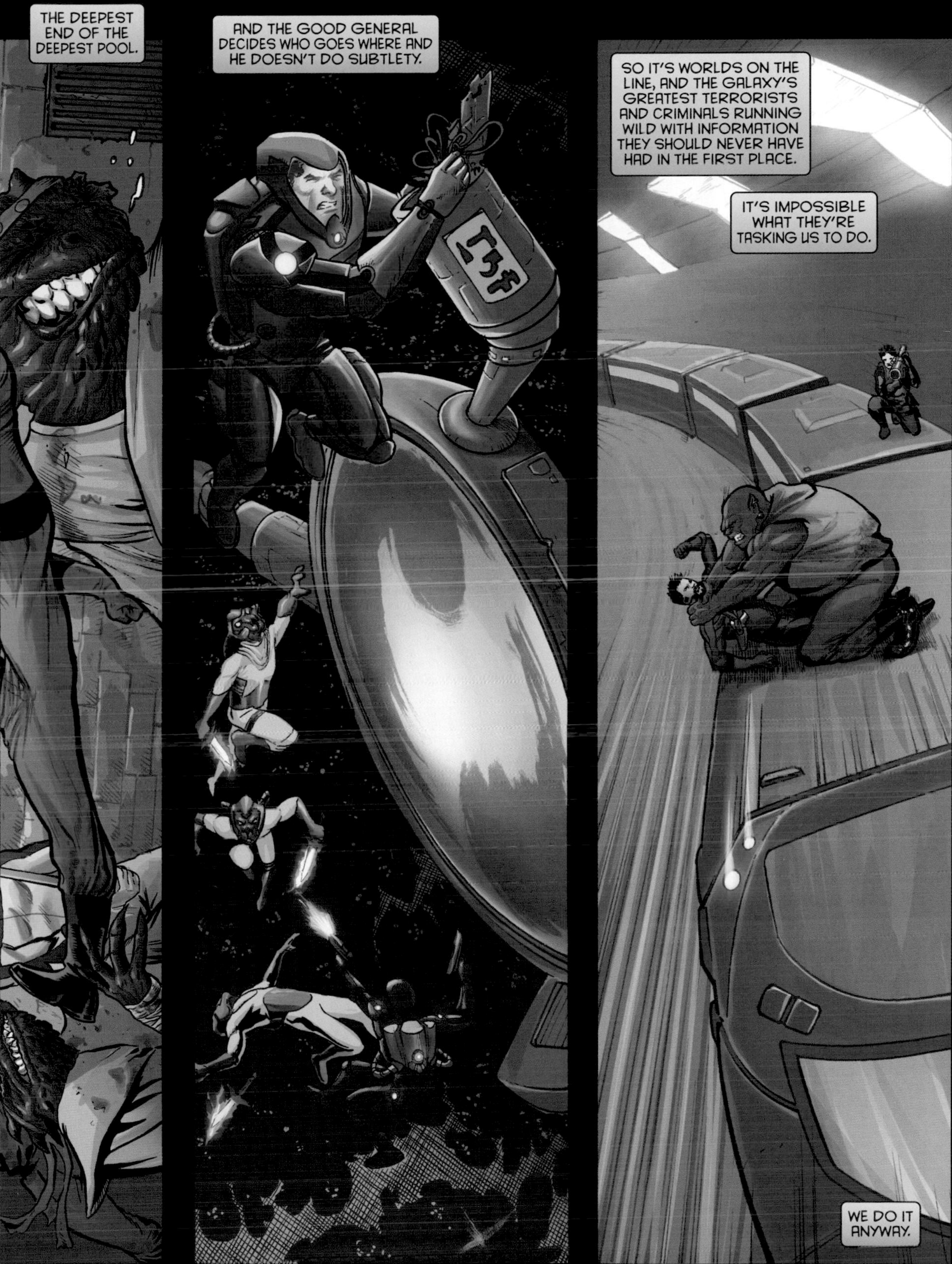
THE DEEPEST END OF THE DEEPEST POOL.
AND THE GOOD GENERAL DECIDES WHO GOES WHERE AND HE DOESN'T DO SUBTLETY.
SO IT'S WORLDS ON THE LINE, AND THE GALAXY'S GREATEST TERRORISTS AND CRIMINALS RUNNING WILD WITH INFORMATION THEY SHOULD NEVER HAVE HAD IN THE FIRST PLACE.
IT'S IMPOSSIBLE WHAT THEY'RE TASKING US TO DO.
WE DO IT ANYWAY.

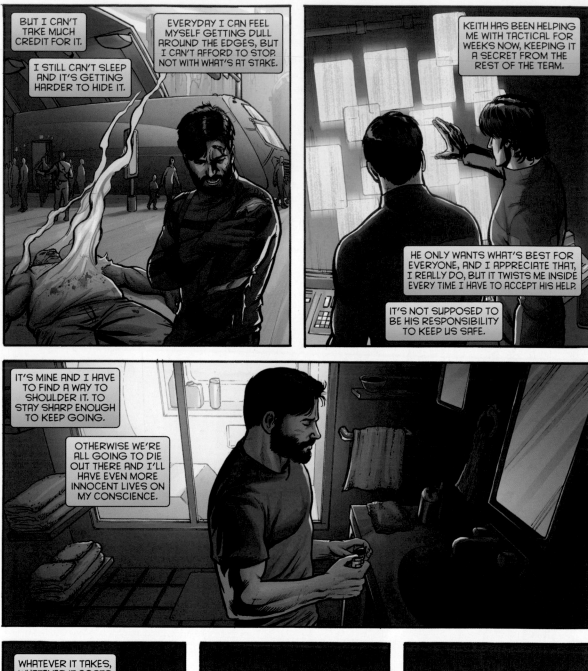

BUT I CAN'T TAKE MUCH CREDIT FOR IT.

I STILL CAN'T SLEEP AND IT'S GETTING HARDER TO HIDE IT.

EVERYDAY I CAN FEEL MYSELF GETTING DULL AROUND THE EDGES, BUT I CAN'T AFFORD TO STOP. NOT WITH WHAT'S AT STAKE.

KEITH HAS BEEN HELPING ME WITH TACTICAL FOR WEEKS NOW, KEEPING IT A SECRET FROM THE REST OF THE TEAM.

HE ONLY WANTS WHAT'S BEST FOR EVERYONE, AND I APPRECIATE THAT, I REALLY DO, BUT IT TWISTS ME INSIDE EVERY TIME I HAVE TO ACCEPT HIS HELP.

IT'S NOT SUPPOSED TO BE HIS RESPONSIBILITY TO KEEP US SAFE.

IT'S MINE AND I HAVE TO FIND A WAY TO SHOULDER IT. TO STAY SHARP ENOUGH TO KEEP GOING.

OTHERWISE WE'RE ALL GOING TO DIE OUT THERE AND I'LL HAVE EVEN MORE INNOCENT LIVES ON MY CONSCIENCE.

WHATEVER IT TAKES, WHATEVER IT COSTS ME--I WILL DO ANYTHING TO KEEP MY TEAM SAFE.

ANYTHING.

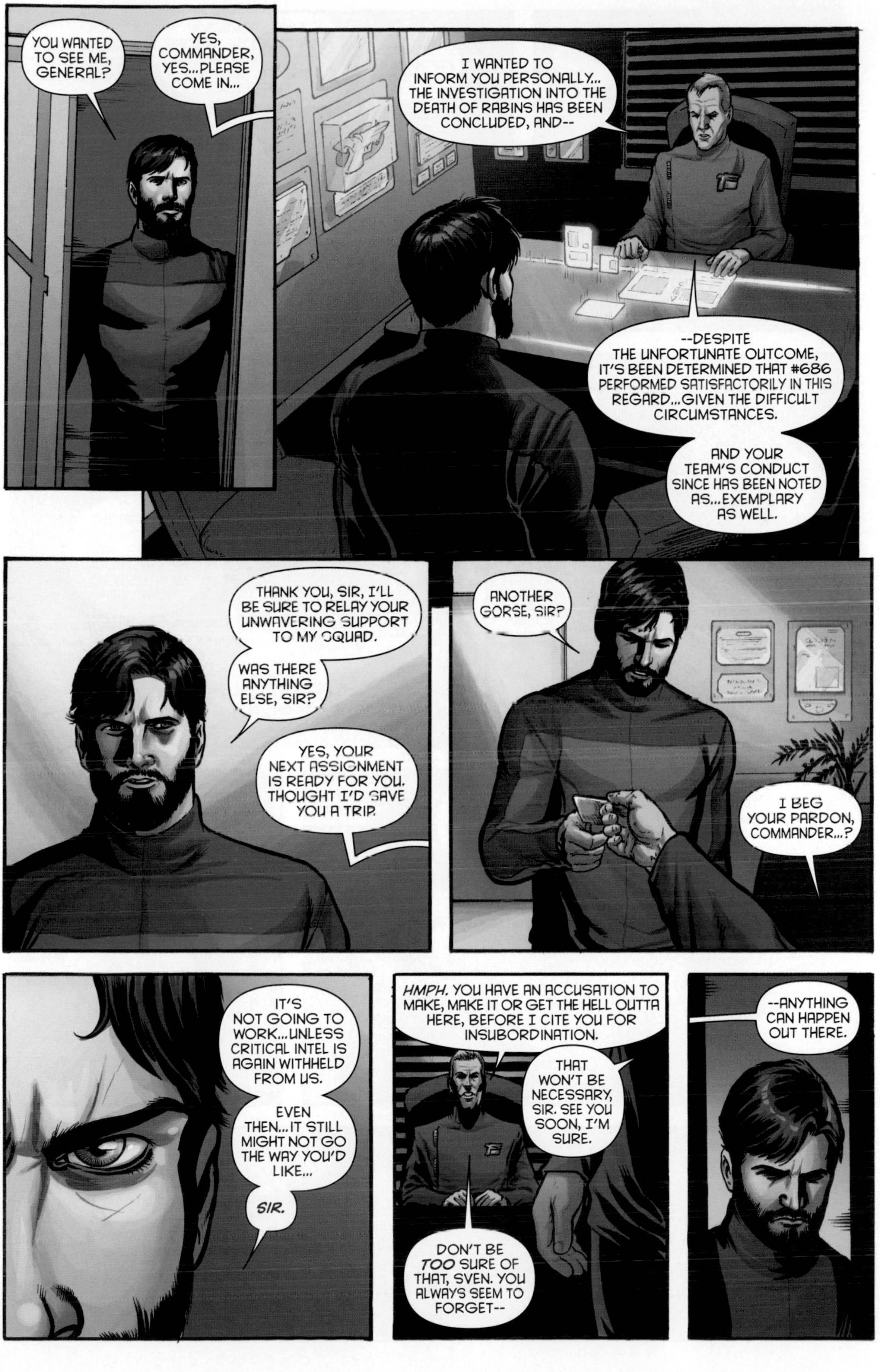
YOU WANTED TO SEE ME, GENERAL?
YES, COMMANDER, YES...PLEASE COME IN...
I WANTED TO INFORM YOU PERSONALLY... THE INVESTIGATION INTO THE DEATH OF RABINS HAS BEEN CONCLUDED, AND--
--DESPITE THE UNFORTUNATE OUTCOME, IT'S BEEN DETERMINED THAT #686 PERFORMED SATISFACTORILY IN THIS REGARD...GIVEN THE DIFFICULT CIRCUMSTANCES.
AND YOUR TEAM'S CONDUCT SINCE HAS BEEN NOTED AS...EXEMPLARY AS WELL.
THANK YOU, SIR, I'LL BE SURE TO RELAY YOUR UNWAVERING SUPPORT TO MY SQUAD.
WAS THERE ANYTHING ELSE, SIR?
YES, YOUR NEXT ASSIGNMENT IS READY FOR YOU. THOUGHT I'D SAVE YOU A TRIP.
ANOTHER GORSE, SIR?
I BEG YOUR PARDON, COMMANDER...?
IT'S NOT GOING TO WORK...UNLESS CRITICAL INTEL IS AGAIN WITHHELD FROM US.
EVEN THEN...IT STILL MIGHT NOT GO THE WAY YOU'D LIKE...
SIR.
HMPH. YOU HAVE AN ACCUSATION TO MAKE, MAKE IT OR GET THE HELL OUTTA HERE, BEFORE I CITE YOU FOR INSUBORDINATION.
THAT WON'T BE NECESSARY, SIR. SEE YOU SOON, I'M SURE.
DON'T BE TOO SURE OF THAT, SVEN. YOU ALWAYS SEEM TO FORGET--
--ANYTHING CAN HAPPEN OUT THERE.

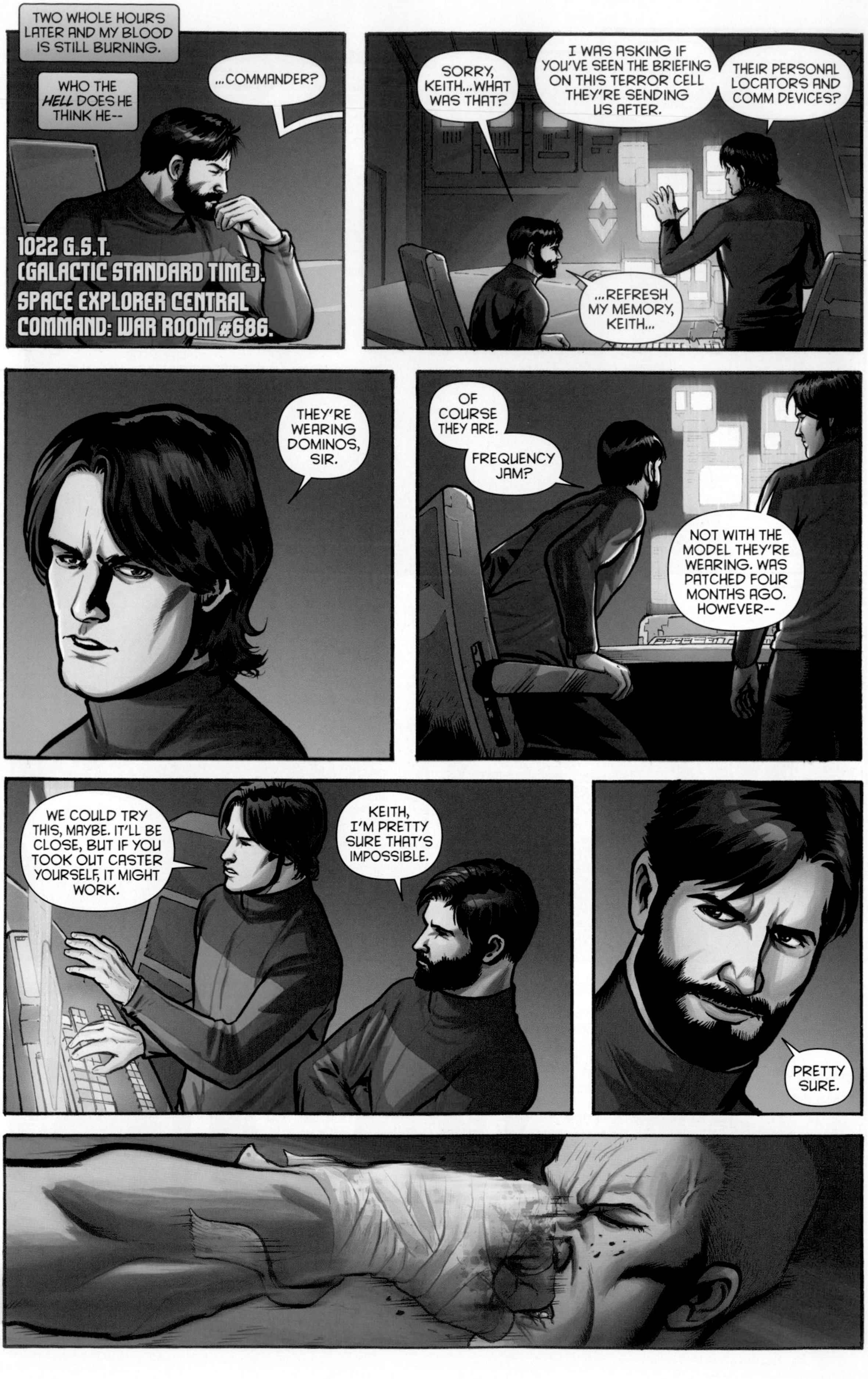
TWO WHOLE HOURS LATER AND MY BLOOD IS STILL BURNING.
WHO THE HELL DOES HE THINK HE--
...COMMANDER?
1022 G.S.T. (GALACTIC STANDARD TIME).
SPACE EXPLORER CENTRAL COMMAND: WAR ROOM #686.
SORRY, KEITH...WHAT WAS THAT?
I WAS ASKING IF YOU'VE SEEN THE BRIEFING ON THIS TERROR CELL THEY'RE SENDING US AFTER.
THEIR PERSONAL LOCATORS AND COMM DEVICES?
...REFRESH MY MEMORY, KEITH...
THEY'RE WEARING DOMINOS, SIR.
OF COURSE THEY ARE.
FREQUENCY JAM?
NOT WITH THE MODEL THEY'RE WEARING. WAS PATCHED FOUR MONTHS AGO. HOWEVER--
WE COULD TRY THIS, MAYBE. IT'LL BE CLOSE, BUT IF YOU TOOK OUT CASTER YOURSELF, IT MIGHT WORK.
KEITH, I'M PRETTY SURE THAT'S IMPOSSIBLE.
PRETTY SURE.

PLANET PILERIA,
ALLIANCE ID CODE #006.

2152 G.S.T.
BASEMENT OF
CASTER INC. BUILDING.

NAME: *MILTON WELLIVER*
AGE: *47*
CHARGES: *DOMESTIC TERRORISM,
AGGRAVATED ASSAULT, MURDER*
GROUP AFFILIATION: *TWO SUNS*
LOCATOR ID TAG *#317864259*

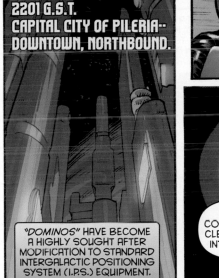

PLANET PILERIA,
ALLIANCE ID CODE #006.

2201 G.S.T.
CAPITAL CITY OF PILERIA--
DOWNTOWN, NORTHBOUND.

"DOMINOS" HAVE BECOME A HIGHLY SOUGHT AFTER MODIFICATION TO STANDARD INTERGALACTIC POSITIONING SYSTEM (I.P.S.) EQUIPMENT.

SPACE EXPLORERS USE THEM PRIMARILY FOR DEEP COVER OPERATIONS, OR FOR RETIRED AGENTS COMMAND FEELS MIGHT HAVE TROUBLE STAYING OUT OF TROUBLE.

SAY YOU'RE RUNNING A SLEEPER CELL, WITH MEMBERS AND AFFILIATES SPREAD ACROSS NEIGHBORING PLANETS AND SYSTEMS.

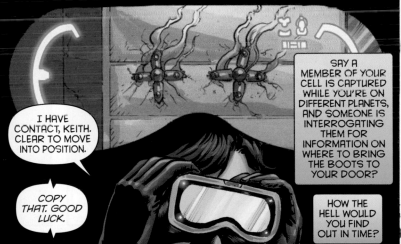

I HAVE CONTACT, KEITH. CLEAR TO MOVE INTO POSITION.

COPY THAT. GOOD LUCK.

SAY A MEMBER OF YOUR CELL IS CAPTURED WHILE YOU'RE ON DIFFERENT PLANETS, AND SOMEONE IS INTERROGATING THEM FOR INFORMATION ON WHERE TO BRING THE BOOTS TO YOUR DOOR?

HOW THE HELL WOULD YOU FIND OUT IN TIME?

YOUR SEAT, SIR.

THANK YOU.

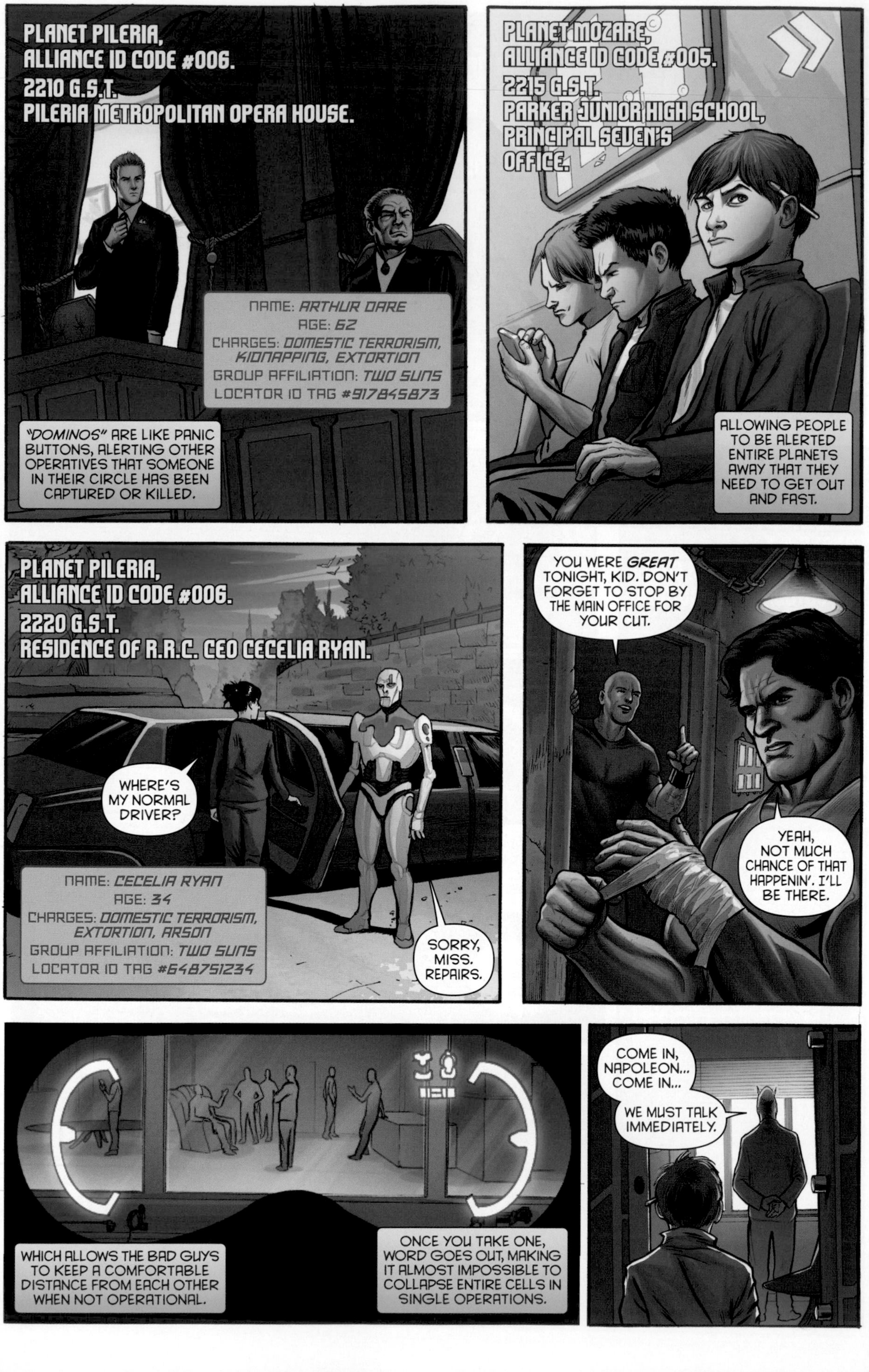
PLANET PILERIA,
ALLIANCE ID CODE #006.
2210 G.S.T.
PILERIA METROPOLITAN OPERA HOUSE.
NAME: ARTHUR DARE
AGE: 62
CHARGES: DOMESTIC TERRORISM, KIDNAPPING, EXTORTION
GROUP AFFILIATION: TWO SUNS
LOCATOR ID TAG #917845873
"DOMINOS" ARE LIKE PANIC BUTTONS, ALERTING OTHER OPERATIVES THAT SOMEONE IN THEIR CIRCLE HAS BEEN CAPTURED OR KILLED.
PLANET MOZARE,
ALLIANCE ID CODE #005.
2215 G.S.T.
PARKER JUNIOR HIGH SCHOOL,
PRINCIPAL SEVEN'S OFFICE.
ALLOWING PEOPLE TO BE ALERTED ENTIRE PLANETS AWAY THAT THEY NEED TO GET OUT AND FAST.
PLANET PILERIA,
ALLIANCE ID CODE #006.
2220 G.S.T.
RESIDENCE OF R.R.C. CEO CECELIA RYAN.
WHERE'S MY NORMAL DRIVER?
NAME: CECELIA RYAN
AGE: 34
CHARGES: DOMESTIC TERRORISM, EXTORTION, ARSON
GROUP AFFILIATION: TWO SUNS
LOCATOR ID TAG #648751234
SORRY, MISS. REPAIRS.
YOU WERE GREAT TONIGHT, KID. DON'T FORGET TO STOP BY THE MAIN OFFICE FOR YOUR CUT.
YEAH, NOT MUCH CHANCE OF THAT HAPPENIN'. I'LL BE THERE.
WHICH ALLOWS THE BAD GUYS TO KEEP A COMFORTABLE DISTANCE FROM EACH OTHER WHEN NOT OPERATIONAL.
ONCE YOU TAKE ONE, WORD GOES OUT, MAKING IT ALMOST IMPOSSIBLE TO COLLAPSE ENTIRE CELLS IN SINGLE OPERATIONS.
COME IN, NAPOLEON... COME IN...
WE MUST TALK IMMEDIATELY.

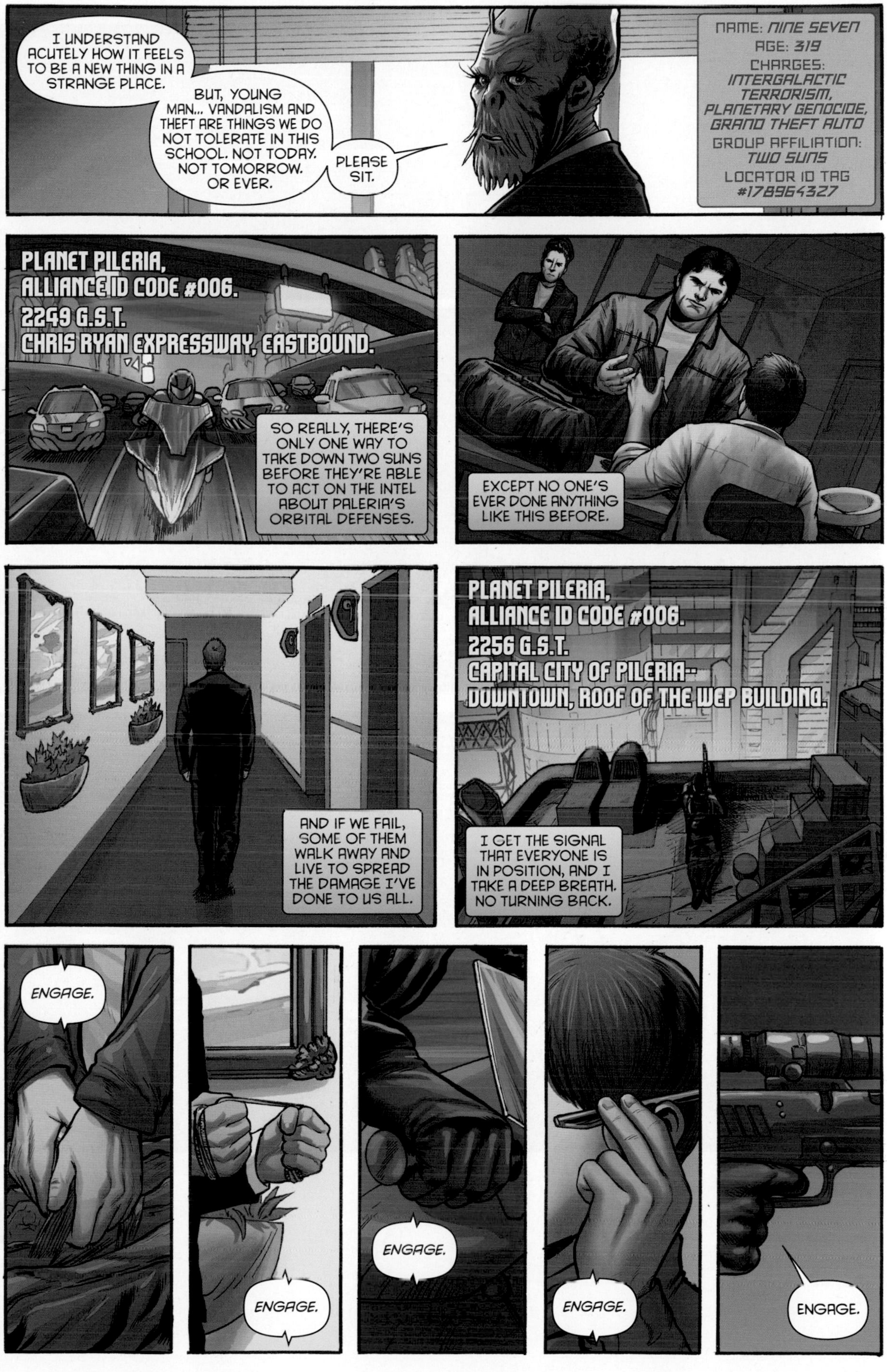
I UNDERSTAND ACUTELY HOW IT FEELS TO BE A NEW THING IN A STRANGE PLACE.
BUT, YOUNG MAN... VANDALISM AND THEFT ARE THINGS WE DO NOT TOLERATE IN THIS SCHOOL. NOT TODAY. NOT TOMORROW. OR EVER.
PLEASE SIT.
NAME: NINE SEVEN AGE: 319 CHARGES: INTERGALACTIC TERRORISM, PLANETARY GENOCIDE, GRAND THEFT AUTO GROUP AFFILIATION: TWO SUNS LOCATOR ID TAG #178964327
PLANET PILERIA, ALLIANCE ID CODE #006. 2249 G.S.T. CHRIS RYAN EXPRESSWAY, EASTBOUND.
SO REALLY, THERE'S ONLY ONE WAY TO TAKE DOWN TWO SUNS BEFORE THEY'RE ABLE TO ACT ON THE INTEL ABOUT PALERIA'S ORBITAL DEFENSES.
EXCEPT NO ONE'S EVER DONE ANYTHING LIKE THIS BEFORE.
AND IF WE FAIL, SOME OF THEM WALK AWAY AND LIVE TO SPREAD THE DAMAGE I'VE DONE TO US ALL.
PLANET PILERIA, ALLIANCE ID CODE #006. 2256 G.S.T. CAPITAL CITY OF PILERIA-- DOWNTOWN, ROOF OF THE WEP BUILDING.
I GET THE SIGNAL THAT EVERYONE IS IN POSITION, AND I TAKE A DEEP BREATH. NO TURNING BACK.
ENGAGE.
ENGAGE.
ENGAGE.
ENGAGE.
ENGAGE.

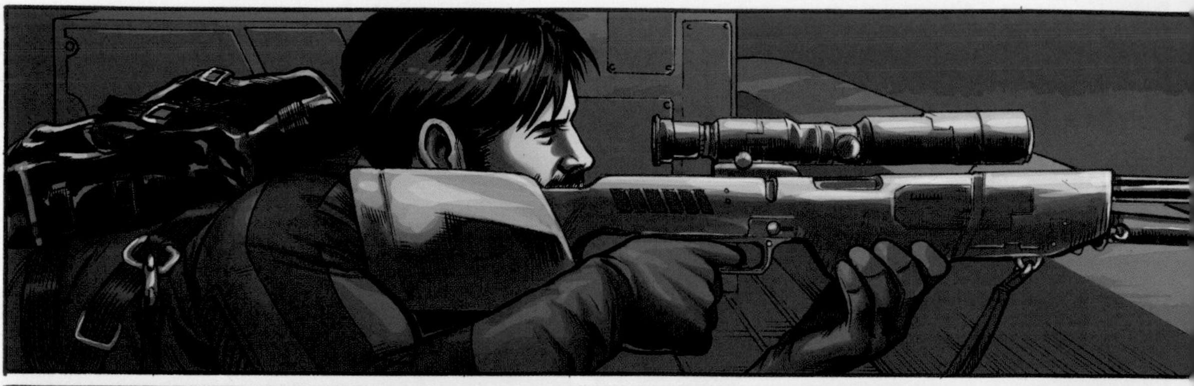
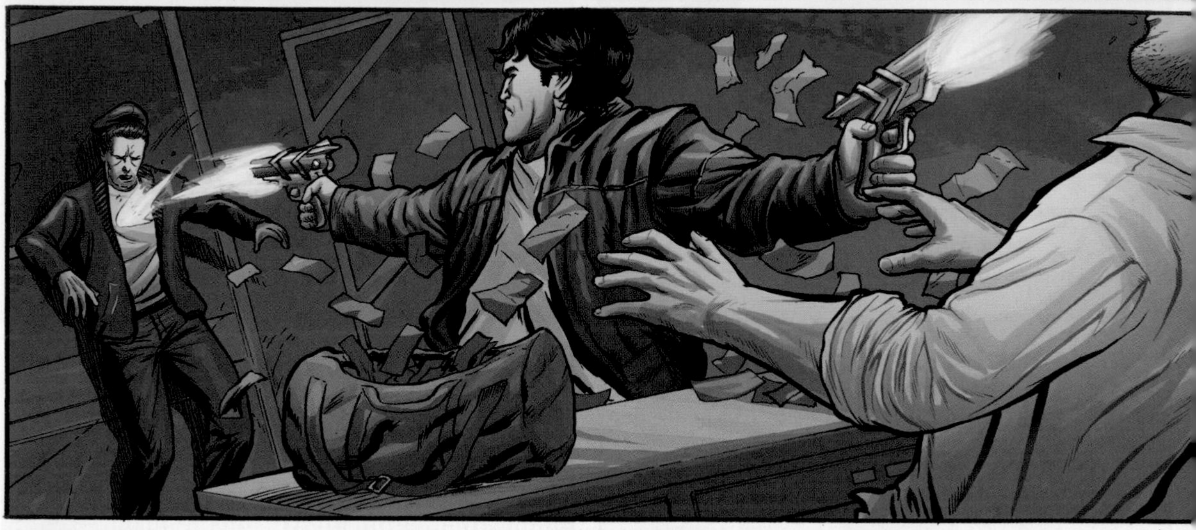
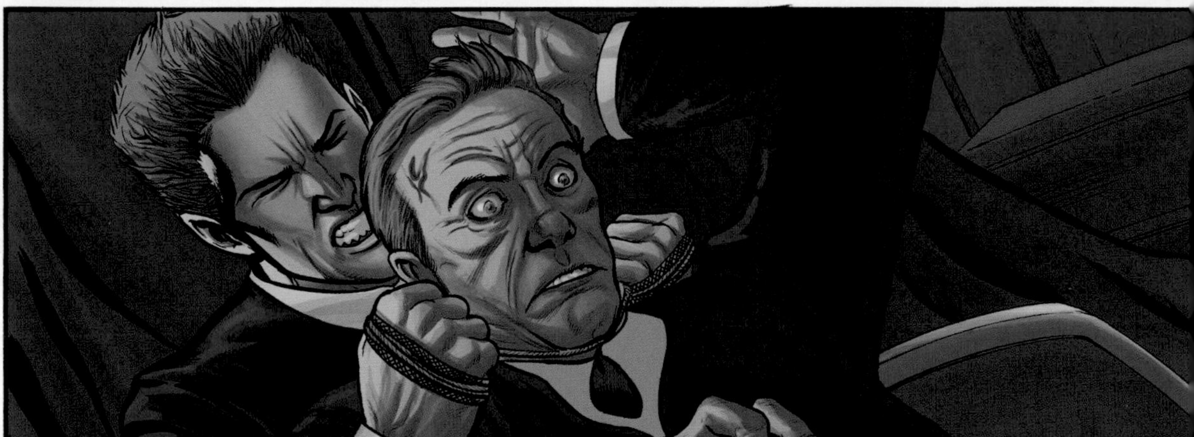
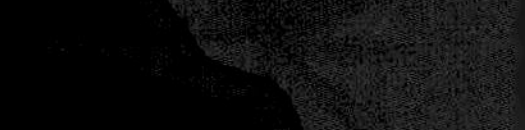

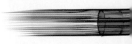

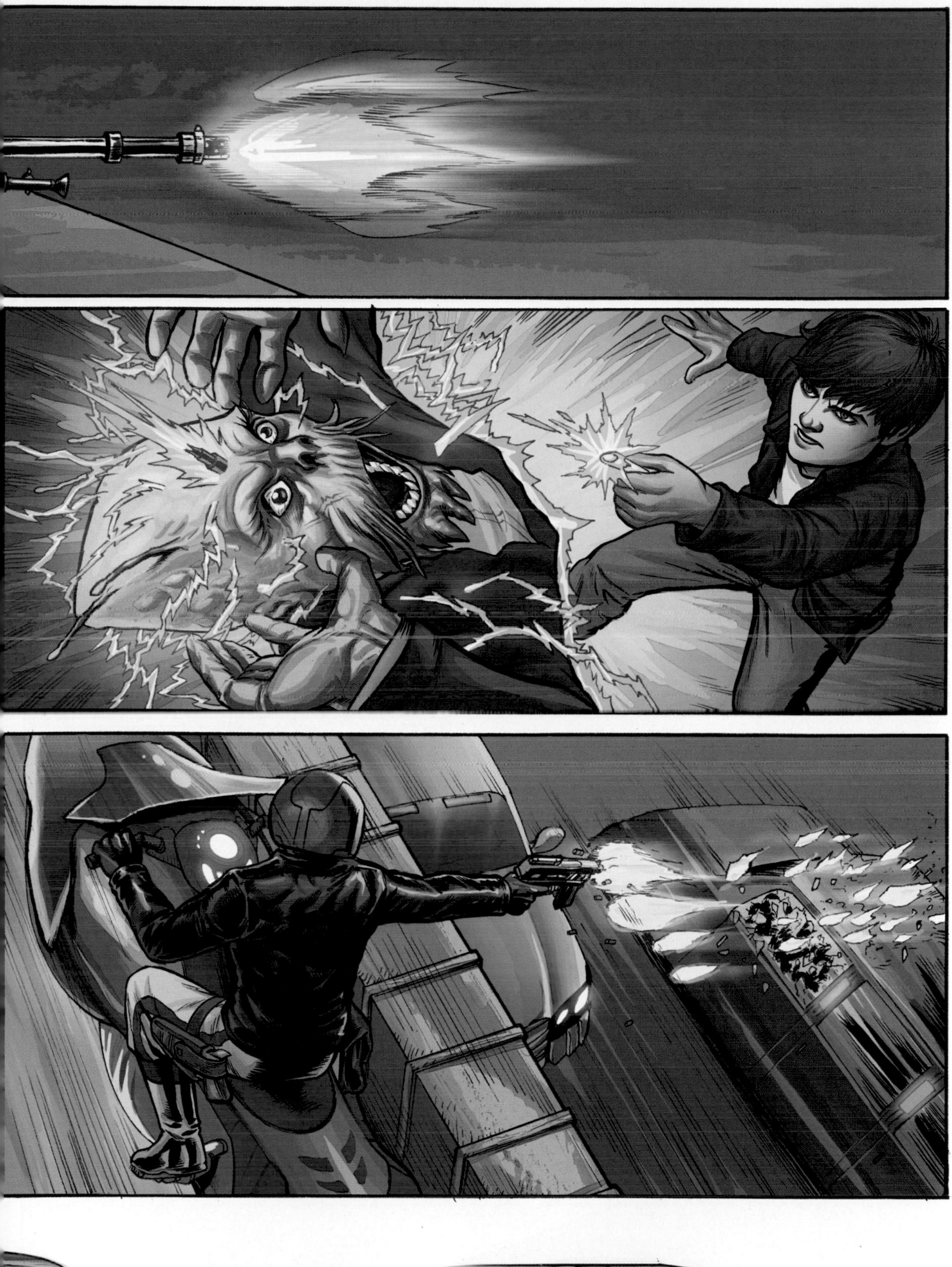

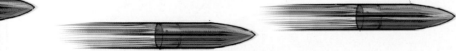

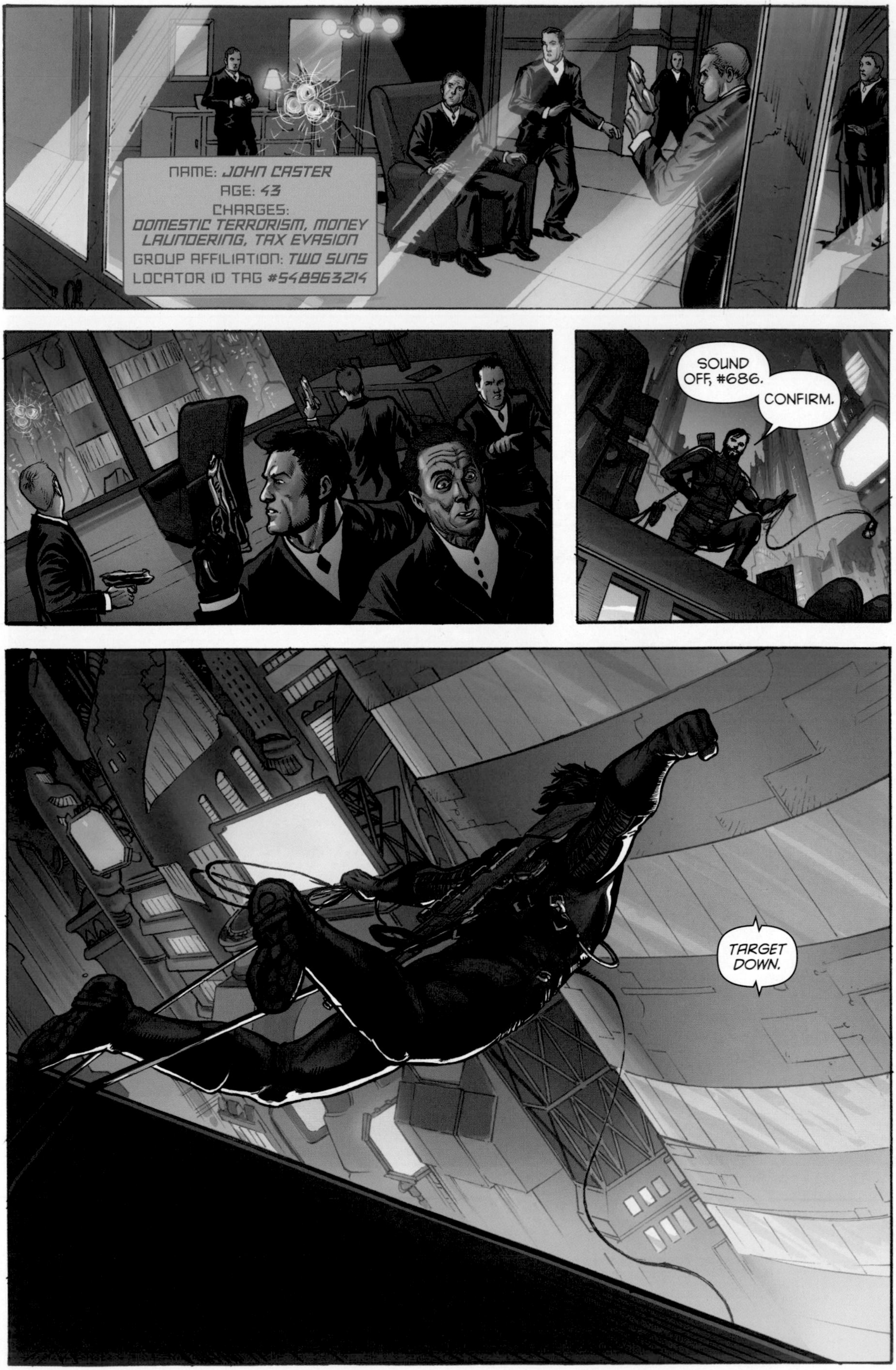
NAME: JOHN CASTER
AGE: 43
CHARGES:
DOMESTIC TERRORISM, MONEY LAUNDERING, TAX EVASION
GROUP AFFILIATION: TWO SUNS
LOCATOR ID TAG #548963214
SOUND OFF, #686.
CONFIRM.
TARGET DOWN.

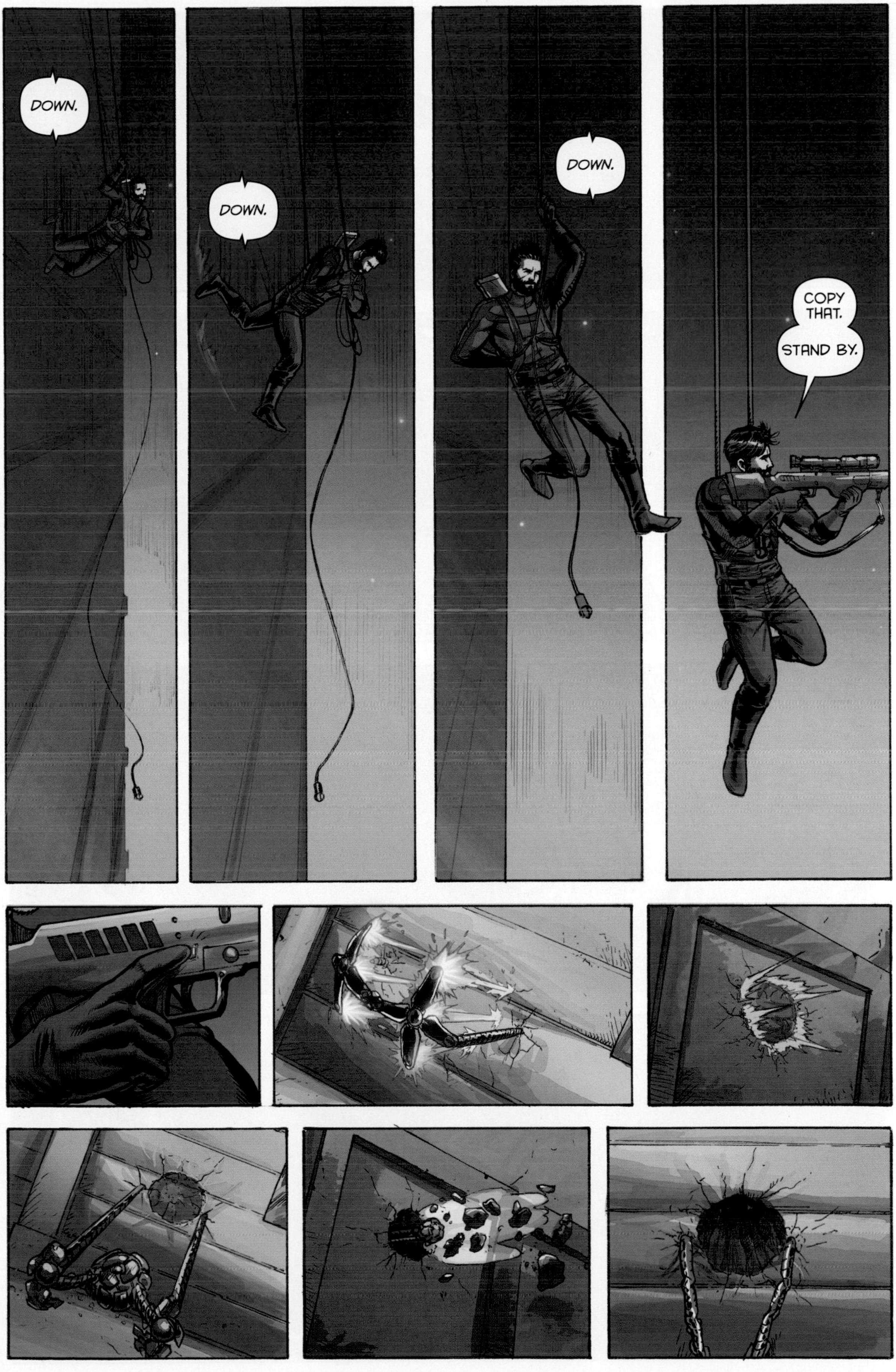
DOWN.
DOWN.
DOWN.
COPY THAT.
STAND BY.

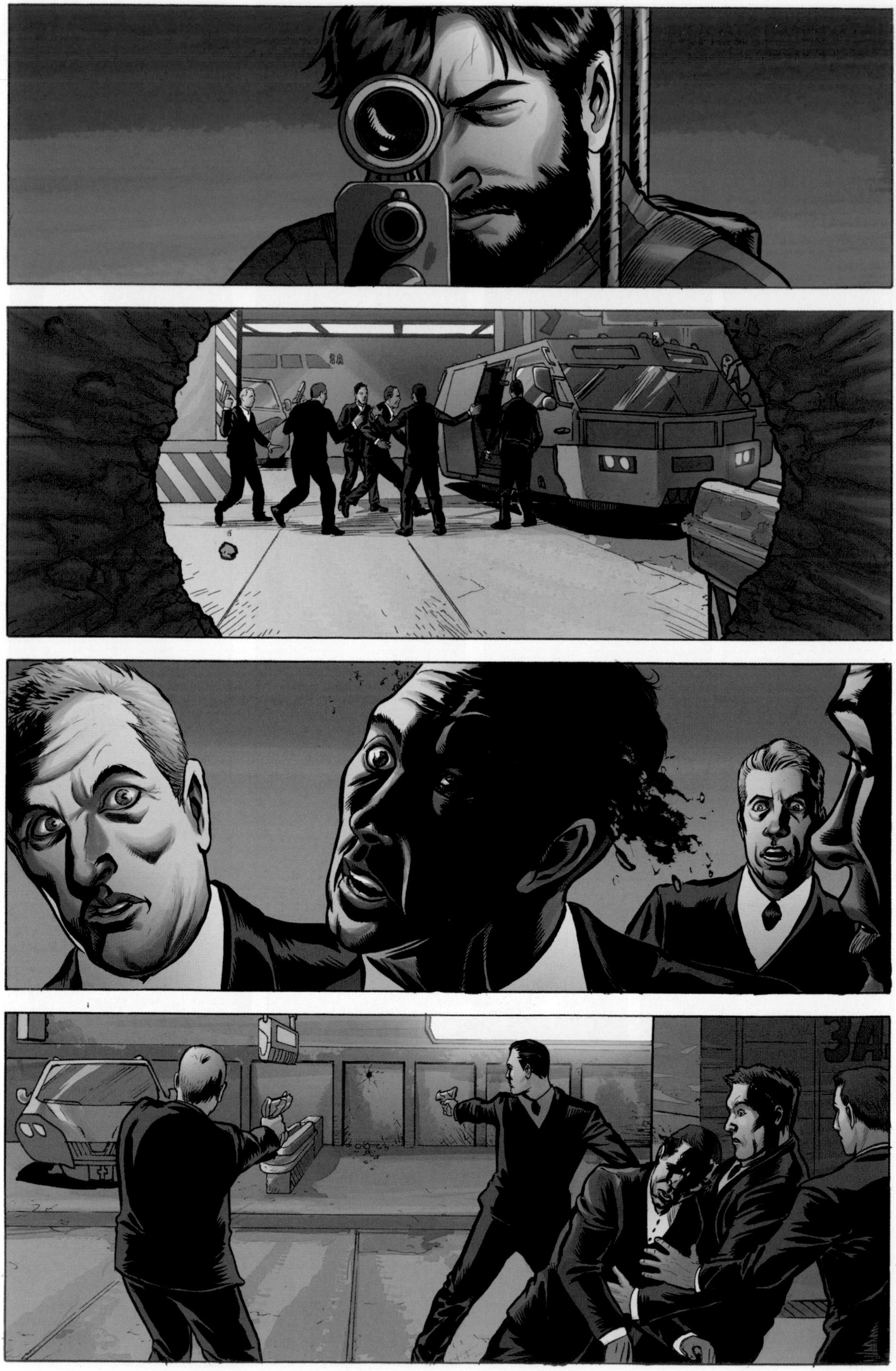
3A
3A

FIVE DOWN.

GOOD WORK, GENTLEMEN.

EVERYONE OFF-PLANET AND BACK IN THE OPS ROOM AT 0900.

SHARP.

IT WOULD BE HOURS BEFORE I'D REALIZE WHAT WE'D JUST DONE.

AND I KNOW THERE WAS NO REAL WAY TO KNOW, THAT WAS THE ENTIRE POINT, BUT STILL...THE TWO SUNS MISSION CHANGED EVERYTHING FOR ALL OF US...

I KNOW THAT NOW.

PLANET EARTH, ALLIANCE ID CODE #001.

0850 G.6.T.
SPACE EXPLORER CENTRAL COMMAND: WAR ROOM #686

I SHOULD FIND ANOTHER WAY.

THERE'LL BE NO TURNING BACK FROM THIS. NOT IF I'M RIGHT.

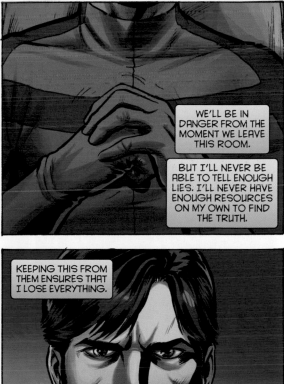

WE'LL BE IN DANGER FROM THE MOMENT WE LEAVE THIS ROOM.

BUT I'LL NEVER BE ABLE TO TELL ENOUGH LIES. I'LL NEVER HAVE ENOUGH RESOURCES ON MY OWN TO FIND THE TRUTH.

KEEPING THIS FROM THEM ENSURES THAT I LOSE EVERYTHING.

TELLING THEM ENSURES--

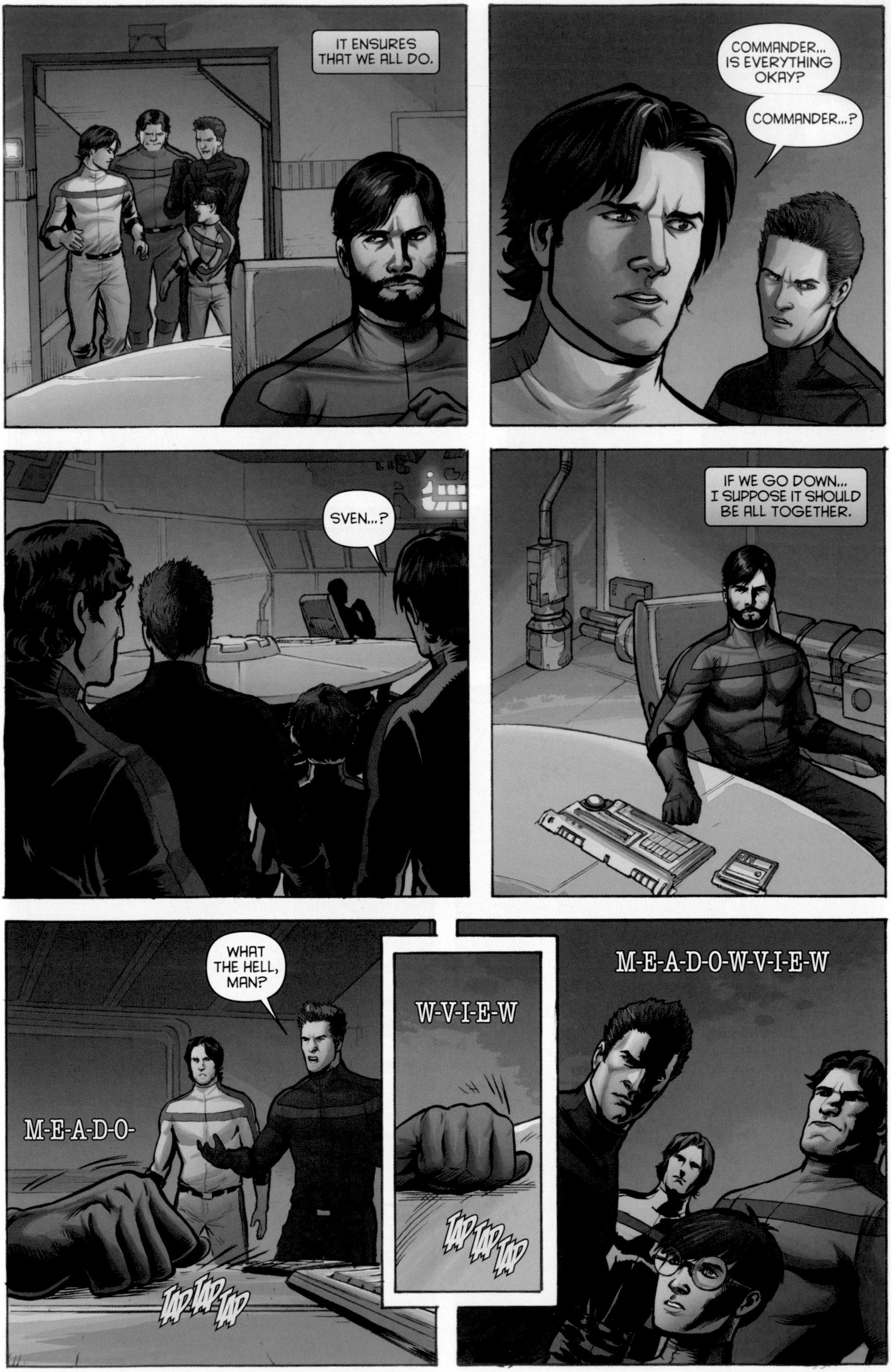
IT ENSURES THAT WE ALL DO.
COMMANDER... IS EVERYTHING OKAY?
COMMANDER...?
SVEN...?
IF WE GO DOWN... I SUPPOSE IT SHOULD BE ALL TOGETHER.
WHAT THE HELL, MAN?
M-E-A-D-O-
TAP TAP TAP
W-V-I-E-W
TAP TAP TAP
M-E-A-D-O-W-V-I-E-W

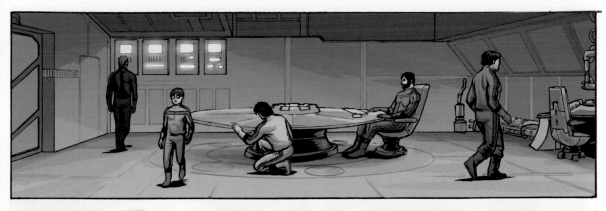

A-L-L-C-L-E-A-R.

G-O.

TAP TAP TAP

GENERAL EVERS IS A TRAITOR TO THE ALLIANCE, AND I NEED EVERYONE'S HELP TO PROVE IT.

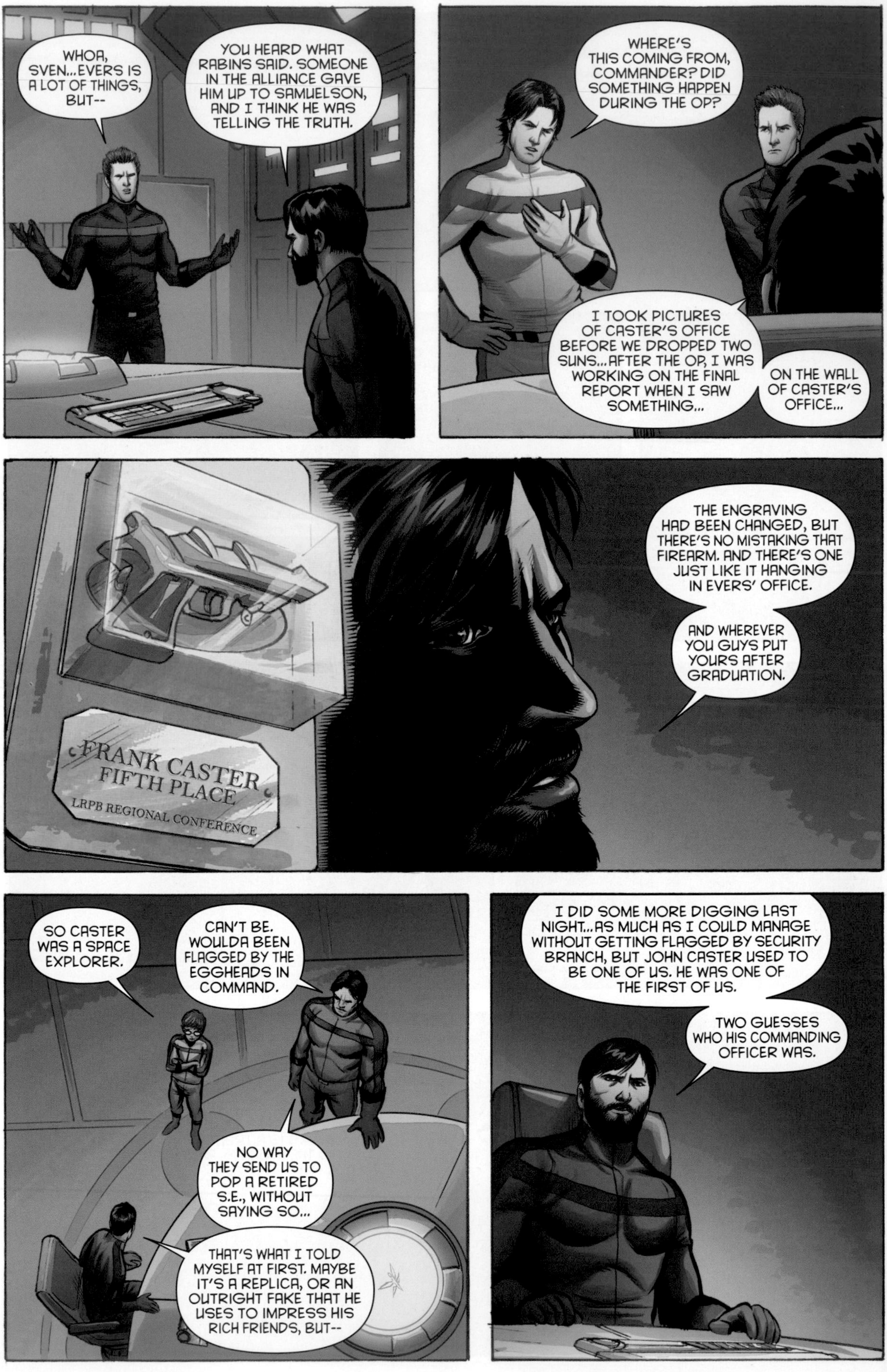
WHOA, SVEN...EVERS IS A LOT OF THINGS, BUT--
YOU HEARD WHAT RABINS SAID. SOMEONE IN THE ALLIANCE GAVE HIM UP TO SAMUELSON, AND I THINK HE WAS TELLING THE TRUTH.
WHERE'S THIS COMING FROM, COMMANDER? DID SOMETHING HAPPEN DURING THE OP?
I TOOK PICTURES OF CASTER'S OFFICE BEFORE WE DROPPED TWO SUNS...AFTER THE OP, I WAS WORKING ON THE FINAL REPORT WHEN I SAW SOMETHING...
ON THE WALL OF CASTER'S OFFICE...
FRANK CASTER FIFTH PLACE
LRPB REGIONAL CONFERENCE
THE ENGRAVING HAD BEEN CHANGED, BUT THERE'S NO MISTAKING THAT FIREARM. AND THERE'S ONE JUST LIKE IT HANGING IN EVERS' OFFICE.
AND WHEREVER YOU GUYS PUT YOURS AFTER GRADUATION.
SO CASTER WAS A SPACE EXPLORER.
CAN'T BE. WOULDA BEEN FLAGGED BY THE EGGHEADS IN COMMAND.
NO WAY THEY SEND US TO POP A RETIRED S.E., WITHOUT SAYING SO...
THAT'S WHAT I TOLD MYSELF AT FIRST. MAYBE IT'S A REPLICA, OR AN OUTRIGHT FAKE THAT HE USES TO IMPRESS HIS RICH FRIENDS, BUT--
I DID SOME MORE DIGGING LAST NIGHT...AS MUCH AS I COULD MANAGE WITHOUT GETTING FLAGGED BY SECURITY BRANCH, BUT JOHN CASTER USED TO BE ONE OF US. HE WAS ONE OF THE FIRST OF US.
TWO GUESSES WHO HIS COMMANDING OFFICER WAS.

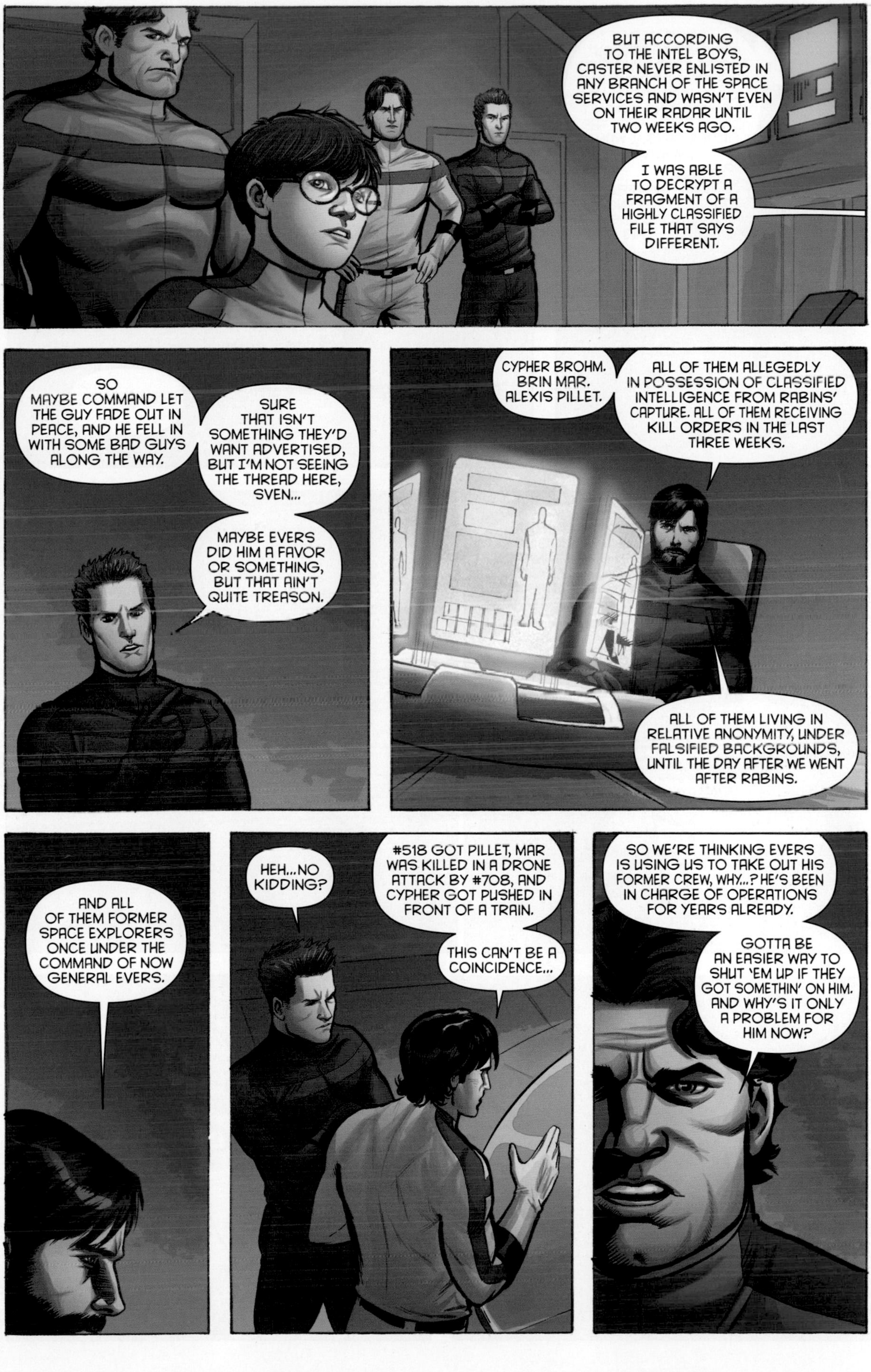
BUT ACCORDING TO THE INTEL BOYS, CASTER NEVER ENLISTED IN ANY BRANCH OF THE SPACE SERVICES AND WASN'T EVEN ON THEIR RADAR UNTIL TWO WEEKS AGO.
I WAS ABLE TO DECRYPT A FRAGMENT OF A HIGHLY CLASSIFIED FILE THAT SAYS DIFFERENT.
SO MAYBE COMMAND LET THE GUY FADE OUT IN PEACE, AND HE FELL IN WITH SOME BAD GUYS ALONG THE WAY.
SURE THAT ISN'T SOMETHING THEY'D WANT ADVERTISED, BUT I'M NOT SEEING THE THREAD HERE, SVEN...
MAYBE EVERS DID HIM A FAVOR OR SOMETHING, BUT THAT AIN'T QUITE TREASON.
CYPHER BROHM. BRIN MAR. ALEXIS PILLET.
ALL OF THEM ALLEGEDLY IN POSSESSION OF CLASSIFIED INTELLIGENCE FROM RABINS' CAPTURE. ALL OF THEM RECEIVING KILL ORDERS IN THE LAST THREE WEEKS.
ALL OF THEM LIVING IN RELATIVE ANONYMITY, UNDER FALSIFIED BACKGROUNDS, UNTIL THE DAY AFTER WE WENT AFTER RABINS.
AND ALL OF THEM FORMER SPACE EXPLORERS ONCE UNDER THE COMMAND OF NOW GENERAL EVERS.
HEH...NO KIDDING?
#518 GOT PILLET, MAR WAS KILLED IN A DRONE ATTACK BY #708, AND CYPHER GOT PUSHED IN FRONT OF A TRAIN.
THIS CAN'T BE A COINCIDENCE...
SO WE'RE THINKING EVERS IS USING US TO TAKE OUT HIS FORMER CREW, WHY...? HE'S BEEN IN CHARGE OF OPERATIONS FOR YEARS ALREADY.
GOTTA BE AN EASIER WAY TO SHUT 'EM UP IF THEY GOT SOMETHIN' ON HIM. AND WHY'S IT ONLY A PROBLEM FOR HIM NOW?

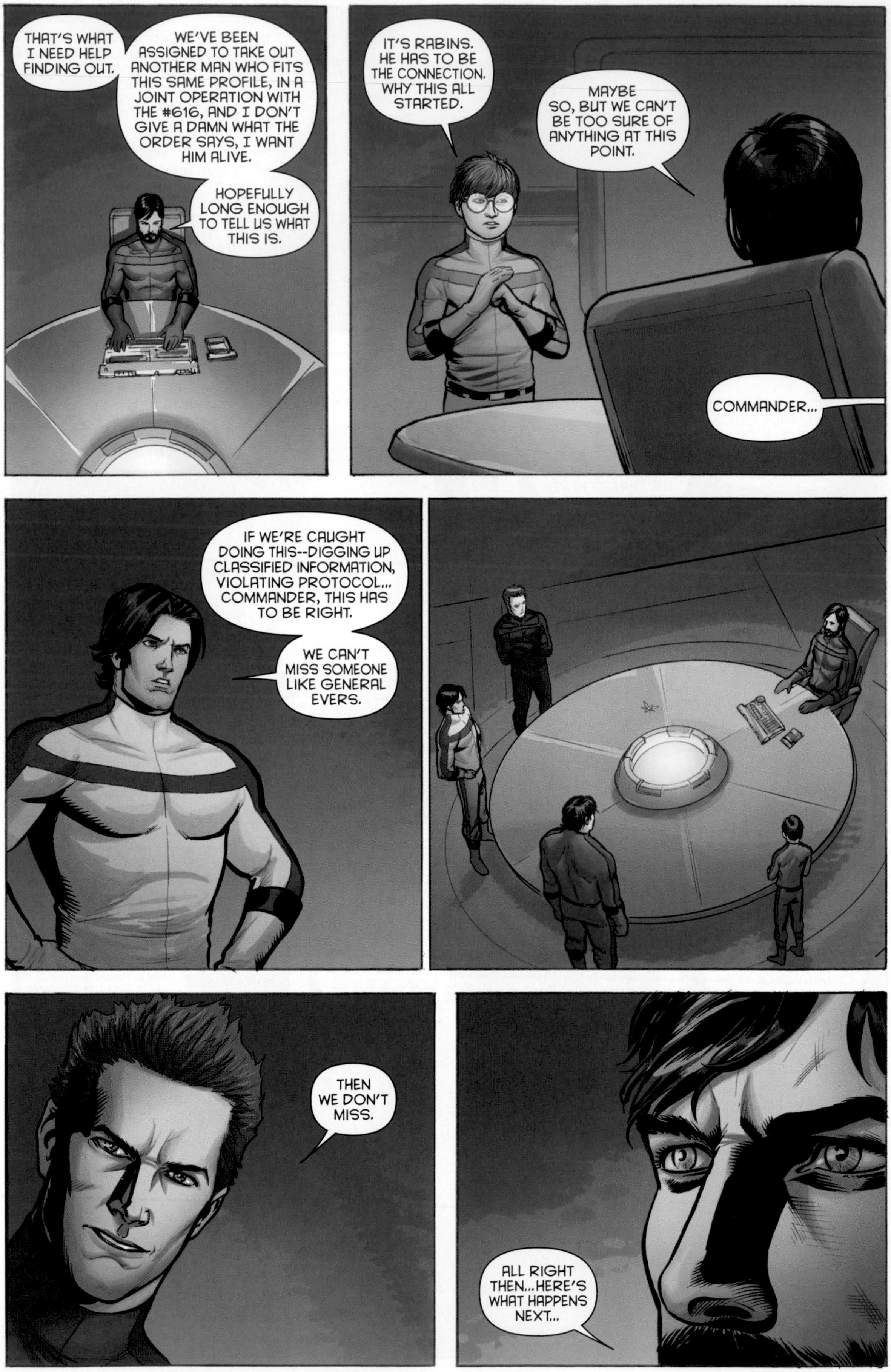
THAT'S WHAT I NEED HELP FINDING OUT.
WE'VE BEEN ASSIGNED TO TAKE OUT ANOTHER MAN WHO FITS THIS SAME PROFILE, IN A JOINT OPERATION WITH THE #616, AND I DON'T GIVE A DAMN WHAT THE ORDER SAYS, I WANT HIM ALIVE.
HOPEFULLY LONG ENOUGH TO TELL US WHAT THIS IS.
IT'S RABINS. HE HAS TO BE THE CONNECTION. WHY THIS ALL STARTED.
MAYBE SO, BUT WE CAN'T BE TOO SURE OF ANYTHING AT THIS POINT.
COMMANDER...
IF WE'RE CAUGHT DOING THIS--DIGGING UP CLASSIFIED INFORMATION, VIOLATING PROTOCOL... COMMANDER, THIS HAS TO BE RIGHT.
WE CAN'T MISS SOMEONE LIKE GENERAL EVERS.
THEN WE DON'T MISS.
ALL RIGHT THEN... HERE'S WHAT HAPPENS NEXT...

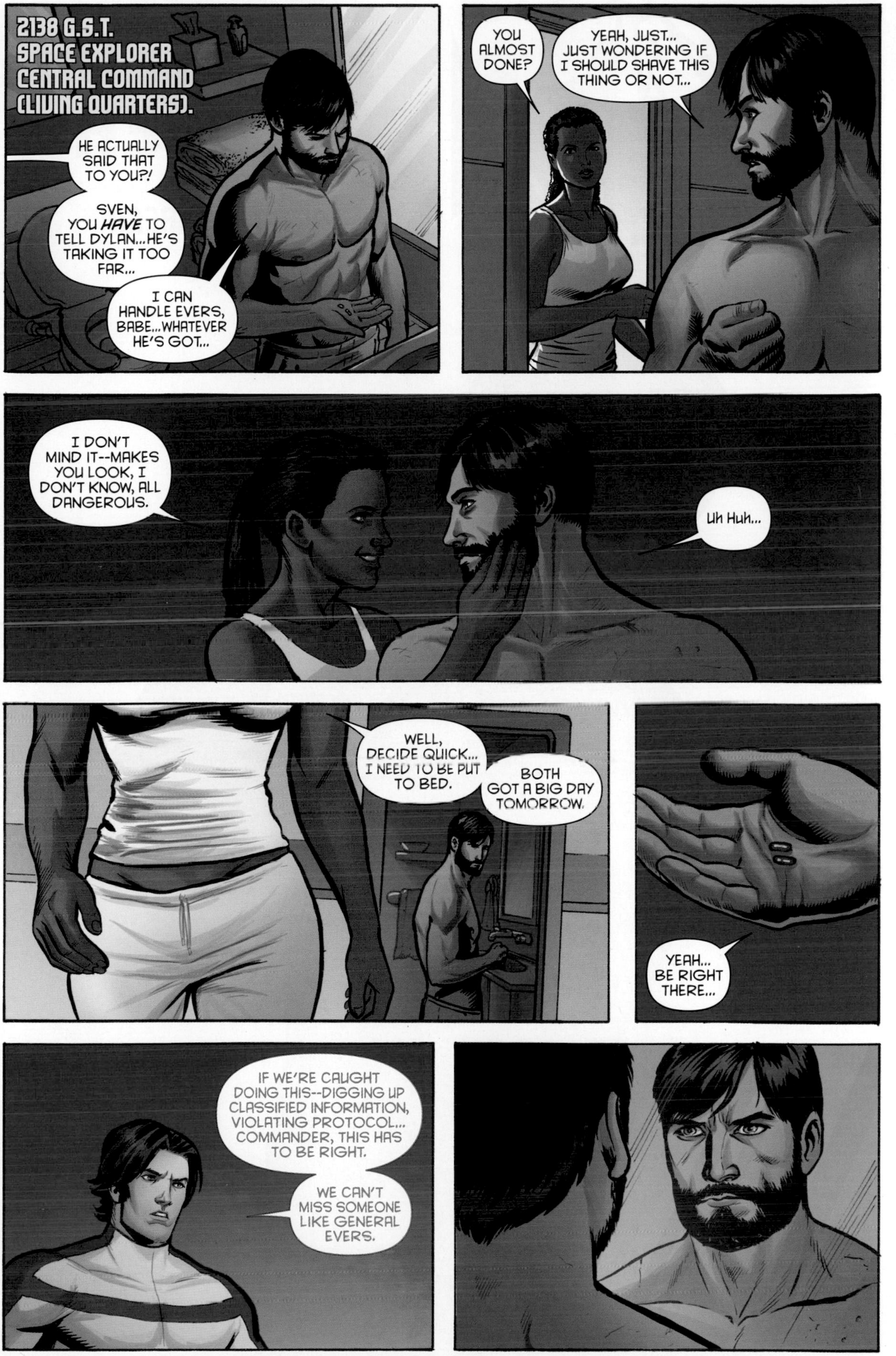
2138 G.S.T.
SPACE EXPLORER
CENTRAL COMMAND
(LIVING QUARTERS).
HE ACTUALLY SAID THAT TO YOU?!
SVEN, YOU HAVE TO TELL DYLAN...HE'S TAKING IT TOO FAR...
I CAN HANDLE EVERS, BABE...WHATEVER HE'S GOT...
YOU ALMOST DONE?
YEAH, JUST... JUST WONDERING IF I SHOULD SHAVE THIS THING OR NOT...
I DON'T MIND IT--MAKES YOU LOOK, I DON'T KNOW, ALL DANGEROUS.
Uh Huh...
WELL, DECIDE QUICK... I NEED TO BE PUT TO BED.
BOTH GOT A BIG DAY TOMORROW.
YEAH... BE RIGHT THERE...
IF WE'RE CAUGHT DOING THIS--DIGGING UP CLASSIFIED INFORMATION, VIOLATING PROTOCOL... COMMANDER, THIS HAS TO BE RIGHT.
WE CAN'T MISS SOMEONE LIKE GENERAL EVERS.

VOLTRON YEAR ONE

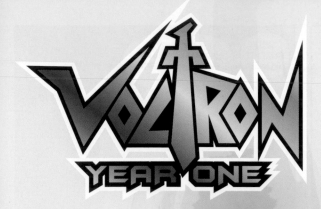

FEARLESS LEADER

3: THE THREAD

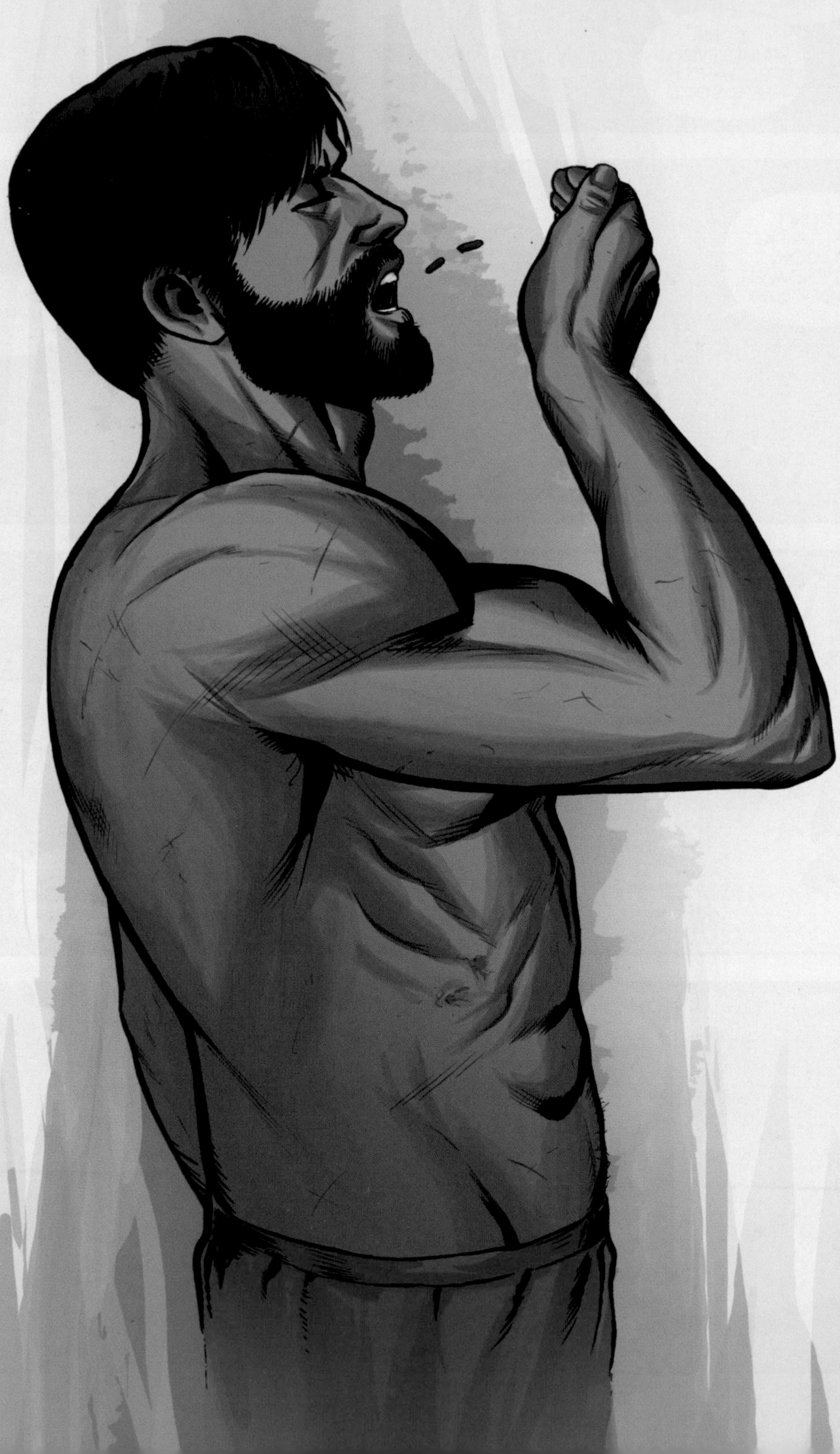

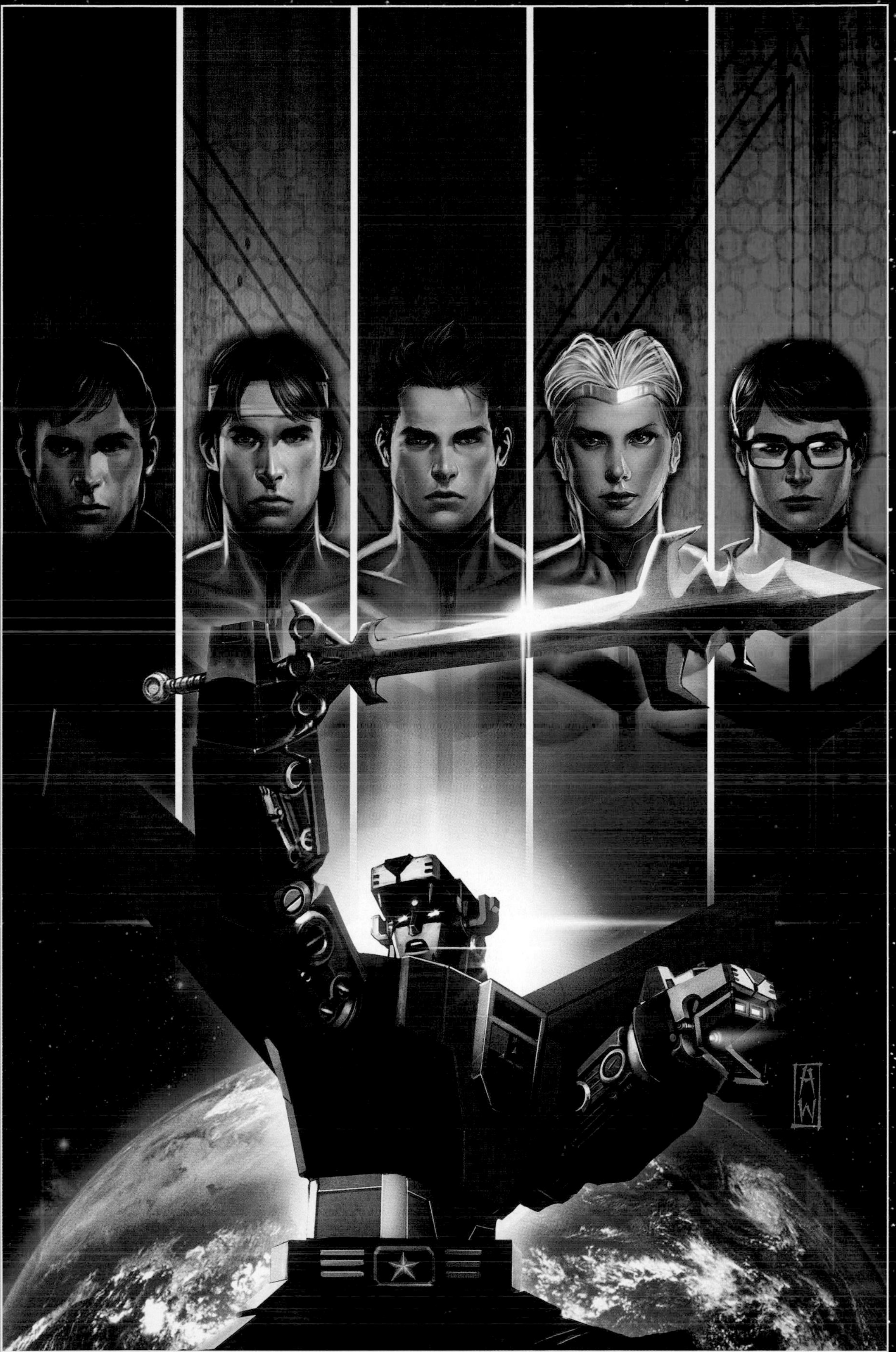
AW

Issue #4 cover by ADMIRA WIJAYA

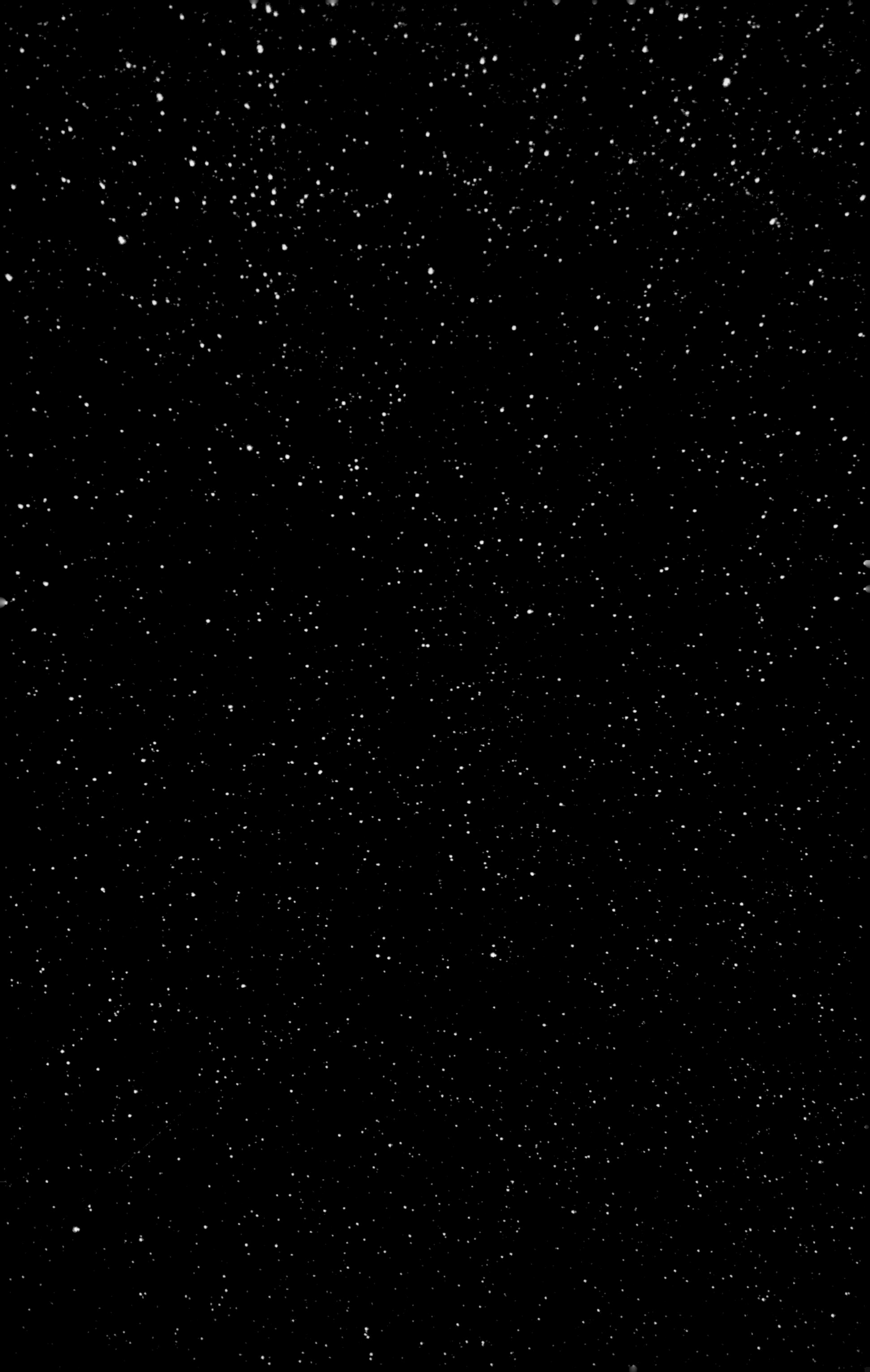

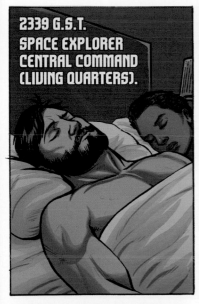

2339 G.S.T.
SPACE EXPLORER
CENTRAL COMMAND
(LIVING QUARTERS).

0057 G.S.T.

0143 G.S.T.

0228 G.S.T.

0315 G.S.T.

0454 G.S.T.

0551 G.S.T.

0627 G.S.T.

0732 G.S.T.

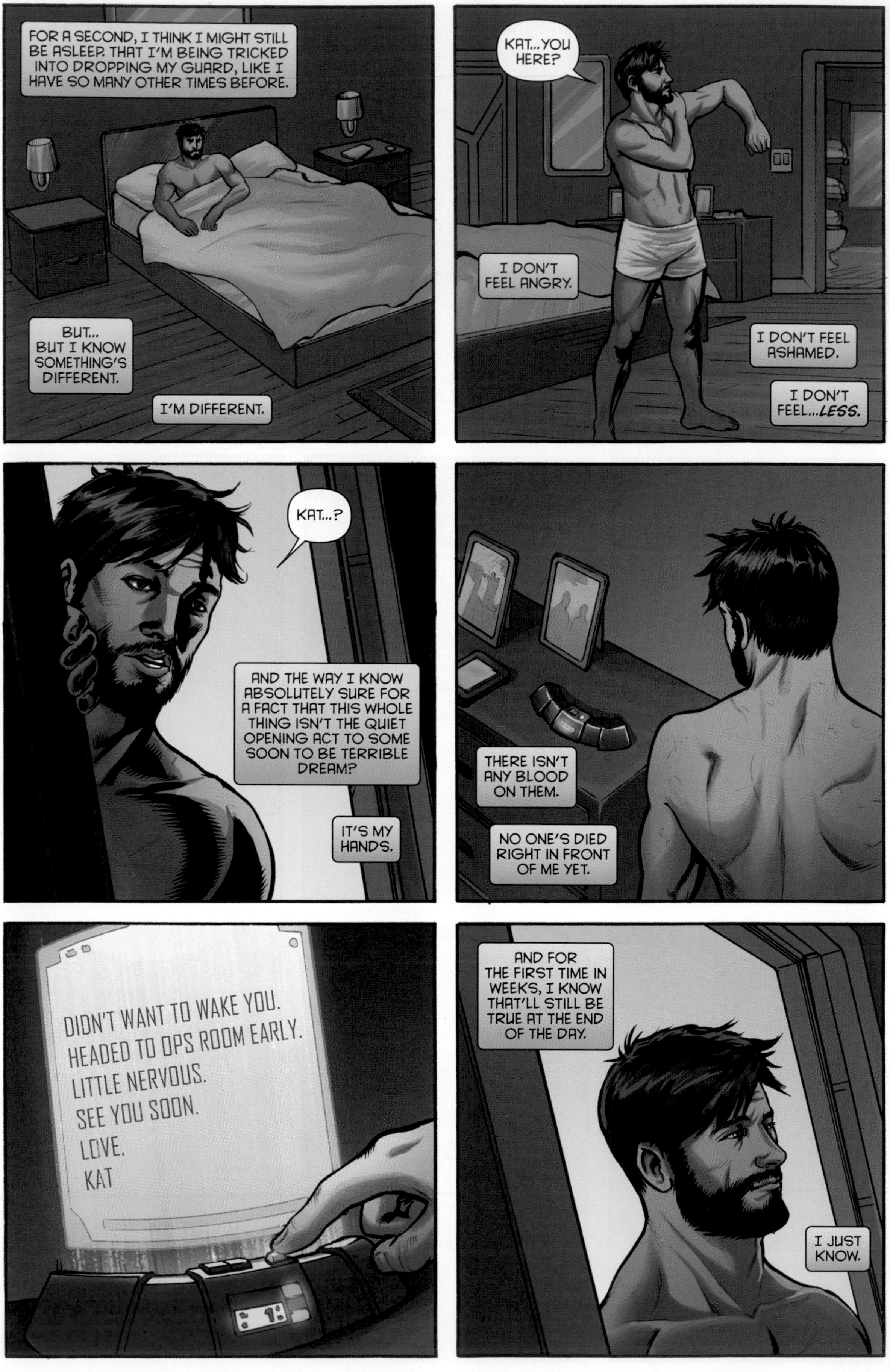
FOR A SECOND, I THINK I MIGHT STILL BE ASLEEP. THAT I'M BEING TRICKED INTO DROPPING MY GUARD, LIKE I HAVE SO MANY OTHER TIMES BEFORE.
BUT... BUT I KNOW SOMETHING'S DIFFERENT.
I'M DIFFERENT.
KAT...YOU HERE?
I DON'T FEEL ANGRY.
I DON'T FEEL ASHAMED.
I DON'T FEEL...*LESS.*
KAT...?
AND THE WAY I KNOW ABSOLUTELY SURE FOR A FACT THAT THIS WHOLE THING ISN'T THE QUIET OPENING ACT TO SOME SOON TO BE TERRIBLE DREAM?
IT'S MY HANDS.
THERE ISN'T ANY BLOOD ON THEM.
NO ONE'S DIED RIGHT IN FRONT OF ME YET.
DIDN'T WANT TO WAKE YOU.
HEADED TO OPS ROOM EARLY.
LITTLE NERVOUS.
SEE YOU SOON.
LOVE,
KAT
AND FOR THE FIRST TIME IN WEEKS, I KNOW THAT'LL STILL BE TRUE AT THE END OF THE DAY.
I JUST KNOW.

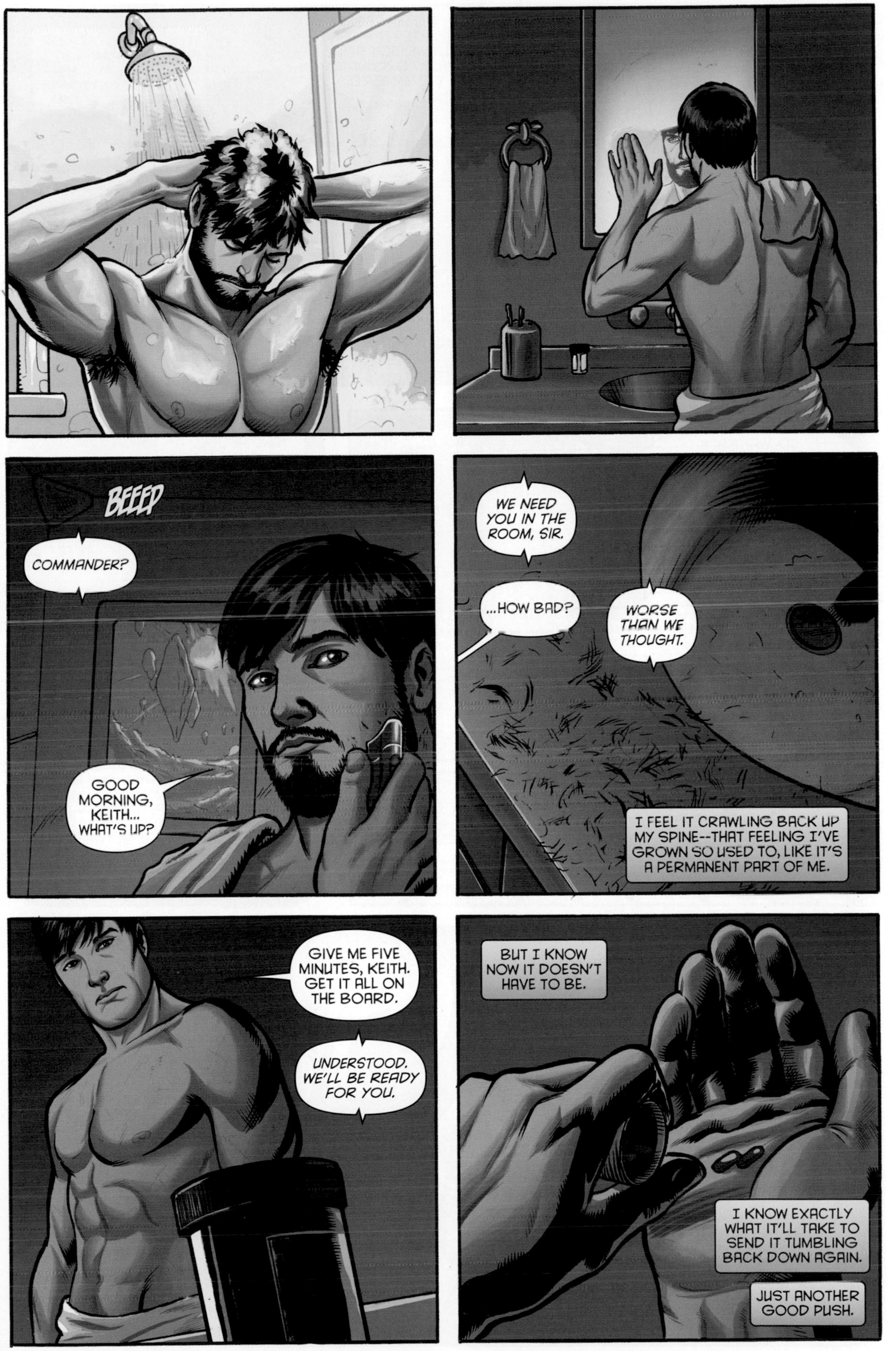
BEEEP
COMMANDER?
GOOD MORNING, KEITH... WHAT'S UP?
WE NEED YOU IN THE ROOM, SIR.
...HOW BAD?
WORSE THAN WE THOUGHT.
I FEEL IT CRAWLING BACK UP MY SPINE--THAT FEELING I'VE GROWN SO USED TO, LIKE IT'S A PERMANENT PART OF ME.
GIVE ME FIVE MINUTES, KEITH. GET IT ALL ON THE BOARD.
UNDERSTOOD. WE'LL BE READY FOR YOU.
BUT I KNOW NOW IT DOESN'T HAVE TO BE.
I KNOW EXACTLY WHAT IT'LL TAKE TO SEND IT TUMBLING BACK DOWN AGAIN.
JUST ANOTHER GOOD PUSH.

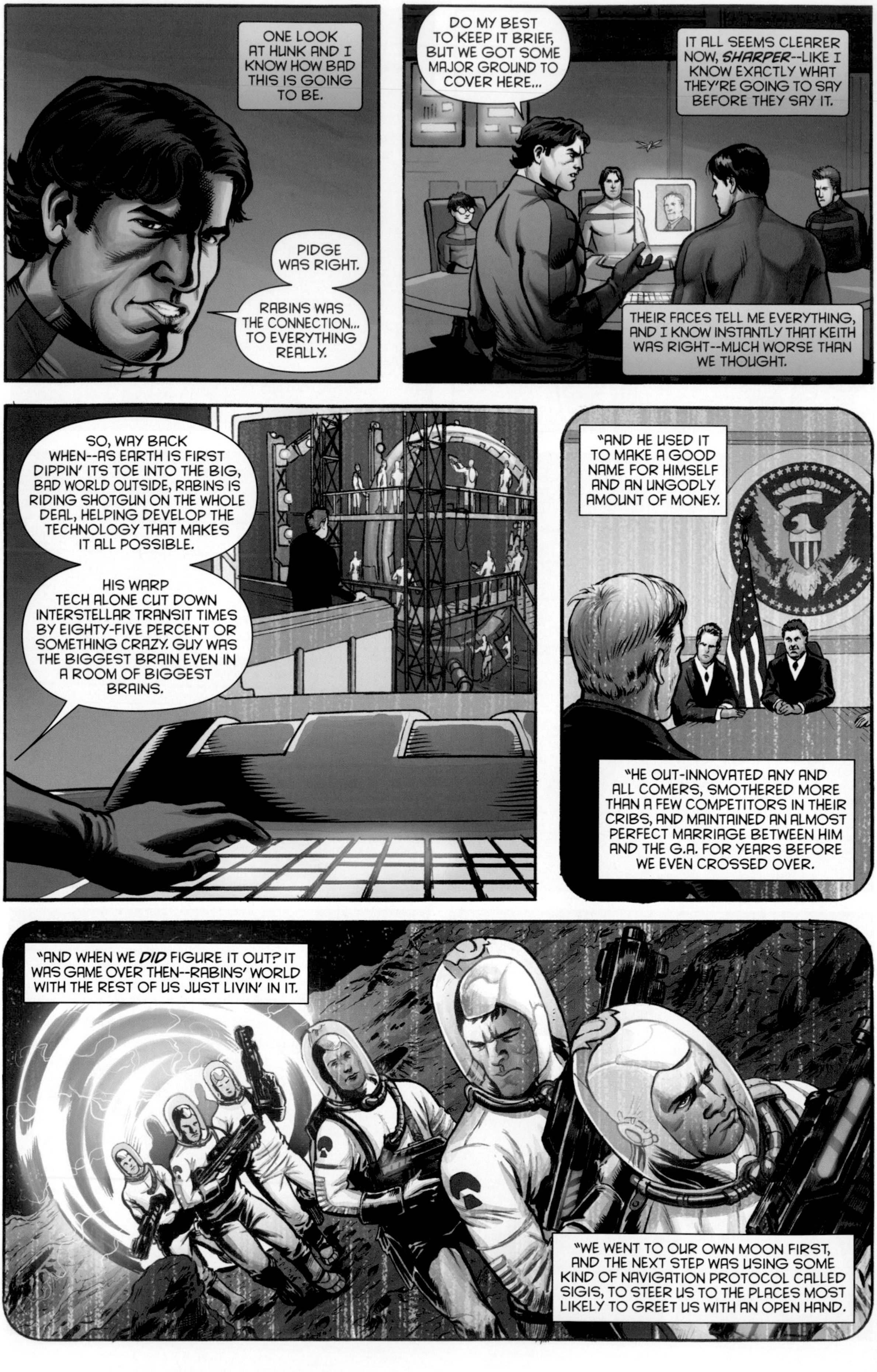
ONE LOOK AT HUNK AND I KNOW HOW BAD THIS IS GOING TO BE.
PIDGE WAS RIGHT.
RABINS WAS THE CONNECTION... TO EVERYTHING REALLY.
DO MY BEST TO KEEP IT BRIEF, BUT WE GOT SOME MAJOR GROUND TO COVER HERE...
IT ALL SEEMS CLEARER NOW, SHARPER--LIKE I KNOW EXACTLY WHAT THEY'RE GOING TO SAY BEFORE THEY SAY IT.
THEIR FACES TELL ME EVERYTHING, AND I KNOW INSTANTLY THAT KEITH WAS RIGHT--MUCH WORSE THAN WE THOUGHT.
SO, WAY BACK WHEN--AS EARTH IS FIRST DIPPIN' ITS TOE INTO THE BIG, BAD WORLD OUTSIDE, RABINS IS RIDING SHOTGUN ON THE WHOLE DEAL, HELPING DEVELOP THE TECHNOLOGY THAT MAKES IT ALL POSSIBLE.
HIS WARP TECH ALONE CUT DOWN INTERSTELLAR TRANSIT TIMES BY EIGHTY-FIVE PERCENT OR SOMETHING CRAZY. GUY WAS THE BIGGEST BRAIN EVEN IN A ROOM OF BIGGEST BRAINS.
"AND HE USED IT TO MAKE A GOOD NAME FOR HIMSELF AND AN UNGODLY AMOUNT OF MONEY.
"HE OUT-INNOVATED ANY AND ALL COMERS, SMOTHERED MORE THAN A FEW COMPETITORS IN THEIR CRIBS, AND MAINTAINED AN ALMOST PERFECT MARRIAGE BETWEEN HIM AND THE G.A. FOR YEARS BEFORE WE EVEN CROSSED OVER.
"AND WHEN WE DID FIGURE IT OUT? IT WAS GAME OVER THEN--RABINS' WORLD WITH THE REST OF US JUST LIVIN' IN IT.
"WE WENT TO OUR OWN MOON FIRST, AND THE NEXT STEP WAS USING SOME KIND OF NAVIGATION PROTOCOL CALLED SIGIS, TO STEER US TO THE PLACES MOST LIKELY TO GREET US WITH AN OPEN HAND.

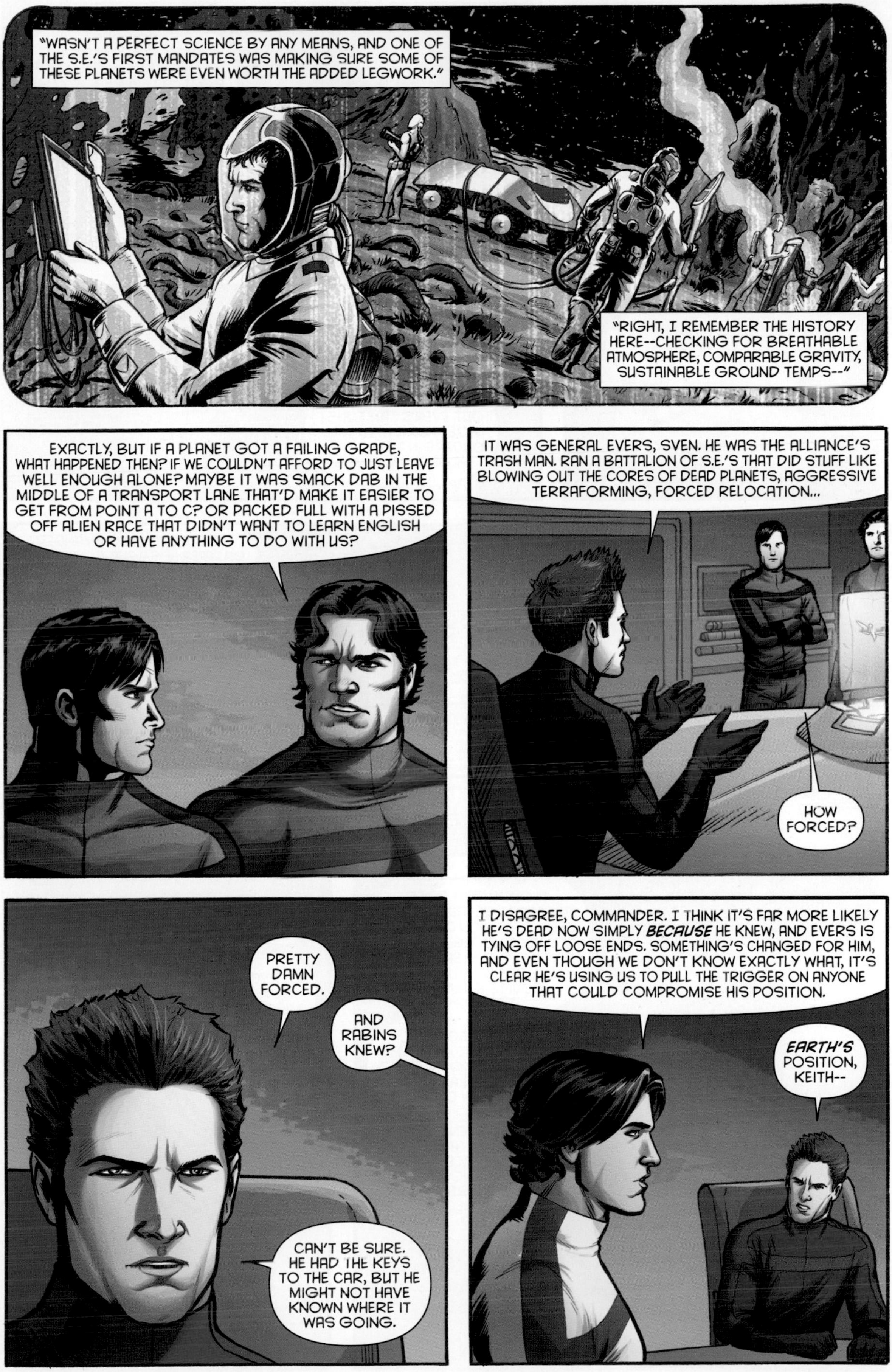
"WASN'T A PERFECT SCIENCE BY ANY MEANS, AND ONE OF THE S.E.'S FIRST MANDATES WAS MAKING SURE SOME OF THESE PLANETS WERE EVEN WORTH THE ADDED LEGWORK."
"RIGHT, I REMEMBER THE HISTORY HERE--CHECKING FOR BREATHABLE ATMOSPHERE, COMPARABLE GRAVITY, SUSTAINABLE GROUND TEMPS--"
EXACTLY, BUT IF A PLANET GOT A FAILING GRADE, WHAT HAPPENED THEN? IF WE COULDN'T AFFORD TO JUST LEAVE WELL ENOUGH ALONE? MAYBE IT WAS SMACK DAB IN THE MIDDLE OF A TRANSPORT LANE THAT'D MAKE IT EASIER TO GET FROM POINT A TO C? OR PACKED FULL WITH A PISSED OFF ALIEN RACE THAT DIDN'T WANT TO LEARN ENGLISH OR HAVE ANYTHING TO DO WITH US?
IT WAS GENERAL EVERS, SVEN. HE WAS THE ALLIANCE'S TRASH MAN. RAN A BATTALION OF S.E.'S THAT DID STUFF LIKE BLOWING OUT THE CORES OF DEAD PLANETS, AGGRESSIVE TERRAFORMING, FORCED RELOCATION...
HOW FORCED?
PRETTY DAMN FORCED.
AND RABINS KNEW?
CAN'T BE SURE. HE HAD THE KEYS TO THE CAR, BUT HE MIGHT NOT HAVE KNOWN WHERE IT WAS GOING.
I DISAGREE, COMMANDER. I THINK IT'S FAR MORE LIKELY HE'S DEAD NOW SIMPLY *BECAUSE* HE KNEW, AND EVERS IS TYING OFF LOOSE ENDS. SOMETHING'S CHANGED FOR HIM, AND EVEN THOUGH WE DON'T KNOW EXACTLY WHAT, IT'S CLEAR HE'S USING US TO PULL THE TRIGGER ON ANYONE THAT COULD COMPROMISE HIS POSITION.
EARTH'S POSITION, KEITH--

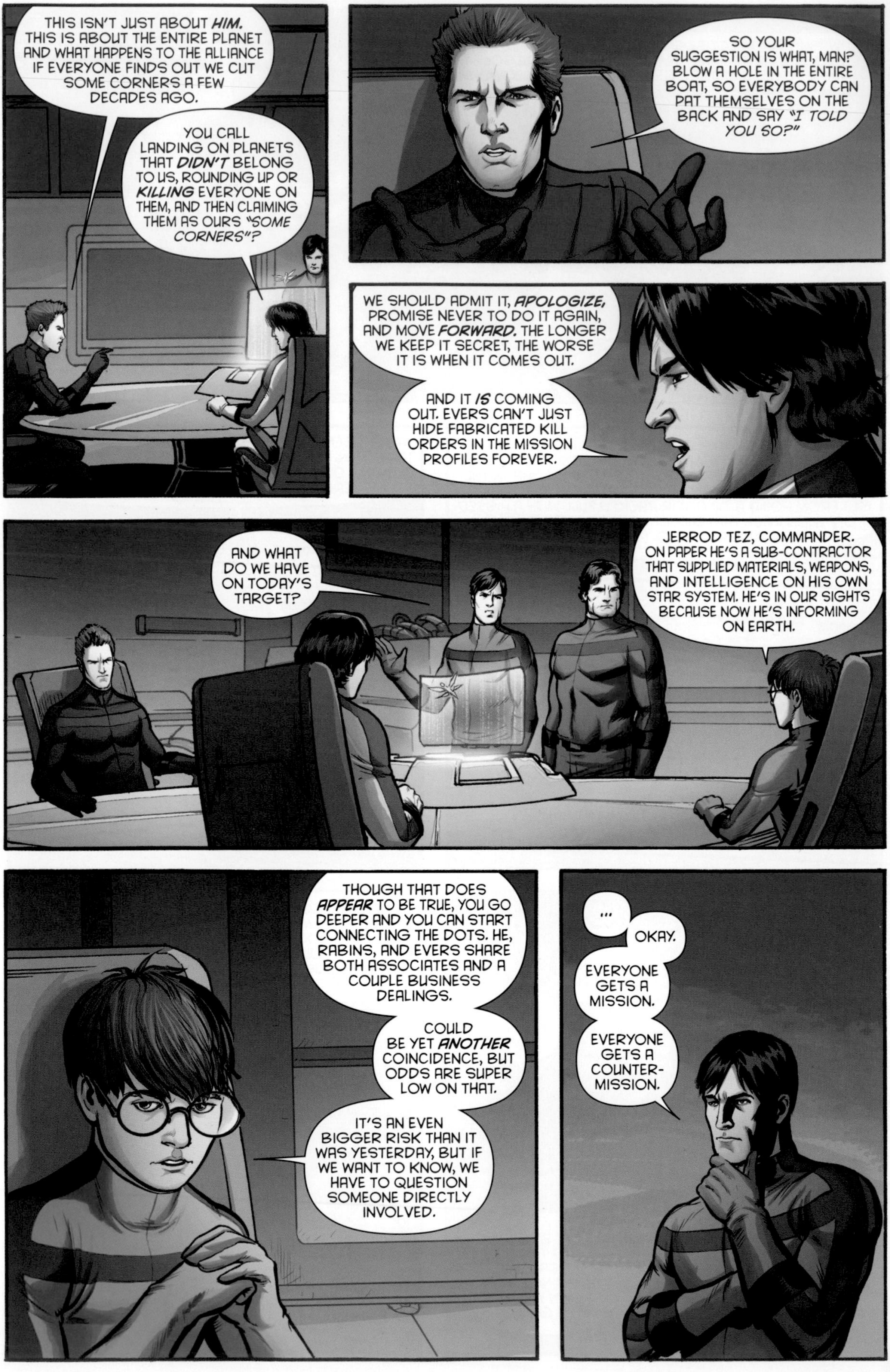
THIS ISN'T JUST ABOUT HIM. THIS IS ABOUT THE ENTIRE PLANET AND WHAT HAPPENS TO THE ALLIANCE IF EVERYONE FINDS OUT WE CUT SOME CORNERS A FEW DECADES AGO.
YOU CALL LANDING ON PLANETS THAT DIDN'T BELONG TO US, ROUNDING UP OR KILLING EVERYONE ON THEM, AND THEN CLAIMING THEM AS OURS "SOME CORNERS"?
SO YOUR SUGGESTION IS WHAT, MAN? BLOW A HOLE IN THE ENTIRE BOAT, SO EVERYBODY CAN PAT THEMSELVES ON THE BACK AND SAY "I TOLD YOU SO?"
WE SHOULD ADMIT IT, APOLOGIZE, PROMISE NEVER TO DO IT AGAIN, AND MOVE FORWARD. THE LONGER WE KEEP IT SECRET, THE WORSE IT IS WHEN IT COMES OUT.
AND IT IS COMING OUT. EVERS CAN'T JUST HIDE FABRICATED KILL ORDERS IN THE MISSION PROFILES FOREVER.
AND WHAT DO WE HAVE ON TODAY'S TARGET?
JERROD TEZ, COMMANDER. ON PAPER HE'S A SUB-CONTRACTOR THAT SUPPLIED MATERIALS, WEAPONS, AND INTELLIGENCE ON HIS OWN STAR SYSTEM. HE'S IN OUR SIGHTS BECAUSE NOW HE'S INFORMING ON EARTH.
THOUGH THAT DOES APPEAR TO BE TRUE, YOU GO DEEPER AND YOU CAN START CONNECTING THE DOTS. HE, RABINS, AND EVERS SHARE BOTH ASSOCIATES AND A COUPLE BUSINESS DEALINGS.
COULD BE YET ANOTHER COINCIDENCE, BUT ODDS ARE SUPER LOW ON THAT.
IT'S AN EVEN BIGGER RISK THAN IT WAS YESTERDAY, BUT IF WE WANT TO KNOW, WE HAVE TO QUESTION SOMEONE DIRECTLY INVOLVED.
...
OKAY.
EVERYONE GETS A MISSION.
EVERYONE GETS A COUNTER-MISSION.

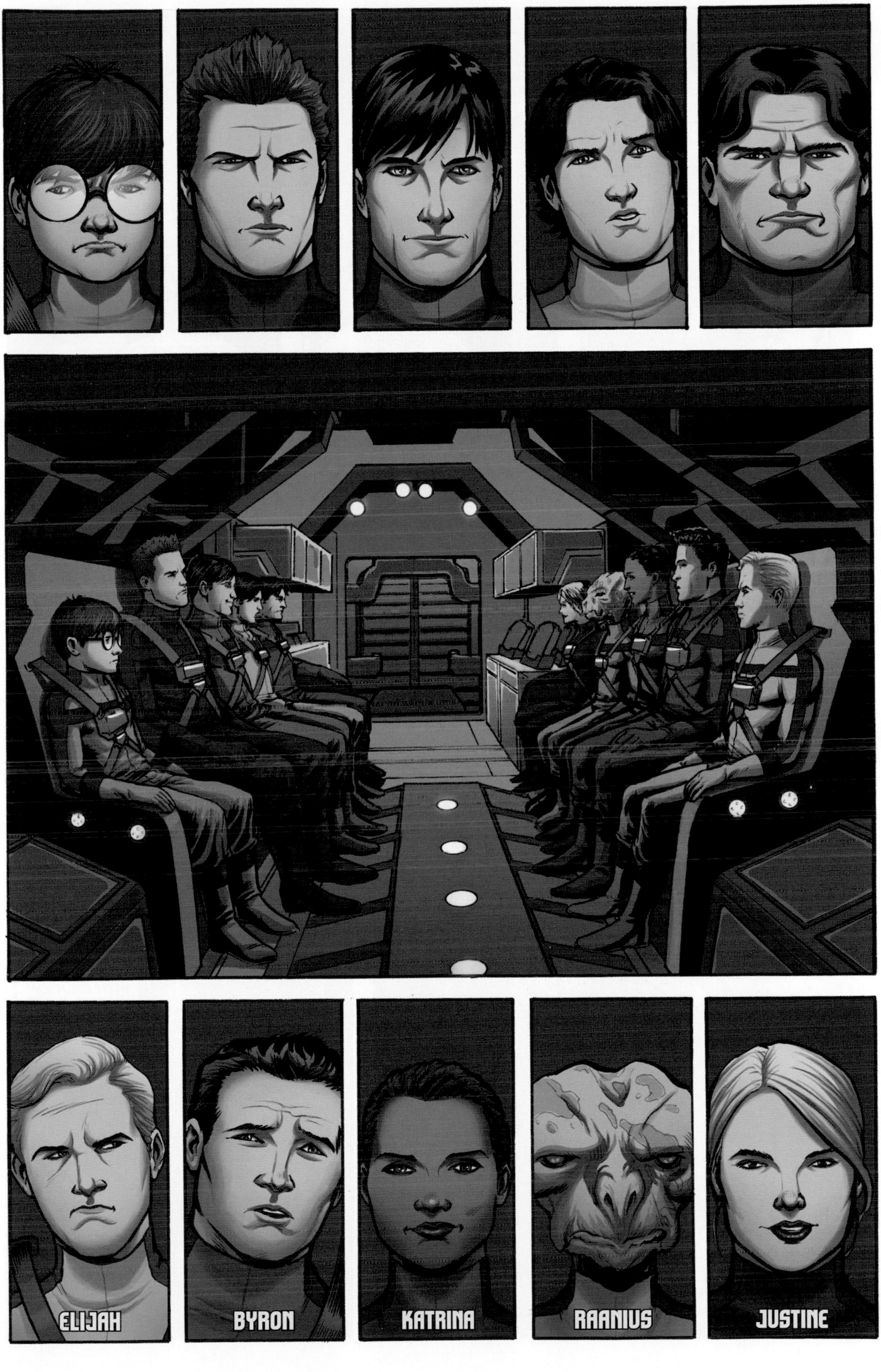
ELIJAH
BYRON
KATRINA
RAANIUS
JUSTINE

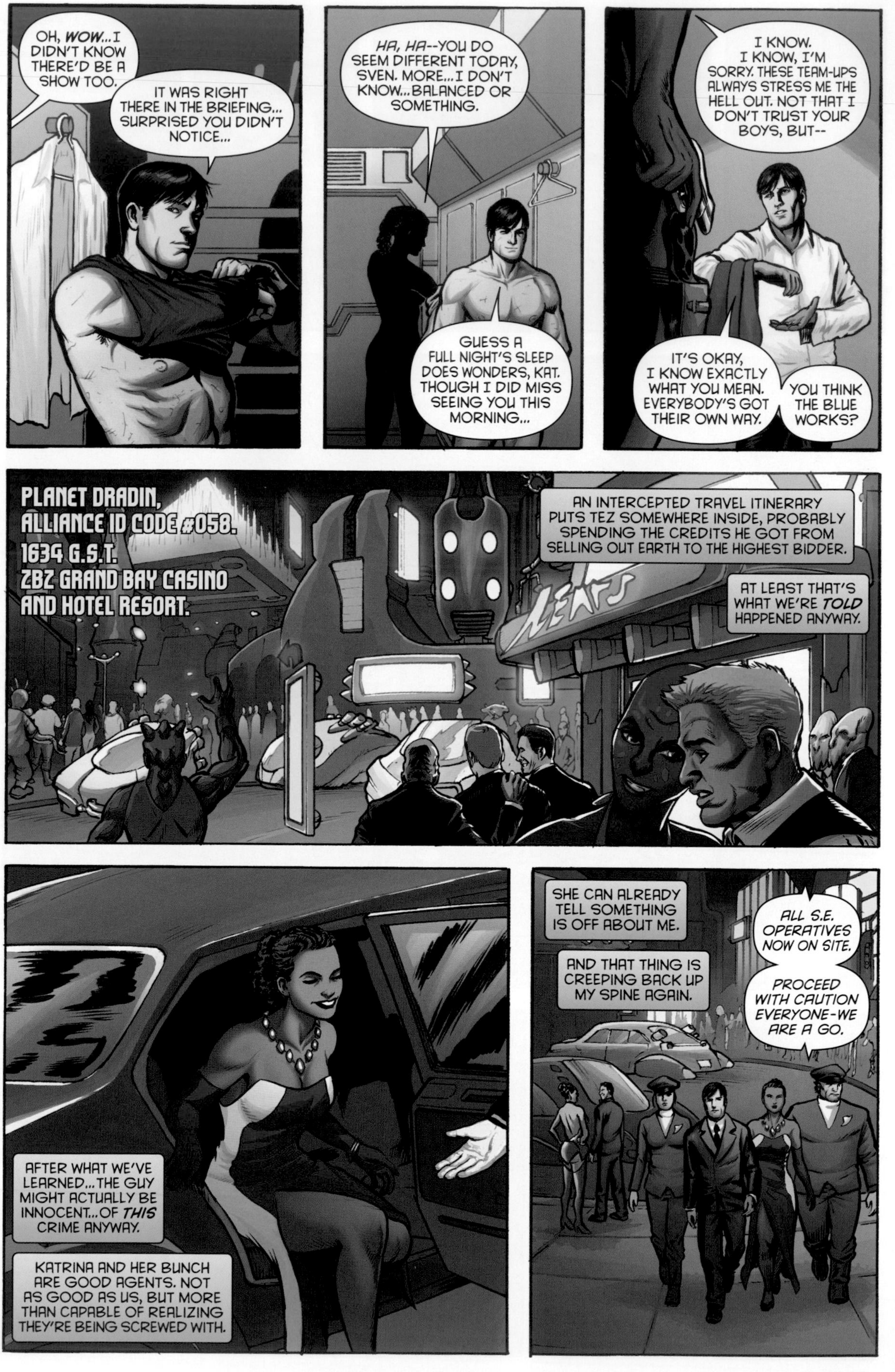

OH, WOW...I DIDN'T KNOW THERE'D BE A SHOW TOO.
IT WAS RIGHT THERE IN THE BRIEFING... SURPRISED YOU DIDN'T NOTICE...
HA, HA--YOU DO SEEM DIFFERENT TODAY, SVEN. MORE...I DON'T KNOW...BALANCED OR SOMETHING.
GUESS A FULL NIGHT'S SLEEP DOES WONDERS, KAT. THOUGH I DID MISS SEEING YOU THIS MORNING...
I KNOW. I KNOW, I'M SORRY. THESE TEAM-UPS ALWAYS STRESS ME THE HELL OUT. NOT THAT I DON'T TRUST YOUR BOYS, BUT--
IT'S OKAY, I KNOW EXACTLY WHAT YOU MEAN. EVERYBODY'S GOT THEIR OWN WAY.
YOU THINK THE BLUE WORKS?
PLANET DRADIN, ALLIANCE ID CODE #058. 1634 G.S.T. ZBZ GRAND BAY CASINO AND HOTEL RESORT.
AN INTERCEPTED TRAVEL ITINERARY PUTS TEZ SOMEWHERE INSIDE, PROBABLY SPENDING THE CREDITS HE GOT FROM SELLING OUT EARTH TO THE HIGHEST BIDDER.
AT LEAST THAT'S WHAT WE'RE TOLD HAPPENED ANYWAY.
AFTER WHAT WE'VE LEARNED...THE GUY MIGHT ACTUALLY BE INNOCENT...OF THIS CRIME ANYWAY.
KATRINA AND HER BUNCH ARE GOOD AGENTS. NOT AS GOOD AS US, BUT MORE THAN CAPABLE OF REALIZING THEY'RE BEING SCREWED WITH.
SHE CAN ALREADY TELL SOMETHING IS OFF ABOUT ME.
AND THAT THING IS CREEPING BACK UP MY SPINE AGAIN.
ALL S.E. OPERATIVES NOW ON SITE.
PROCEED WITH CAUTION EVERYONE-WE ARE A GO.

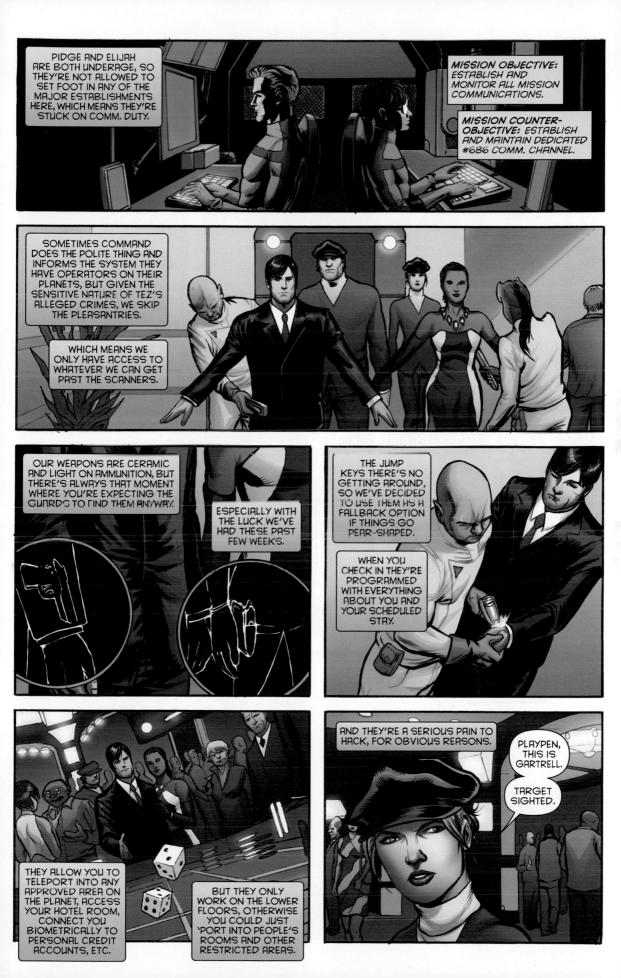

PIDGE AND ELIJAH ARE BOTH UNDERAGE, SO THEY'RE NOT ALLOWED TO SET FOOT IN ANY OF THE MAJOR ESTABLISHMENTS HERE, WHICH MEANS THEY'RE STUCK ON COMM. DUTY.

MISSION OBJECTIVE: ESTABLISH AND MONITOR ALL MISSION COMMUNICATIONS.

MISSION COUNTER-OBJECTIVE: ESTABLISH AND MAINTAIN DEDICATED #686 COMM. CHANNEL.

SOMETIMES COMMAND DOES THE POLITE THING AND INFORMS THE SYSTEM THEY HAVE OPERATORS ON THEIR PLANETS, BUT GIVEN THE SENSITIVE NATURE OF TEZ'S ALLEGED CRIMES, WE SKIP THE PLEASANTRIES.

WHICH MEANS WE ONLY HAVE ACCESS TO WHATEVER WE CAN GET PAST THE SCANNERS.

OUR WEAPONS ARE CERAMIC AND LIGHT ON AMMUNITION, BUT THERE'S ALWAYS THAT MOMENT WHERE YOU'RE EXPECTING THE GUARDS TO FIND THEM ANYWAY.

ESPECIALLY WITH THE LUCK WE'VE HAD THESE PAST FEW WEEKS.

THE JUMP KEYS THERE'S NO GETTING AROUND, SO WE'VE DECIDED TO USE THEM AS A FALLBACK OPTION IF THINGS GO PEAR-SHAPED.

WHEN YOU CHECK IN THEY'RE PROGRAMMED WITH EVERYTHING ABOUT YOU AND YOUR SCHEDULED STAY.

THEY ALLOW YOU TO TELEPORT INTO ANY APPROVED AREA ON THE PLANET, ACCESS YOUR HOTEL ROOM, CONNECT YOU BIOMETRICALLY TO PERSONAL CREDIT ACCOUNTS, ETC.

BUT THEY ONLY WORK ON THE LOWER FLOORS, OTHERWISE YOU COULD JUST 'PORT INTO PEOPLE'S ROOMS AND OTHER RESTRICTED AREAS.

AND THEY'RE A SERIOUS PAIN TO HACK, FOR OBVIOUS REASONS.

PLAYPEN, THIS IS GARTRELL.

TARGET SIGHTED.

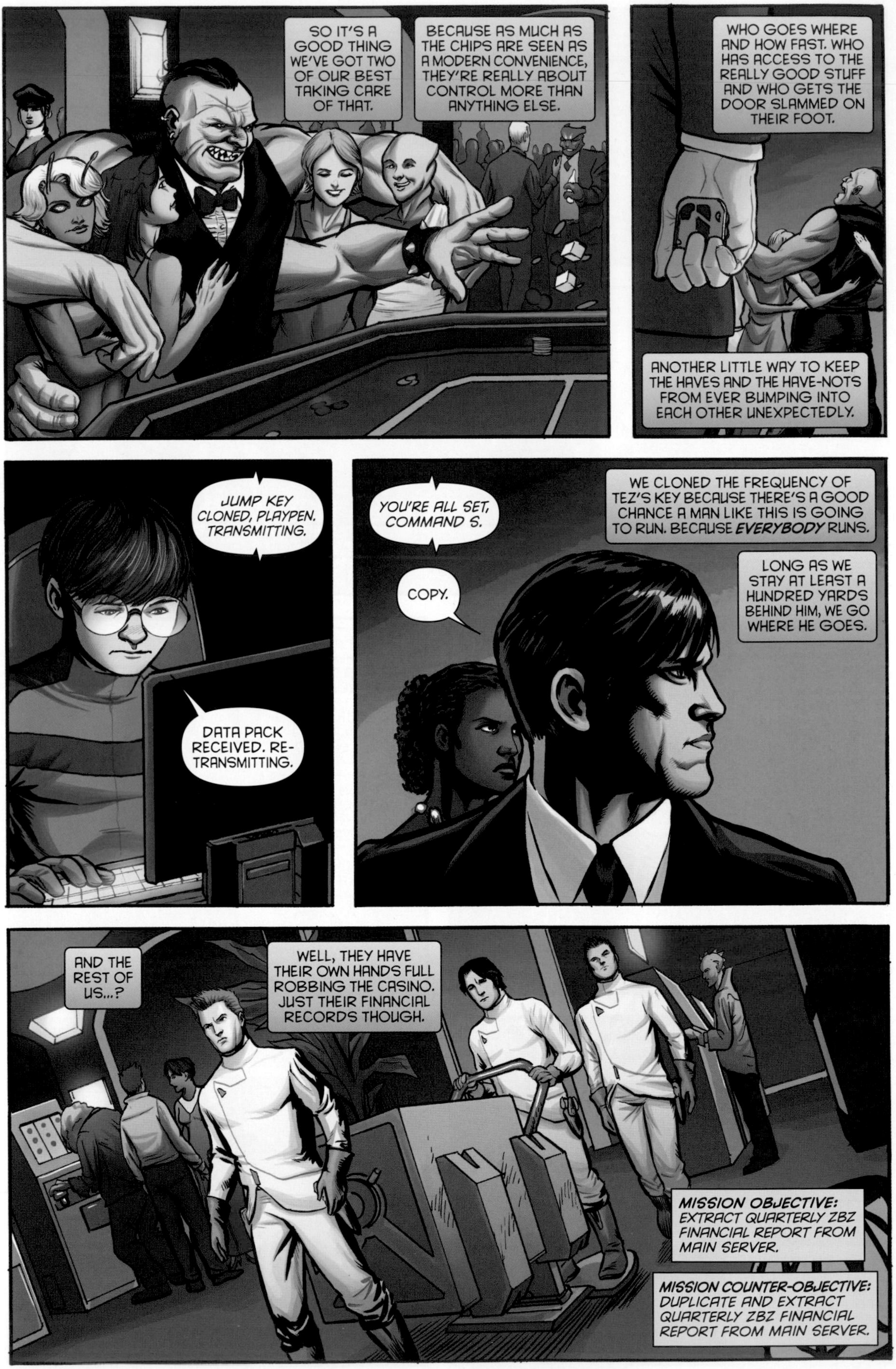
SO IT'S A GOOD THING WE'VE GOT TWO OF OUR BEST TAKING CARE OF THAT.
BECAUSE AS MUCH AS THE CHIPS ARE SEEN AS A MODERN CONVENIENCE, THEY'RE REALLY ABOUT CONTROL MORE THAN ANYTHING ELSE.
WHO GOES WHERE AND HOW FAST. WHO HAS ACCESS TO THE REALLY GOOD STUFF AND WHO GETS THE DOOR SLAMMED ON THEIR FOOT.
ANOTHER LITTLE WAY TO KEEP THE HAVES AND THE HAVE-NOTS FROM EVER BUMPING INTO EACH OTHER UNEXPECTEDLY.
JUMP KEY CLONED, PLAYPEN. TRANSMITTING.
DATA PACK RECEIVED. RE-TRANSMITTING.
YOU'RE ALL SET, COMMAND S.
COPY.
WE CLONED THE FREQUENCY OF TEZ'S KEY BECAUSE THERE'S A GOOD CHANCE A MAN LIKE THIS IS GOING TO RUN. BECAUSE EVERYBODY RUNS.
LONG AS WE STAY AT LEAST A HUNDRED YARDS BEHIND HIM, WE GO WHERE HE GOES.
AND THE REST OF US...?
WELL, THEY HAVE THEIR OWN HANDS FULL ROBBING THE CASINO. JUST THEIR FINANCIAL RECORDS THOUGH.
MISSION OBJECTIVE: EXTRACT QUARTERLY ZBZ FINANCIAL REPORT FROM MAIN SERVER.
MISSION COUNTER-OBJECTIVE: DUPLICATE AND EXTRACT QUARTERLY ZBZ FINANCIAL REPORT FROM MAIN SERVER.

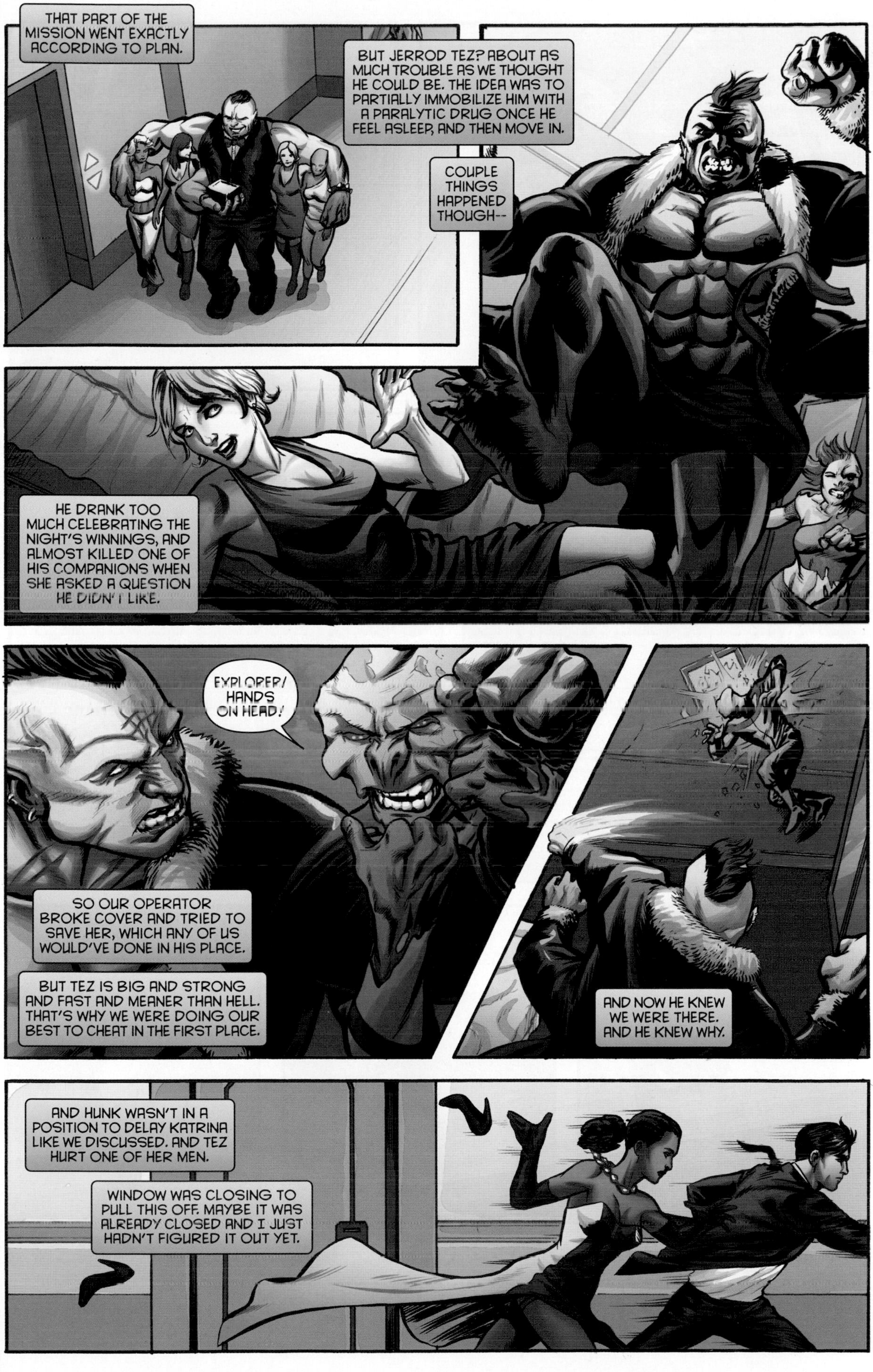

THAT PART OF THE MISSION WENT EXACTLY ACCORDING TO PLAN.
BUT JERROD TEZ? ABOUT AS MUCH TROUBLE AS WE THOUGHT HE COULD BE. THE IDEA WAS TO PARTIALLY IMMOBILIZE HIM WITH A PARALYTIC DRUG ONCE HE FEEL ASLEEP, AND THEN MOVE IN.
COUPLE THINGS HAPPENED THOUGH--
HE DRANK TOO MUCH CELEBRATING THE NIGHT'S WINNINGS, AND ALMOST KILLED ONE OF HIS COMPANIONS WHEN SHE ASKED A QUESTION HE DIDN'T LIKE.
EXPLORER! HANDS ON HEAD!
SO OUR OPERATOR BROKE COVER AND TRIED TO SAVE HER, WHICH ANY OF US WOULD'VE DONE IN HIS PLACE.
BUT TEZ IS BIG AND STRONG AND FAST AND MEANER THAN HELL. THAT'S WHY WE WERE DOING OUR BEST TO CHEAT IN THE FIRST PLACE.
AND NOW HE KNEW WE WERE THERE. AND HE KNEW WHY.
AND HUNK WASN'T IN A POSITION TO DELAY KATRINA LIKE WE DISCUSSED. AND TEZ HURT ONE OF HER MEN.
WINDOW WAS CLOSING TO PULL THIS OFF. MAYBE IT WAS ALREADY CLOSED AND I JUST HADN'T FIGURED IT OUT YET.

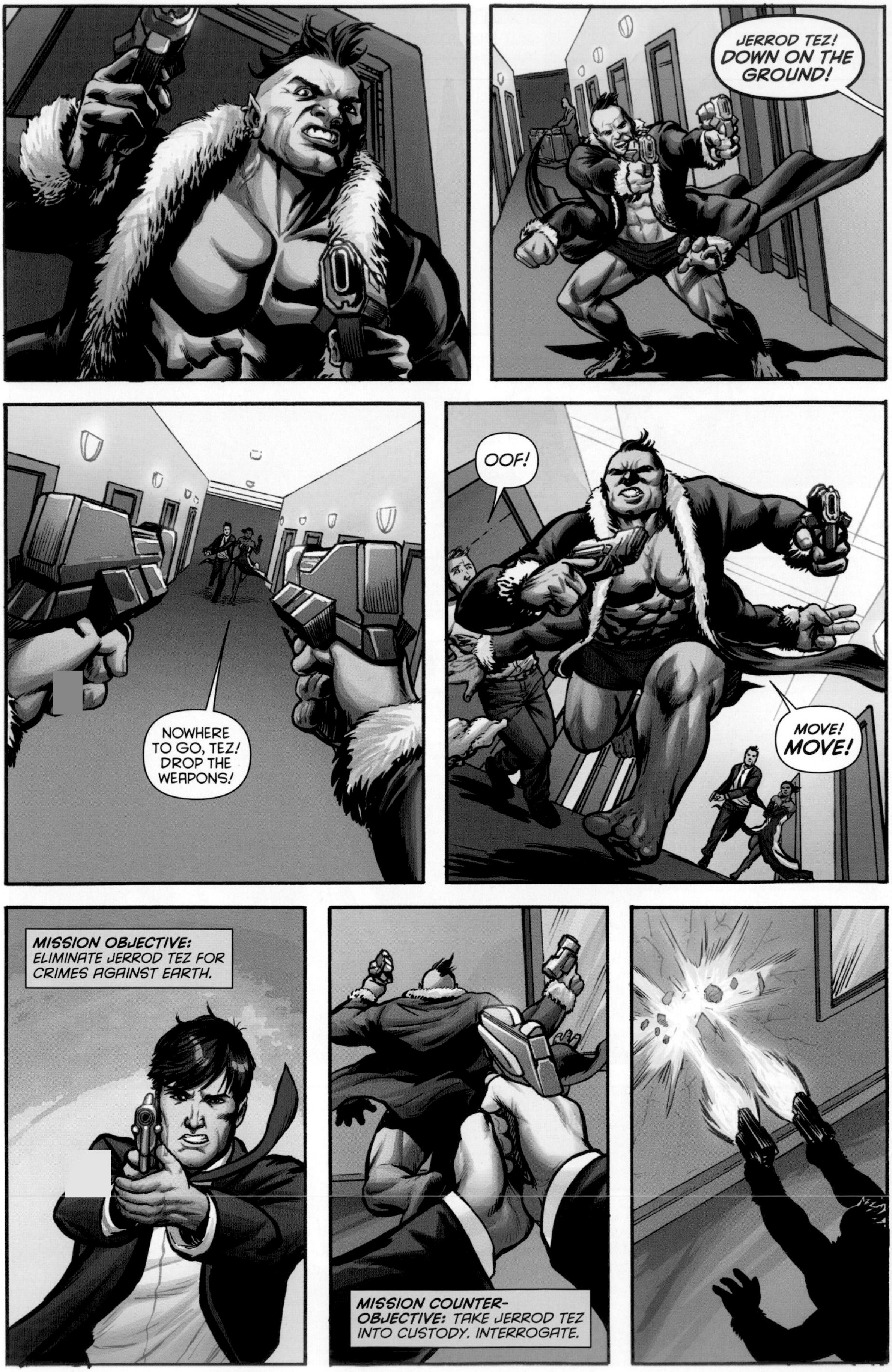
JERROD TEZ! DOWN ON THE GROUND!
NOWHERE TO GO, TEZ! DROP THE WEAPONS!
OOF!
MOVE! MOVE!
MISSION OBJECTIVE: ELIMINATE JERROD TEZ FOR CRIMES AGAINST EARTH.
MISSION COUNTER-OBJECTIVE: TAKE JERROD TEZ INTO CUSTODY. INTERROGATE.

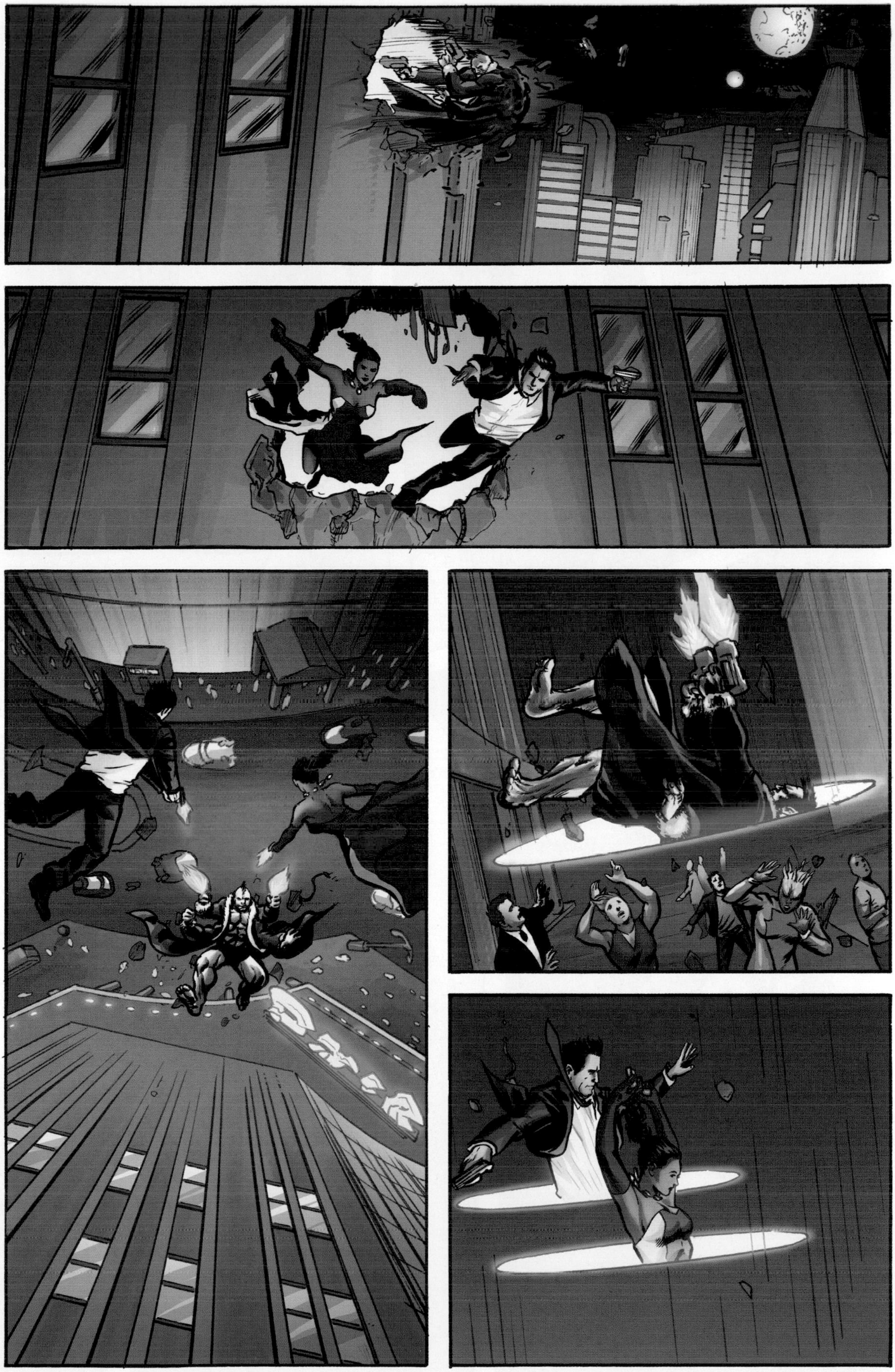

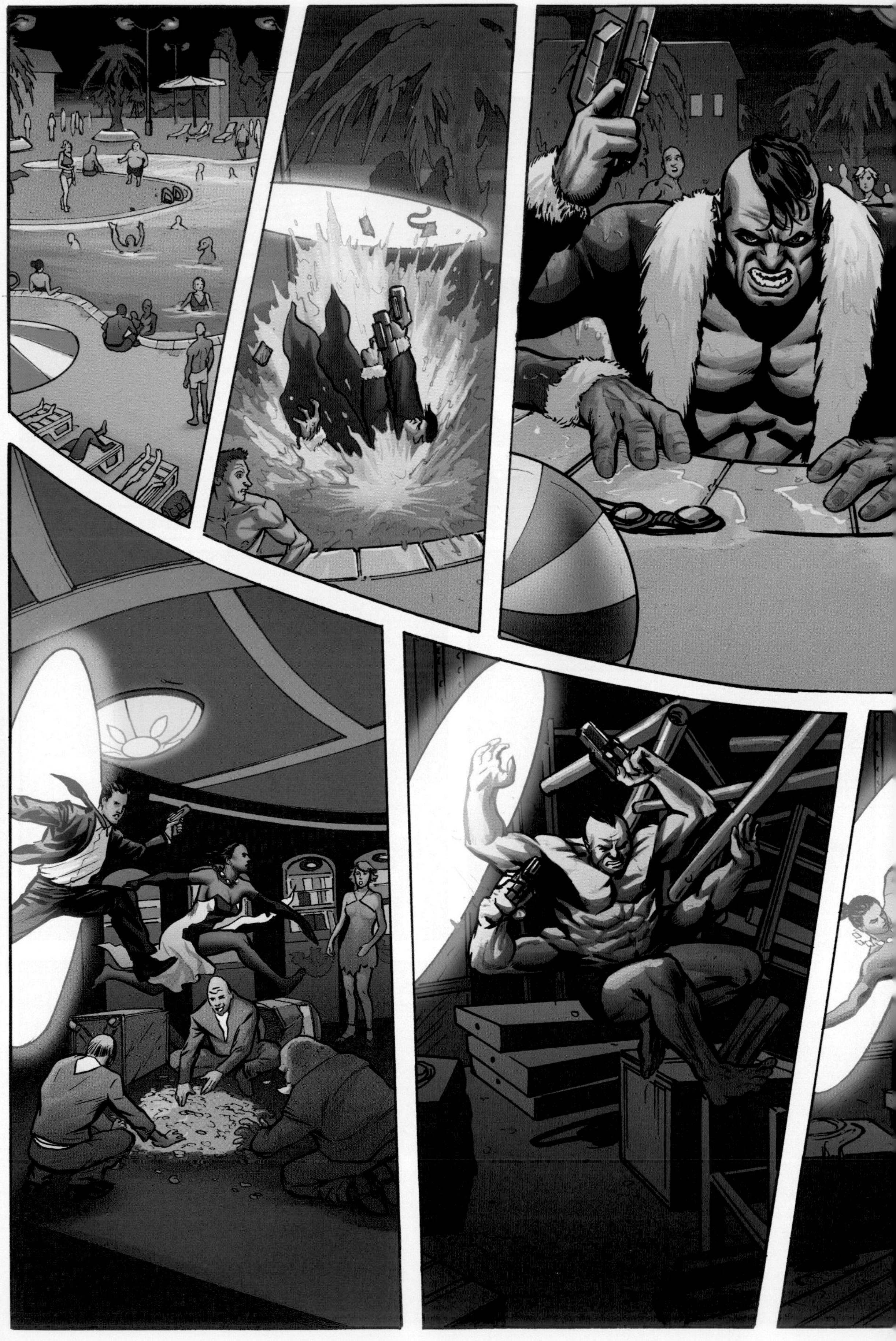

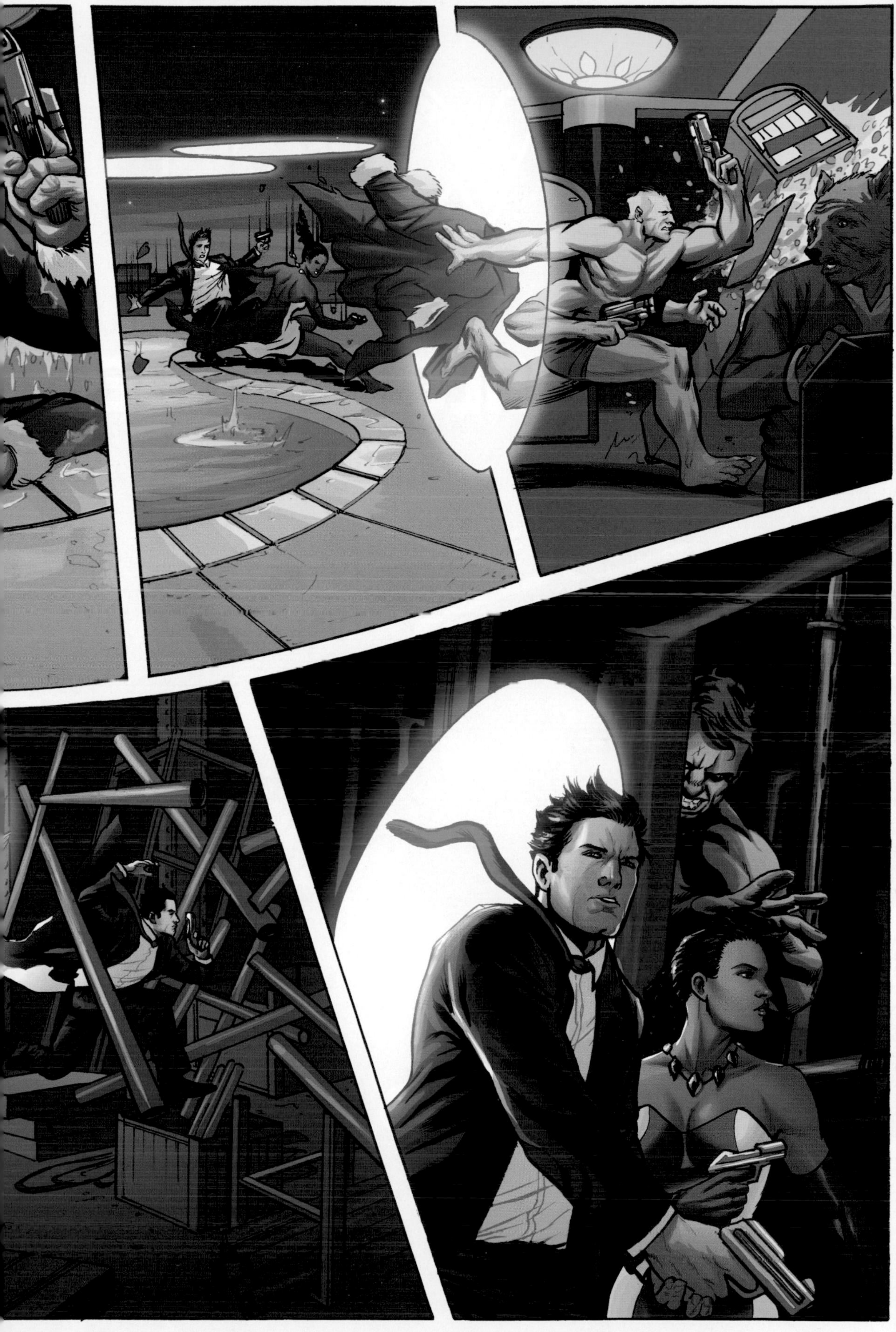

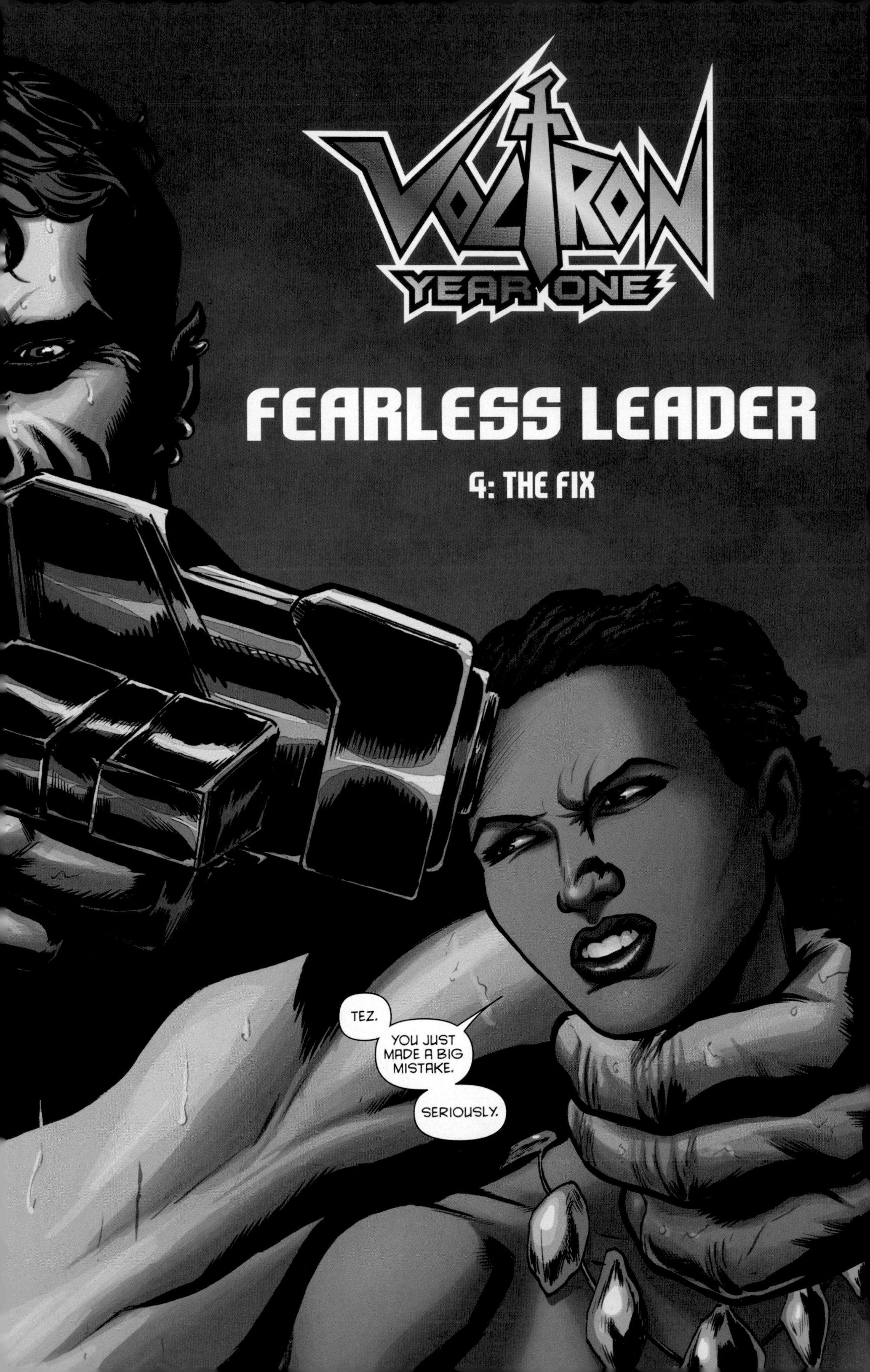
VOLTRON
YEAR ONE
FEARLESS LEADER
4: THE FIX
TEZ.
YOU JUST MADE A BIG MISTAKE.
SERIOUSLY.

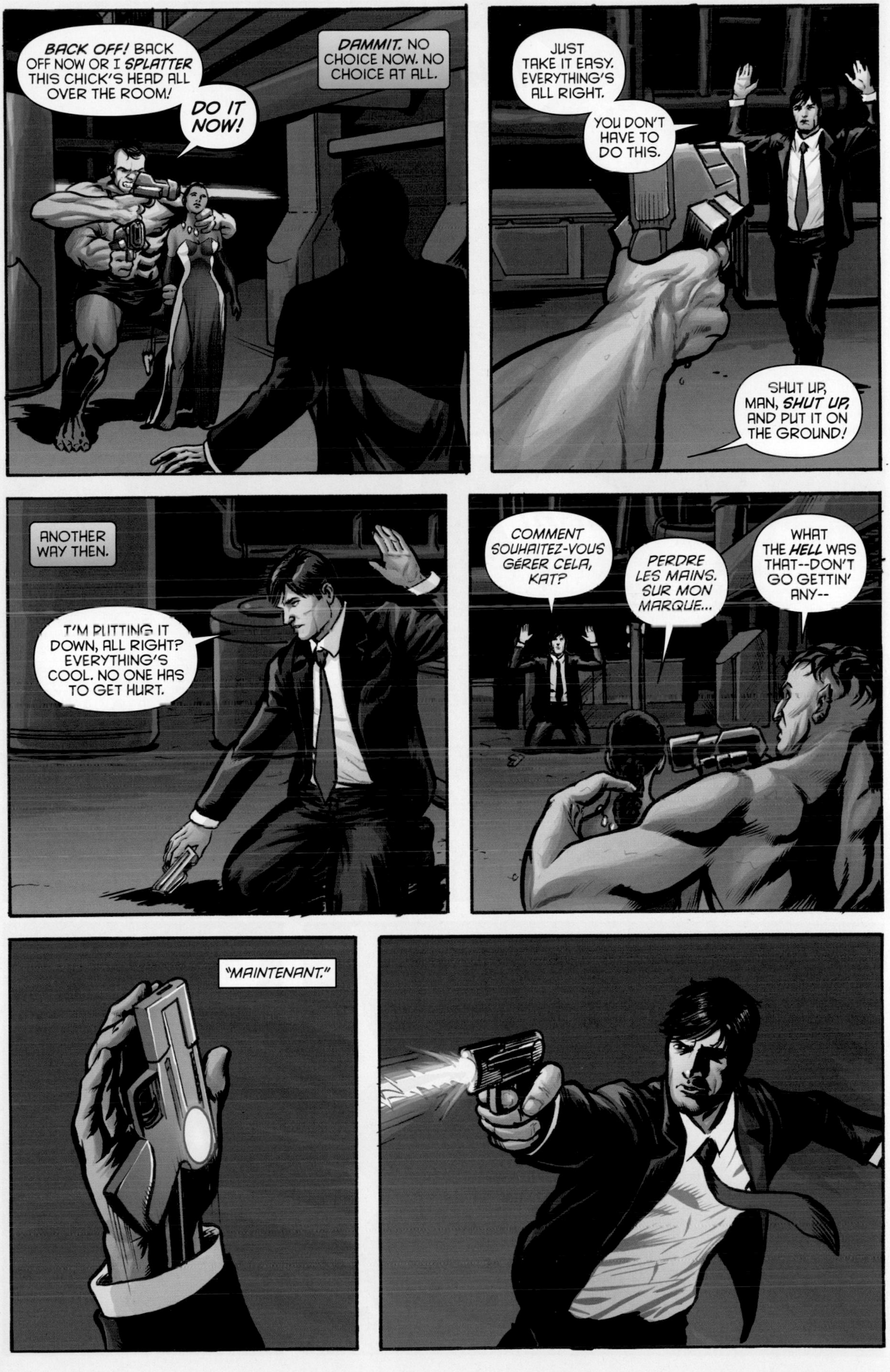
BACK OFF! BACK OFF NOW OR I SPLATTER THIS CHICK'S HEAD ALL OVER THE ROOM!
DO IT NOW!
DAMMIT. NO CHOICE NOW. NO CHOICE AT ALL.
JUST TAKE IT EASY. EVERYTHING'S ALL RIGHT.
YOU DON'T HAVE TO DO THIS.
SHUT UP, MAN, SHUT UP, AND PUT IT ON THE GROUND!
ANOTHER WAY THEN.
I'M PUTTING IT DOWN, ALL RIGHT? EVERYTHING'S COOL. NO ONE HAS TO GET HURT.
COMMENT SOUHAITEZ-VOUS GÉRER CELA, KAT?
PERDRE LES MAINS. SUR MON MARQUE...
WHAT THE HELL WAS THAT--DON'T GO GETTIN' ANY--
"MAINTENANT."

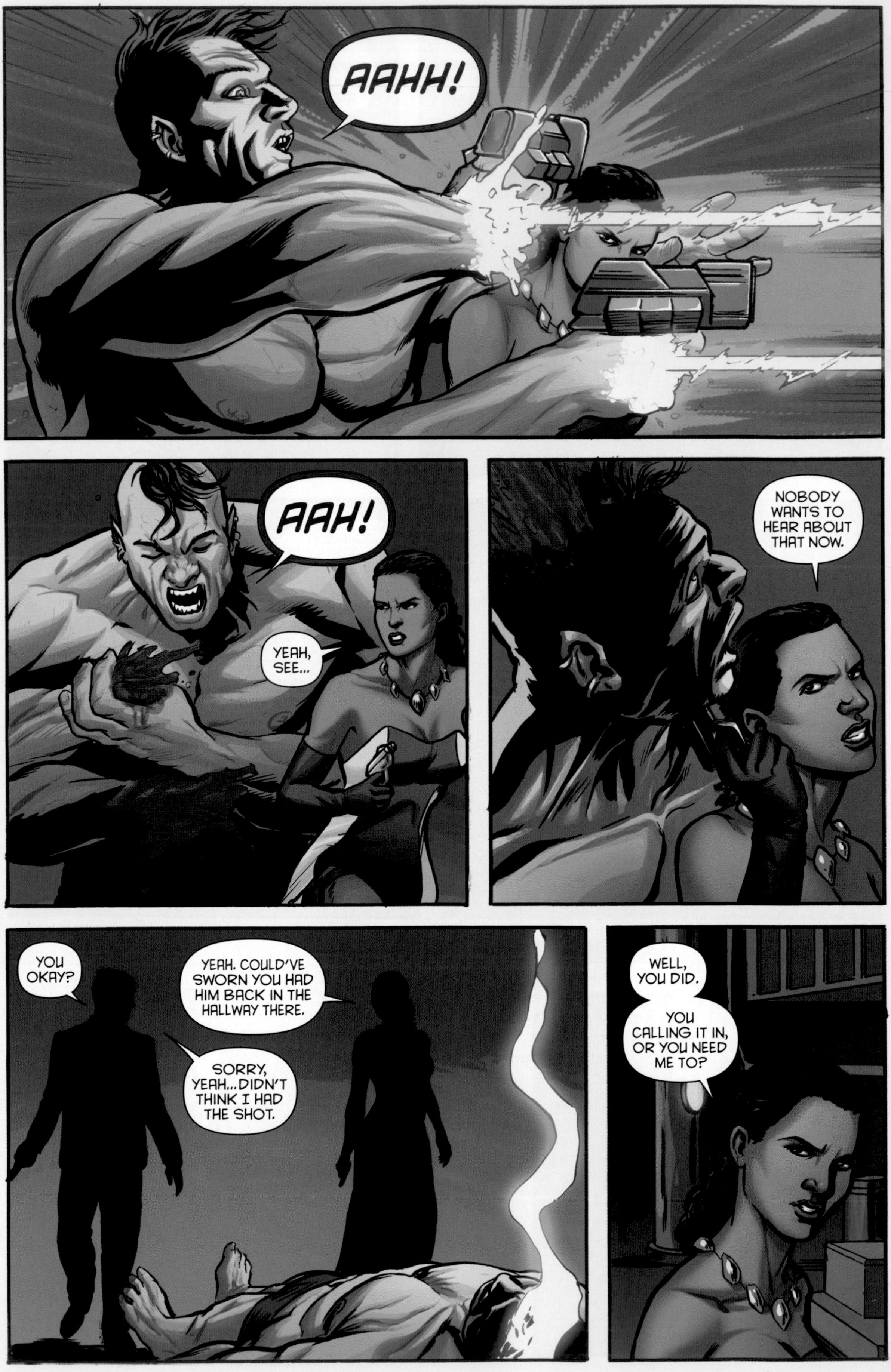
AAHH!
AAH!
YEAH, SEE...
NOBODY WANTS TO HEAR ABOUT THAT NOW.
YOU OKAY?
YEAH. COULD'VE SWORN YOU HAD HIM BACK IN THE HALLWAY THERE.
SORRY, YEAH...DIDN'T THINK I HAD THE SHOT.
WELL, YOU DID.
YOU CALLING IT IN, OR YOU NEED ME TO?

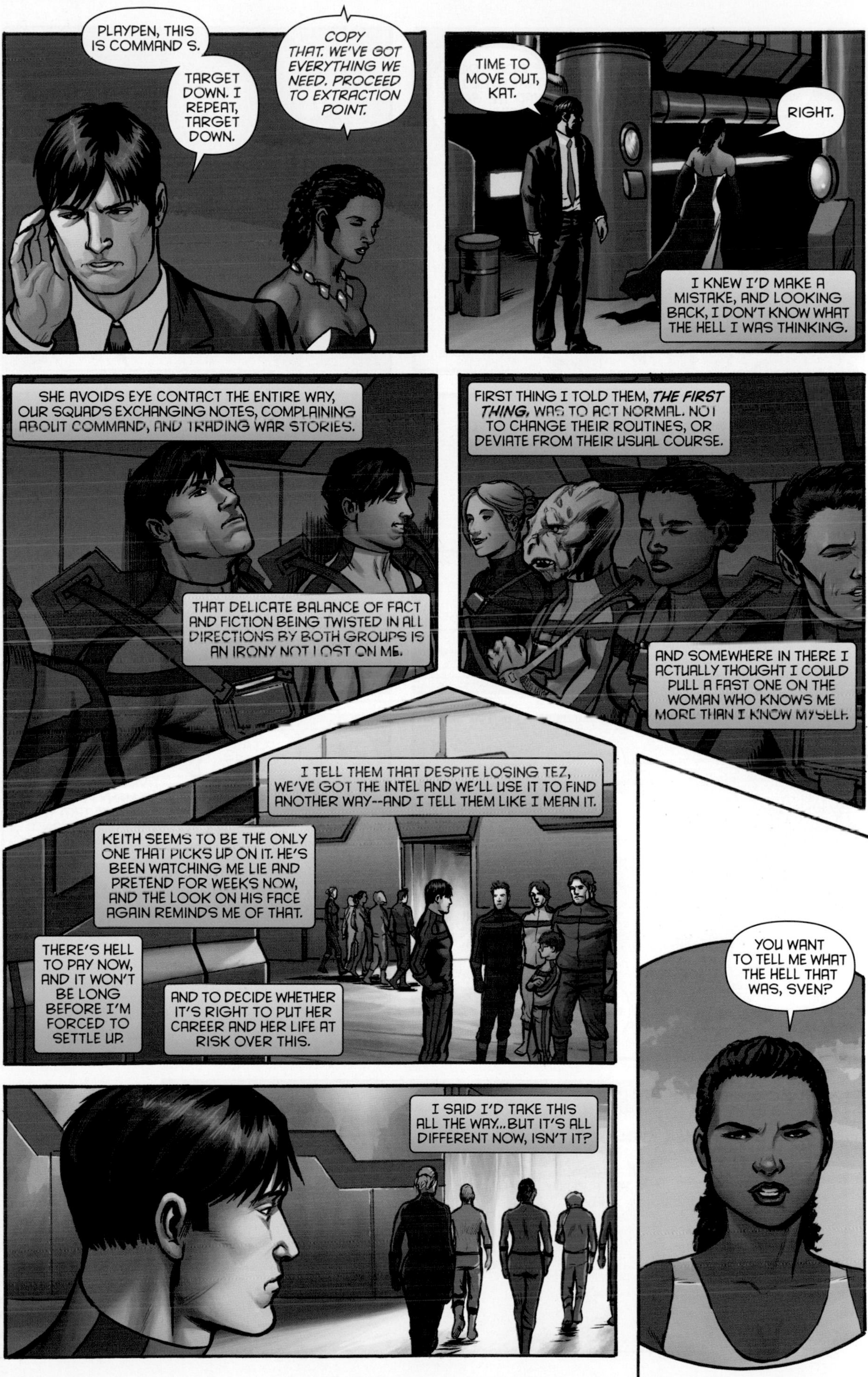
PLAYPEN, THIS IS COMMAND S.
TARGET DOWN. I REPEAT, TARGET DOWN.
COPY THAT. WE'VE GOT EVERYTHING WE NEED. PROCEED TO EXTRACTION POINT.
TIME TO MOVE OUT, KAT.
RIGHT.
I KNEW I'D MAKE A MISTAKE, AND LOOKING BACK, I DON'T KNOW WHAT THE HELL I WAS THINKING.
SHE AVOIDS EYE CONTACT THE ENTIRE WAY, OUR SQUADS EXCHANGING NOTES, COMPLAINING ABOUT COMMAND, AND TRADING WAR STORIES.
THAT DELICATE BALANCE OF FACT AND FICTION BEING TWISTED IN ALL DIRECTIONS BY BOTH GROUPS IS AN IRONY NOT LOST ON ME.
FIRST THING I TOLD THEM, *THE FIRST THING,* WAS TO ACT NORMAL. NOT TO CHANGE THEIR ROUTINES, OR DEVIATE FROM THEIR USUAL COURSE.
AND SOMEWHERE IN THERE I ACTUALLY THOUGHT I COULD PULL A FAST ONE ON THE WOMAN WHO KNOWS ME MORE THAN I KNOW MYSELF.
I TELL THEM THAT DESPITE LOSING TEZ, WE'VE GOT THE INTEL AND WE'LL USE IT TO FIND ANOTHER WAY--AND I TELL THEM LIKE I MEAN IT.
KEITH SEEMS TO BE THE ONLY ONE THAT PICKS UP ON IT. HE'S BEEN WATCHING ME LIE AND PRETEND FOR WEEKS NOW, AND THE LOOK ON HIS FACE AGAIN REMINDS ME OF THAT.
THERE'S HELL TO PAY NOW, AND IT WON'T BE LONG BEFORE I'M FORCED TO SETTLE UP.
AND TO DECIDE WHETHER IT'S RIGHT TO PUT HER CAREER AND HER LIFE AT RISK OVER THIS.
YOU WANT TO TELL ME WHAT THE HELL THAT WAS, SVEN?
I SAID I'D TAKE THIS ALL THE WAY... BUT IT'S ALL DIFFERENT NOW, ISN'T IT?

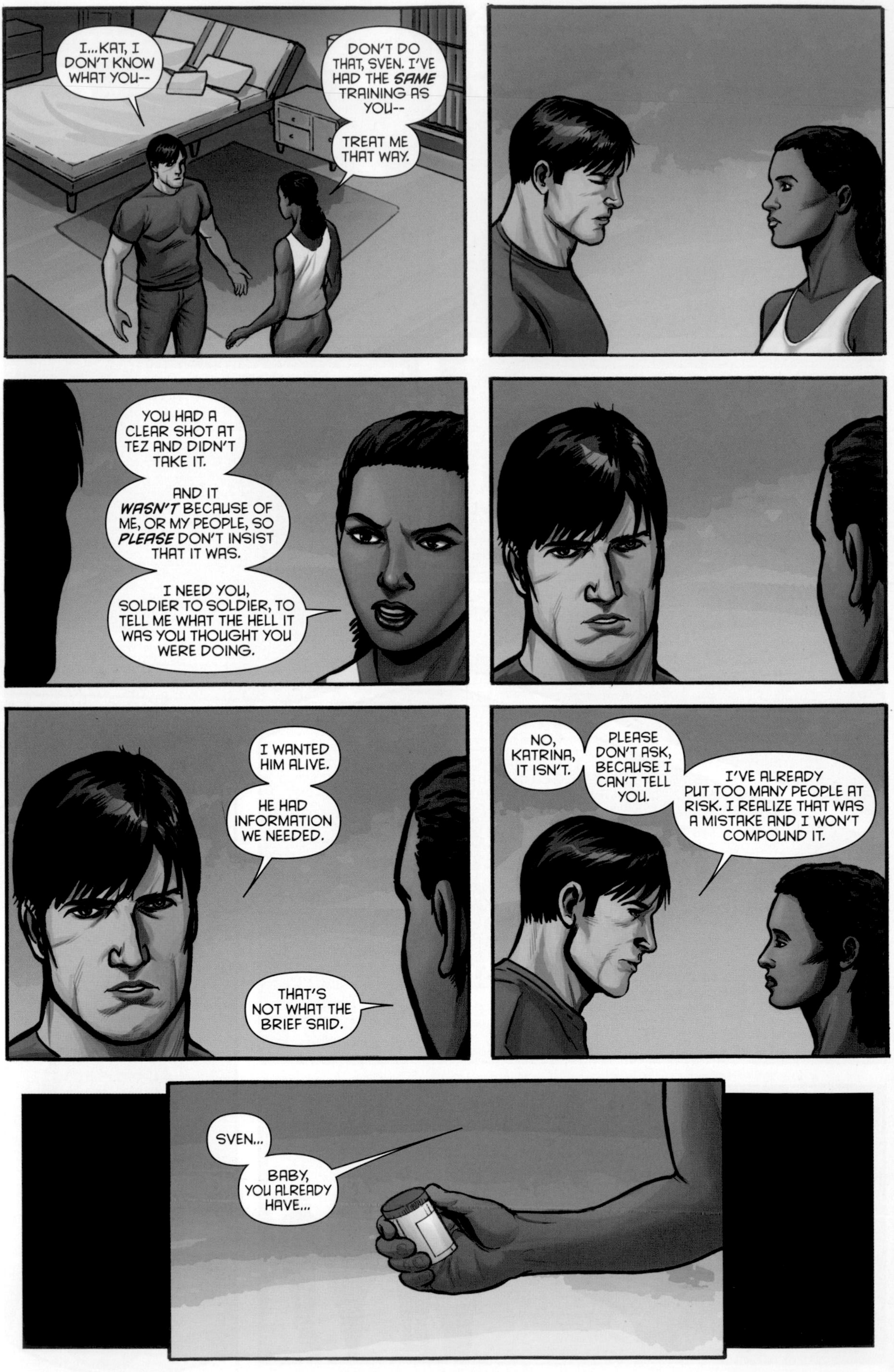
I...KAT, I DON'T KNOW WHAT YOU--
DON'T DO THAT, SVEN. I'VE HAD THE *SAME* TRAINING AS YOU--
TREAT ME THAT WAY.
YOU HAD A CLEAR SHOT AT TEZ AND DIDN'T TAKE IT.
AND IT *WASN'T* BECAUSE OF ME, OR MY PEOPLE, SO *PLEASE* DON'T INSIST THAT IT WAS.
I NEED YOU, SOLDIER TO SOLDIER, TO TELL ME WHAT THE HELL IT WAS YOU THOUGHT YOU WERE DOING.
I WANTED HIM ALIVE.
HE HAD INFORMATION WE NEEDED.
THAT'S NOT WHAT THE BRIEF SAID.
NO, KATRINA, IT ISN'T.
PLEASE DON'T ASK, BECAUSE I CAN'T TELL YOU.
I'VE ALREADY PUT TOO MANY PEOPLE AT RISK. I REALIZE THAT WAS A MISTAKE AND I WON'T COMPOUND IT.
SVEN...
BABY, YOU ALREADY HAVE...

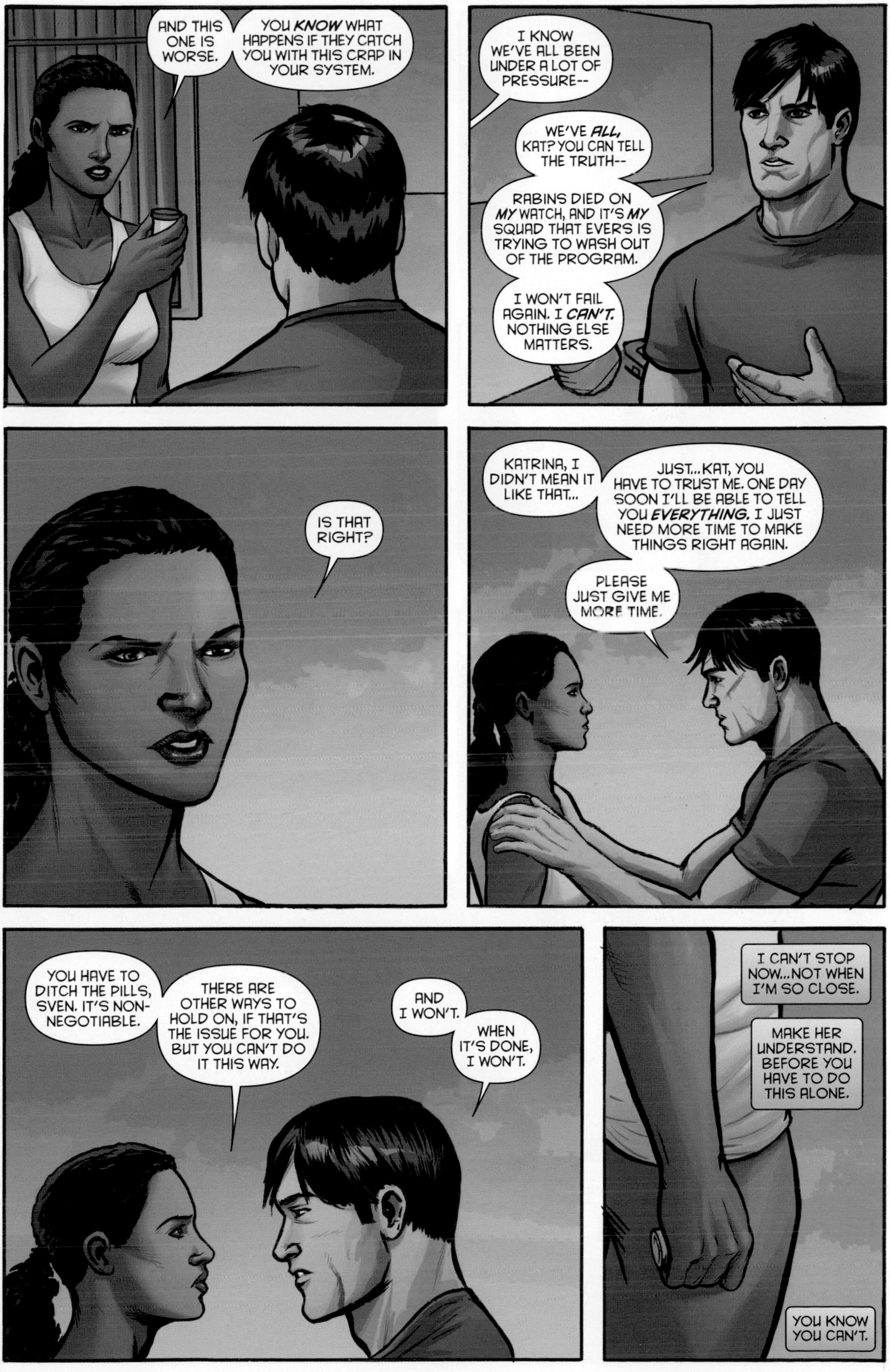
AND THIS ONE IS WORSE.
YOU KNOW WHAT HAPPENS IF THEY CATCH YOU WITH THIS CRAP IN YOUR SYSTEM.
I KNOW WE'VE ALL BEEN UNDER A LOT OF PRESSURE--
WE'VE ALL, KAT? YOU CAN TELL THE TRUTH--
RABINS DIED ON MY WATCH, AND IT'S MY SQUAD THAT EVERS IS TRYING TO WASH OUT OF THE PROGRAM.
I WON'T FAIL AGAIN. I CAN'T. NOTHING ELSE MATTERS.
IS THAT RIGHT?
KATRINA, I DIDN'T MEAN IT LIKE THAT...
JUST...KAT, YOU HAVE TO TRUST ME. ONE DAY SOON I'LL BE ABLE TO TELL YOU EVERYTHING. I JUST NEED MORE TIME TO MAKE THINGS RIGHT AGAIN.
PLEASE JUST GIVE ME MORE TIME.
YOU HAVE TO DITCH THE PILLS, SVEN. IT'S NON-NEGOTIABLE.
THERE ARE OTHER WAYS TO HOLD ON, IF THAT'S THE ISSUE FOR YOU. BUT YOU CAN'T DO IT THIS WAY.
AND I WON'T.
WHEN IT'S DONE, I WON'T.
I CAN'T STOP NOW...NOT WHEN I'M SO CLOSE.
MAKE HER UNDERSTAND. BEFORE YOU HAVE TO DO THIS ALONE.
YOU KNOW YOU CAN'T.

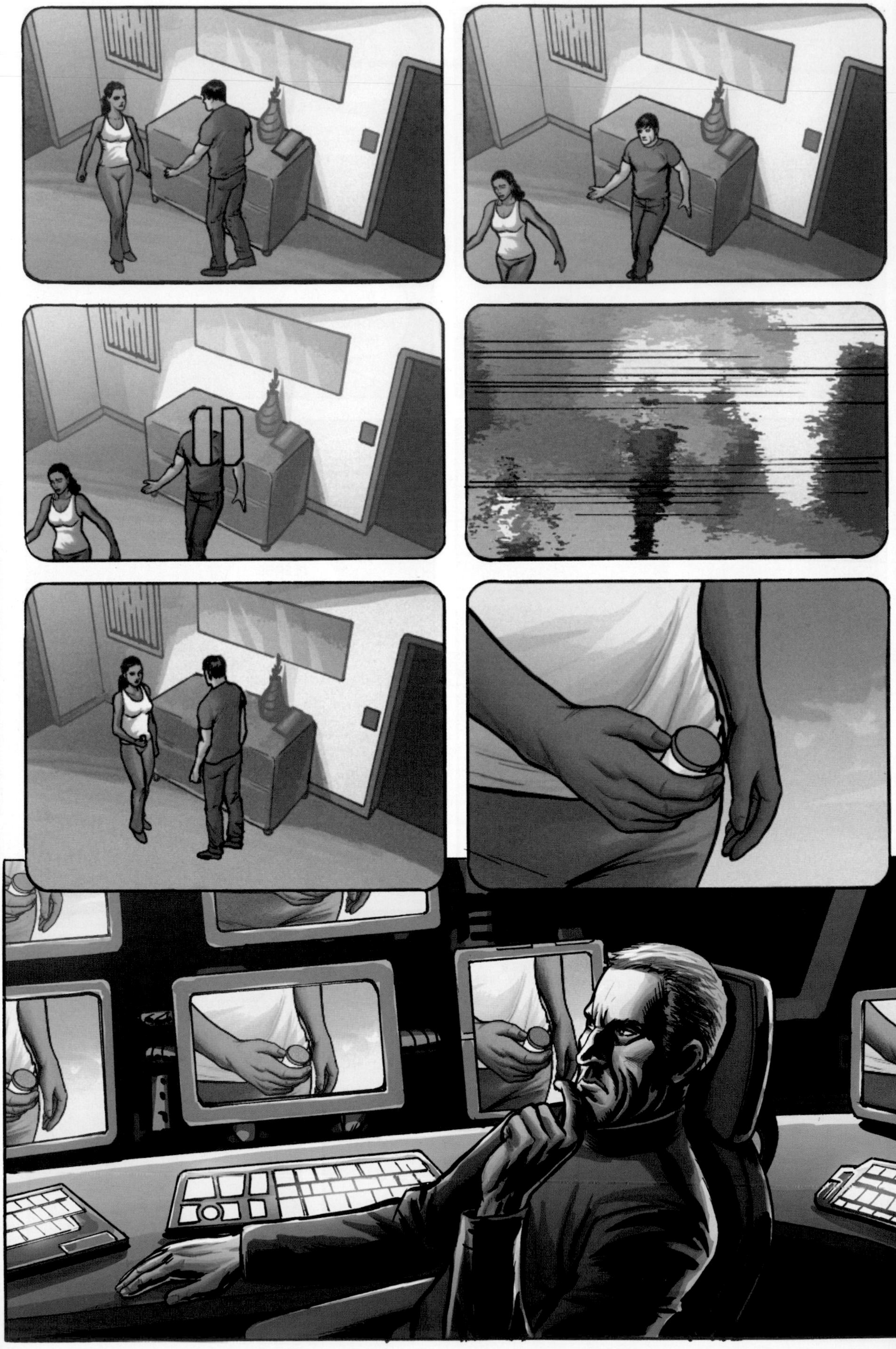

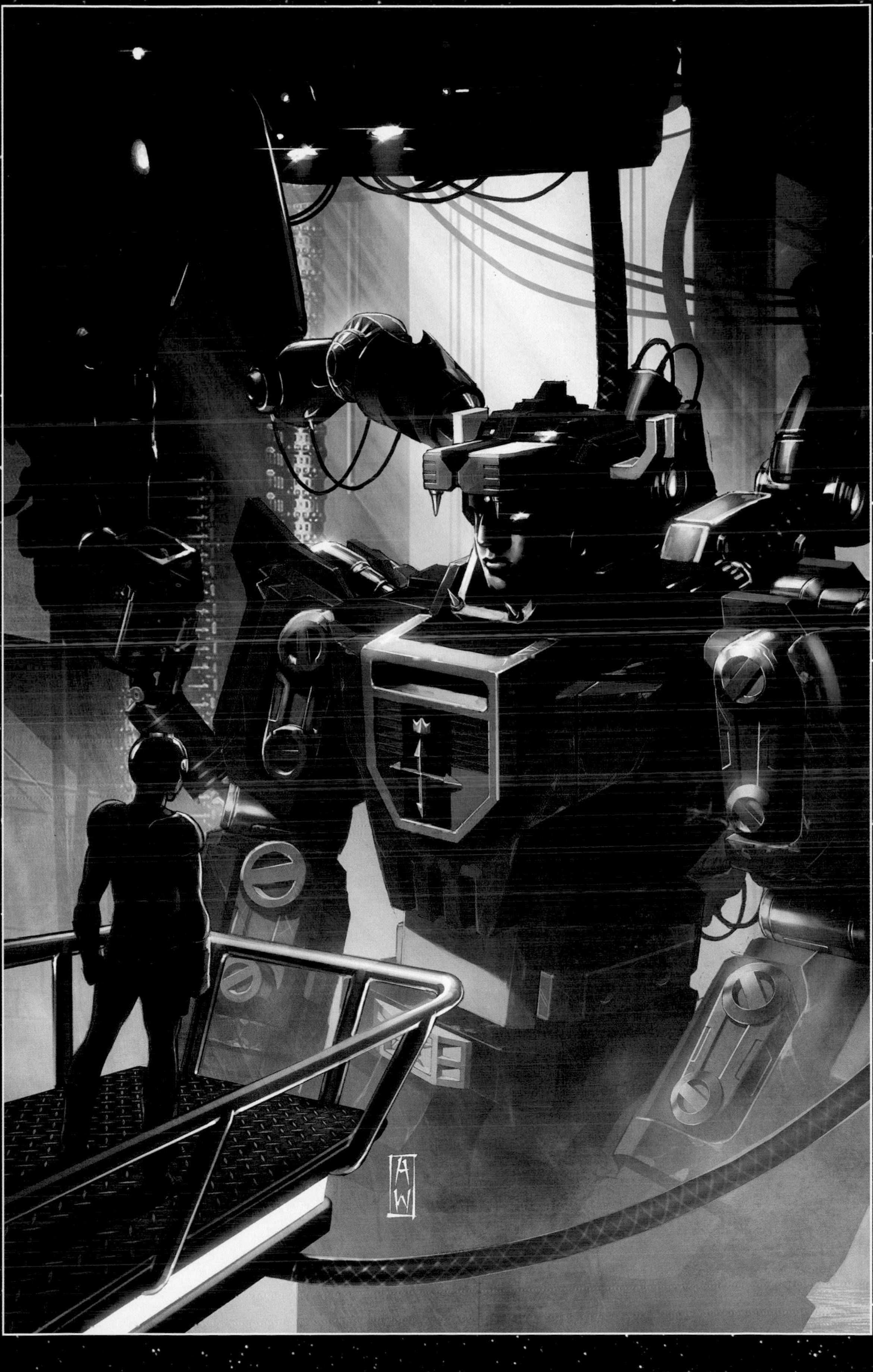
AW

Issue #5 cover by ADMIRA WIJAYA

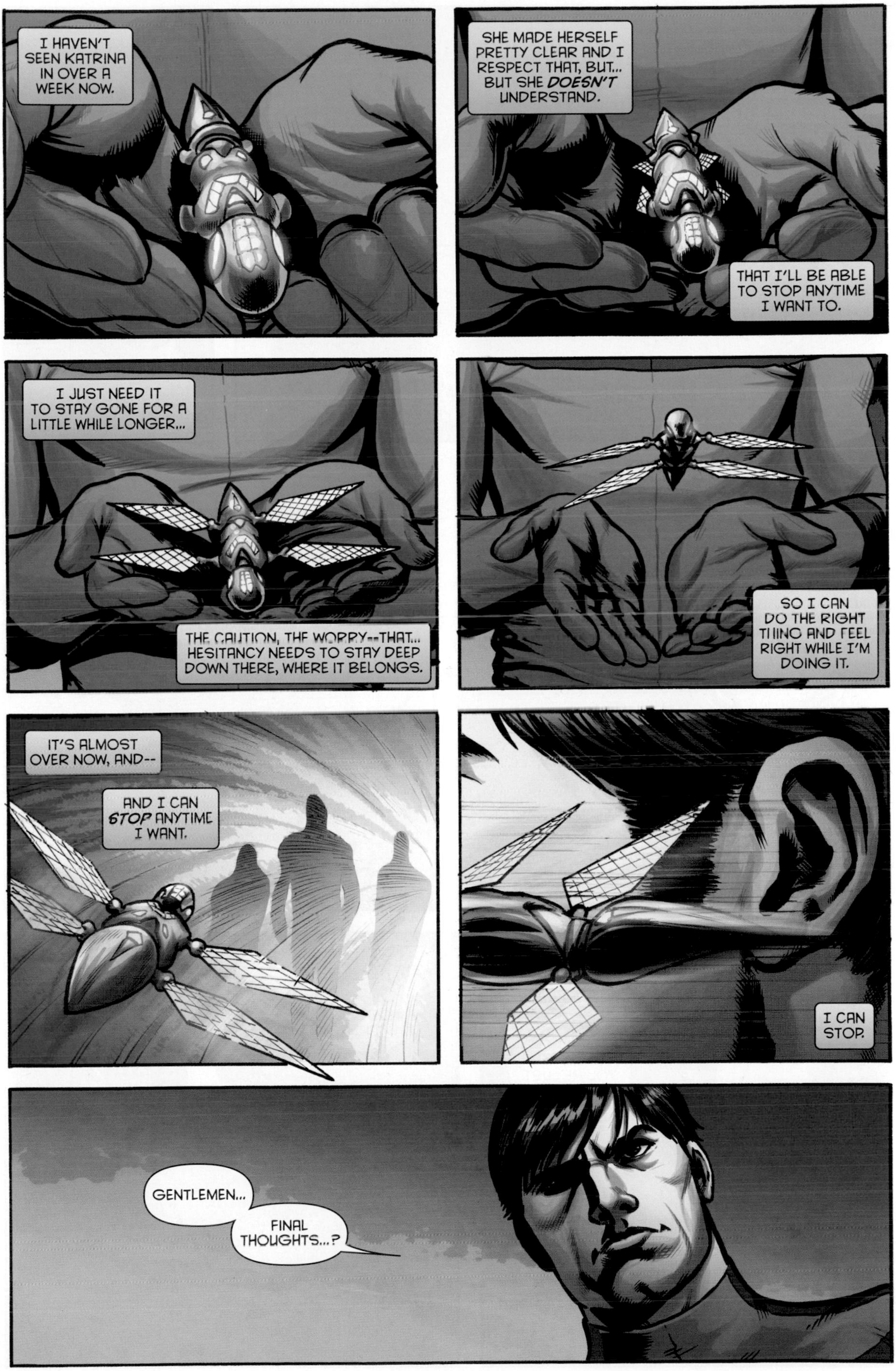
I HAVEN'T SEEN KATRINA IN OVER A WEEK NOW.
SHE MADE HERSELF PRETTY CLEAR AND I RESPECT THAT, BUT... BUT SHE *DOESN'T* UNDERSTAND.
THAT I'LL BE ABLE TO STOP ANYTIME I WANT TO.
I JUST NEED IT TO STAY GONE FOR A LITTLE WHILE LONGER...
THE CAUTION, THE WORRY--THAT... HESITANCY NEEDS TO STAY DEEP DOWN THERE, WHERE IT BELONGS.
SO I CAN DO THE RIGHT THING AND FEEL RIGHT WHILE I'M DOING IT.
IT'S ALMOST OVER NOW, AND--
AND I CAN *STOP* ANYTIME I WANT.
I CAN STOP.
GENTLEMEN...
FINAL THOUGHTS...?

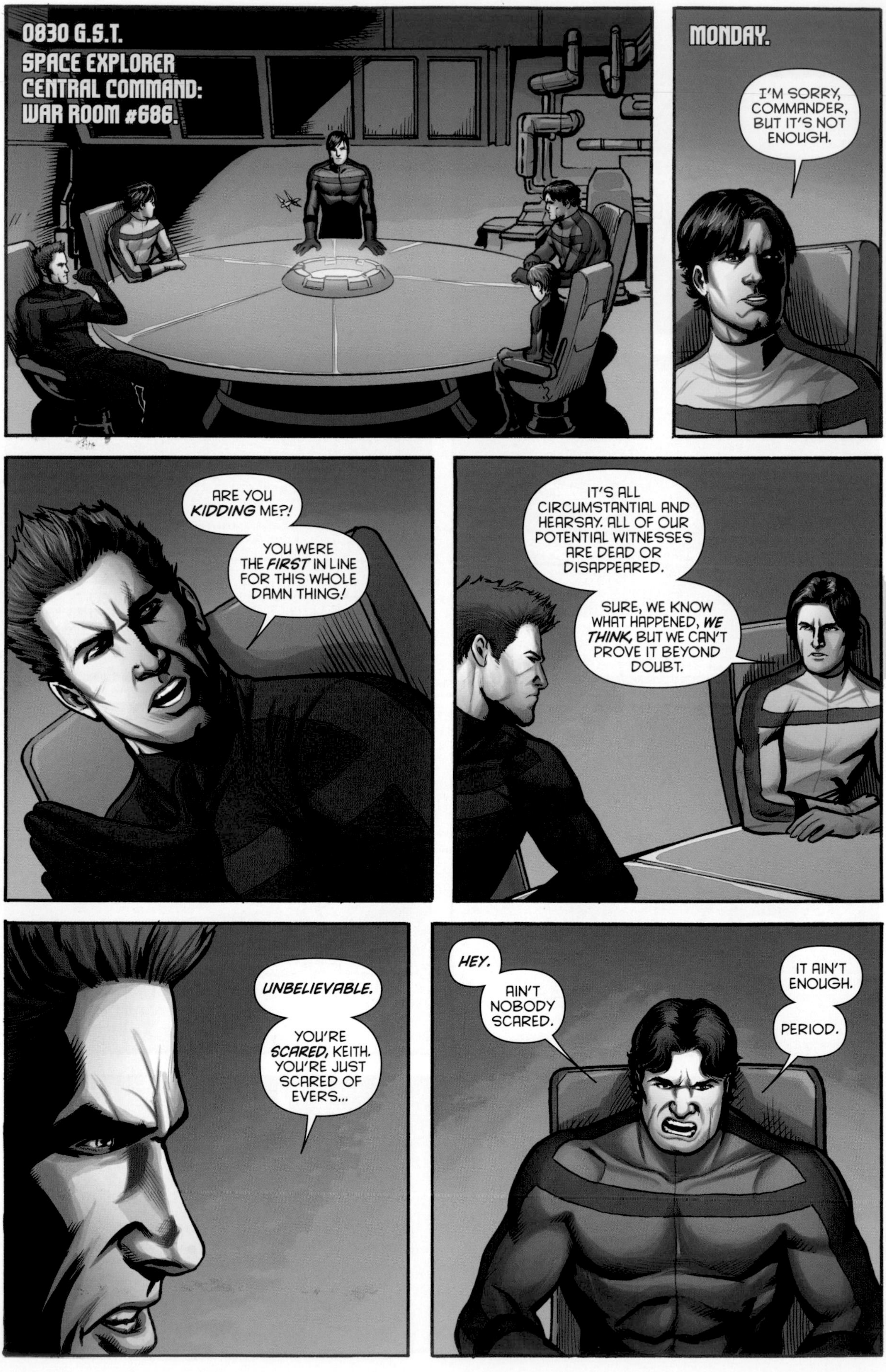
0830 G.S.T.
SPACE EXPLORER CENTRAL COMMAND: WAR ROOM #686.
MONDAY.
I'M SORRY, COMMANDER, BUT IT'S NOT ENOUGH.
ARE YOU KIDDING ME?!
YOU WERE THE FIRST IN LINE FOR THIS WHOLE DAMN THING!
IT'S ALL CIRCUMSTANTIAL AND HEARSAY. ALL OF OUR POTENTIAL WITNESSES ARE DEAD OR DISAPPEARED.
SURE, WE KNOW WHAT HAPPENED, WE THINK, BUT WE CAN'T PROVE IT BEYOND DOUBT.
UNBELIEVABLE.
YOU'RE SCARED, KEITH. YOU'RE JUST SCARED OF EVERS...
HEY.
AIN'T NOBODY SCARED.
IT AIN'T ENOUGH.
PERIOD.

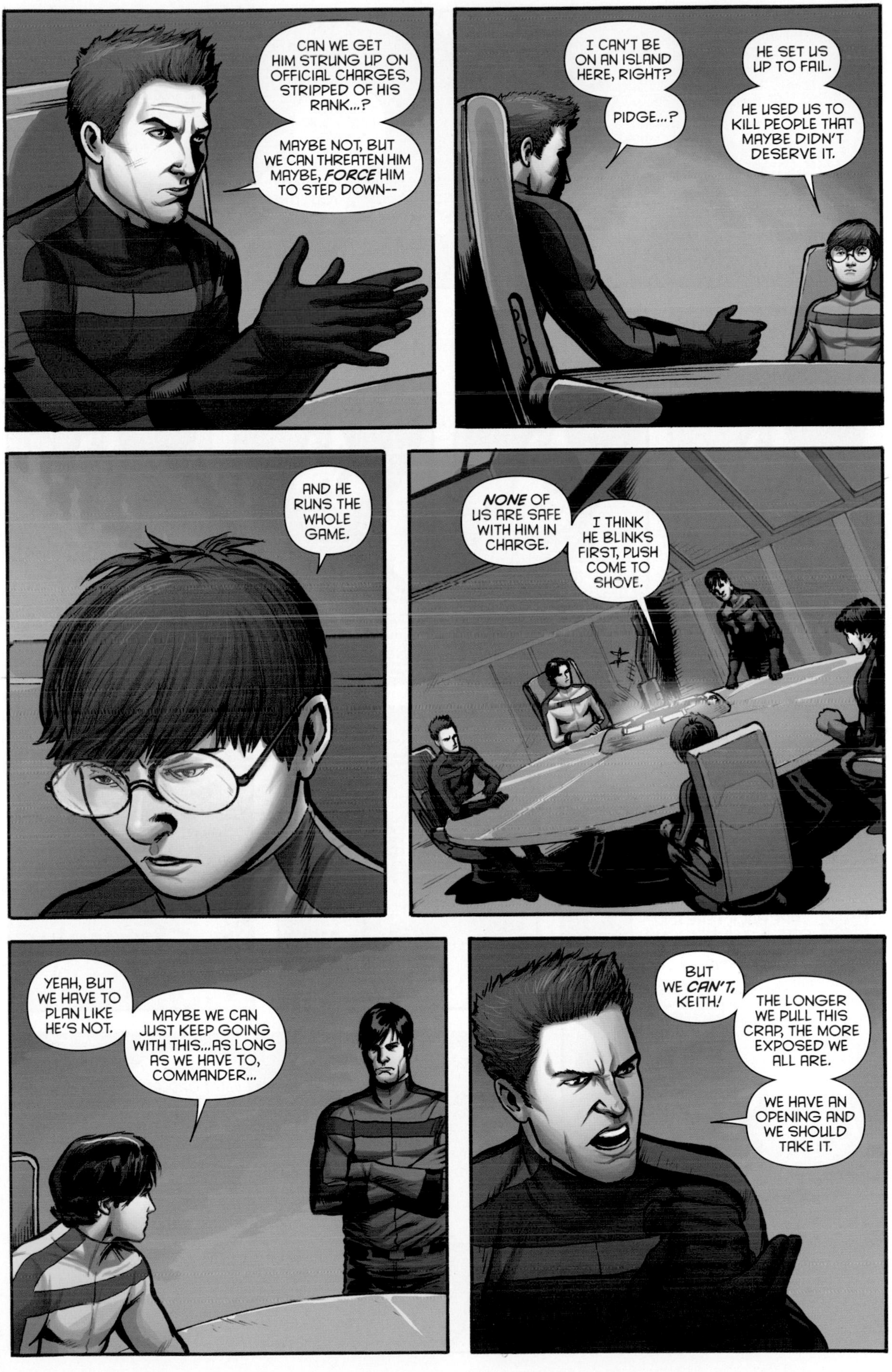
CAN WE GET HIM STRUNG UP ON OFFICIAL CHARGES, STRIPPED OF HIS RANK...?
MAYBE NOT, BUT WE CAN THREATEN HIM MAYBE, *FORCE* HIM TO STEP DOWN--
I CAN'T BE ON AN ISLAND HERE, RIGHT?
PIDGE...?
HE SET US UP TO FAIL.
HE USED US TO KILL PEOPLE THAT MAYBE DIDN'T DESERVE IT.
AND HE RUNS THE WHOLE GAME.
NONE OF US ARE SAFE WITH HIM IN CHARGE.
I THINK HE BLINKS FIRST, PUSH COME TO SHOVE.
YEAH, BUT WE HAVE TO PLAN LIKE HE'S NOT.
MAYBE WE CAN JUST KEEP GOING WITH THIS...AS LONG AS WE HAVE TO, COMMANDER...
BUT WE *CAN'T*, KEITH!
THE LONGER WE PULL THIS CRAP, THE MORE EXPOSED WE ALL ARE.
WE HAVE AN OPENING AND WE SHOULD TAKE IT.

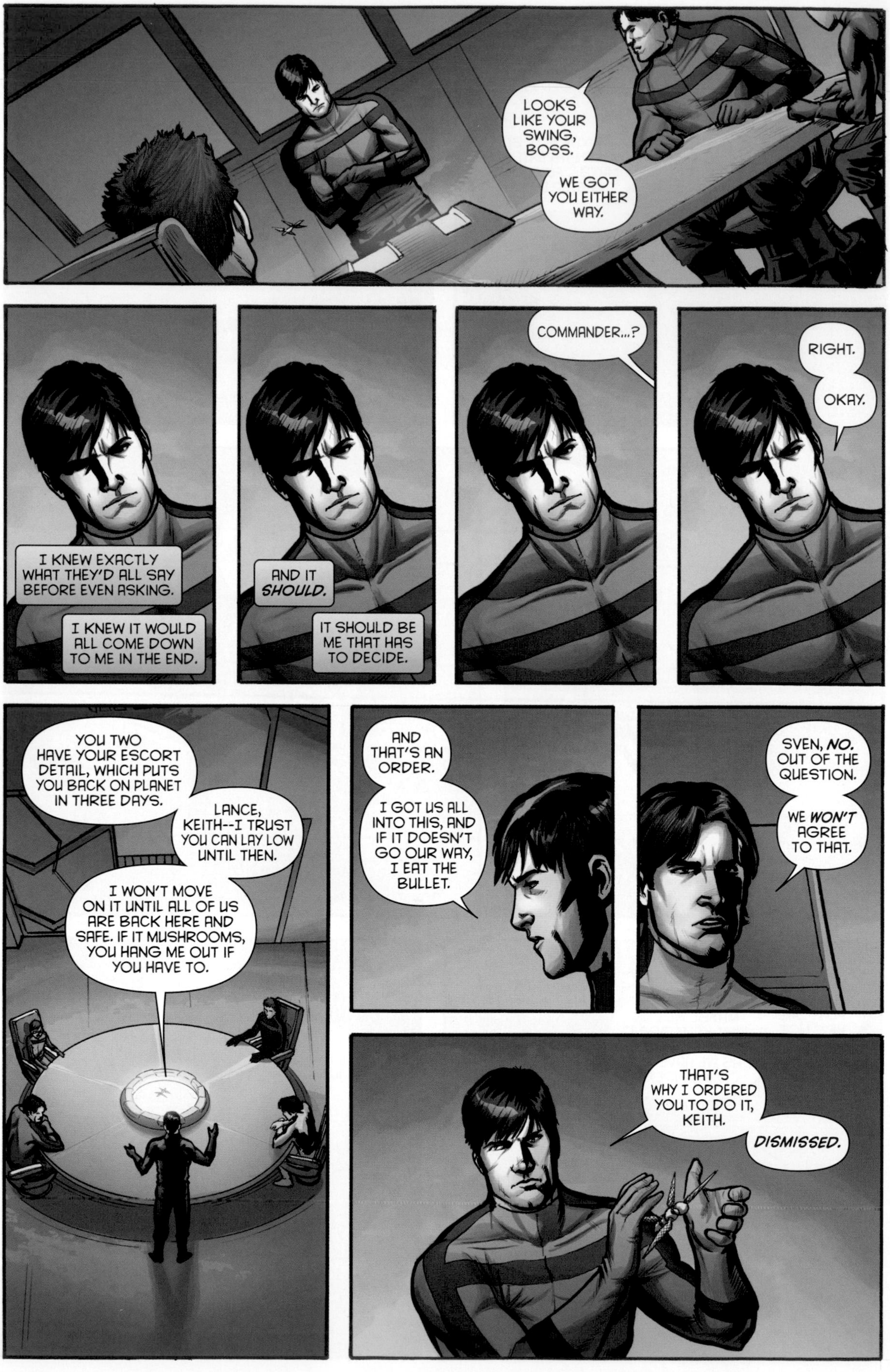
LOOKS LIKE YOUR SWING, BOSS.
WE GOT YOU EITHER WAY.
I KNEW EXACTLY WHAT THEY'D ALL SAY BEFORE EVEN ASKING.
I KNEW IT WOULD ALL COME DOWN TO ME IN THE END.
AND IT SHOULD.
IT SHOULD BE ME THAT HAS TO DECIDE.
COMMANDER...?
RIGHT.
OKAY.
YOU TWO HAVE YOUR ESCORT DETAIL, WHICH PUTS YOU BACK ON PLANET IN THREE DAYS.
LANCE, KEITH--I TRUST YOU CAN LAY LOW UNTIL THEN.
I WON'T MOVE ON IT UNTIL ALL OF US ARE BACK HERE AND SAFE. IF IT MUSHROOMS, YOU HANG ME OUT IF YOU HAVE TO.
AND THAT'S AN ORDER.
I GOT US ALL INTO THIS, AND IF IT DOESN'T GO OUR WAY, I EAT THE BULLET.
SVEN, NO. OUT OF THE QUESTION.
WE WON'T AGREE TO THAT.
THAT'S WHY I ORDERED YOU TO DO IT, KEITH.
DISMISSED.

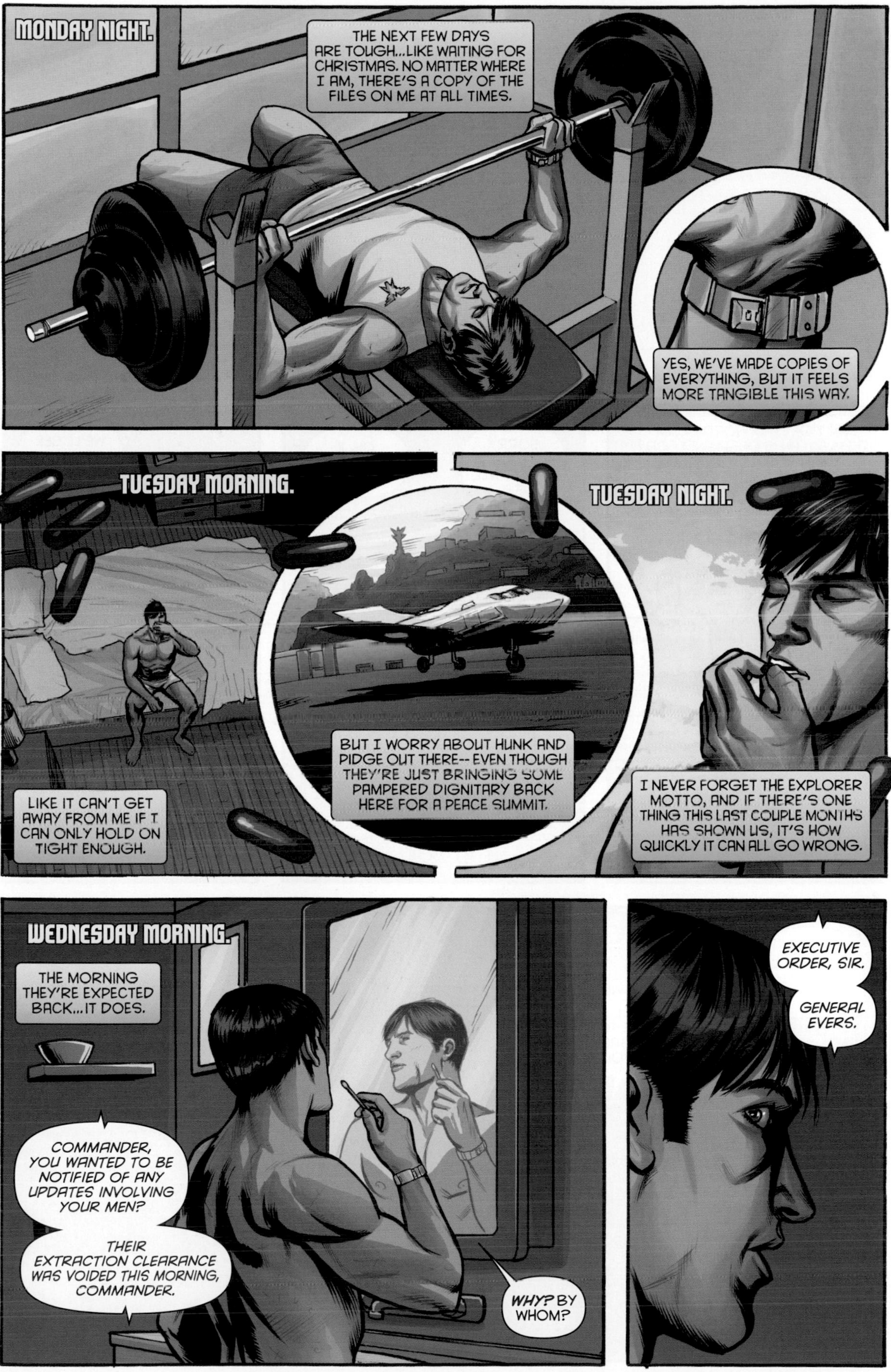
MONDAY NIGHT.
THE NEXT FEW DAYS ARE TOUGH...LIKE WAITING FOR CHRISTMAS. NO MATTER WHERE I AM, THERE'S A COPY OF THE FILES ON ME AT ALL TIMES.
YES, WE'VE MADE COPIES OF EVERYTHING, BUT IT FEELS MORE TANGIBLE THIS WAY.
TUESDAY MORNING.
LIKE IT CAN'T GET AWAY FROM ME IF I CAN ONLY HOLD ON TIGHT ENOUGH.
BUT I WORRY ABOUT HUNK AND PIDGE OUT THERE-- EVEN THOUGH THEY'RE JUST BRINGING SOME PAMPERED DIGNITARY BACK HERE FOR A PEACE SUMMIT.
TUESDAY NIGHT.
I NEVER FORGET THE EXPLORER MOTTO, AND IF THERE'S ONE THING THIS LAST COUPLE MONTHS HAS SHOWN US, IT'S HOW QUICKLY IT CAN ALL GO WRONG.
WEDNESDAY MORNING.
THE MORNING THEY'RE EXPECTED BACK...IT DOES.
COMMANDER, YOU WANTED TO BE NOTIFIED OF ANY UPDATES INVOLVING YOUR MEN?
THEIR EXTRACTION CLEARANCE WAS VOIDED THIS MORNING, COMMANDER.
WHY? BY WHOM?
EXECUTIVE ORDER, SIR.
GENERAL EVERS.

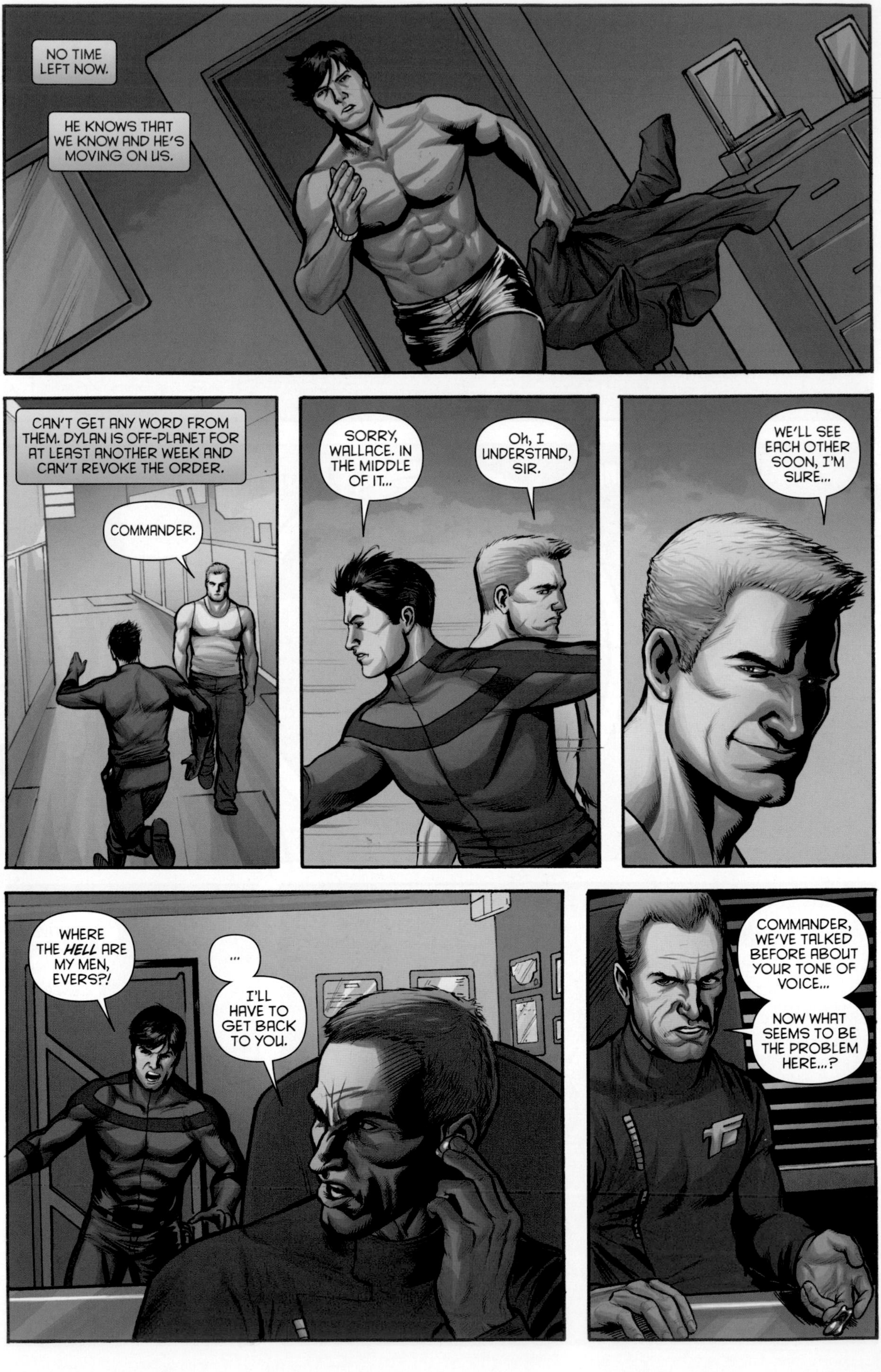
NO TIME LEFT NOW.
HE KNOWS THAT WE KNOW AND HE'S MOVING ON US.
CAN'T GET ANY WORD FROM THEM. DYLAN IS OFF-PLANET FOR AT LEAST ANOTHER WEEK AND CAN'T REVOKE THE ORDER.
COMMANDER.
SORRY, WALLACE. IN THE MIDDLE OF IT...
Oh, I UNDERSTAND, SIR.
WE'LL SEE EACH OTHER SOON, I'M SURE...
WHERE THE *HELL* ARE MY MEN, EVERS?!
...
I'LL HAVE TO GET BACK TO YOU.
COMMANDER, WE'VE TALKED BEFORE ABOUT YOUR TONE OF VOICE...
NOW WHAT SEEMS TO BE THE PROBLEM HERE...?

EXTRACTION FOR HUNK AND PIDGE WAS *CANCELED* THIS MORNING BY EXECUTIVE ORDER, AND I'D LIKE AN EXPLANATION.

AN *EXPLANATION*, COMMANDER? JUST WHO THE HELL DO YOU THINK YOU ARE?

I WANT THEM ON A TRANSPORT *SAFE* IN THE NEXT FIFTEEN MINUTES, OR THIS GOES INTO THE HAND OF EVERY MEMBER OF THE SECURITY COUNCIL.

AND WHAT'S ON IT?

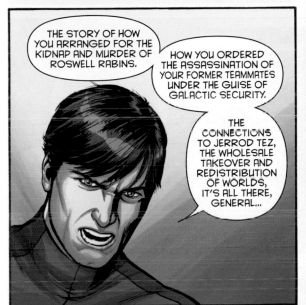

THE STORY OF HOW YOU ARRANGED FOR THE KIDNAP AND MURDER OF ROSWELL RABINS.

HOW YOU ORDERED THE ASSASSINATION OF YOUR FORMER TEAMMATES UNDER THE GUISE OF GALACTIC SECURITY.

THE CONNECTIONS TO JERROD TEZ, THE WHOLESALE TAKEOVER AND REDISTRIBUTION OF WORLDS, IT'S ALL THERE, GENERAL...

I DON'T KNOW IF YOU'RE AWARE OF THIS, BUT YOUR FIRST RESPONSIBILITY AS AN S.E. COMMANDER IS TO PROTECT THE BRAVE MEN AND WOMEN UNDER YOUR CARE.

IT'S THE FIRST AND MOST IMPORTANT MANDATE SOMEONE LIKE US CAN EVER BE GIVEN.

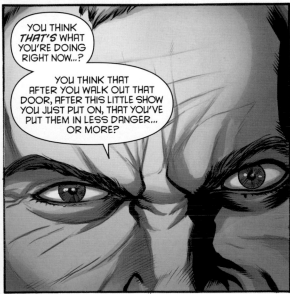

YOU THINK *THAT'S* WHAT YOU'RE DOING RIGHT NOW...?

YOU THINK THAT AFTER YOU WALK OUT THAT DOOR, AFTER THIS LITTLE SHOW YOU JUST PUT ON, THAT YOU'VE PUT THEM IN LESS DANGER... OR MORE?

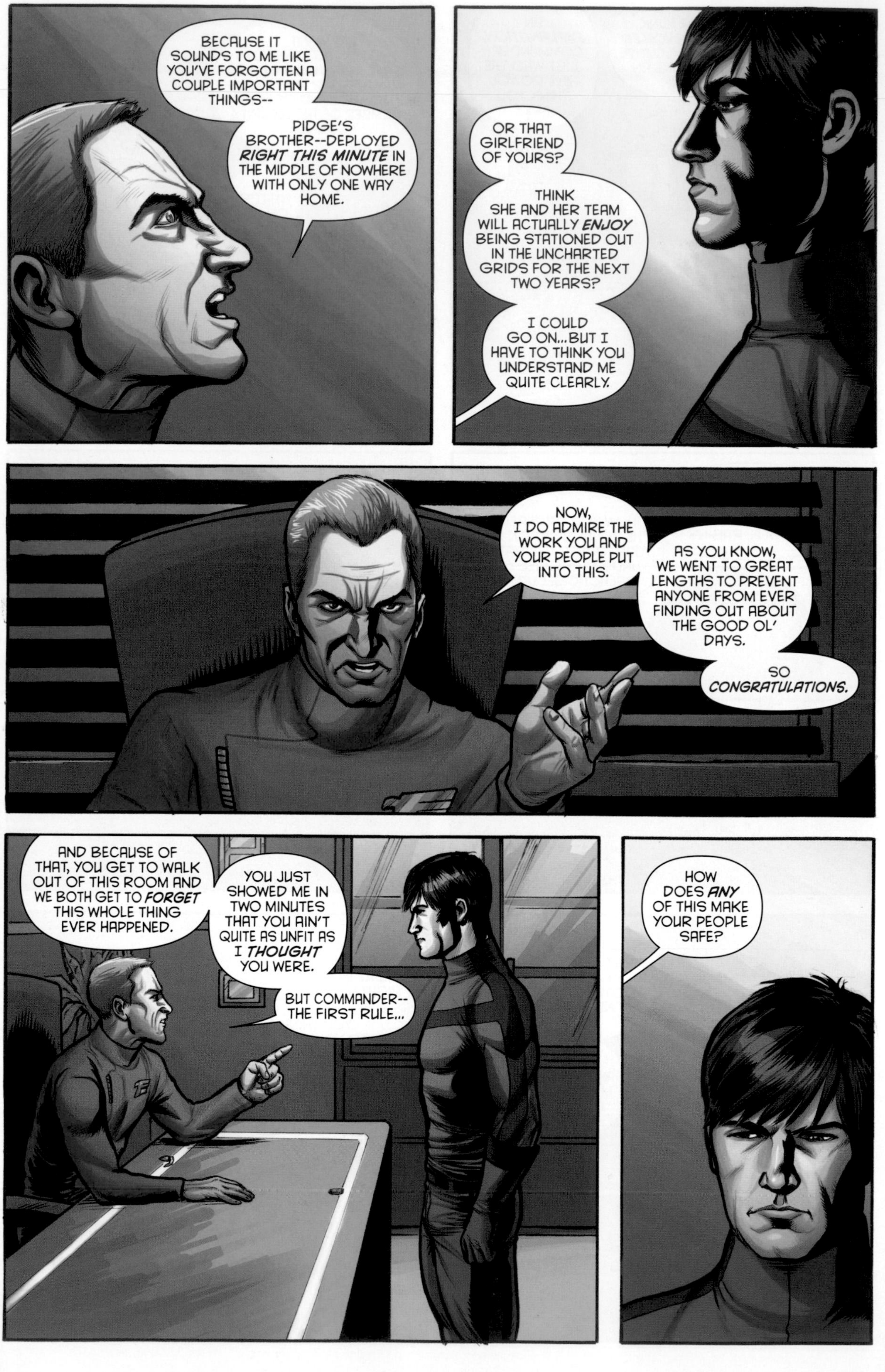
BECAUSE IT SOUNDS TO ME LIKE YOU'VE FORGOTTEN A COUPLE IMPORTANT THINGS--
PIDGE'S BROTHER--DEPLOYED *RIGHT THIS MINUTE* IN THE MIDDLE OF NOWHERE WITH ONLY ONE WAY HOME.
OR THAT GIRLFRIEND OF YOURS?
THINK SHE AND HER TEAM WILL ACTUALLY *ENJOY* BEING STATIONED OUT IN THE UNCHARTED GRIDS FOR THE NEXT TWO YEARS?
I COULD GO ON...BUT I HAVE TO THINK YOU UNDERSTAND ME QUITE CLEARLY.
NOW, I DO ADMIRE THE WORK YOU AND YOUR PEOPLE PUT INTO THIS.
AS YOU KNOW, WE WENT TO GREAT LENGTHS TO PREVENT ANYONE FROM EVER FINDING OUT ABOUT THE GOOD OL' DAYS.
SO *CONGRATULATIONS.*
AND BECAUSE OF THAT, YOU GET TO WALK OUT OF THIS ROOM AND WE BOTH GET TO *FORGET* THIS WHOLE THING EVER HAPPENED.
YOU JUST SHOWED ME IN TWO MINUTES THAT YOU AIN'T QUITE AS UNFIT AS I *THOUGHT* YOU WERE.
BUT COMMANDER-- THE FIRST RULE...
HOW DOES *ANY* OF THIS MAKE YOUR PEOPLE SAFE?

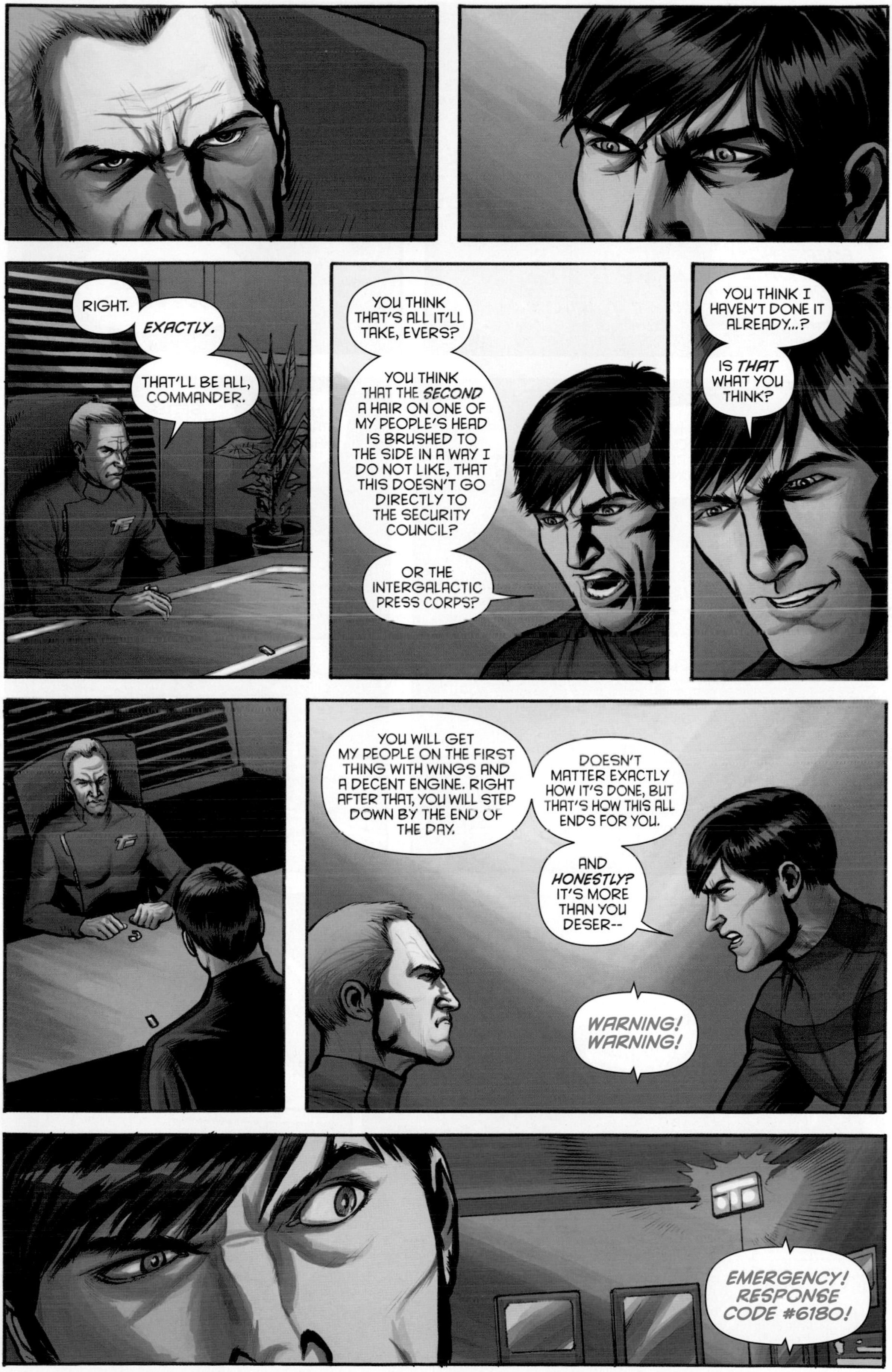
RIGHT.
EXACTLY.
THAT'LL BE ALL, COMMANDER.
YOU THINK THAT'S ALL IT'LL TAKE, EVERS?
YOU THINK THAT THE *SECOND* A HAIR ON ONE OF MY PEOPLE'S HEAD IS BRUSHED TO THE SIDE IN A WAY I DO NOT LIKE, THAT THIS DOESN'T GO DIRECTLY TO THE SECURITY COUNCIL?
OR THE INTERGALACTIC PRESS CORPS?
YOU THINK I HAVEN'T DONE IT ALREADY...?
IS *THAT* WHAT YOU THINK?
YOU WILL GET MY PEOPLE ON THE FIRST THING WITH WINGS AND A DECENT ENGINE. RIGHT AFTER THAT, YOU WILL STEP DOWN BY THE END OF THE DAY.
DOESN'T MATTER EXACTLY HOW IT'S DONE, BUT THAT'S HOW THIS ALL ENDS FOR YOU.
AND *HONESTLY?* IT'S MORE THAN YOU DESER--
WARNING! WARNING!
EMERGENCY! RESPONSE CODE #6180!

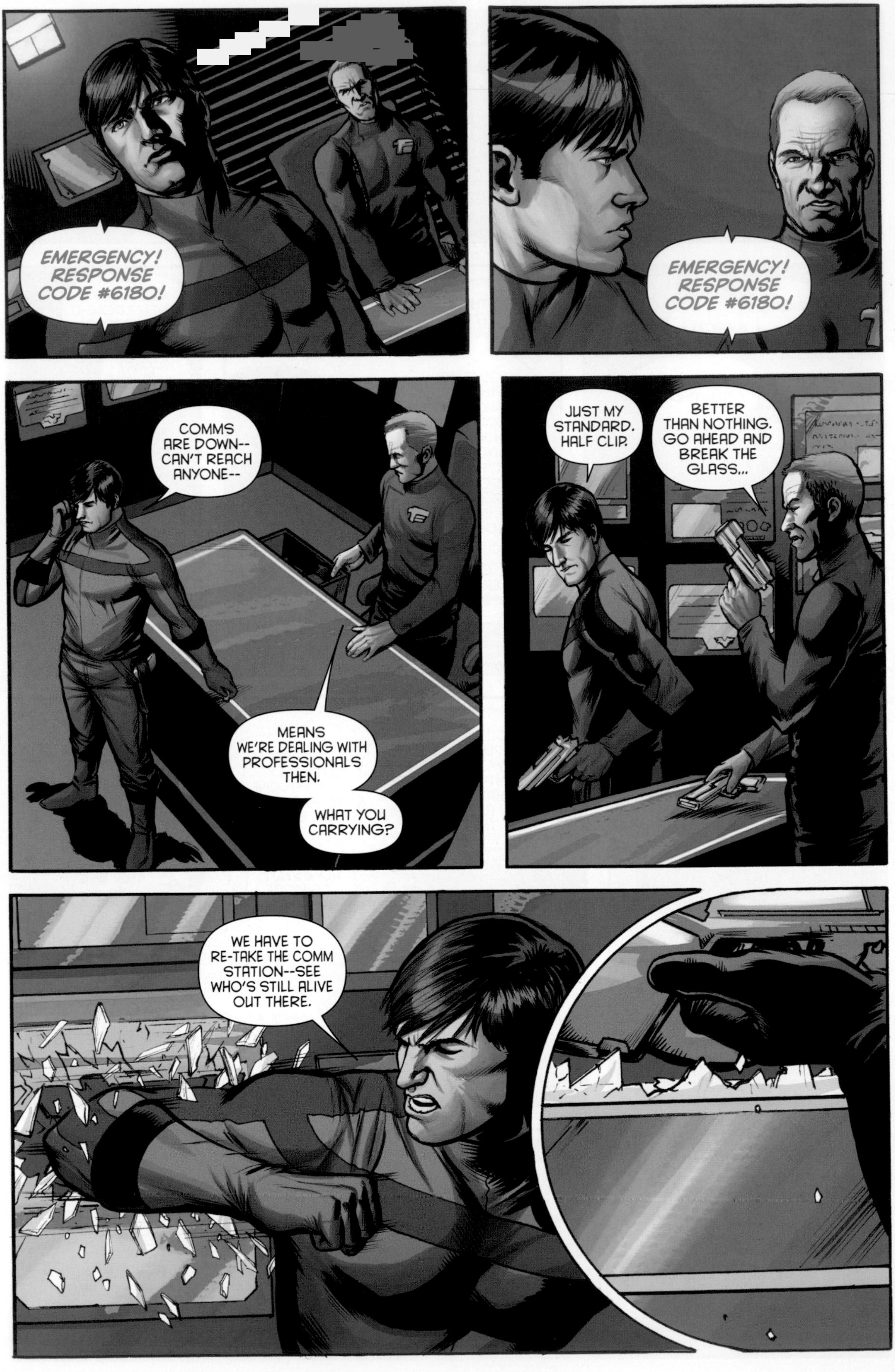
EMERGENCY! RESPONSE CODE #6180!
EMERGENCY! RESPONSE CODE #6180!
COMMS ARE DOWN-- CAN'T REACH ANYONE--
MEANS WE'RE DEALING WITH PROFESSIONALS THEN.
WHAT YOU CARRYING?
JUST MY STANDARD. HALF CLIP.
BETTER THAN NOTHING. GO AHEAD AND BREAK THE GLASS...
WE HAVE TO RE-TAKE THE COMM STATION--SEE WHO'S STILL ALIVE OUT THERE.

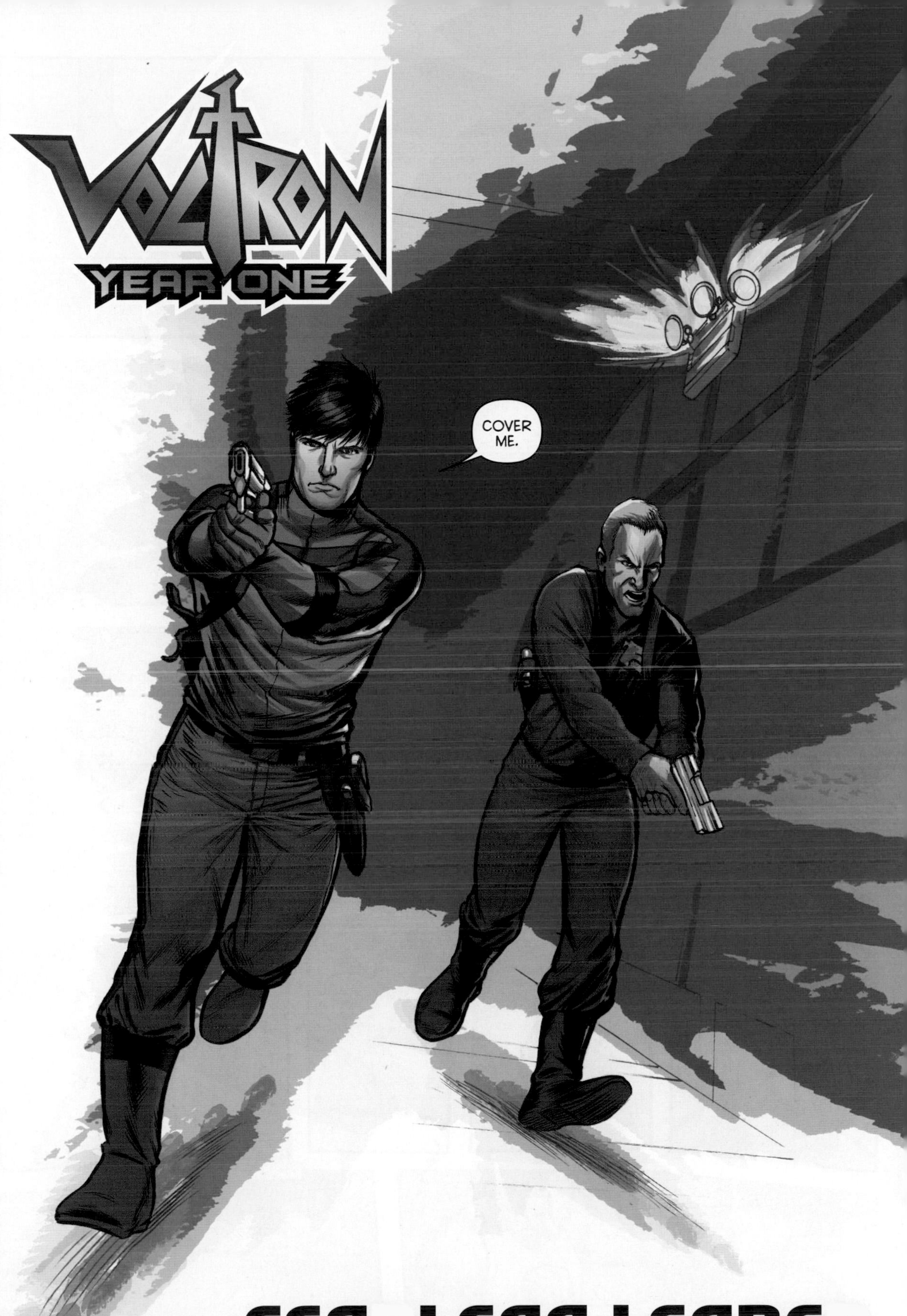
VOLTRON
YEAR ONE
COVER ME.

FEA LESS LEADE

5: THE COST

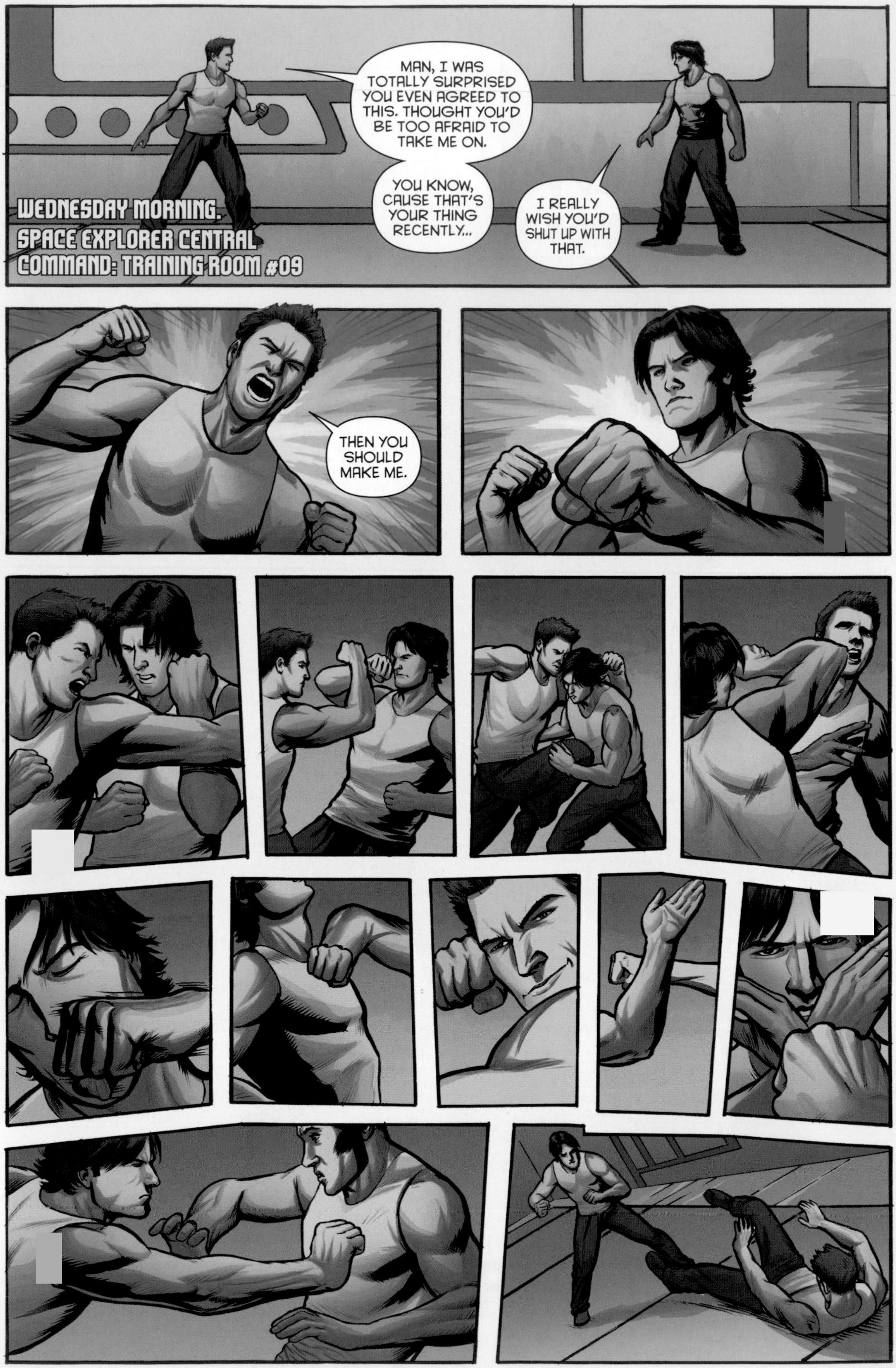
WEDNESDAY MORNING.
SPACE EXPLORER CENTRAL COMMAND: TRAINING ROOM #09
MAN, I WAS TOTALLY SURPRISED YOU EVEN AGREED TO THIS. THOUGHT YOU'D BE TOO AFRAID TO TAKE ME ON.
YOU KNOW, CAUSE THAT'S YOUR THING RECENTLY...
I REALLY WISH YOU'D SHUT UP WITH THAT.
THEN YOU SHOULD MAKE ME.

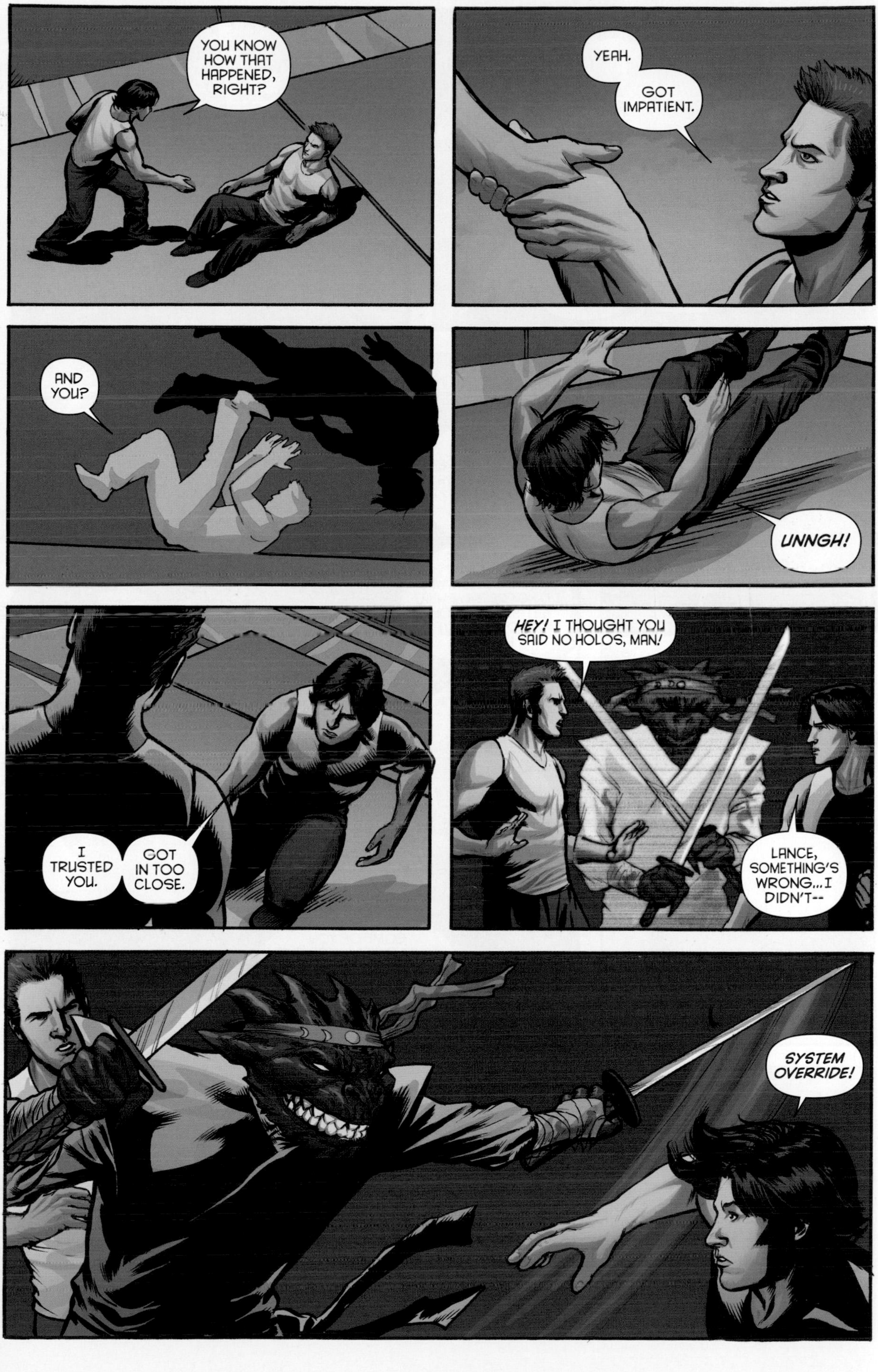
YOU KNOW HOW THAT HAPPENED, RIGHT?
YEAH.
GOT IMPATIENT.
AND YOU?
UNNGH!
I TRUSTED YOU.
GOT IN TOO CLOSE.
HEY! I THOUGHT YOU SAID NO HOLOS, MAN!
LANCE, SOMETHING'S WRONG...I DIDN'T--
SYSTEM OVERRIDE!

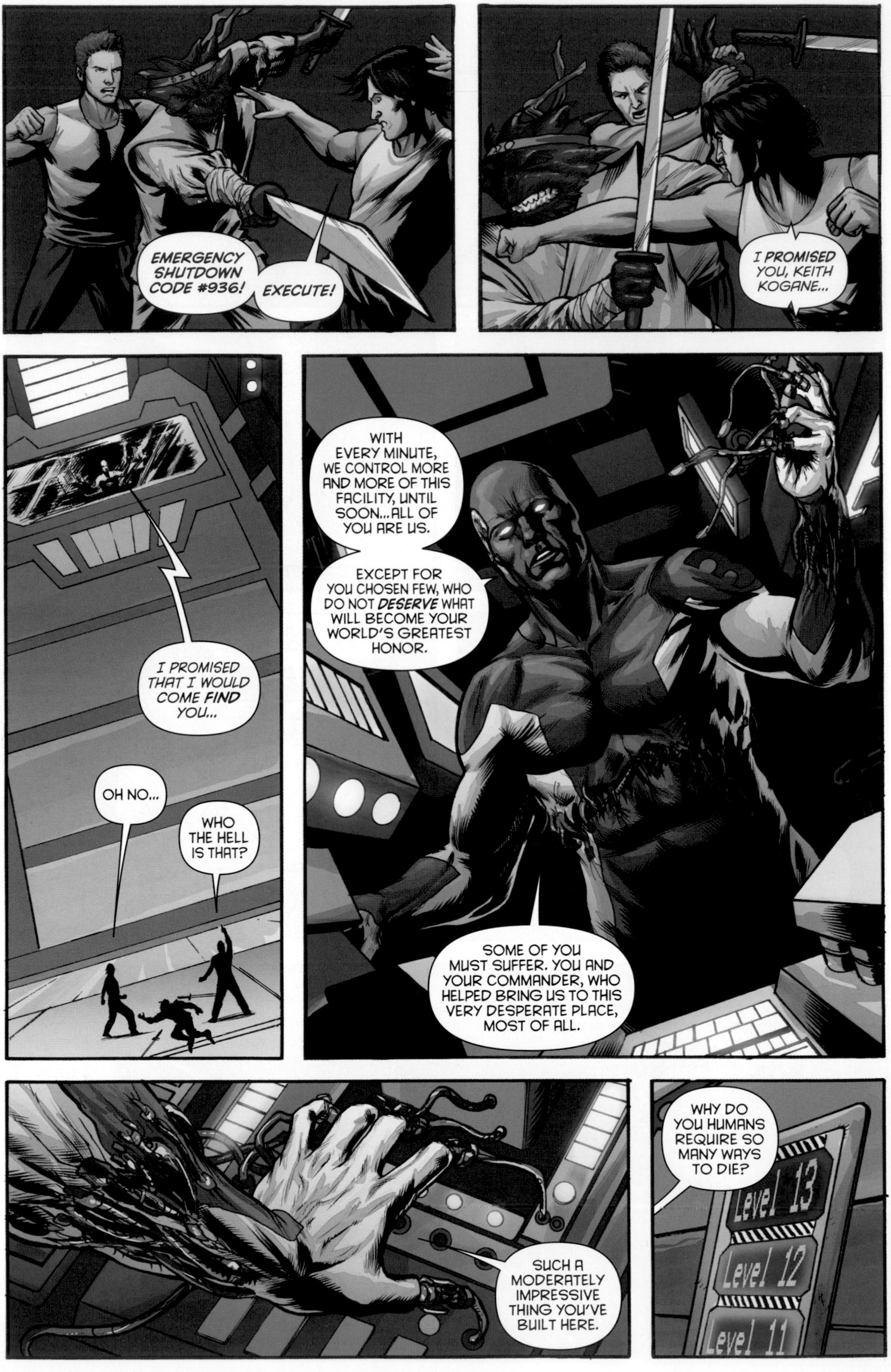
EMERGENCY SHUTDOWN CODE #936!
EXECUTE!
I PROMISED YOU, KEITH KOGANE...
I PROMISED THAT I WOULD COME FIND YOU...
OH NO...
WHO THE HELL IS THAT?
WITH EVERY MINUTE, WE CONTROL MORE AND MORE OF THIS FACILITY, UNTIL SOON...ALL OF YOU ARE US.
EXCEPT FOR YOU CHOSEN FEW, WHO DO NOT DESERVE WHAT WILL BECOME YOUR WORLD'S GREATEST HONOR.
SOME OF YOU MUST SUFFER. YOU AND YOUR COMMANDER, WHO HELPED BRING US TO THIS VERY DESPERATE PLACE, MOST OF ALL.
SUCH A MODERATELY IMPRESSIVE THING YOU'VE BUILT HERE.
WHY DO YOU HUMANS REQUIRE SO MANY WAYS TO DIE?
Level 13
Level 12
Level 11

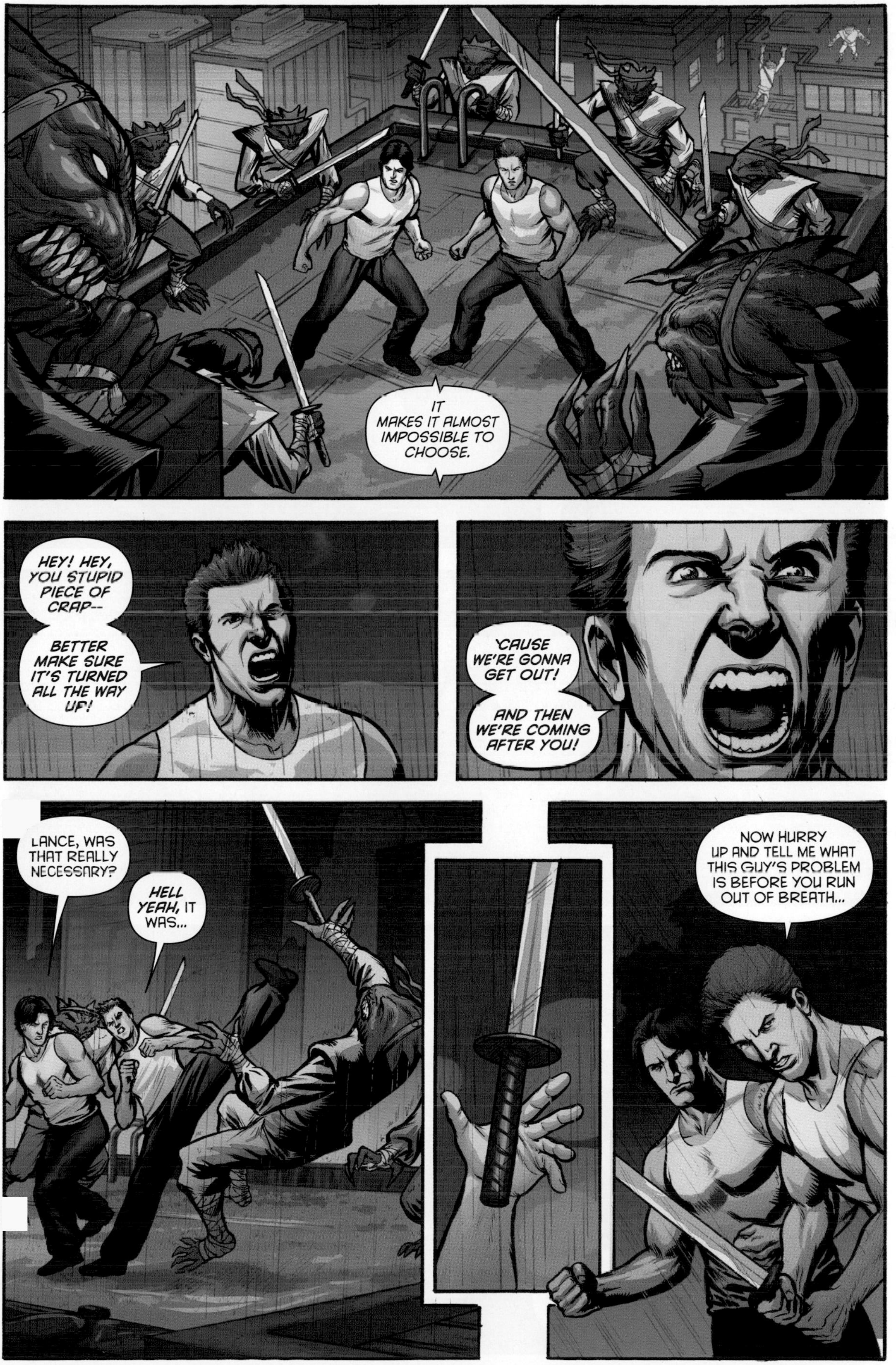
IT MAKES IT ALMOST IMPOSSIBLE TO CHOOSE.
HEY! HEY, YOU STUPID PIECE OF CRAP--
BETTER MAKE SURE IT'S TURNED ALL THE WAY UP!
'CAUSE WE'RE GONNA GET OUT!
AND THEN WE'RE COMING AFTER YOU!
LANCE, WAS THAT REALLY NECESSARY?
HELL YEAH, IT WAS...
NOW HURRY UP AND TELL ME WHAT THIS GUY'S PROBLEM IS BEFORE YOU RUN OUT OF BREATH...

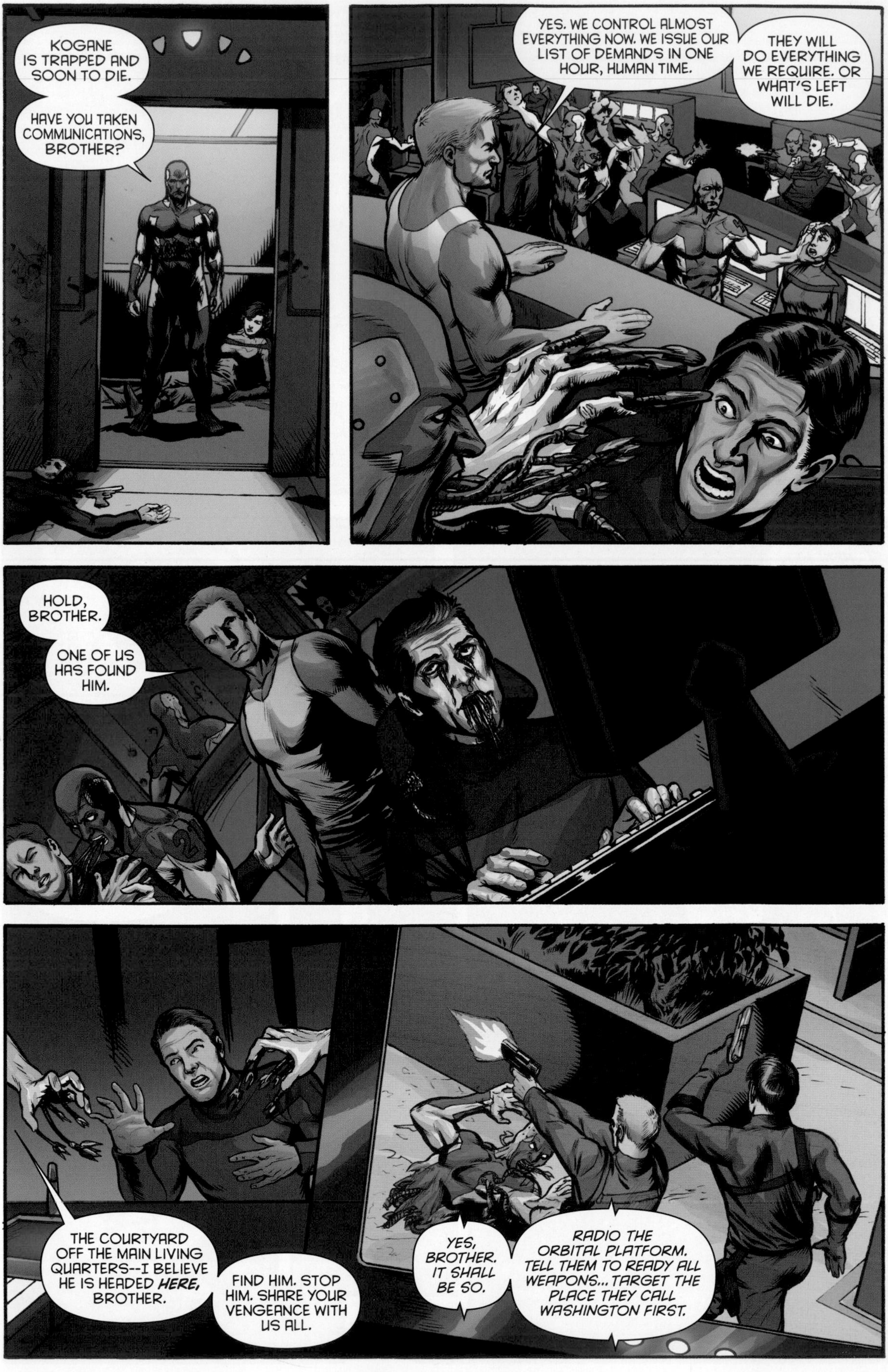
KOGANE IS TRAPPED AND SOON TO DIE.
HAVE YOU TAKEN COMMUNICATIONS, BROTHER?
YES. WE CONTROL ALMOST EVERYTHING NOW. WE ISSUE OUR LIST OF DEMANDS IN ONE HOUR, HUMAN TIME.
THEY WILL DO EVERYTHING WE REQUIRE. OR WHAT'S LEFT WILL DIE.
HOLD, BROTHER.
ONE OF US HAS FOUND HIM.
THE COURTYARD OFF THE MAIN LIVING QUARTERS--I BELIEVE HE IS HEADED *HERE,* BROTHER.
FIND HIM. STOP HIM. SHARE YOUR VENGEANCE WITH US ALL.
YES, BROTHER. IT SHALL BE SO.
RADIO THE ORBITAL PLATFORM. TELL THEM TO READY ALL WEAPONS... TARGET THE PLACE THEY CALL WASHINGTON FIRST.

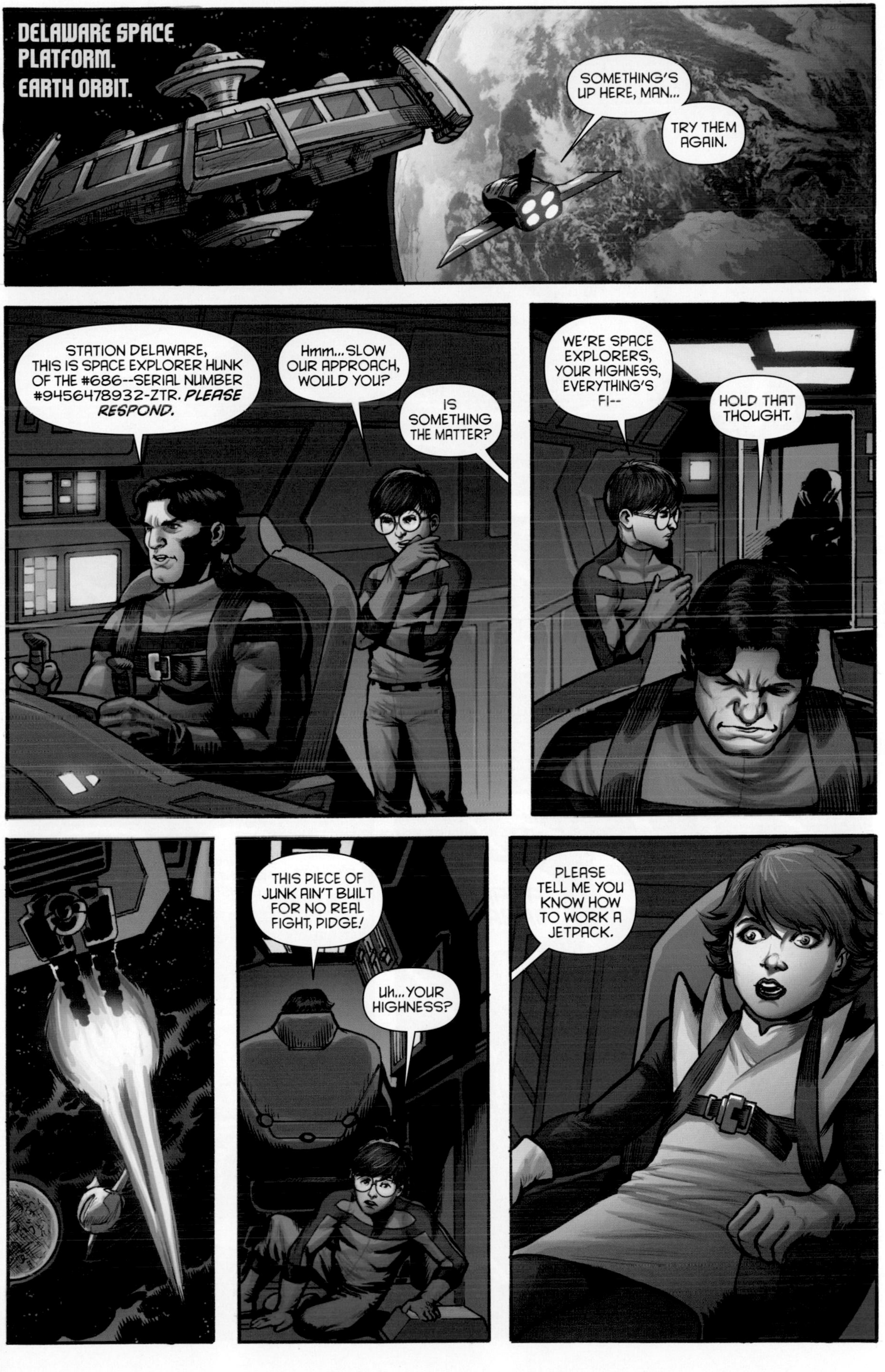

DELAWARE SPACE PLATFORM. EARTH ORBIT.
SOMETHING'S UP HERE, MAN...
TRY THEM AGAIN.
STATION DELAWARE, THIS IS SPACE EXPLORER HUNK OF THE #686--SERIAL NUMBER #9456478932-ZTR. PLEASE RESPOND.
Hmm... SLOW OUR APPROACH, WOULD YOU?
IS SOMETHING THE MATTER?
WE'RE SPACE EXPLORERS, YOUR HIGHNESS, EVERYTHING'S FI--
HOLD THAT THOUGHT.
THIS PIECE OF JUNK AIN'T BUILT FOR NO REAL FIGHT, PIDGE!
Uh... YOUR HIGHNESS?
PLEASE TELL ME YOU KNOW HOW TO WORK A JETPACK.

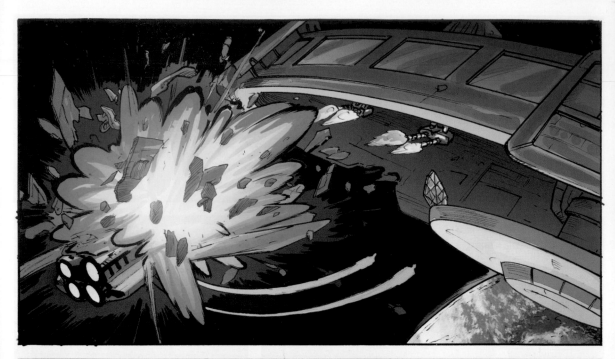

HUNK, THERE'S A BLIND SPOT NEAR THE AIRLOCK ON THE SOUTHEAST CORNER.

WE'LL PUNCH IN THERE.

HOW YOU DOING, YOUR HIGHNESS?

AAAAAA! AAAAAAA!

FAIR ENOUGH.

STILL NOTHING FROM THE GUYS?

NOPE. COMM SYSTEM IS COMPLETELY DOWN.

SEEMING KINDA INTENTIONAL AT THIS POINT...

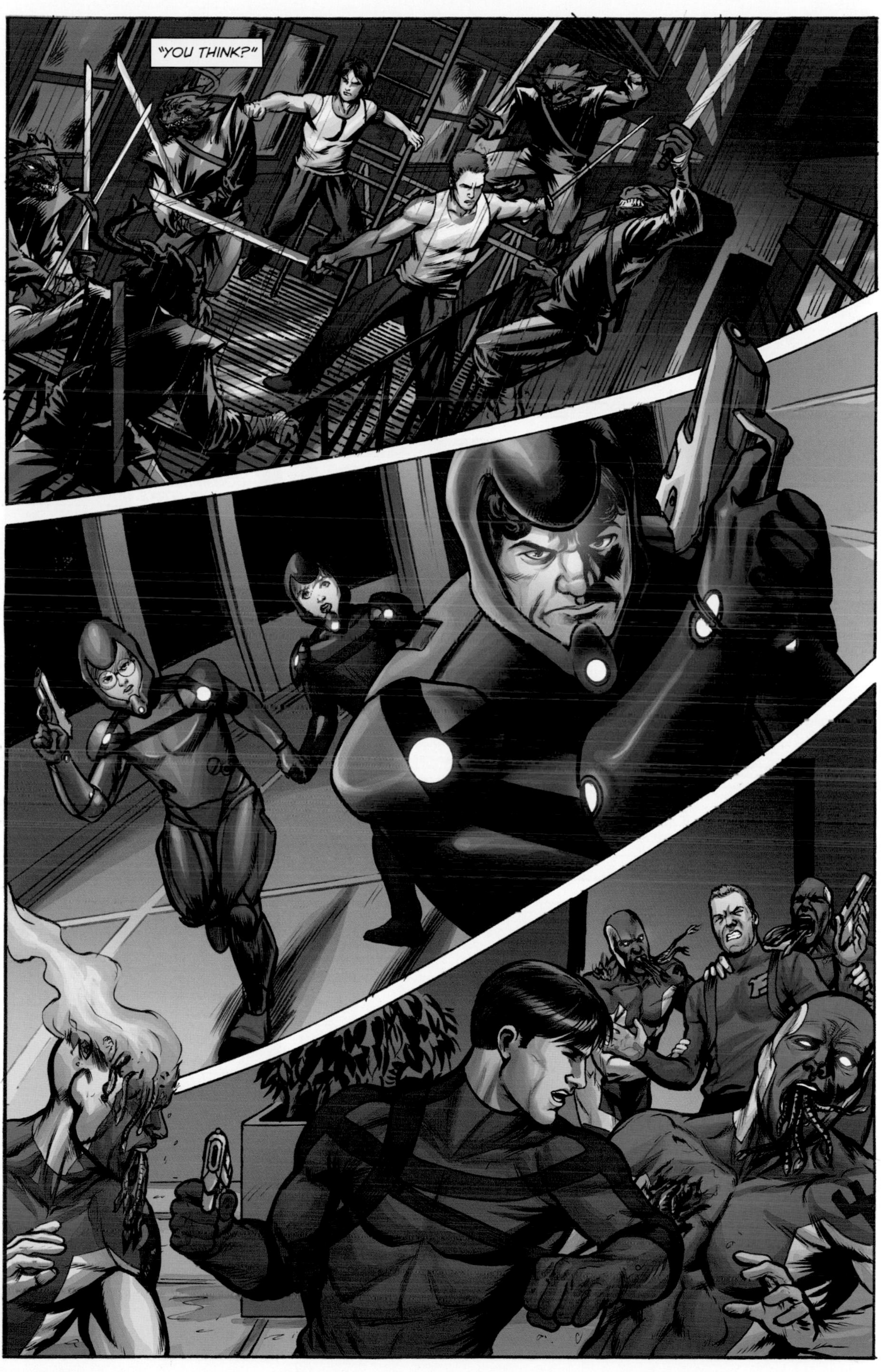
"YOU THINK?"

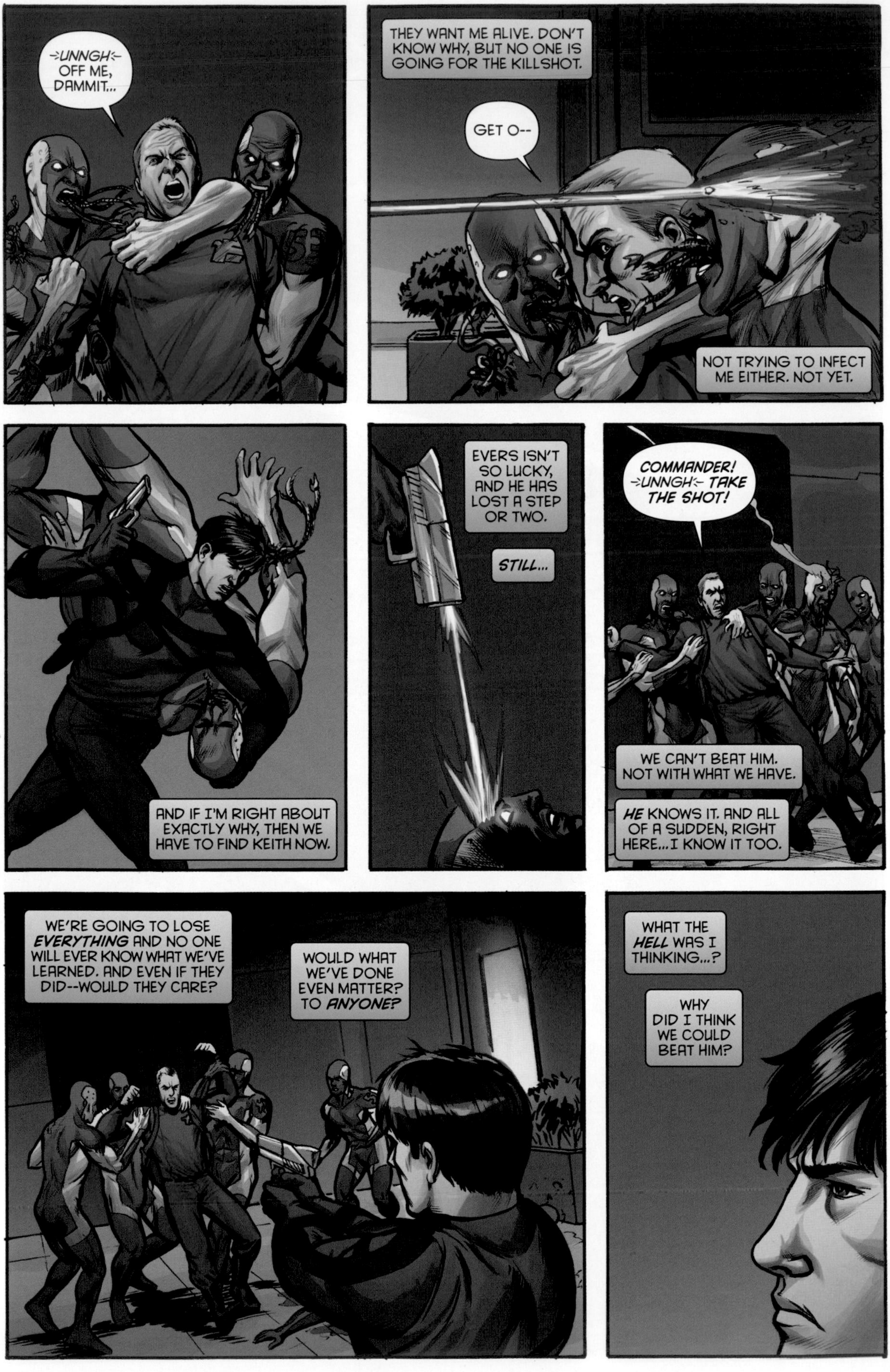

-UNNGH- OFF ME, DAMMIT...
THEY WANT ME ALIVE. DON'T KNOW WHY, BUT NO ONE IS GOING FOR THE KILLSHOT.
GET O--
NOT TRYING TO INFECT ME EITHER. NOT YET.
AND IF I'M RIGHT ABOUT EXACTLY WHY, THEN WE HAVE TO FIND KEITH NOW.
EVERS ISN'T SO LUCKY, AND HE HAS LOST A STEP OR TWO.
STILL...
COMMANDER! -UNNGH- TAKE THE SHOT!
WE CAN'T BEAT HIM. NOT WITH WHAT WE HAVE.
HE KNOWS IT. AND ALL OF A SUDDEN, RIGHT HERE...I KNOW IT TOO.
WE'RE GOING TO LOSE EVERYTHING AND NO ONE WILL EVER KNOW WHAT WE'VE LEARNED. AND EVEN IF THEY DID--WOULD THEY CARE?
WOULD WHAT WE'VE DONE EVEN MATTER? TO ANYONE?
WHAT THE HELL WAS I THINKING...?
WHY DID I THINK WE COULD BEAT HIM?

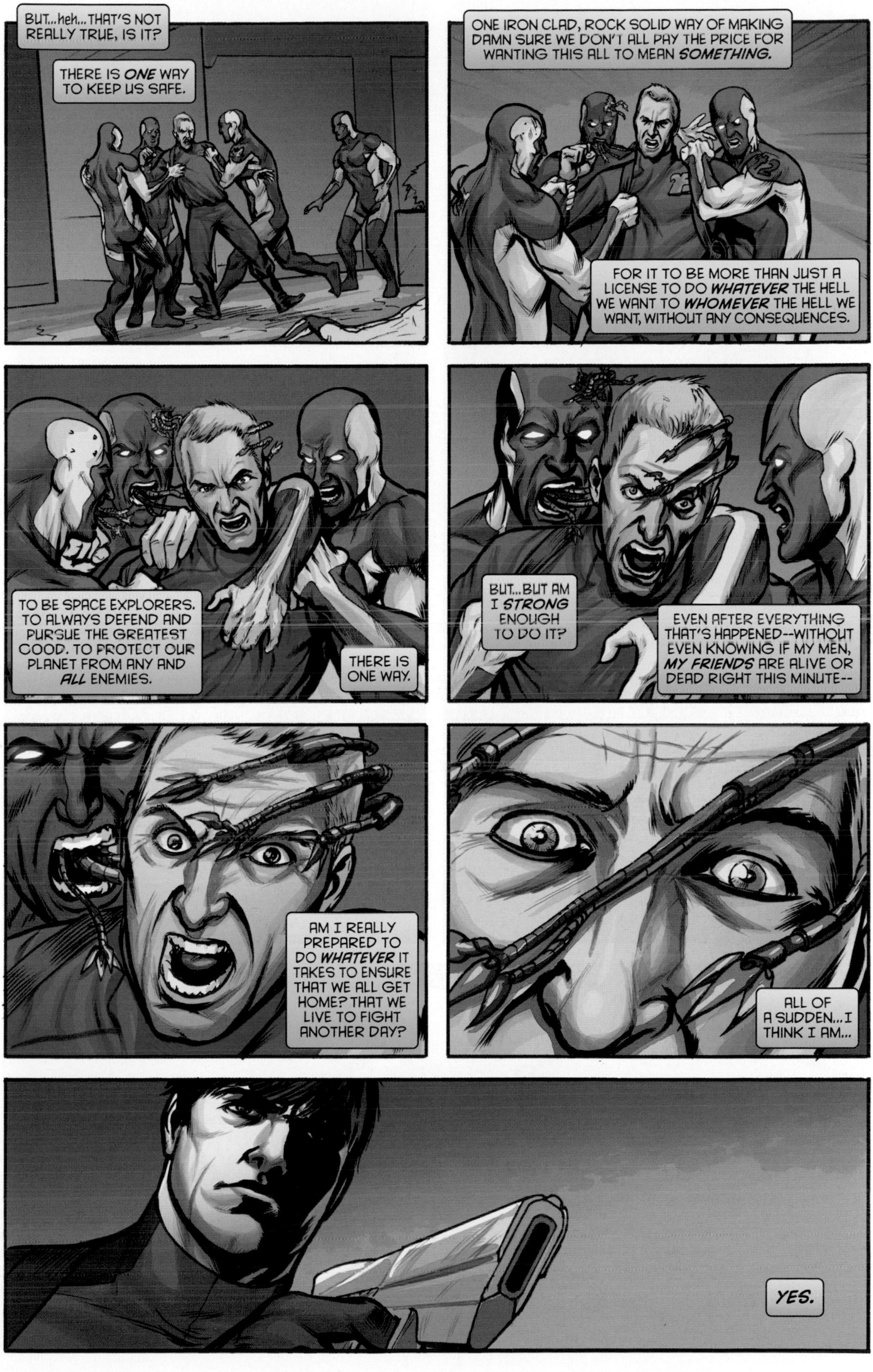
BUT...heh...THAT'S NOT REALLY TRUE, IS IT?
THERE IS *ONE* WAY TO KEEP US SAFE.
ONE IRON CLAD, ROCK SOLID WAY OF MAKING DAMN SURE WE DON'T ALL PAY THE PRICE FOR WANTING THIS ALL TO MEAN *SOMETHING.*
FOR IT TO BE MORE THAN JUST A LICENSE TO DO *WHATEVER* THE HELL WE WANT TO *WHOMEVER* THE HELL WE WANT, WITHOUT ANY CONSEQUENCES.
TO BE SPACE EXPLORERS. TO ALWAYS DEFEND AND PURSUE THE GREATEST GOOD. TO PROTECT OUR PLANET FROM ANY AND *ALL* ENEMIES.
THERE IS ONE WAY.
BUT...BUT AM I *STRONG* ENOUGH TO DO IT?
EVEN AFTER EVERYTHING THAT'S HAPPENED--WITHOUT EVEN KNOWING IF MY MEN, *MY FRIENDS* ARE ALIVE OR DEAD RIGHT THIS MINUTE--
AM I REALLY PREPARED TO DO *WHATEVER* IT TAKES TO ENSURE THAT WE ALL GET HOME? THAT WE LIVE TO FIGHT ANOTHER DAY?
ALL OF A SUDDEN...I THINK I AM...
YES.

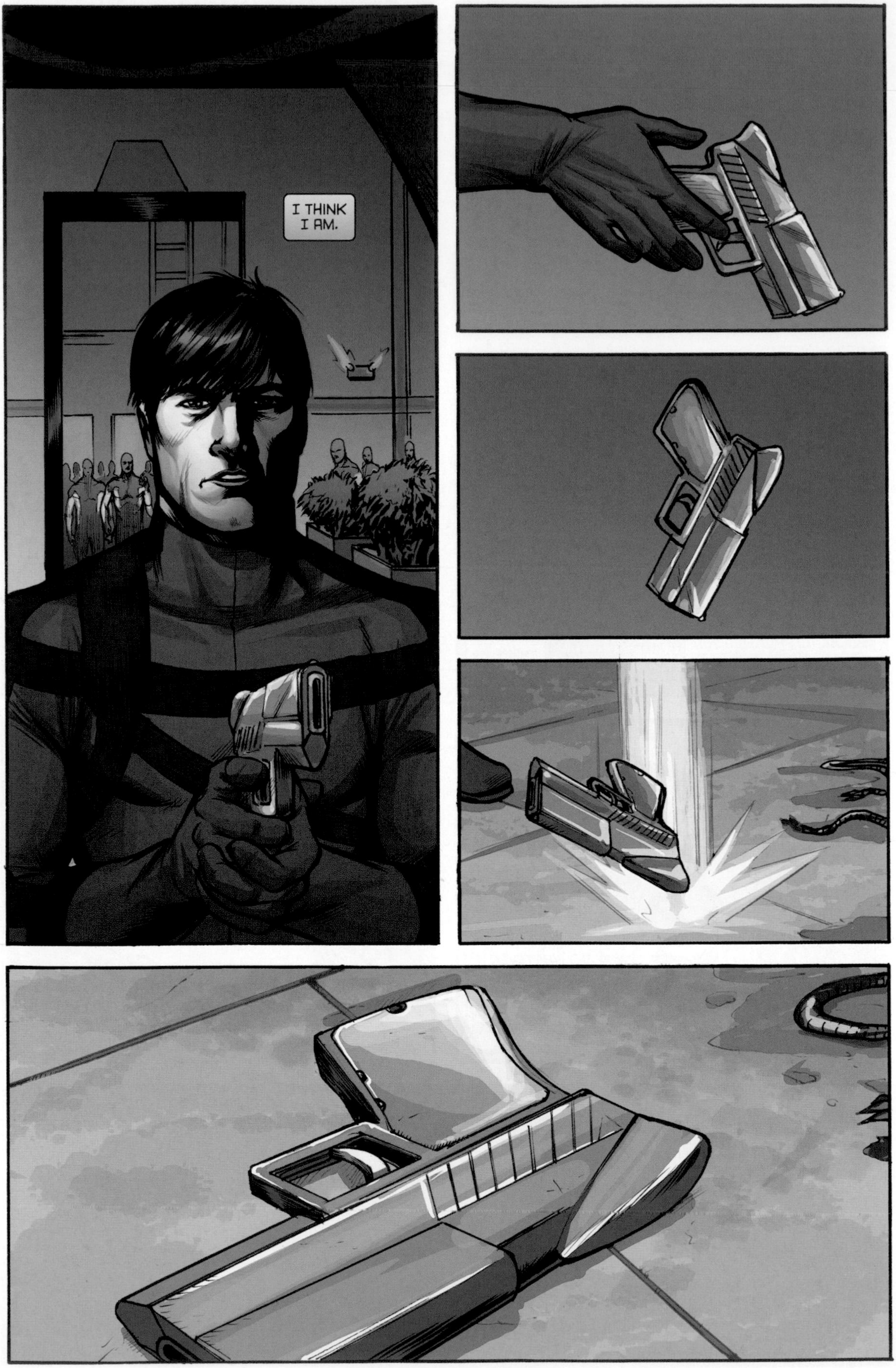
I THINK I AM.

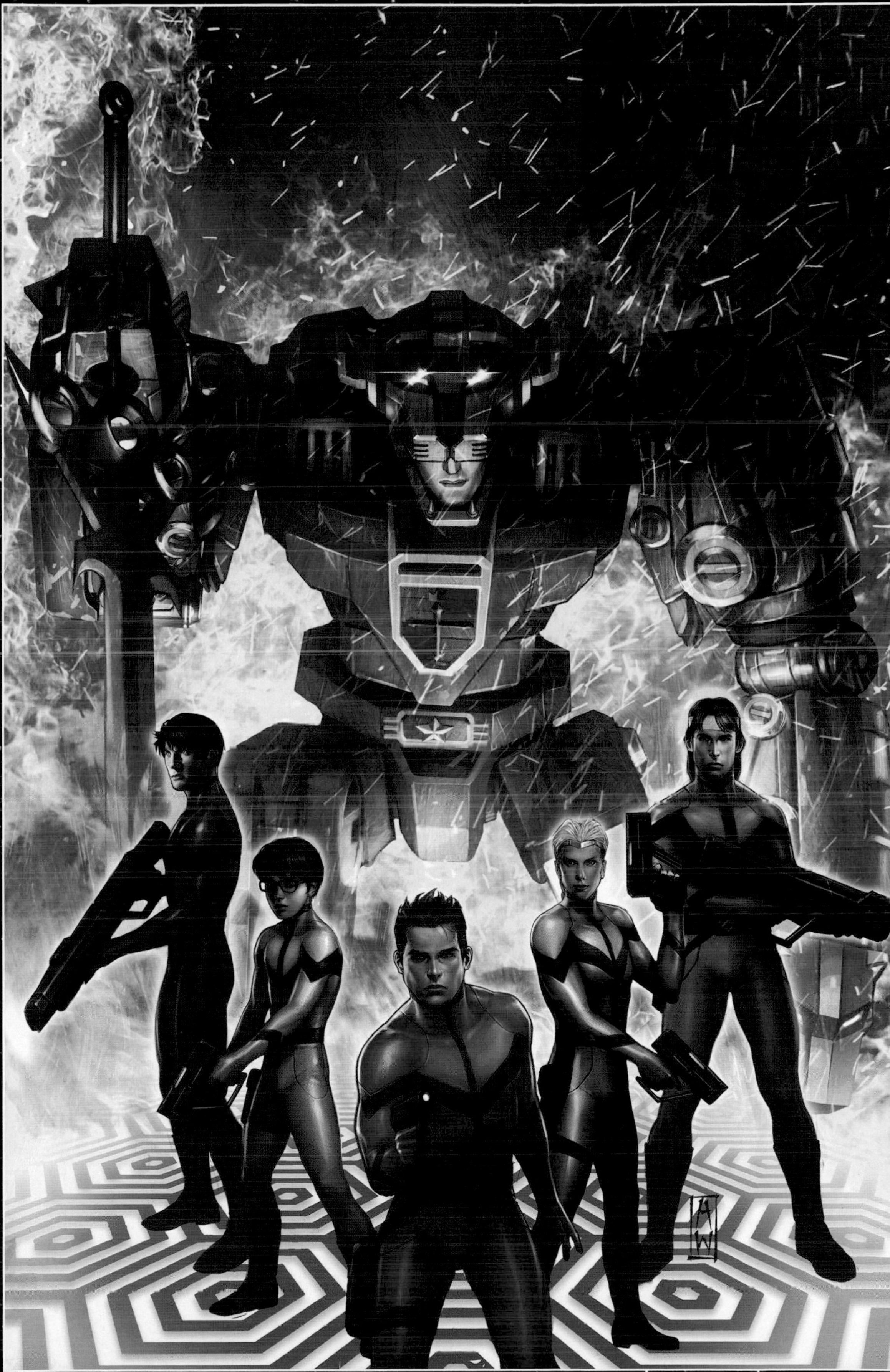

Issue #6 cover by **ADMIRA WIJAYA**

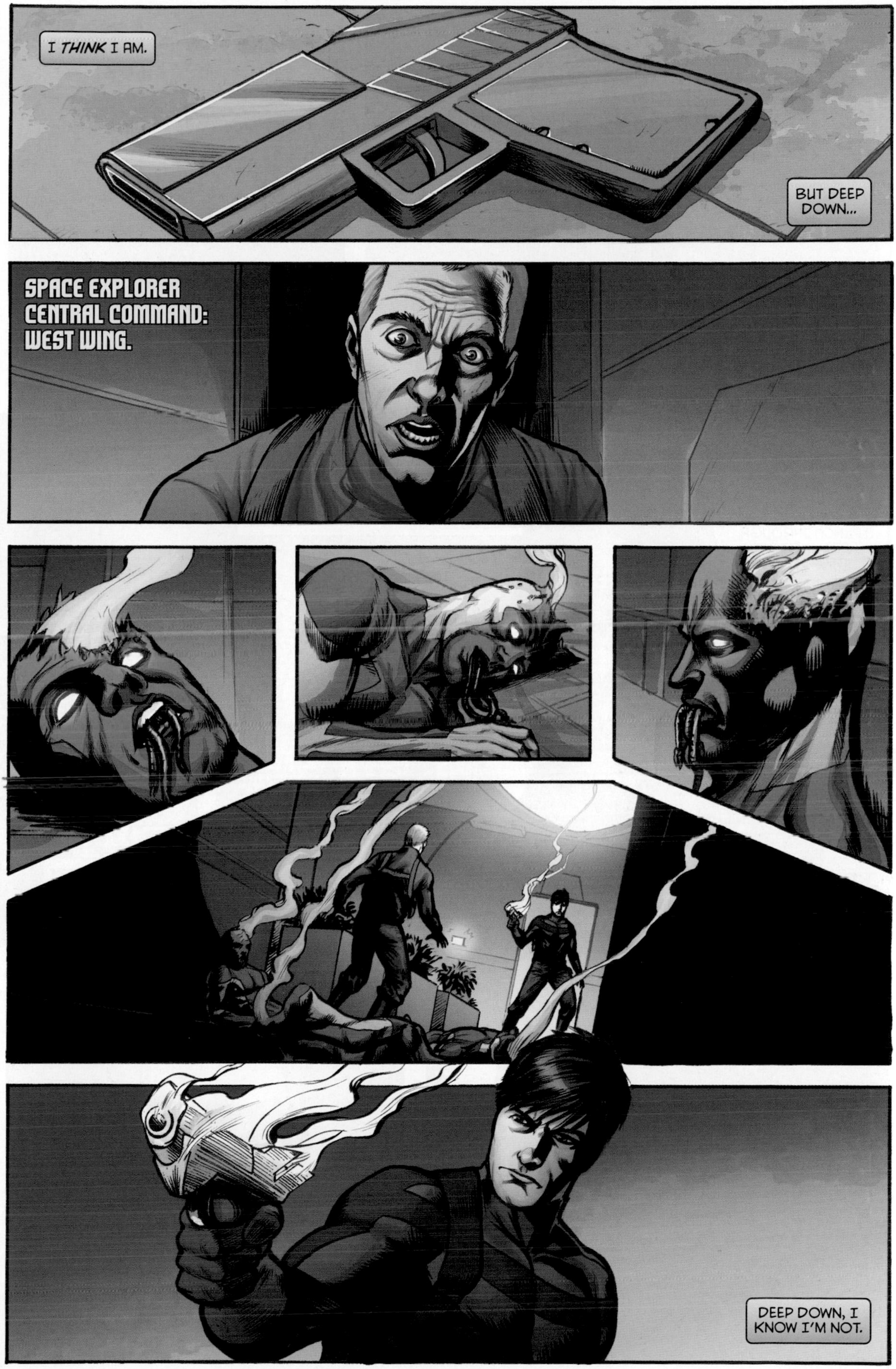
I THINK I AM.
BUT DEEP DOWN...
SPACE EXPLORER CENTRAL COMMAND: WEST WING.
DEEP DOWN, I KNOW I'M NOT.

KID--HOLY *CRAP*, KID--

I THOUGHT--

I TOLD YOU THERE WAS ONLY HALF A CLIP IN IT.

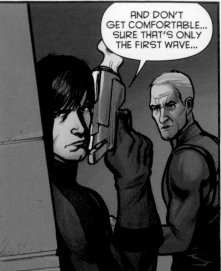

AND DON'T GET COMFORTABLE... SURE THAT'S ONLY THE FIRST WAVE...

YEAH, I'M LOOKING AT INCOMING, AND I RECOGNIZE THE GUY OUT FRONT. WE CAN'T PUNCH THROUGH HERE--NOT WITH THIS ANTIQUE.

YOU KNOW ANY OTHER ROUTE TO COMM?

"ANYTHING THAT'S BEEN ADDED TO THE ORIGINAL LAYOUT OVER THE YEARS? SECONDARY ACCESS POINTS MAYBE?"

"GENERAL...?"

EVERS, THEY'LL BE ON TOP OF US ANY SECOND. IF YOU KNOW--

...

TIME TO WASHINGTON, D.C. STRIKE: 47 MINUTES.

FOLLOW ME.

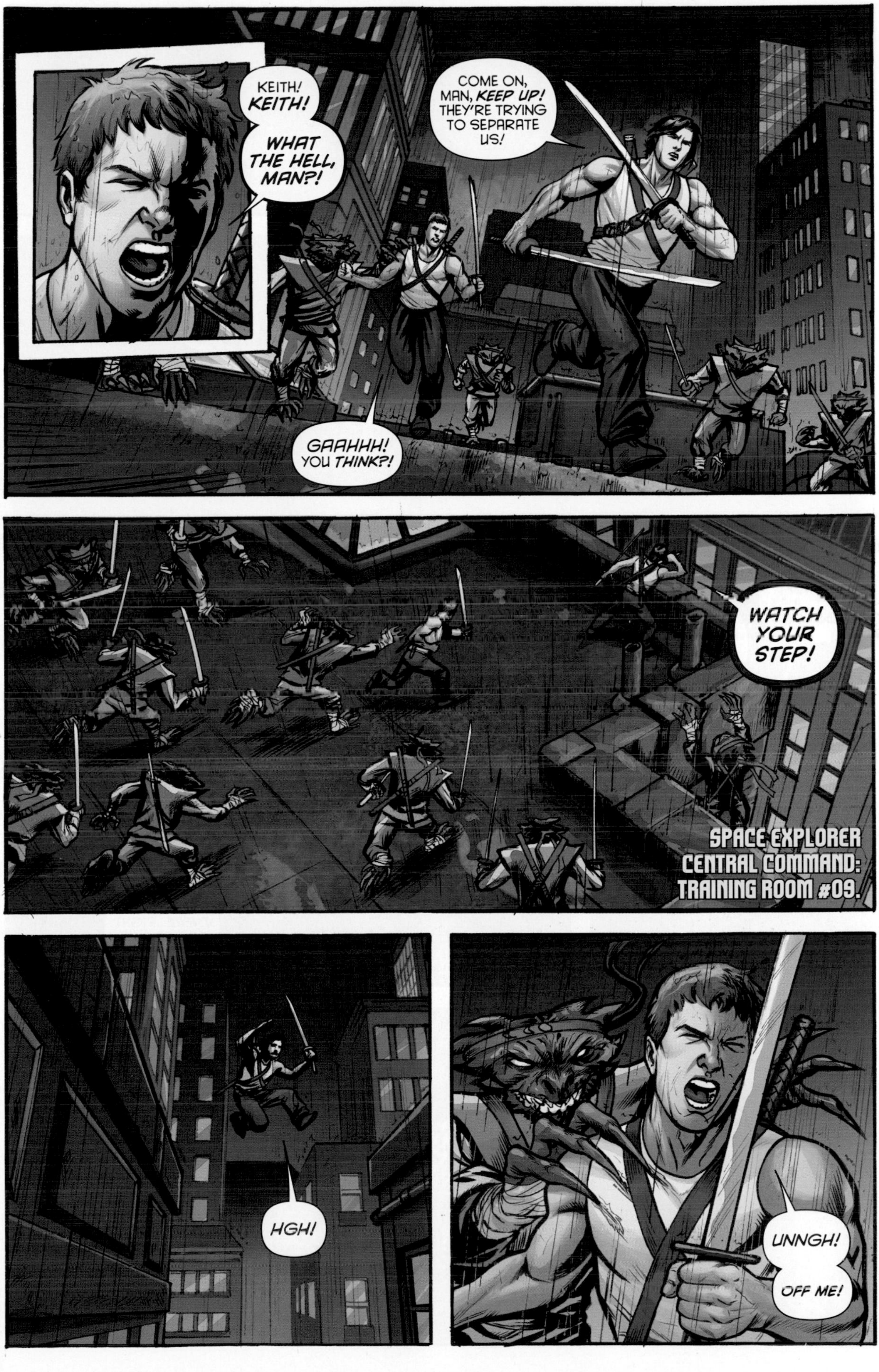
KEITH! KEITH!
WHAT THE HELL, MAN?!
COME ON, MAN, KEEP UP! THEY'RE TRYING TO SEPARATE US!
GAAHHH! YOU THINK?!
WATCH YOUR STEP!
SPACE EXPLORER CENTRAL COMMAND: TRAINING ROOM #09.
HGH!
UNNGH!
OFF ME!

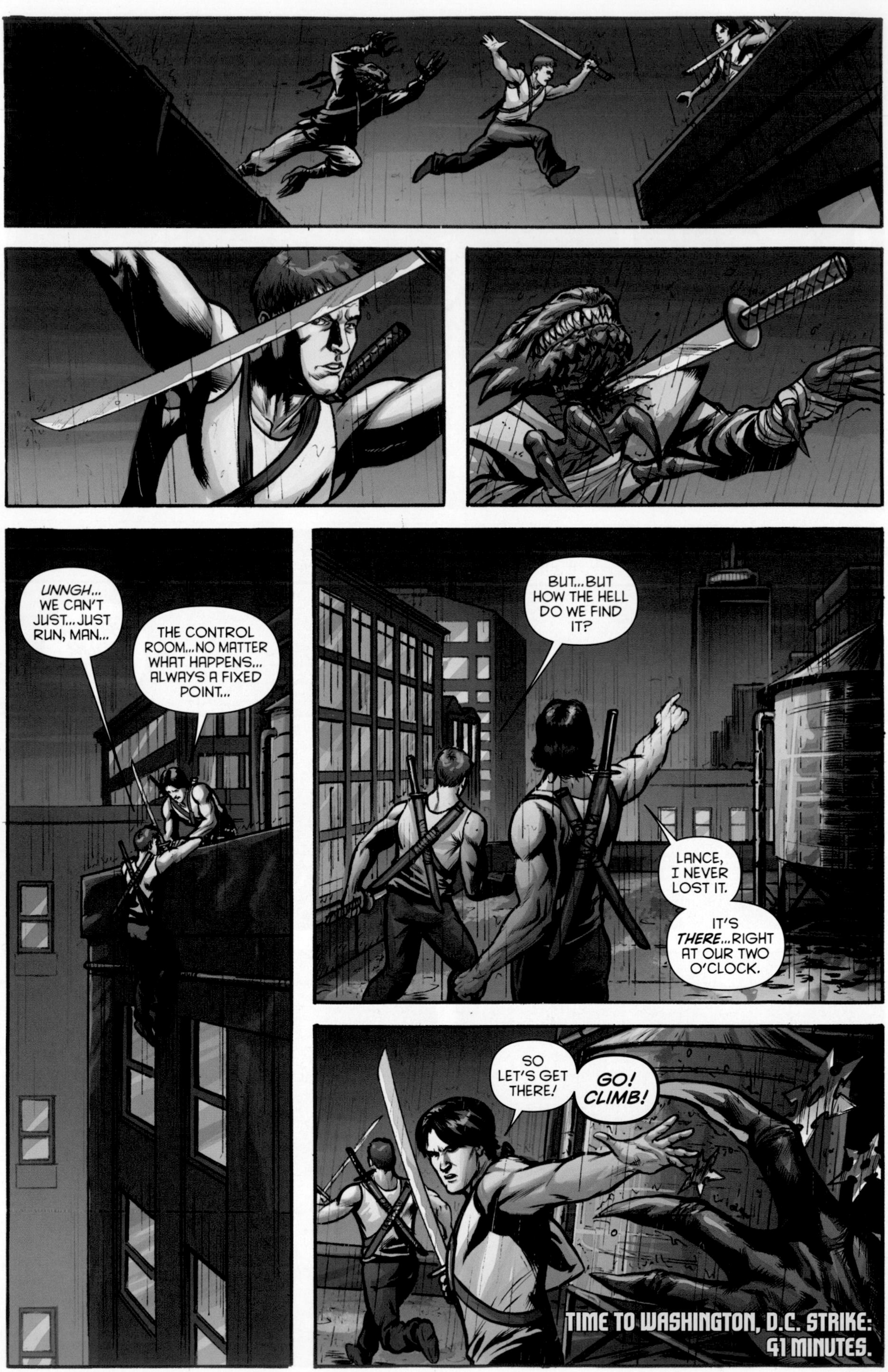
UNNGH... WE CAN'T JUST... JUST RUN, MAN...
THE CONTROL ROOM... NO MATTER WHAT HAPPENS... ALWAYS A FIXED POINT...
BUT... BUT HOW THE HELL DO WE FIND IT?
LANCE, I NEVER LOST IT.
IT'S *THERE*... RIGHT AT OUR TWO O'CLOCK.
SO LET'S GET THERE!
GO! CLIMB!
TIME TO WASHINGTON, D.C. STRIKE: 41 MINUTES.

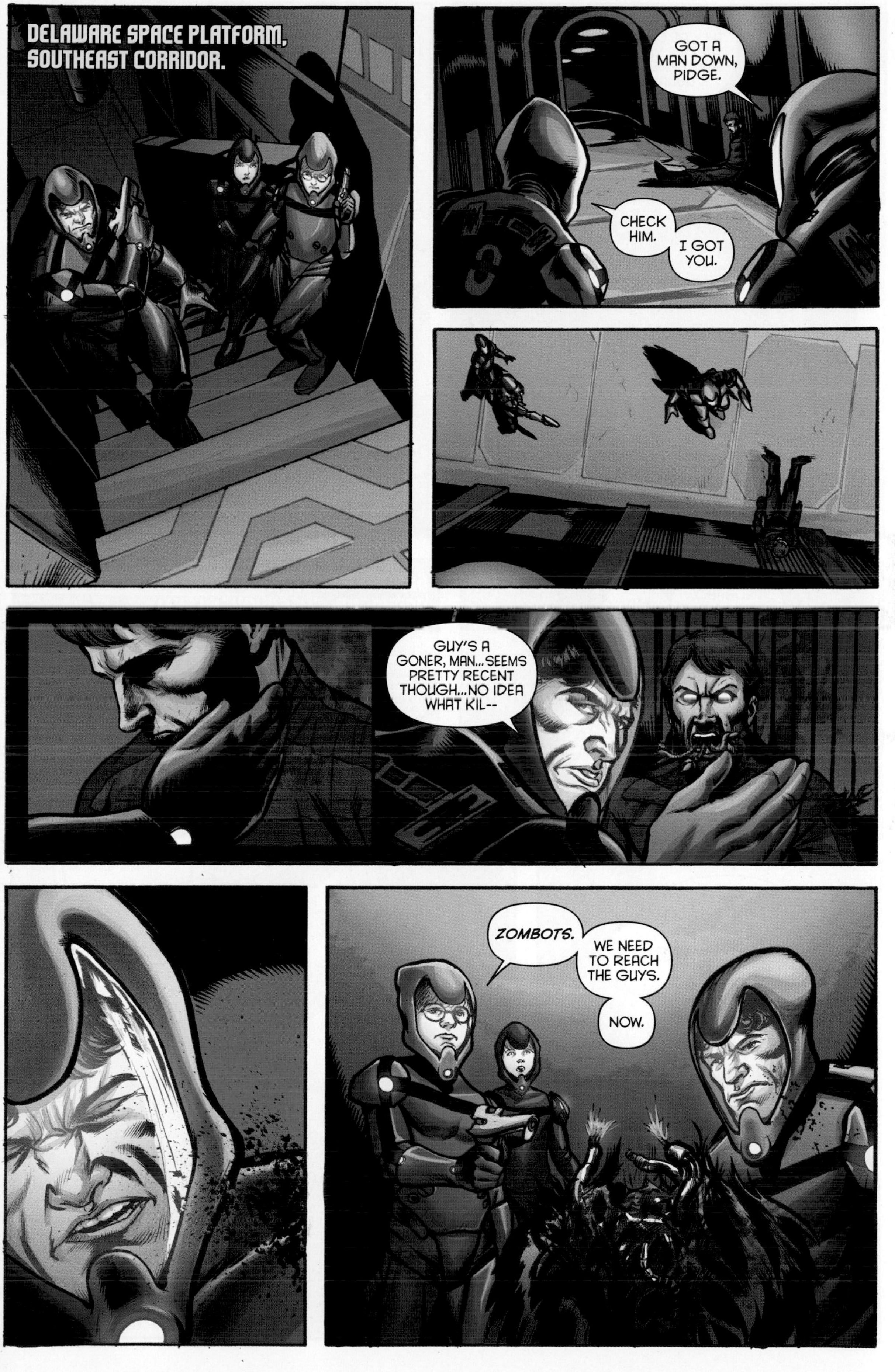
DELAWARE SPACE PLATFORM, SOUTHEAST CORRIDOR.
GOT A MAN DOWN, PIDGE.
CHECK HIM.
I GOT YOU.
GUY'S A GONER, MAN... SEEMS PRETTY RECENT THOUGH... NO IDEA WHAT KIL--
ZOMBOTS.
WE NEED TO REACH THE GUYS.
NOW.

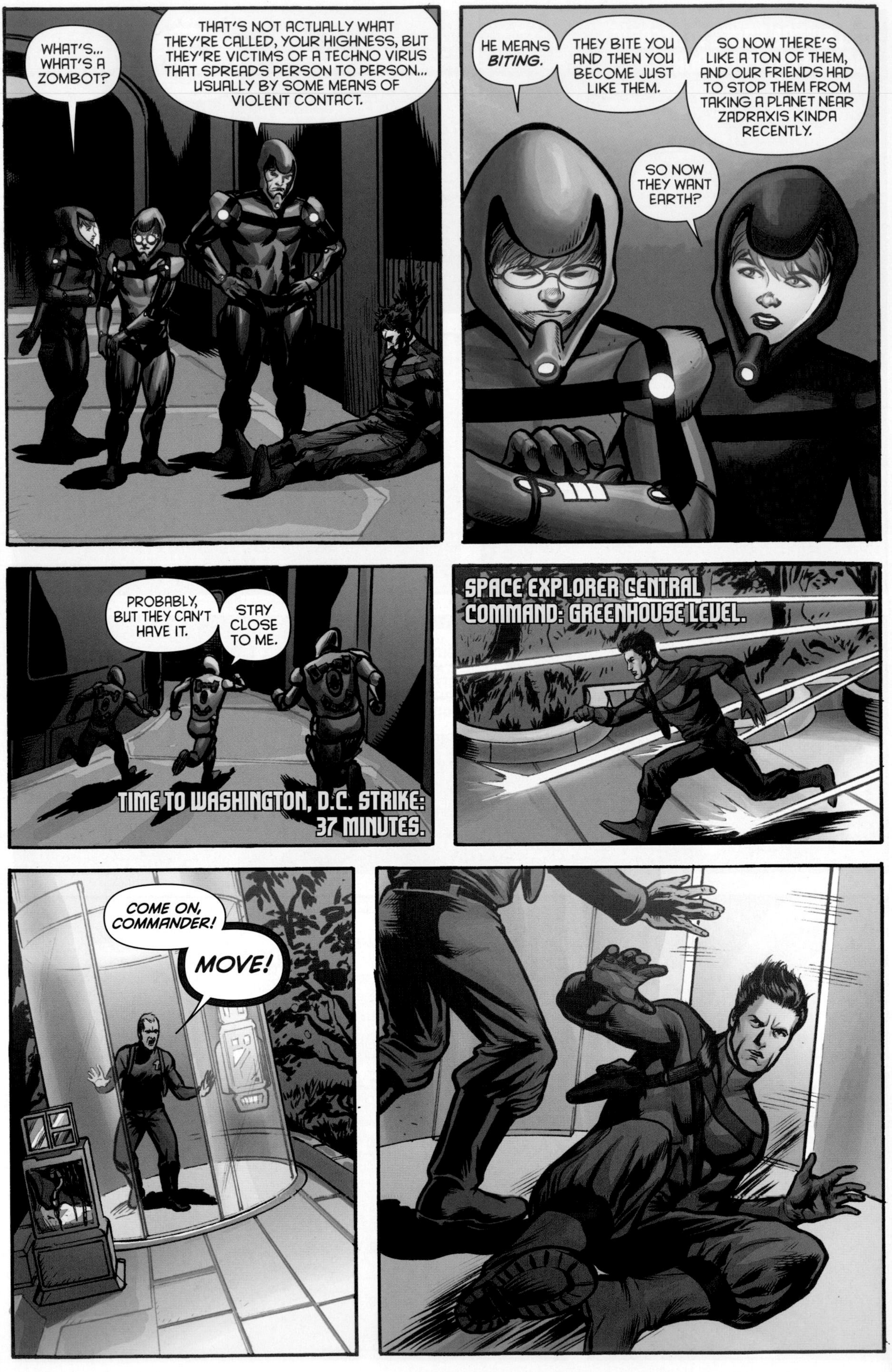
WHAT'S... WHAT'S A ZOMBOT?
THAT'S NOT ACTUALLY WHAT THEY'RE CALLED, YOUR HIGHNESS, BUT THEY'RE VICTIMS OF A TECHNO VIRUS THAT SPREADS PERSON TO PERSON... USUALLY BY SOME MEANS OF VIOLENT CONTACT.
HE MEANS *BITING.*
THEY BITE YOU AND THEN YOU BECOME JUST LIKE THEM.
SO NOW THERE'S LIKE A TON OF THEM, AND OUR FRIENDS HAD TO STOP THEM FROM TAKING A PLANET NEAR ZADRAXIS KINDA RECENTLY.
SO NOW THEY WANT EARTH?
PROBABLY, BUT THEY CAN'T HAVE IT.
STAY CLOSE TO ME.
TIME TO WASHINGTON, D.C. STRIKE: 37 MINUTES.
SPACE EXPLORER CENTRAL COMMAND: GREENHOUSE LEVEL.
COME ON, COMMANDER!
MOVE!

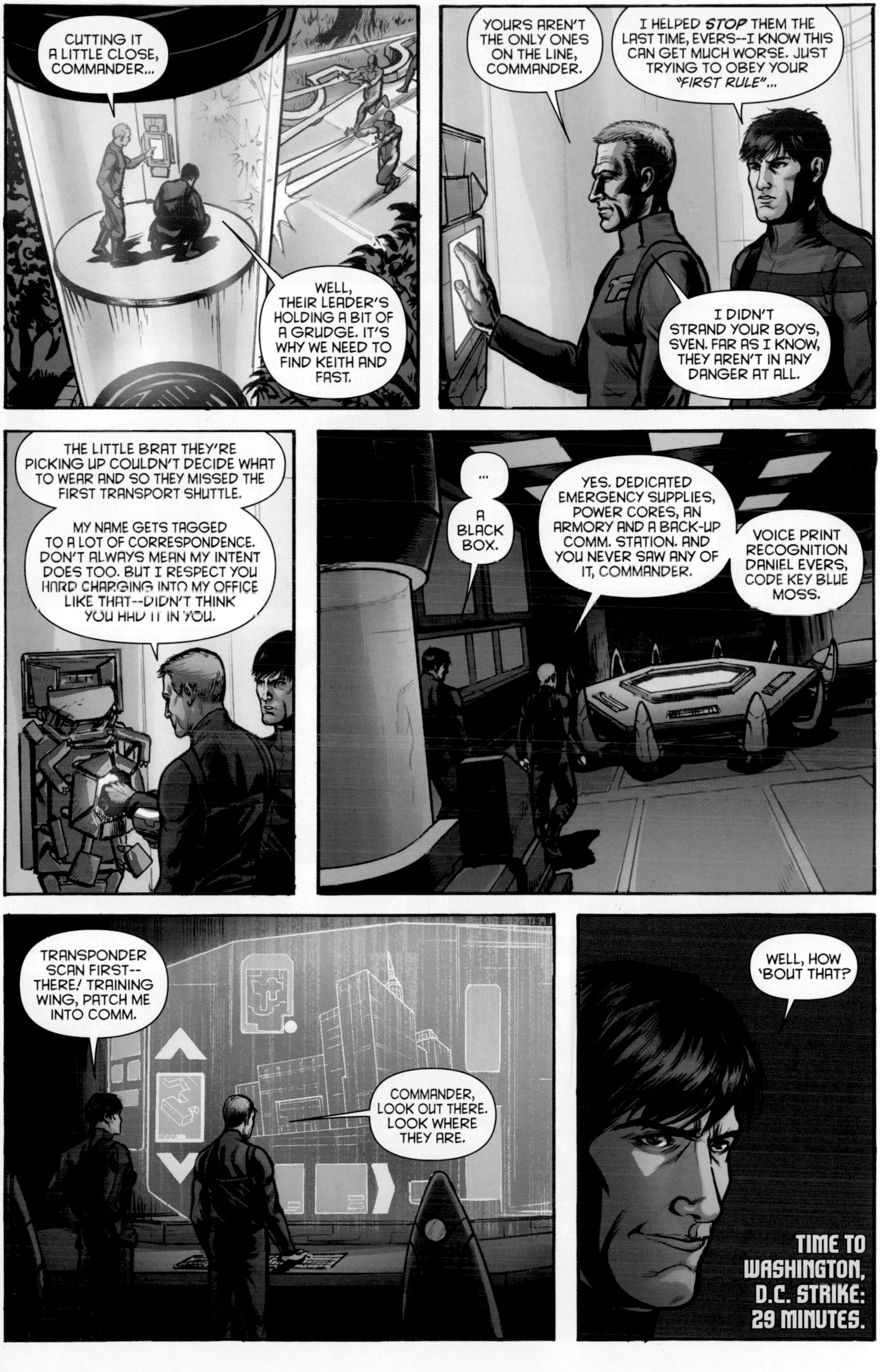
CUTTING IT A LITTLE CLOSE, COMMANDER...
WELL, THEIR LEADER'S HOLDING A BIT OF A GRUDGE. IT'S WHY WE NEED TO FIND KEITH AND FAST.
YOURS AREN'T THE ONLY ONES ON THE LINE, COMMANDER.
I HELPED STOP THEM THE LAST TIME, EVERS--I KNOW THIS CAN GET MUCH WORSE. JUST TRYING TO OBEY YOUR "FIRST RULE"...
I DIDN'T STRAND YOUR BOYS, SVEN. FAR AS I KNOW, THEY AREN'T IN ANY DANGER AT ALL.
THE LITTLE BRAT THEY'RE PICKING UP COULDN'T DECIDE WHAT TO WEAR AND SO THEY MISSED THE FIRST TRANSPORT SHUTTLE.
MY NAME GETS TAGGED TO A LOT OF CORRESPONDENCE. DON'T ALWAYS MEAN MY INTENT DOES TOO. BUT I RESPECT YOU HARD CHARGING INTO MY OFFICE LIKE THAT--DIDN'T THINK YOU HAD IT IN YOU.
...
A BLACK BOX.
YES. DEDICATED EMERGENCY SUPPLIES, POWER CORES, AN ARMORY AND A BACK-UP COMM. STATION. AND YOU NEVER SAW ANY OF IT, COMMANDER.
VOICE PRINT RECOGNITION DANIEL EVERS, CODE KEY BLUE MOSS.
TRANSPONDER SCAN FIRST--THERE! TRAINING WING, PATCH ME INTO COMM.
COMMANDER, LOOK OUT THERE. LOOK WHERE THEY ARE.
WELL, HOW 'BOUT THAT?
TIME TO WASHINGTON, D.C. STRIKE: 29 MINUTES.

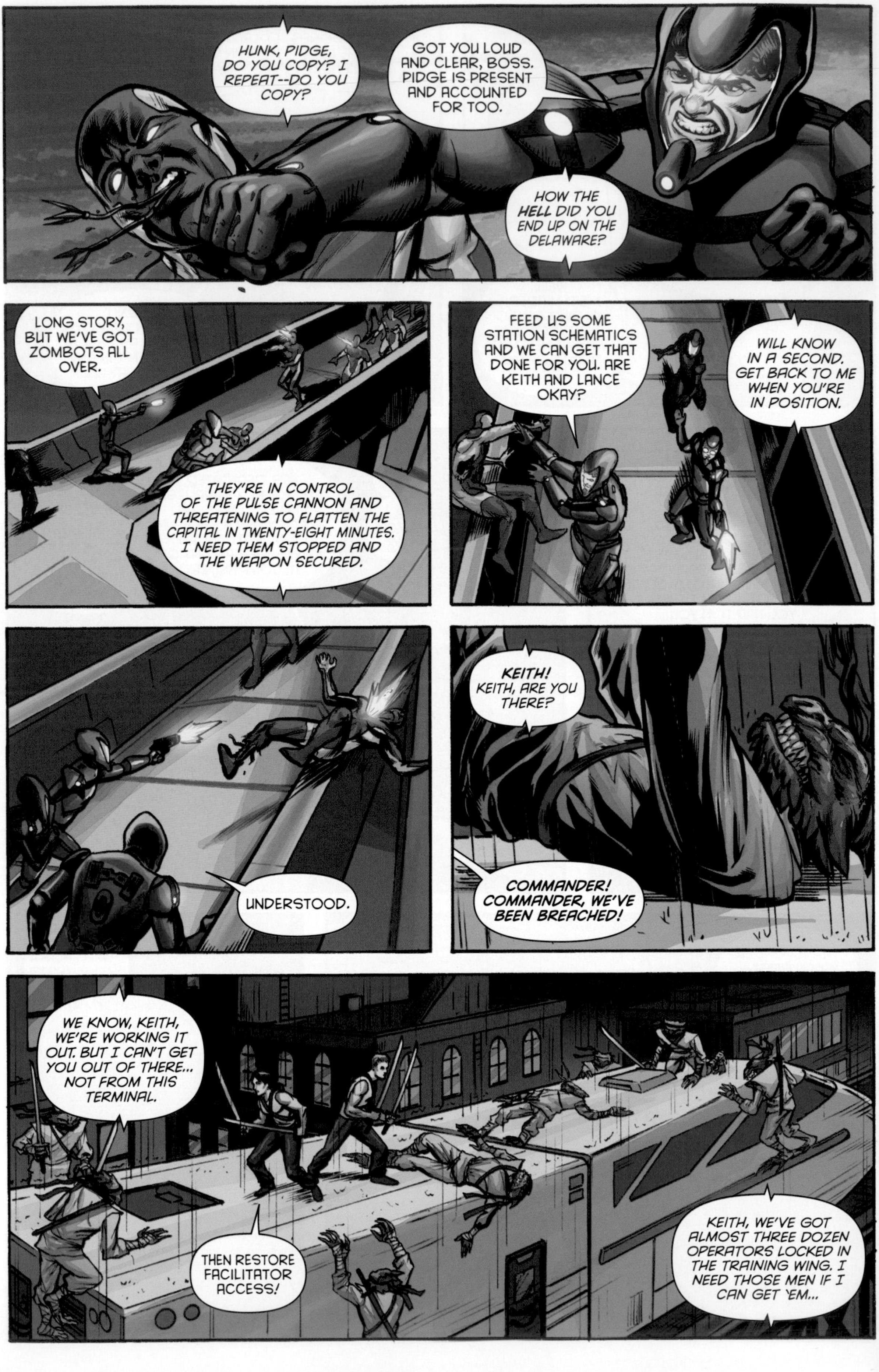
HUNK, PIDGE, DO YOU COPY? I REPEAT--DO YOU COPY?
GOT YOU LOUD AND CLEAR, BOSS. PIDGE IS PRESENT AND ACCOUNTED FOR TOO.
HOW THE **HELL** DID YOU END UP ON THE DELAWARE?
LONG STORY, BUT WE'VE GOT ZOMBOTS ALL OVER.
THEY'RE IN CONTROL OF THE PULSE CANNON AND THREATENING TO FLATTEN THE CAPITAL IN TWENTY-EIGHT MINUTES. I NEED THEM STOPPED AND THE WEAPON SECURED.
FEED US SOME STATION SCHEMATICS AND WE CAN GET THAT DONE FOR YOU. ARE KEITH AND LANCE OKAY?
WILL KNOW IN A SECOND. GET BACK TO ME WHEN YOU'RE IN POSITION.
UNDERSTOOD.
KEITH! KEITH, ARE YOU THERE?
COMMANDER! COMMANDER, WE'VE BEEN BREACHED!
WE KNOW, KEITH, WE'RE WORKING IT OUT. BUT I CAN'T GET YOU OUT OF THERE... NOT FROM THIS TERMINAL.
THEN RESTORE FACILITATOR ACCESS!
KEITH, WE'VE GOT ALMOST THREE DOZEN OPERATORS LOCKED IN THE TRAINING WING. I NEED THOSE MEN IF I CAN GET 'EM...

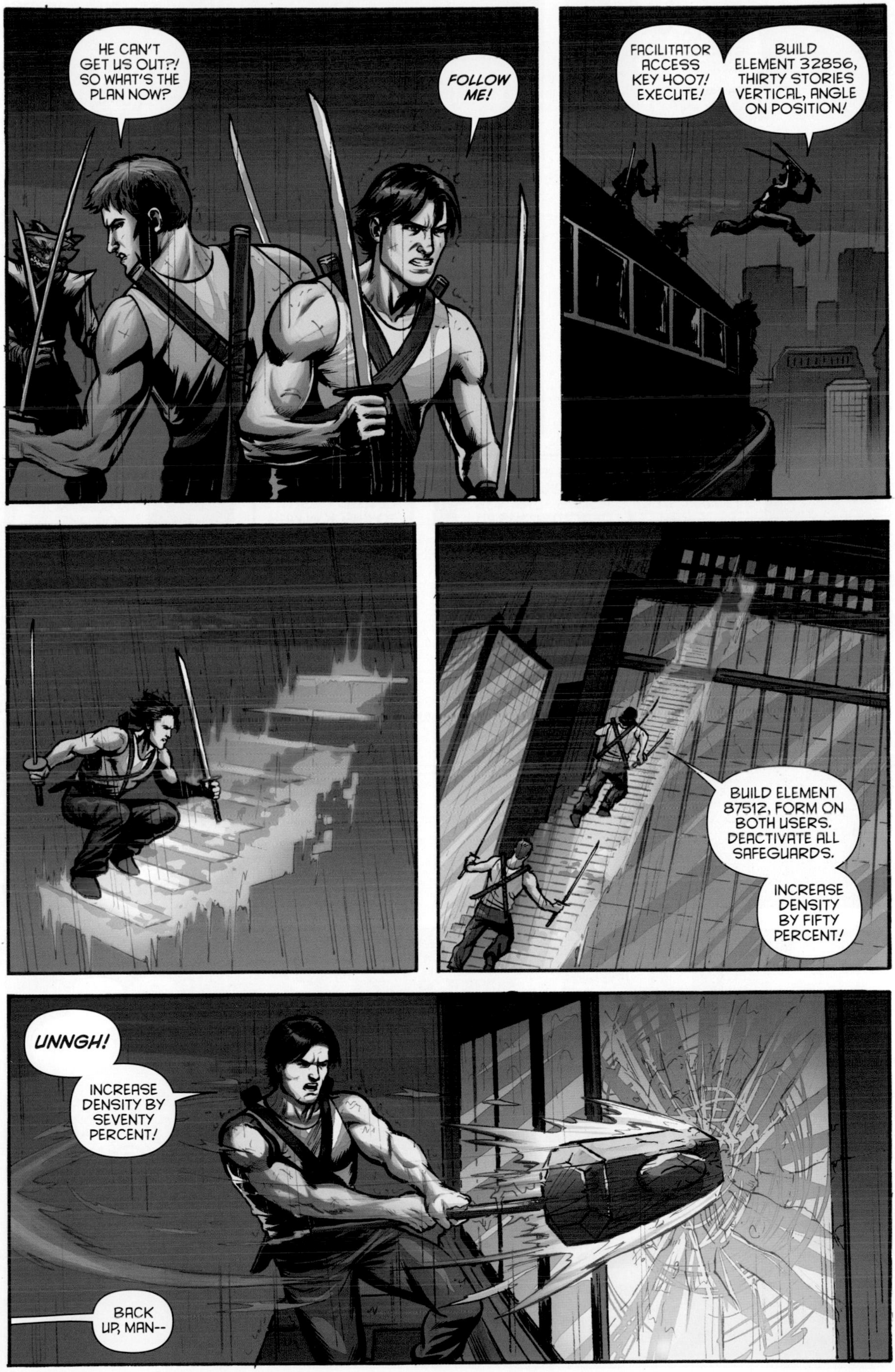
HE CAN'T GET US OUT?! SO WHAT'S THE PLAN NOW?
FOLLOW ME!
FACILITATOR ACCESS KEY 4007! EXECUTE!
BUILD ELEMENT 32856, THIRTY STORIES VERTICAL, ANGLE ON POSITION!
BUILD ELEMENT 87512, FORM ON BOTH USERS. DEACTIVATE ALL SAFEGUARDS.
INCREASE DENSITY BY FIFTY PERCENT!
UNNGH!
INCREASE DENSITY BY SEVENTY PERCENT!
BACK UP, MAN--

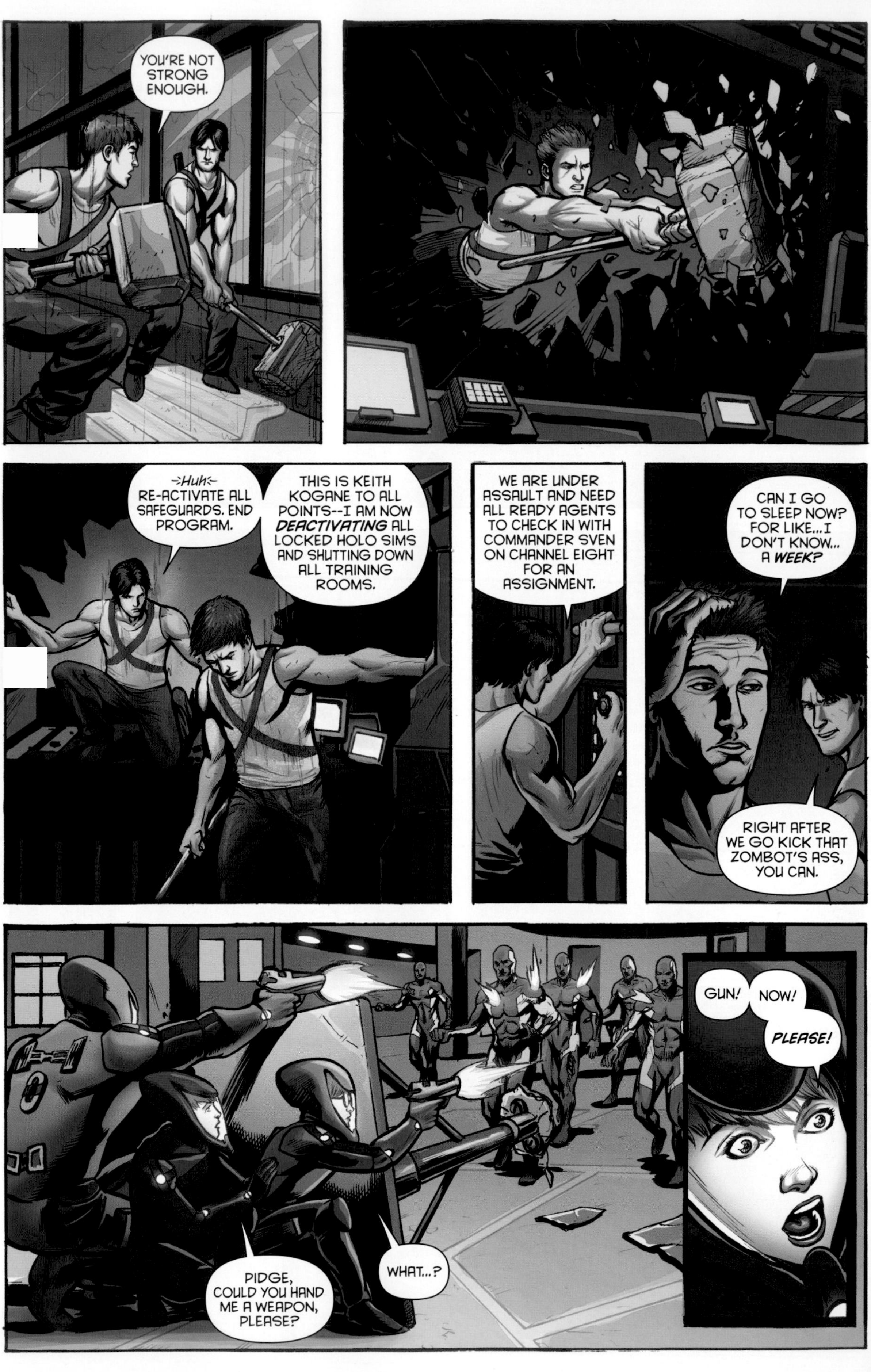
YOU'RE NOT STRONG ENOUGH.
-Huh-
RE-ACTIVATE ALL SAFEGUARDS. END PROGRAM.
THIS IS KEITH KOGANE TO ALL POINTS--I AM NOW DEACTIVATING ALL LOCKED HOLO SIMS AND SHUTTING DOWN ALL TRAINING ROOMS.
WE ARE UNDER ASSAULT AND NEED ALL READY AGENTS TO CHECK IN WITH COMMANDER SVEN ON CHANNEL EIGHT FOR AN ASSIGNMENT.
CAN I GO TO SLEEP NOW? FOR LIKE...I DON'T KNOW... A WEEK?
RIGHT AFTER WE GO KICK THAT ZOMBOT'S ASS, YOU CAN.
PIDGE, COULD YOU HAND ME A WEAPON, PLEASE?
WHAT...?
GUN!
NOW!
PLEASE!

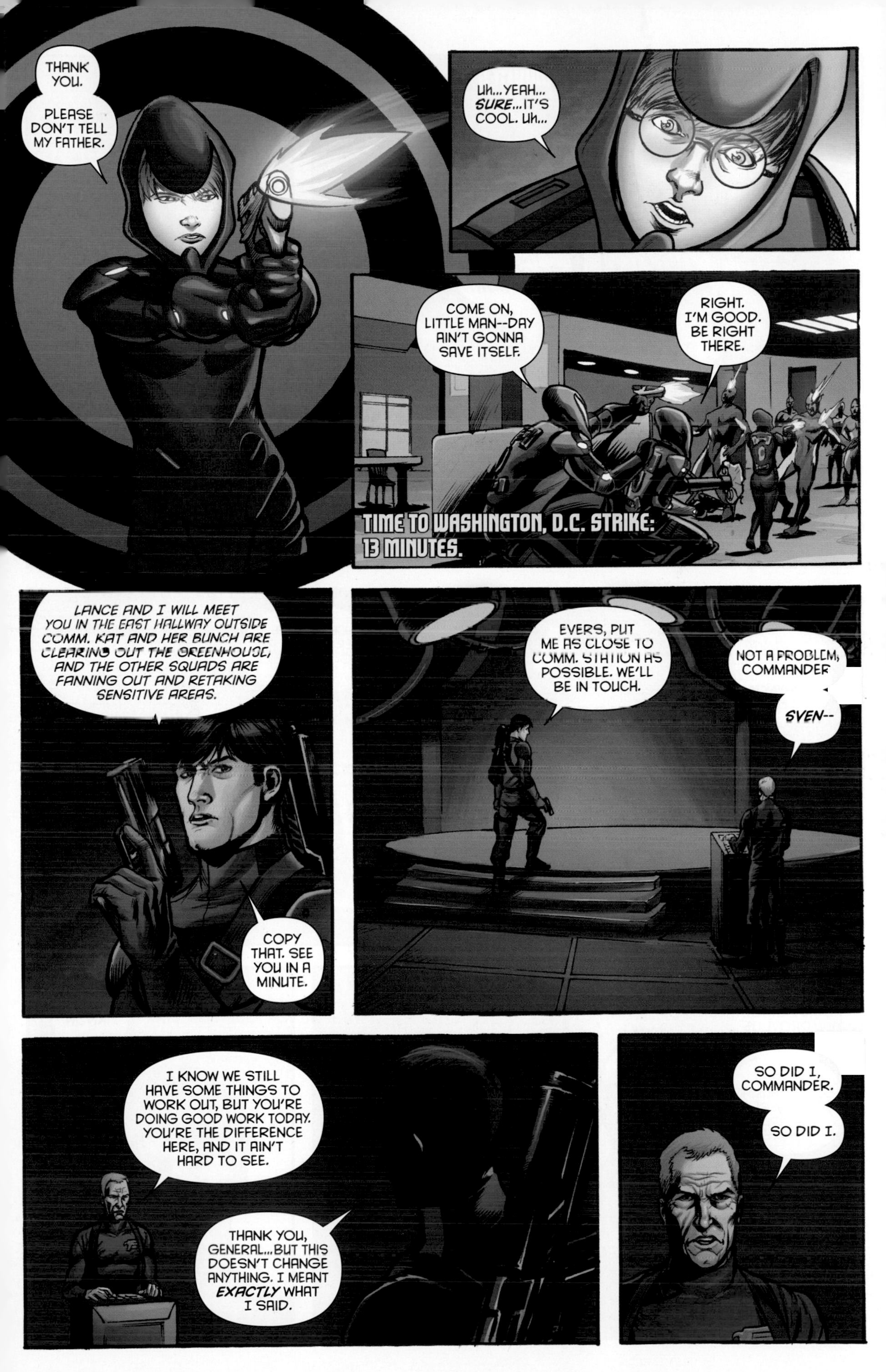
THANK YOU.
PLEASE DON'T TELL MY FATHER.
UH...YEAH... SURE...IT'S COOL. UH...
COME ON, LITTLE MAN--DAY AIN'T GONNA SAVE ITSELF.
RIGHT. I'M GOOD. BE RIGHT THERE.
TIME TO WASHINGTON, D.C. STRIKE: 13 MINUTES.
LANCE AND I WILL MEET YOU IN THE EAST HALLWAY OUTSIDE COMM. KAT AND HER BUNCH ARE CLEARING OUT THE GREENHOUSE, AND THE OTHER SQUADS ARE FANNING OUT AND RETAKING SENSITIVE AREAS.
COPY THAT. SEE YOU IN A MINUTE.
EVERS, PUT ME AS CLOSE TO COMM. STATION AS POSSIBLE. WE'LL BE IN TOUCH.
NOT A PROBLEM, COMMANDER
SVEN--
I KNOW WE STILL HAVE SOME THINGS TO WORK OUT, BUT YOU'RE DOING GOOD WORK TODAY. YOU'RE THE DIFFERENCE HERE, AND IT AIN'T HARD TO SEE.
THANK YOU, GENERAL...BUT THIS DOESN'T CHANGE ANYTHING. I MEANT EXACTLY WHAT I SAID.
SO DID I, COMMANDER.
SO DID I.

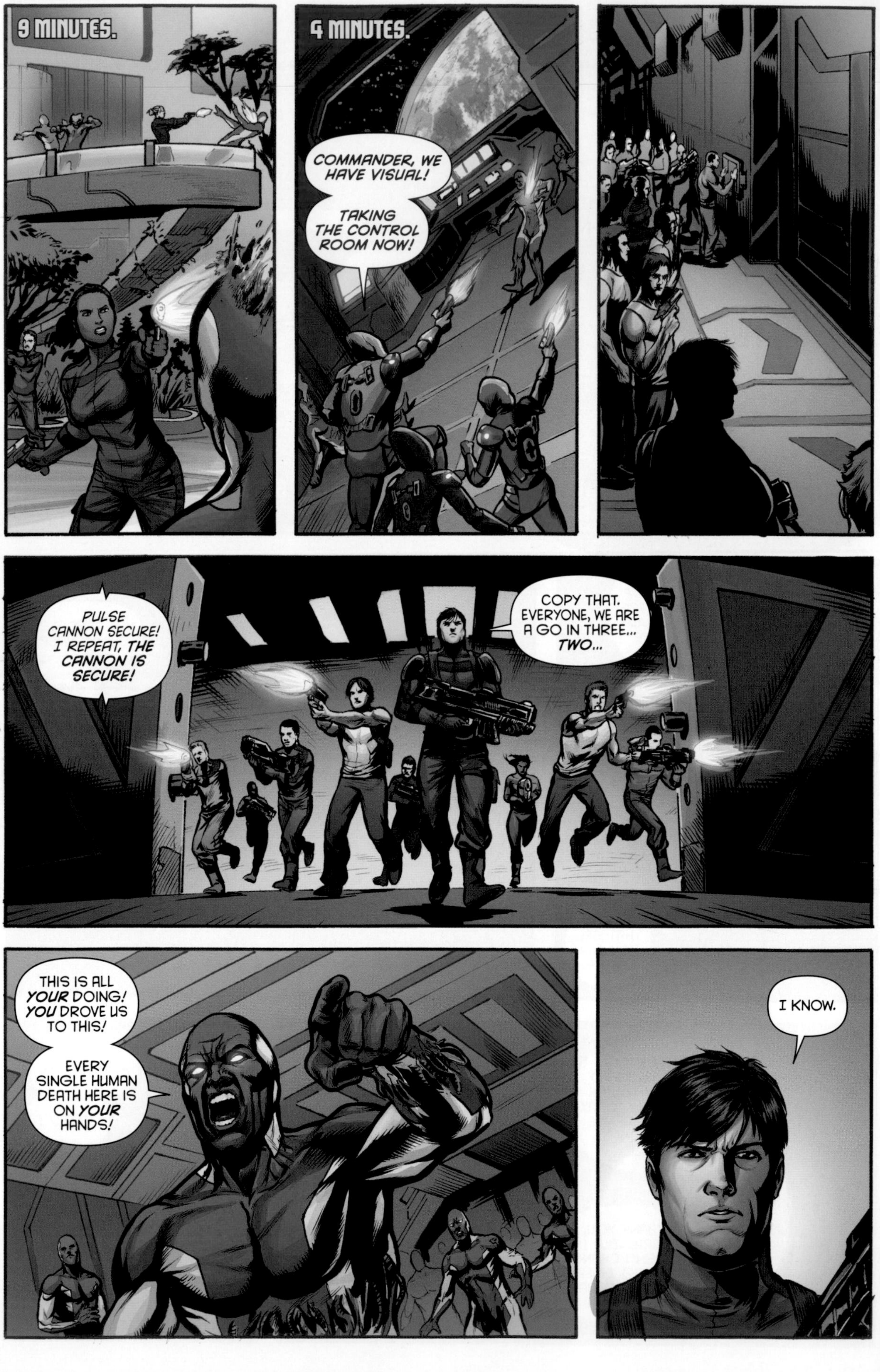
9 MINUTES.
4 MINUTES.
COMMANDER, WE HAVE VISUAL!
TAKING THE CONTROL ROOM NOW!
PULSE CANNON SECURE! I REPEAT, THE CANNON IS SECURE!
COPY THAT. EVERYONE, WE ARE A GO IN THREE... TWO...
THIS IS ALL YOUR DOING! YOU DROVE US TO THIS!
EVERY SINGLE HUMAN DEATH HERE IS ON YOUR HANDS!
I KNOW.

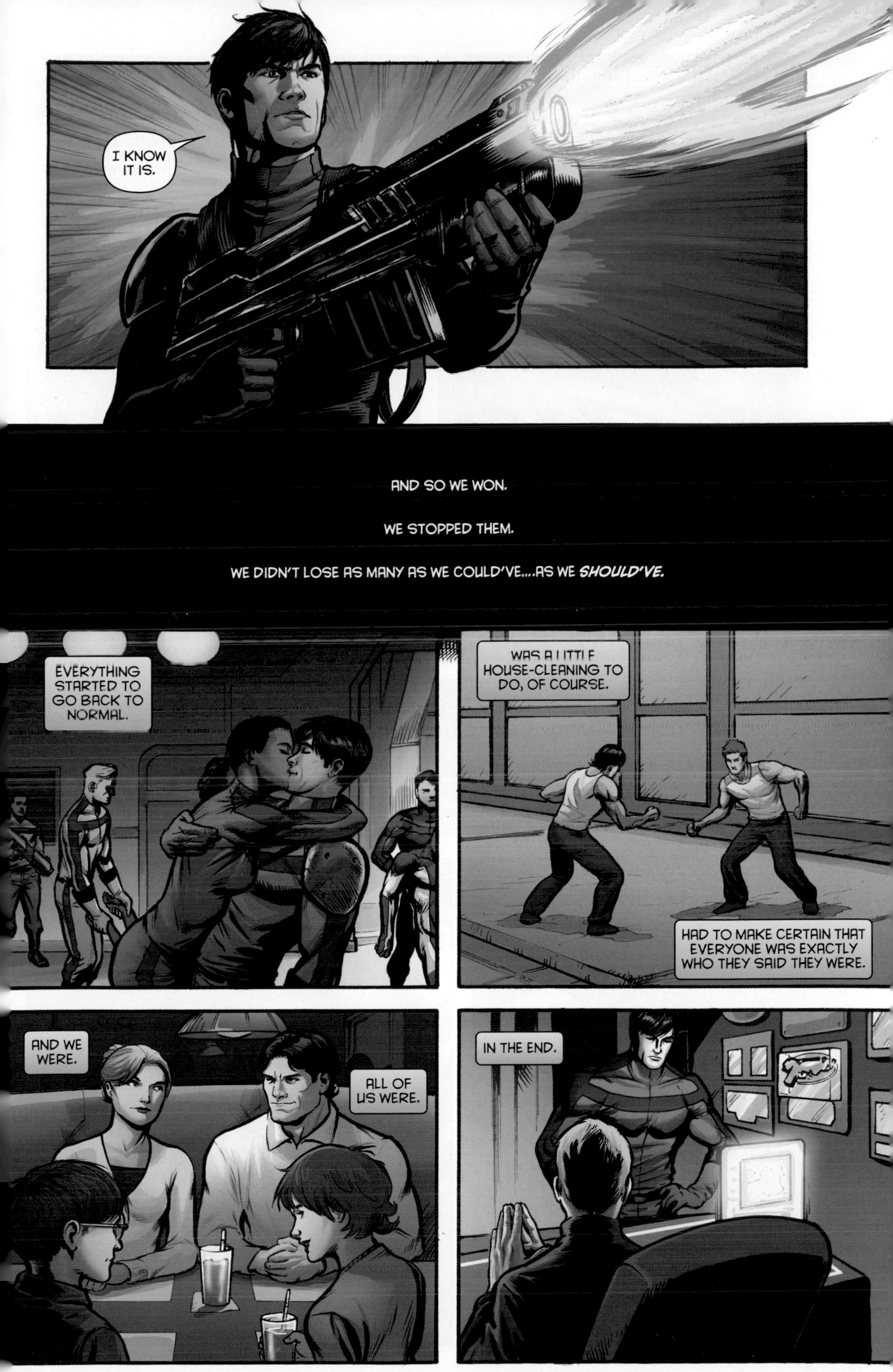
I KNOW IT IS.
AND SO WE WON.
WE STOPPED THEM.
WE DIDN'T LOSE AS MANY AS WE COULD'VE....AS WE *SHOULD'VE.*
EVERYTHING STARTED TO GO BACK TO NORMAL.
WAS A LITTLE HOUSE-CLEANING TO DO, OF COURSE.
HAD TO MAKE CERTAIN THAT EVERYONE WAS EXACTLY WHO THEY SAID THEY WERE.
AND WE WERE.
ALL OF US WERE.
IN THE END.

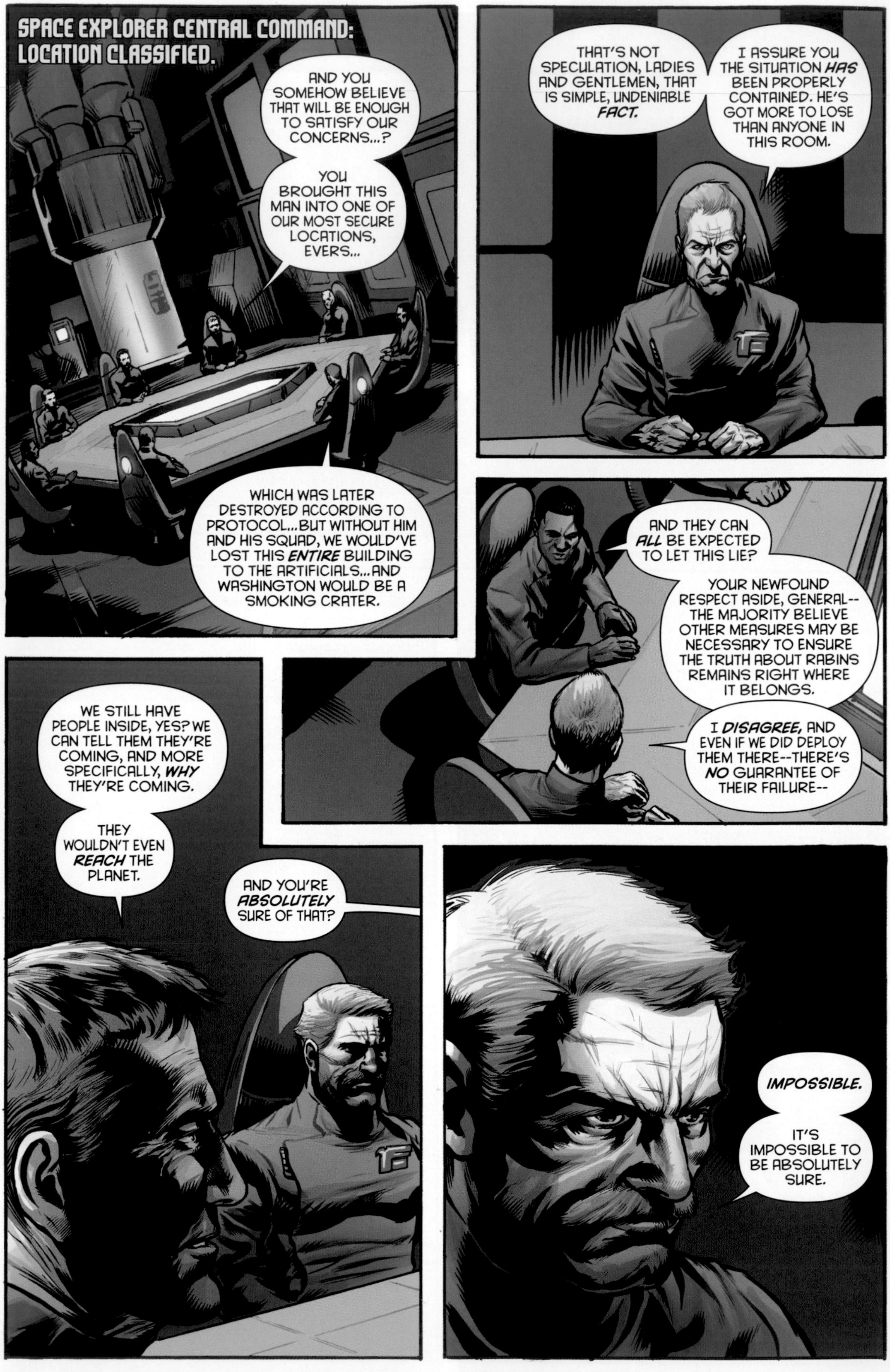
SPACE EXPLORER CENTRAL COMMAND: LOCATION CLASSIFIED.
AND YOU SOMEHOW BELIEVE THAT WILL BE ENOUGH TO SATISFY OUR CONCERNS...?
YOU BROUGHT THIS MAN INTO ONE OF OUR MOST SECURE LOCATIONS, EVERS...
WHICH WAS LATER DESTROYED ACCORDING TO PROTOCOL...BUT WITHOUT HIM AND HIS SQUAD, WE WOULD'VE LOST THIS *ENTIRE* BUILDING TO THE ARTIFICIALS...AND WASHINGTON WOULD BE A SMOKING CRATER.
THAT'S NOT SPECULATION, LADIES AND GENTLEMEN, THAT IS SIMPLE, UNDENIABLE *FACT.*
I ASSURE YOU THE SITUATION *HAS* BEEN PROPERLY CONTAINED. HE'S GOT MORE TO LOSE THAN ANYONE IN THIS ROOM.
AND THEY CAN *ALL* BE EXPECTED TO LET THIS LIE?
YOUR NEWFOUND RESPECT ASIDE, GENERAL-- THE MAJORITY BELIEVE OTHER MEASURES MAY BE NECESSARY TO ENSURE THE TRUTH ABOUT RABINS REMAINS RIGHT WHERE IT BELONGS.
I *DISAGREE,* AND EVEN IF WE DID DEPLOY THEM THERE--THERE'S *NO* GUARANTEE OF THEIR FAILURE--
WE STILL HAVE PEOPLE INSIDE, YES? WE CAN TELL THEM THEY'RE COMING, AND MORE SPECIFICALLY, *WHY* THEY'RE COMING.
THEY WOULDN'T EVEN *REACH* THE PLANET.
AND YOU'RE *ABSOLUTELY* SURE OF THAT?
IMPOSSIBLE.
IT'S IMPOSSIBLE TO BE ABSOLUTELY SURE.

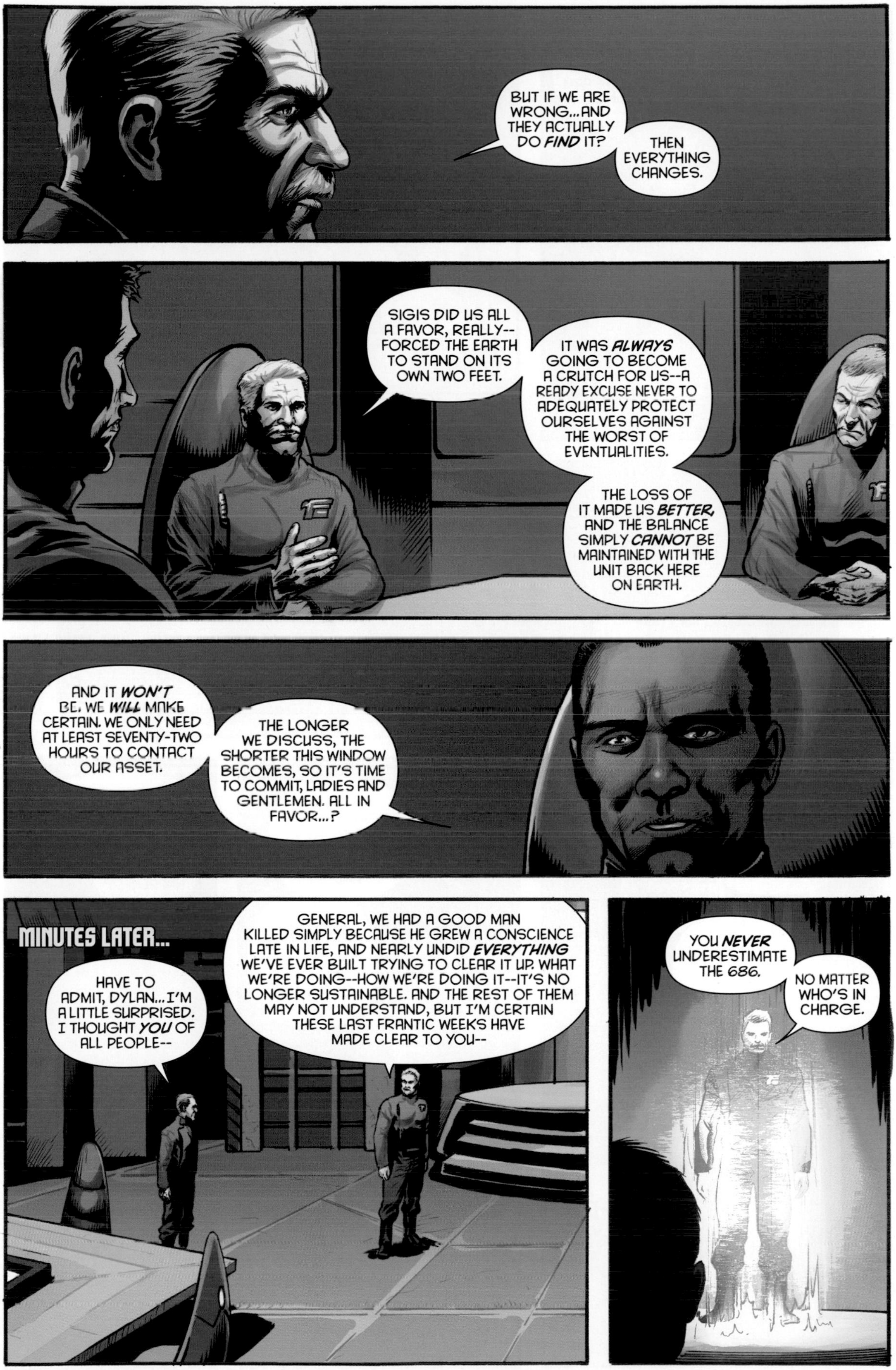
BUT IF WE ARE WRONG...AND THEY ACTUALLY DO *FIND* IT?
THEN EVERYTHING CHANGES.
SIGIS DID US ALL A FAVOR, REALLY--FORCED THE EARTH TO STAND ON ITS OWN TWO FEET.
IT WAS *ALWAYS* GOING TO BECOME A CRUTCH FOR US--A READY EXCUSE NEVER TO ADEQUATELY PROTECT OURSELVES AGAINST THE WORST OF EVENTUALITIES.
THE LOSS OF IT MADE US *BETTER*, AND THE BALANCE SIMPLY *CANNOT* BE MAINTAINED WITH THE UNIT BACK HERE ON EARTH.
AND IT *WON'T* BE. WE *WILL* MAKE CERTAIN. WE ONLY NEED AT LEAST SEVENTY-TWO HOURS TO CONTACT OUR ASSET.
THE LONGER WE DISCUSS, THE SHORTER THIS WINDOW BECOMES, SO IT'S TIME TO COMMIT, LADIES AND GENTLEMEN. ALL IN FAVOR...?
MINUTES LATER...
HAVE TO ADMIT, DYLAN... I'M A LITTLE SURPRISED. I THOUGHT *YOU* OF ALL PEOPLE--
GENERAL, WE HAD A GOOD MAN KILLED SIMPLY BECAUSE HE GREW A CONSCIENCE LATE IN LIFE, AND NEARLY UNDID *EVERYTHING* WE'VE EVER BUILT TRYING TO CLEAR IT UP. WHAT WE'RE DOING--HOW WE'RE DOING IT--IT'S NO LONGER SUSTAINABLE. AND THE REST OF THEM MAY NOT UNDERSTAND, BUT I'M CERTAIN THESE LAST FRANTIC WEEKS HAVE MADE CLEAR TO YOU--
YOU *NEVER* UNDERESTIMATE THE 686.
NO MATTER WHO'S IN CHARGE.

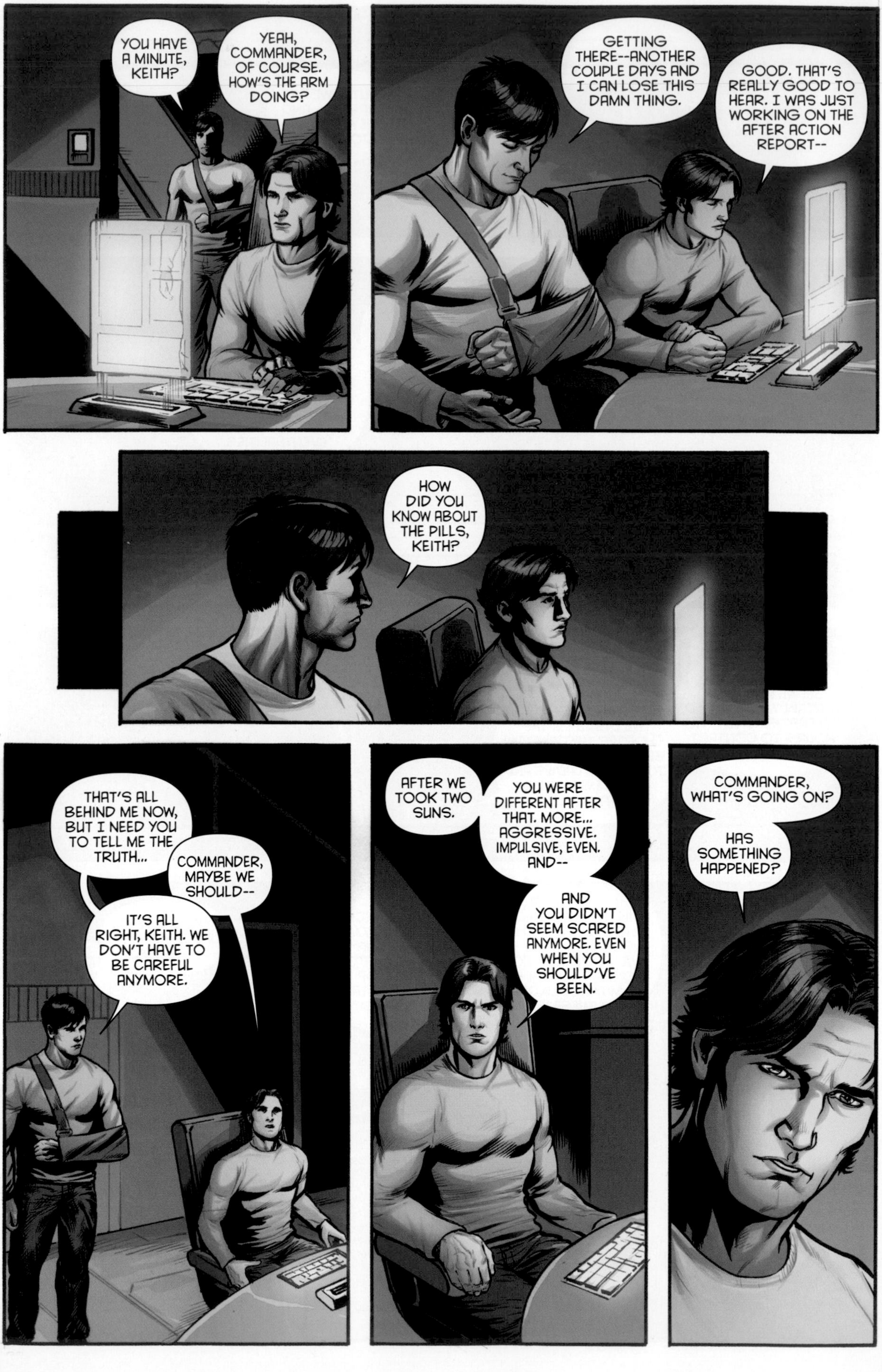
YOU HAVE A MINUTE, KEITH?
YEAH, COMMANDER, OF COURSE. HOW'S THE ARM DOING?
GETTING THERE--ANOTHER COUPLE DAYS AND I CAN LOSE THIS DAMN THING.
GOOD. THAT'S REALLY GOOD TO HEAR. I WAS JUST WORKING ON THE AFTER ACTION REPORT--
HOW DID YOU KNOW ABOUT THE PILLS, KEITH?
THAT'S ALL BEHIND ME NOW, BUT I NEED YOU TO TELL ME THE TRUTH...
COMMANDER, MAYBE WE SHOULD--
IT'S ALL RIGHT, KEITH. WE DON'T HAVE TO BE CAREFUL ANYMORE.
AFTER WE TOOK TWO SUNS.
YOU WERE DIFFERENT AFTER THAT. MORE... AGGRESSIVE. IMPULSIVE, EVEN. AND--
AND YOU DIDN'T SEEM SCARED ANYMORE. EVEN WHEN YOU SHOULD'VE BEEN.
COMMANDER, WHAT'S GOING ON?
HAS SOMETHING HAPPENED?

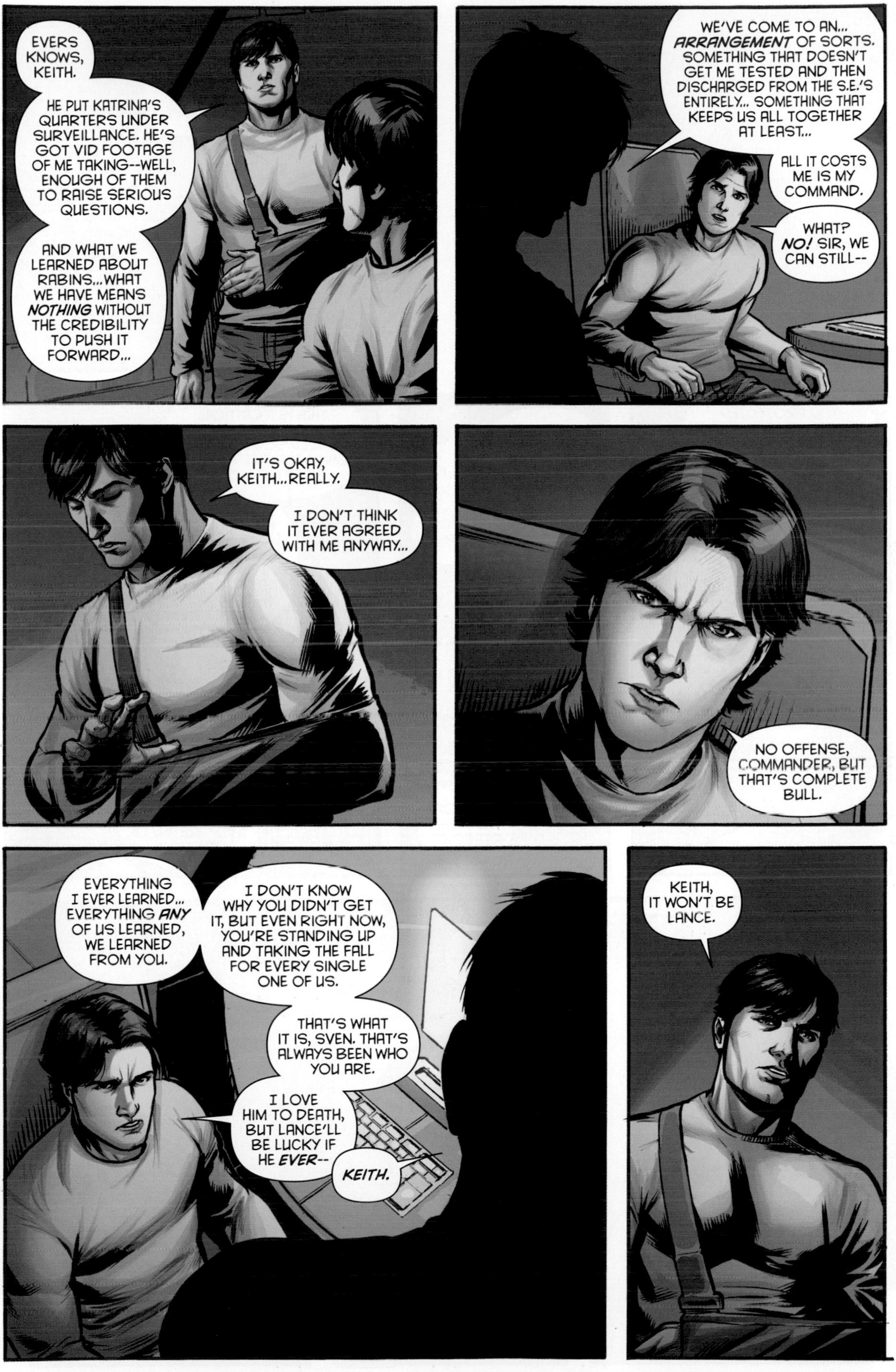
EVERS KNOWS, KEITH.
HE PUT KATRINA'S QUARTERS UNDER SURVEILLANCE. HE'S GOT VID FOOTAGE OF ME TAKING--WELL, ENOUGH OF THEM TO RAISE SERIOUS QUESTIONS.
AND WHAT WE LEARNED ABOUT RABINS...WHAT WE HAVE MEANS NOTHING WITHOUT THE CREDIBILITY TO PUSH IT FORWARD...
WE'VE COME TO AN... ARRANGEMENT OF SORTS. SOMETHING THAT DOESN'T GET ME TESTED AND THEN DISCHARGED FROM THE S.E.'S ENTIRELY... SOMETHING THAT KEEPS US ALL TOGETHER AT LEAST...
ALL IT COSTS ME IS MY COMMAND.
WHAT? NO! SIR, WE CAN STILL--
IT'S OKAY, KEITH...REALLY.
I DON'T THINK IT EVER AGREED WITH ME ANYWAY...
NO OFFENSE, COMMANDER, BUT THAT'S COMPLETE BULL.
EVERYTHING I EVER LEARNED... EVERYTHING ANY OF US LEARNED, WE LEARNED FROM YOU.
I DON'T KNOW WHY YOU DIDN'T GET IT, BUT EVEN RIGHT NOW, YOU'RE STANDING UP AND TAKING THE FALL FOR EVERY SINGLE ONE OF US.
THAT'S WHAT IT IS, SVEN. THAT'S ALWAYS BEEN WHO YOU ARE.
I LOVE HIM TO DEATH, BUT LANCE'LL BE LUCKY IF HE EVER--
KEITH.
KEITH, IT WON'T BE LANCE.

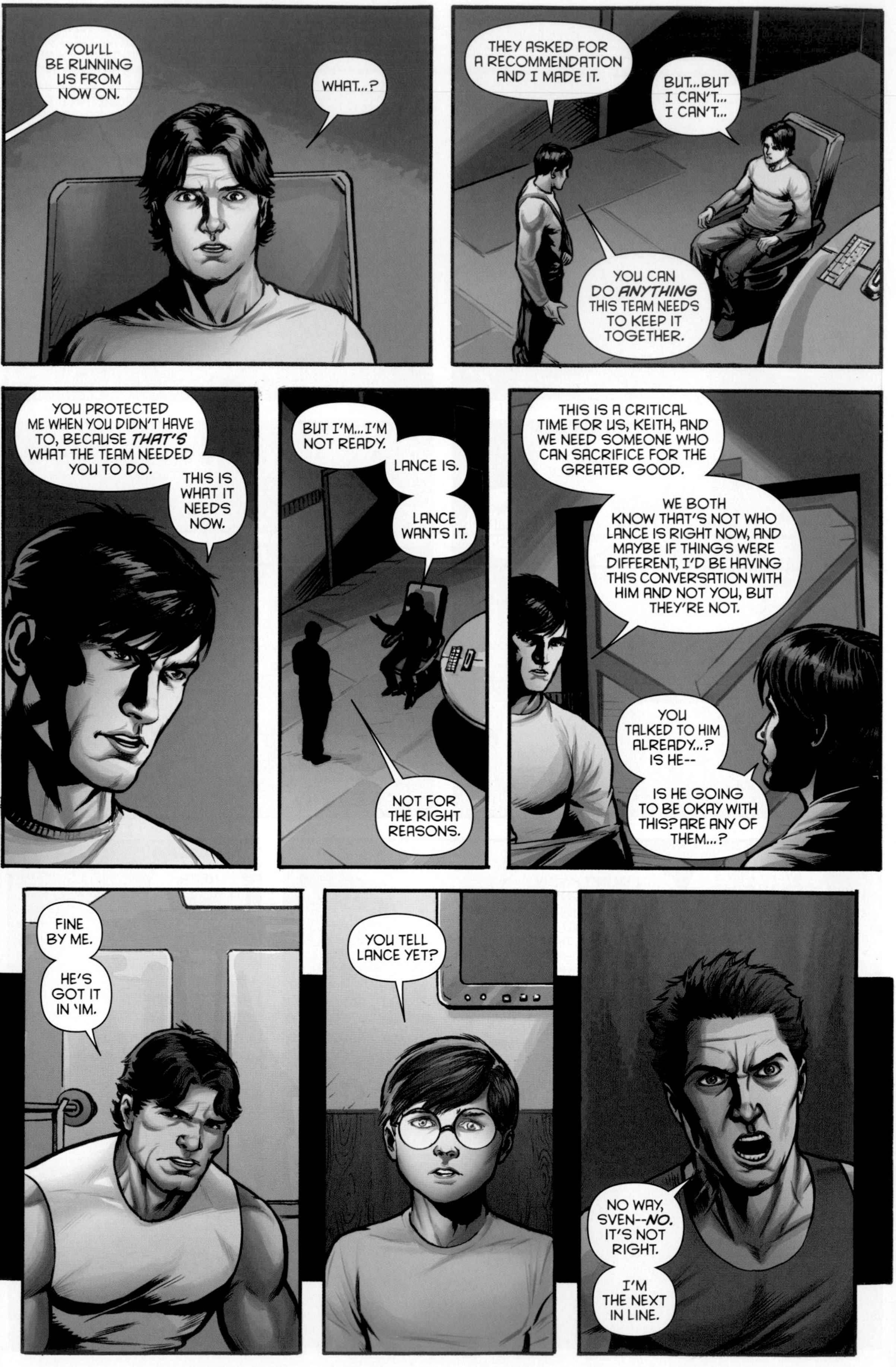
YOU'LL BE RUNNING US FROM NOW ON.
WHAT...?
THEY ASKED FOR A RECOMMENDATION AND I MADE IT.
BUT...BUT I CAN'T... I CAN'T...
YOU CAN DO *ANYTHING* THIS TEAM NEEDS TO KEEP IT TOGETHER.
YOU PROTECTED ME WHEN YOU DIDN'T HAVE TO, BECAUSE *THAT'S* WHAT THE TEAM NEEDED YOU TO DO.
THIS IS WHAT IT NEEDS NOW.
BUT I'M...I'M NOT READY.
LANCE IS.
LANCE WANTS IT.
NOT FOR THE RIGHT REASONS.
THIS IS A CRITICAL TIME FOR US, KEITH, AND WE NEED SOMEONE WHO CAN SACRIFICE FOR THE GREATER GOOD.
WE BOTH KNOW THAT'S NOT WHO LANCE IS RIGHT NOW, AND MAYBE IF THINGS WERE DIFFERENT, I'D BE HAVING THIS CONVERSATION WITH HIM AND NOT YOU, BUT THEY'RE NOT.
YOU TALKED TO HIM ALREADY...? IS HE--
IS HE GOING TO BE OKAY WITH THIS? ARE ANY OF THEM...?
FINE BY ME.
HE'S GOT IT IN 'IM.
YOU TELL LANCE YET?
NO WAY, SVEN--*NO.* IT'S NOT RIGHT.
I'M THE NEXT IN LINE.

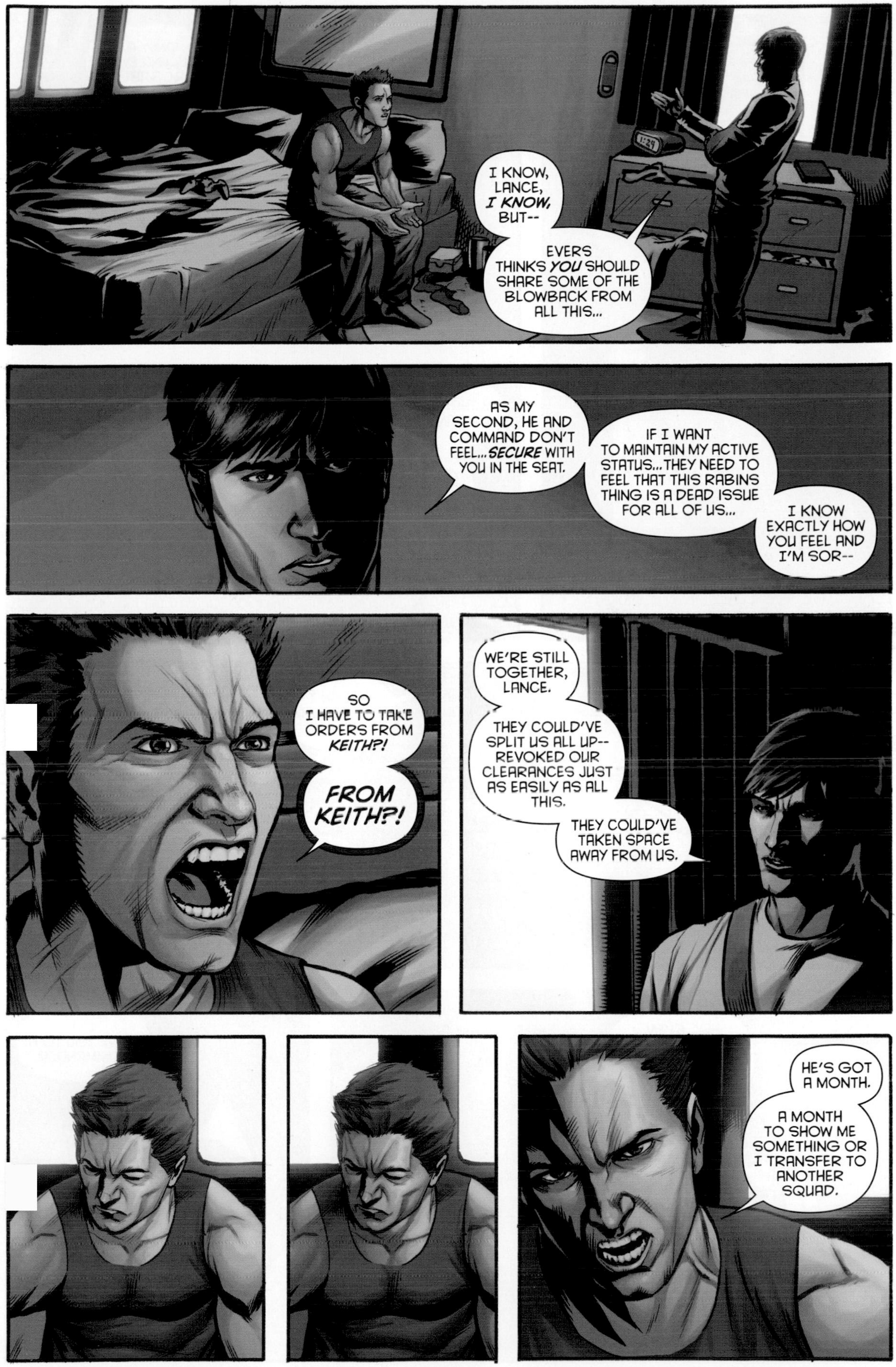
I KNOW, LANCE, I KNOW, BUT--
EVERS THINKS YOU SHOULD SHARE SOME OF THE BLOWBACK FROM ALL THIS...
AS MY SECOND, HE AND COMMAND DON'T FEEL... SECURE WITH YOU IN THE SEAT.
IF I WANT TO MAINTAIN MY ACTIVE STATUS... THEY NEED TO FEEL THAT THIS RABINS THING IS A DEAD ISSUE FOR ALL OF US...
I KNOW EXACTLY HOW YOU FEEL AND I'M SOR--
SO I HAVE TO TAKE ORDERS FROM KEITH?!
FROM KEITH?!
WE'RE STILL TOGETHER, LANCE.
THEY COULD'VE SPLIT US ALL UP-- REVOKED OUR CLEARANCES JUST AS EASILY AS ALL THIS.
THEY COULD'VE TAKEN SPACE AWAY FROM US.
HE'S GOT A MONTH.
A MONTH TO SHOW ME SOMETHING OR I TRANSFER TO ANOTHER SQUAD.

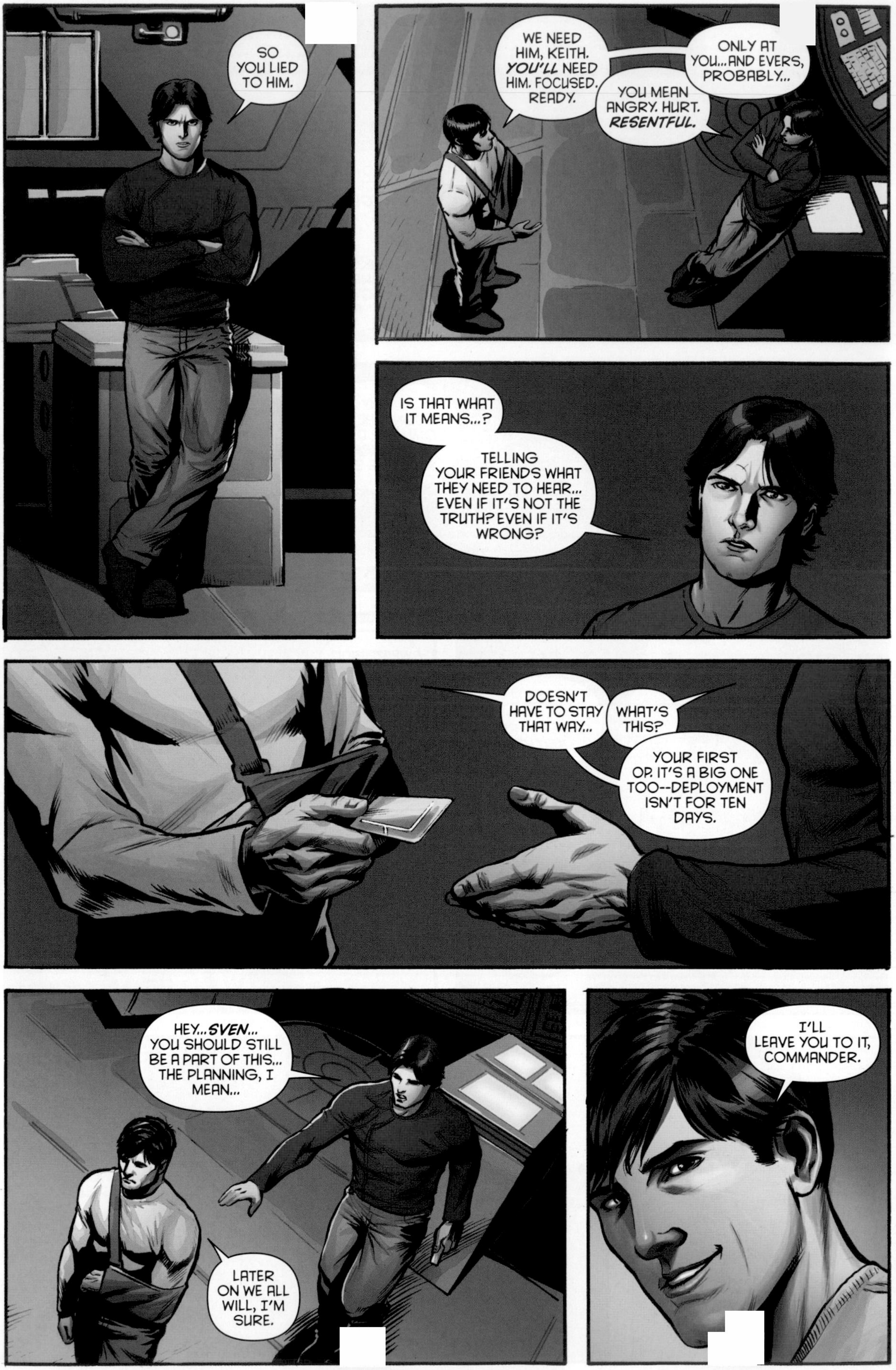
SO YOU LIED TO HIM.
WE NEED HIM, KEITH. YOU'LL NEED HIM. FOCUSED. READY.
YOU MEAN ANGRY. HURT. RESENTFUL.
ONLY AT YOU...AND EVERS, PROBABLY...
IS THAT WHAT IT MEANS...?
TELLING YOUR FRIENDS WHAT THEY NEED TO HEAR... EVEN IF IT'S NOT THE TRUTH? EVEN IF IT'S WRONG?
DOESN'T HAVE TO STAY THAT WAY...
WHAT'S THIS?
YOUR FIRST OP. IT'S A BIG ONE TOO--DEPLOYMENT ISN'T FOR TEN DAYS.
HEY...SVEN... YOU SHOULD STILL BE A PART OF THIS... THE PLANNING, I MEAN...
LATER ON WE ALL WILL, I'M SURE.
I'LL LEAVE YOU TO IT, COMMANDER.

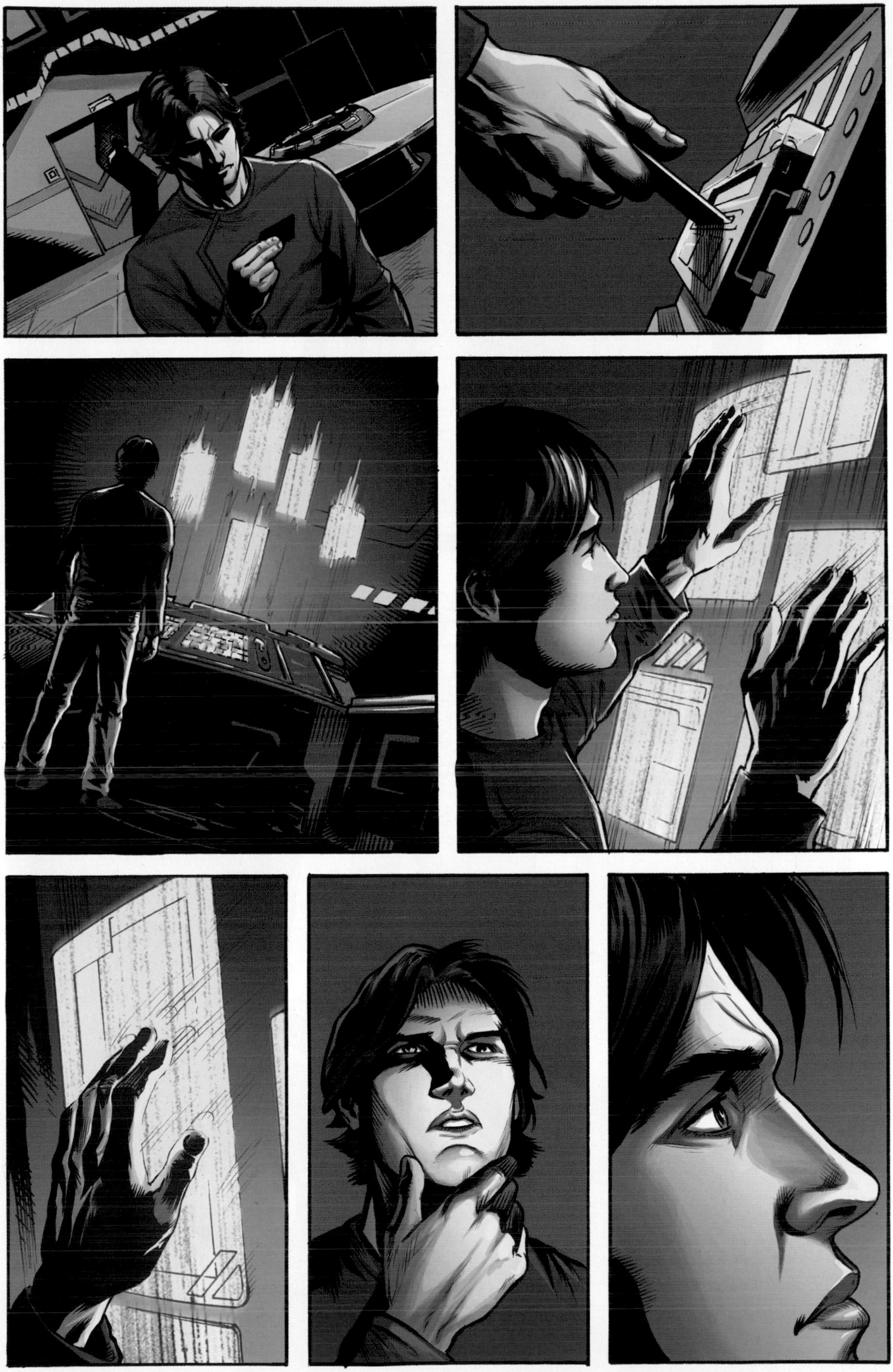

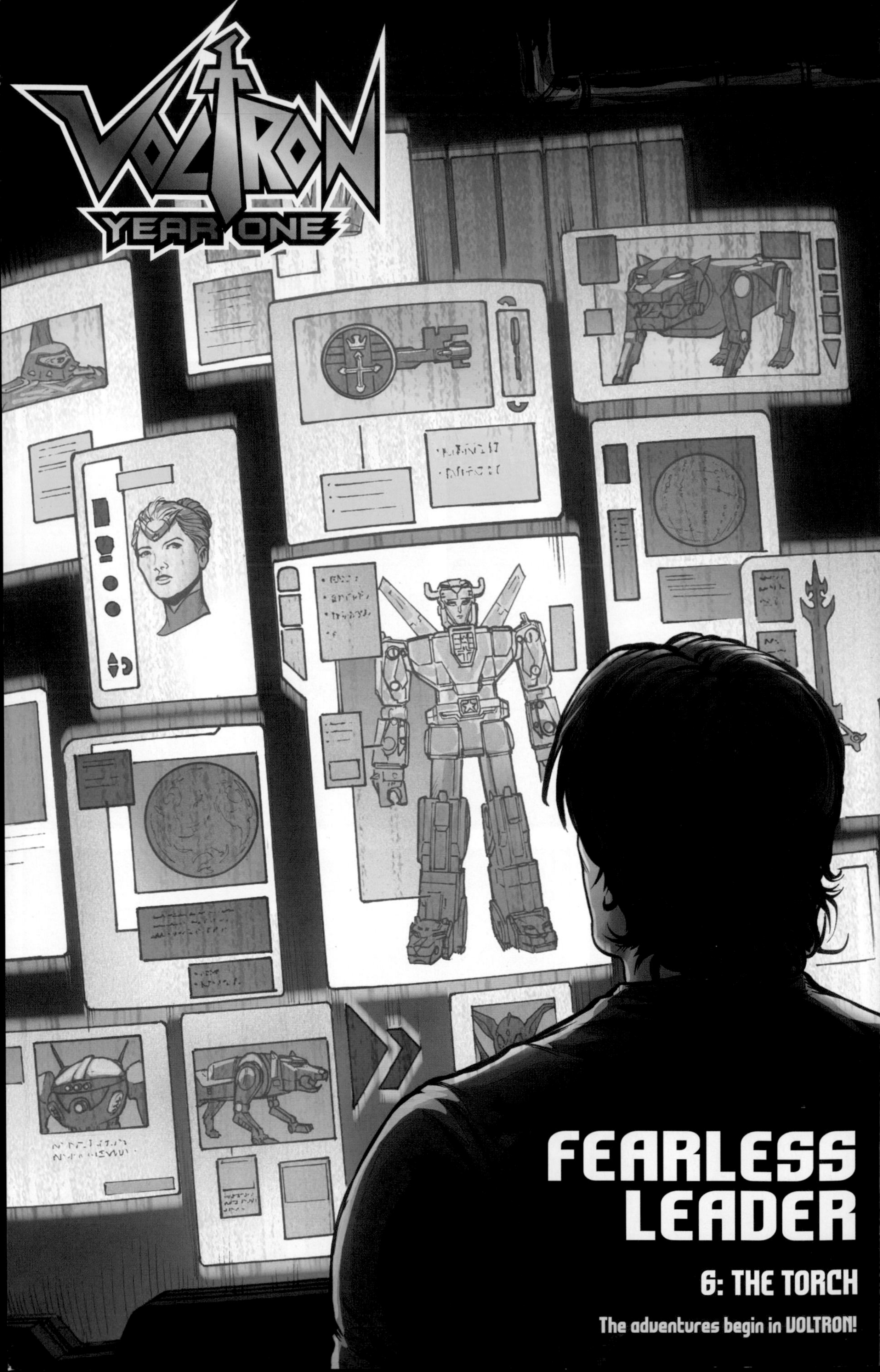
VOLTRON
YEAR ONE
FEARLESS LEADER
6: THE TORCH
The adventures begin in VOLTRON!

COMMENTARY TRACKS
VOLTRON: YEAR ONE #1
By Brandon Thomas

Okay, so my big grand plan for the Year One series was to approach the storytelling in an entirely different way from the main series, and I decided this for a couple reasons. Mainly, I wanted to continue growing and developing as a writer, and didn't want to start writing scripts in a formulaic, predictable way this early on in my career. Really don't think I've established any sort of creative fingerprint yet, and that it'll take some time before that happens organically, but I want to make it as hard on myself as possible, if that makes any sense.

So I took every little storytelling trick that was being used in the main series and decided not to use it here, so don't expect any flashbacks, overly dramatic transitions, and the kind of "jumping around" feeling the regular book has. Also gave myself a codeword ("bullet") for this series that I kept reminding myself of whenever I got the itch to use something like that, and in many respects, writing this book is more similar to writing Miranda Mercury. Something where the goal is always to move forward, and to do so quickly at all times.

And I'm using internal captioning to dig a little further into Sven's head and give us additional information and insights that would otherwise be difficult to inject into the narrative. Along with resisting the urge to methodically plot everything out to the very last detail before I actually write the issues, and preventing myself from re-writing large chunks of dialogue when the art comes back, the idea is to give this series an entirely different feel. Something more organic and immediate, that almost feels like it could be written by a completely different writer.

Also think this series gets off to a much stronger start, as I wrote this first script of Year One after I wrote #4 of the main title, which I felt creatively was a huge turning point for me. Time will tell of course, but here are a few additional thoughts about what went into putting this first script together...

Page 1
Usually want to get off to a fast start, and that was no different here. We're thrown into the pool and launching on an image that we never really saw in the original series—- Sven thrown into a prominent heroic position, doing his best Jack Bauer impression, as his team runs for their lives while under heavy fire. The opportunity to thrust Sven into the spotlight was the thing that attracted me to writing this prequel in the first place, and being trusted with taking him from this place to his inevitable departure from the Voltron Force is a real, real honor. That, naturally, begins with a bloodied, battered Sven screaming at his teammates, "GO!!"

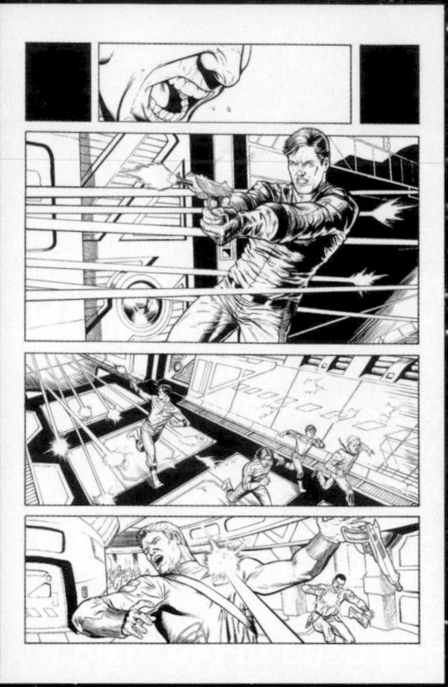

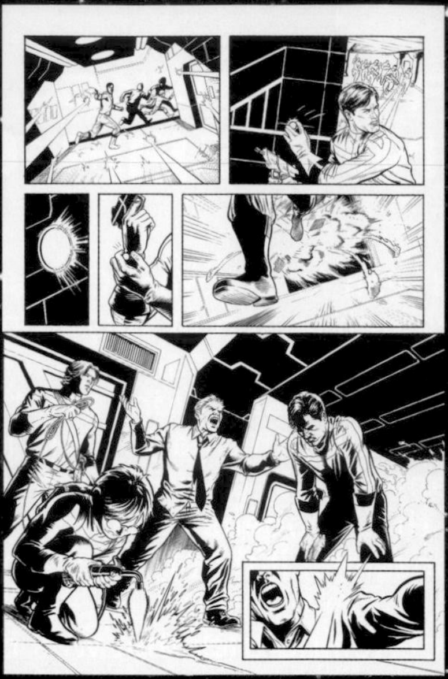

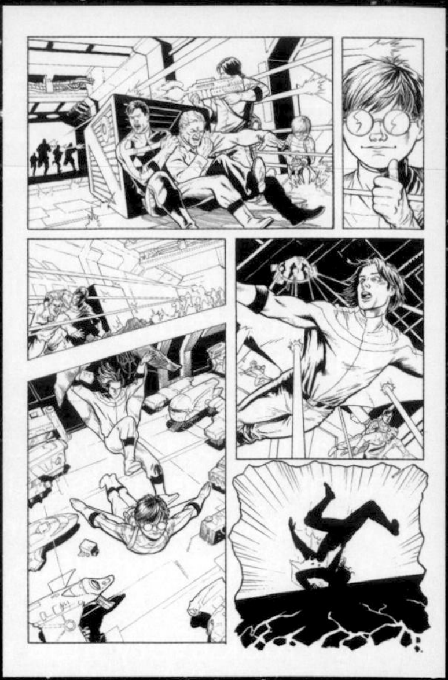

Pages 3-5

Okay, so this is obviously a dream sequence, and unlike most dream sequences, we wanted to tell you something was seriously off before we told you something was off. The first clue is really the shot that hits the man they're supposed to be protecting, as it comes from a direction the characters are facing. In the script, I urged Craig to throttle down on his storytelling instincts and do things that really didn't make any sense visually. Have things literally appear out of nowhere like the giant crate Sven takes cover behind on page 3. Have Keith and Pidge sprout gliding mechanisms out of their jumpsuits that weren't there until the moment they needed them to be there. Break Keith's neck in a terrible fall.

That last bit was a massive indicator something is amiss, but we wanted to stack the impossibilities right on top of each other. Lance dies. Hunk dies. The man they've come to rescue won't stop talking and knows things that he can't possibly know. The fact that no one but him and Sven speak in this entire scene is another intentional thing. Then when the pressure mounts to its highest point, Sven kills the man he's

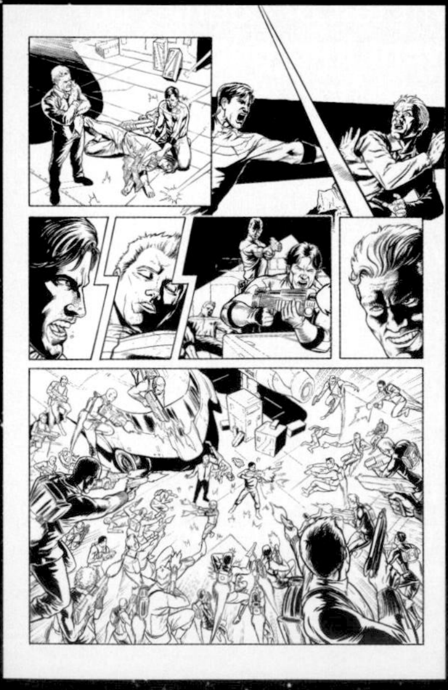

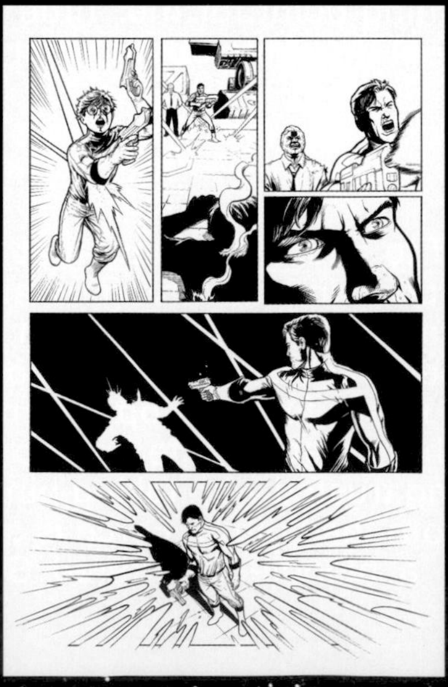

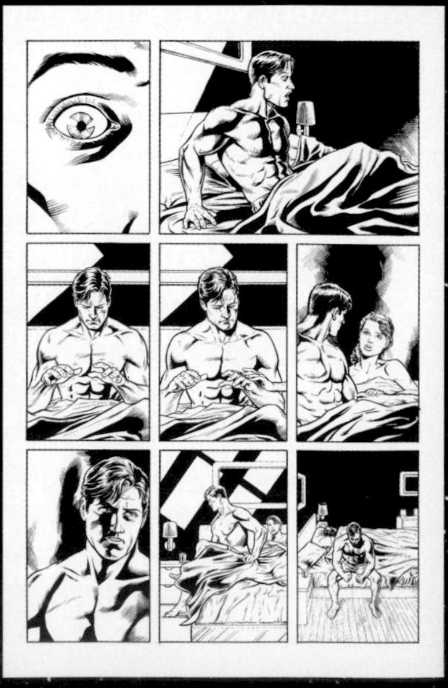

been sent to rescue. That last panel of page 5 is one of my favorite things that Craig drew in the entire issue...he looks like the weight of the world is truly on his shoulders there, seconds before being cut down by a rain of laser blasts with sharpened edges.

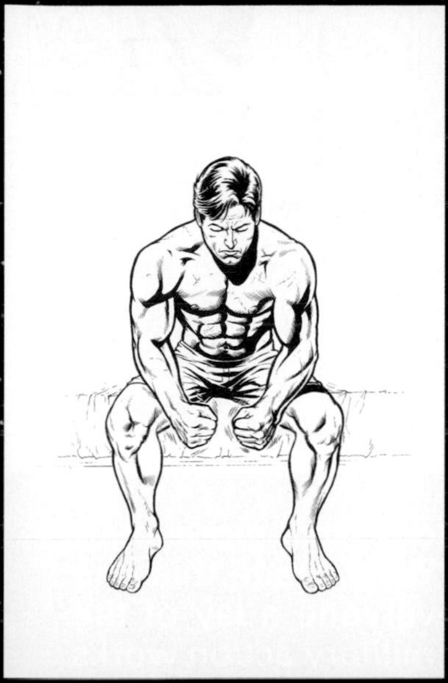

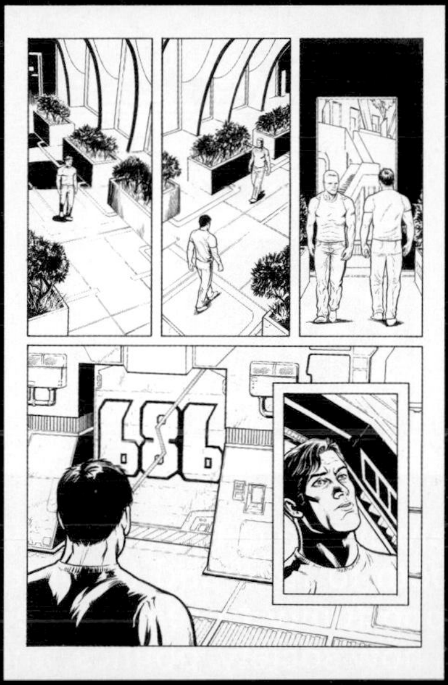

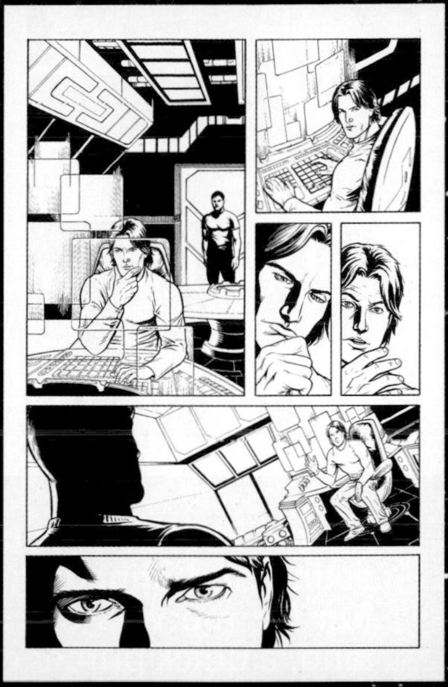

Page 7

All of our title pages in this arc will be formatted something like this, holding on moments where Sven is being overwhelmed by the responsibility placed in his hands. Where everything else falls away and it's just him and his massive inferiority complex all alone somewhere. Sometimes it'll be a moment of great significance, or where he makes a fateful decision, but wanted to do something visually that made the overall vibe and emotions jump out at you. Think our colorist Adriano Lucas also did a great job at giving the image a little more weight and spark, and what he's done for the title page in the next issue is even better.

Pages 9-10

So it was important to quickly establish what the status quo is regarding Sven and Keith in this series, as it's obviously a little different from what we've seen before. The dynamic is pretty similar to an older, wiser brother and his younger sibling, whose ideals and passionate beliefs about right and wrong haven't quite crashed into cold, harsh reality just yet. Despite some naivete on Keith's part, it was critical that you get he's a hard worker, always respects the chain of command, and more than anything, cares deeply about the safety and well-being of his friends and teammates. That is going to be indispensable in subsequent issues when things start to go wrong. Sven is a very different person at the end of this story, and Keith is too.

Pages 11-12

The info dump is of course a time-honored tradition of storytelling, a necessary evil that must be embraced for the story's greater good. Ignoring it is never an answer, and unnecessarily drawing it out over a higher number of pages just wastes space better served for other

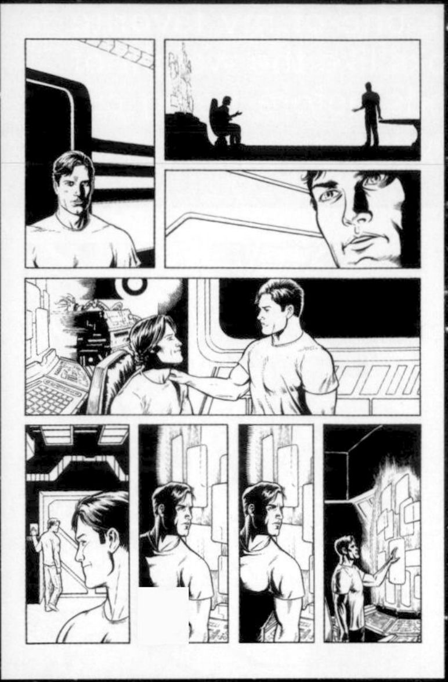
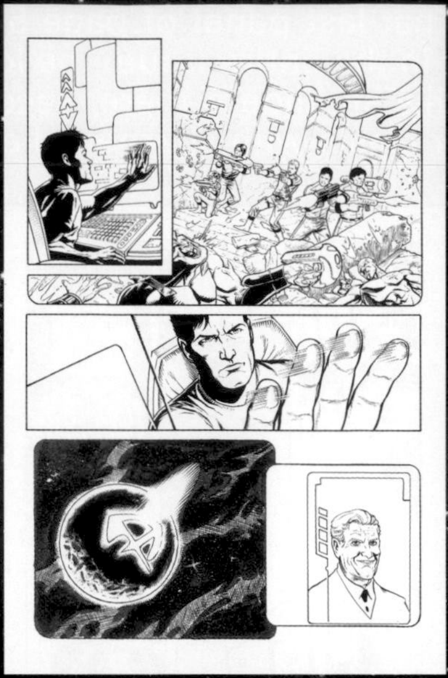
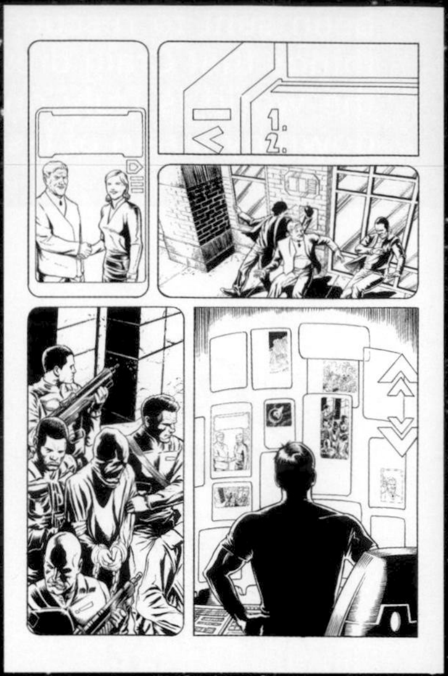

things. That said, you always have to find a way to make it more interesting and engaging both to read and to write. What made this one fun for me was the opportunity to really give everyone a lay of the land, a quick primer on how society, politics, and military action works in the far flung future. The answer to this of course is not very different from how it's conducted today, for better or worse. But the major thing I wanted to impress anyone everyone really comes down to three simple words—-Earth comes first. Now and probably forever. And you'll see that play out in this series, and the main book when the backstage political maneuvering becomes a larger aspect of the story.

Page 13
This is another attempt at conveying a block of information in what I hope was an interesting way. Plan was to do something like this at the beginning of every mission, but the construction of the series changed down the line, so I'm not sure if you'll be seeing it again. Do love how it came out though, and was really happy with the choices letterer Simon Bowland made for the fonts and assorted elements. One of the

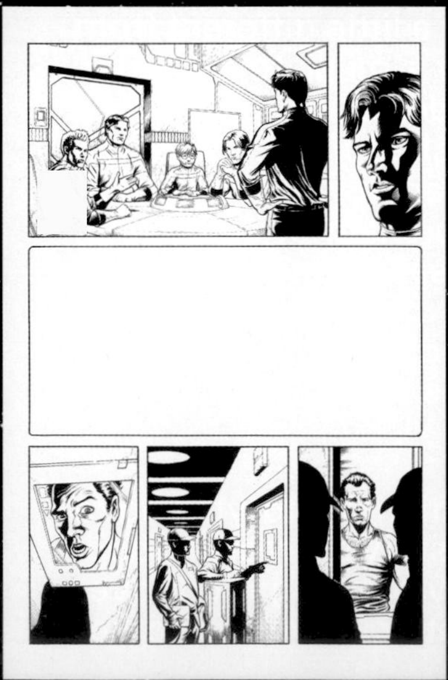
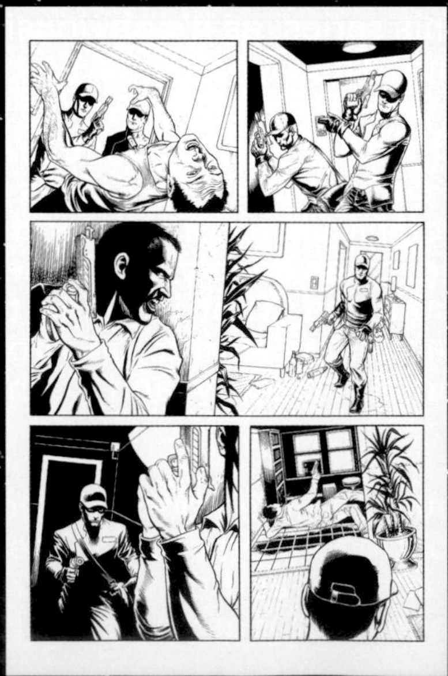
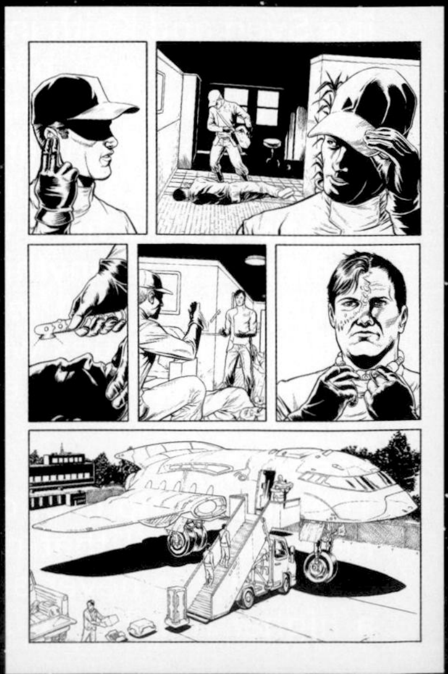

reasons I don't think we'll be doing it again was because it provides a little too much info on what's to come. It essentially lays out the entire remainder of the book, and while it worked okay here, probably would be counter-productive given what comes next. This was one of the last pages I fully scripted out, waiting until the entire story was done before going back and writing out the actual objectives.

Pages 14-15
Started out being obsessed with Keith (and still am) but I'm quickly warming up to the charms of Lance as well. Love his bluntness, so to speak, and in this case, Sven does too. Also wanted to hint that Lance is officially second-in-command of the unit currently, which makes Keith's upcoming ascension even more unpredictable and unexpected. Their quick takedown was fun to script, especially Sven's lines used to distract their targets, which are essentially a bunch of nonsense. Anytime you can write things that don't make a lick of sense, and do so for the cause, it's always a nice feeling.

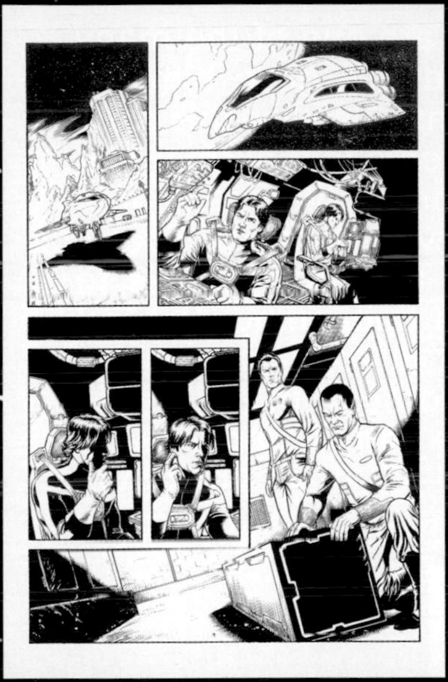
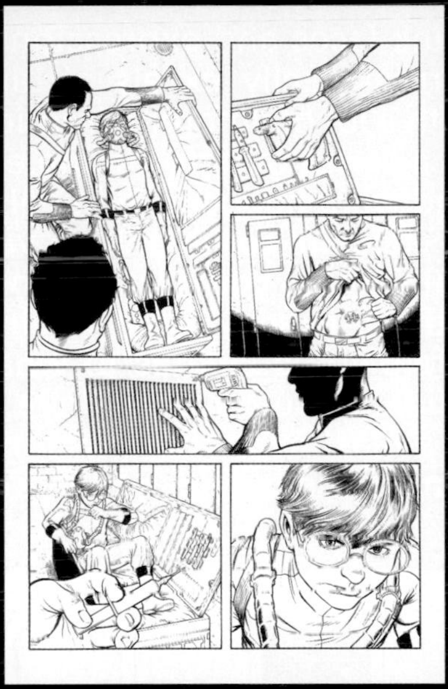
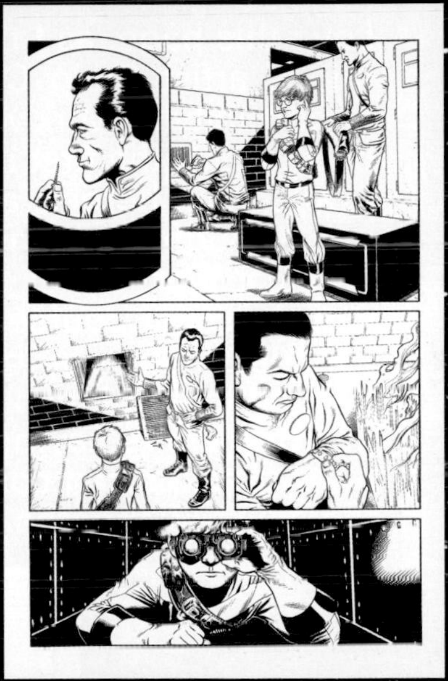

Pages 17-19
Love Pidge. Love 'em, love 'em. To me, this question of, "How the hell did this punk kid end up on a team of Space Explorers," can only be answered the most obvious way...cause he's just that damn awesome. Think what would happen if you took Damien Wayne, Doogie Howser, Barry Ween, and yes, Jack Warning, and smashed them all together? That right there is Pidge to me—a young man who is extremely good at what he does, can only get better, and isn't afraid of letting others know about it. Isn't afraid of much of anything to be honest, which is why he was just perfect for this John McClane moment. Also thought it would fun to have him constantly busting Lance's balls about something, which is a dynamic that's flipped a bit in the main book, where he has to put up with Allura constantly busting his balls.

But he's been good at injecting some levity and moments of humor into the stories, on top of a being a complete bad-ass, of course...

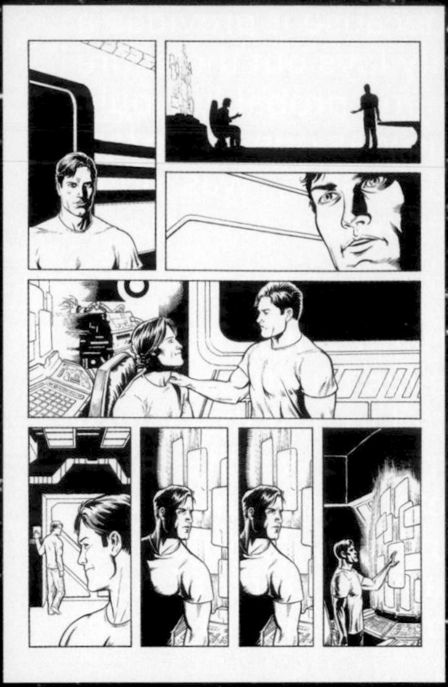
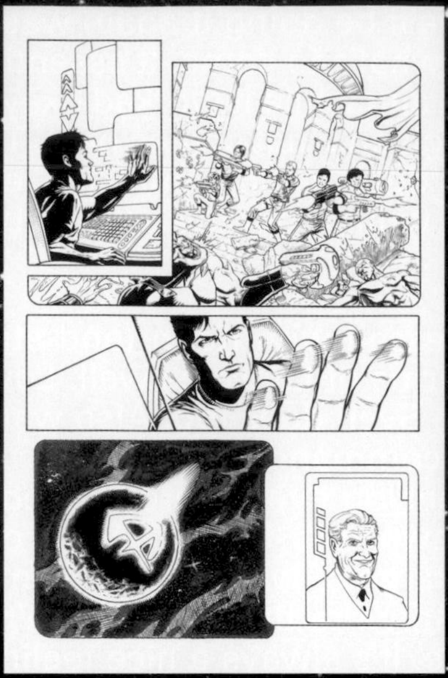
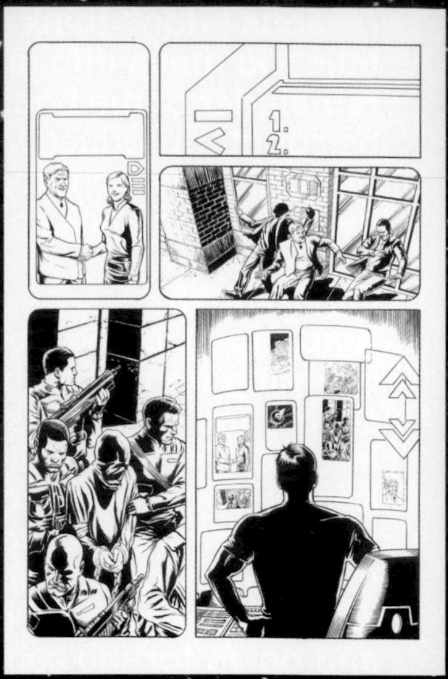

Page 22
Love this page, as I think faces and expressions are one of the many things artist Craig Cermak really excels at, and this gave him the opportunity to work with a lot of different emotions. Also like this page because it's the first in a series of unfortunate events that permanently affect our heroes, and what happens in panel one continues to happen throughout the arc, despite some of their very best efforts. Sven's greatest fear is that things will come apart and he won't be able to stop it, so of course that's exactly what begins happening. Rabins' exhausted apology offers some clue as to what direction things are headed in, but I'mconfident you guys will love some of the surprises in store. We're having a blast exploring this time period, and look for a few unexpected connections between this and the main book over the next few months...

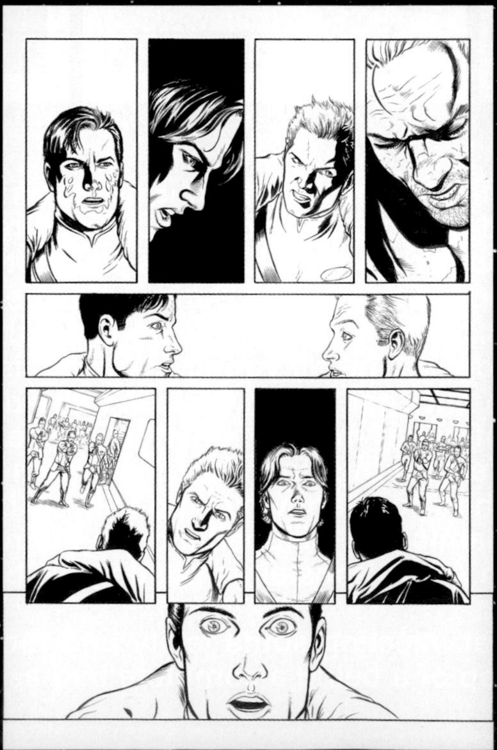

VOLTRON: YEAR ONE #2
By Brandon Thomas

Page 1
Picking up from the exact moment we left off, with Sven still doing the deer in the headlights thing. Luckily, he recovers just in time, and yes, I did sneak the word "Mercury" in there just because. This is also the point where the captioning drops away for a bit, but I really liked that last completely darkened panel with the very final piece of internal text.

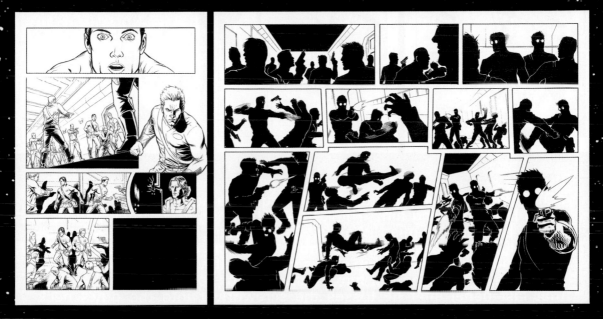

Pages 2 & 3
I'm writing my scripts completely out of sequence now, so I always try to note which page was the last one to get slotted into the final script. There's usually a reason for it, and I like figuring it out in the post-game, so if necessary, I can adjust my overall process going forward. In the case of this script, this "turn on the dark" portion of things was what got done last, and the reason was pretty simple—describing exactly what I was imagining to artist Craig Cermak was pretty damn near impossible.

It's one of those things that happens occasionally, the images look so clear in your head, but describing them on a piece of paper feels particularly daunting. Like you're going to screw it all up trying to transfer this amazing picture you have in your head into someone else's, and it's going to happen because you couldn't find the right words to bring everything across.

Fortunately, Craig is awesome, and was able to make sense of my frenzied descriptions, so the whole thing came out great. Love the eerily green night vision goggles dancing all over the page as Sven and Lance go to work. This was the first double-page spread Craig did for the series, as he made the mistake of telling me that he hadn't done that many in his young career, so obviously I had no choice but to write more and more of them into the later issues. There are two in issue 3, and they are both absolutely beautiful pieces of work. So this one, while dope in its own right, is really just the warm-up for him with this sort of thing.

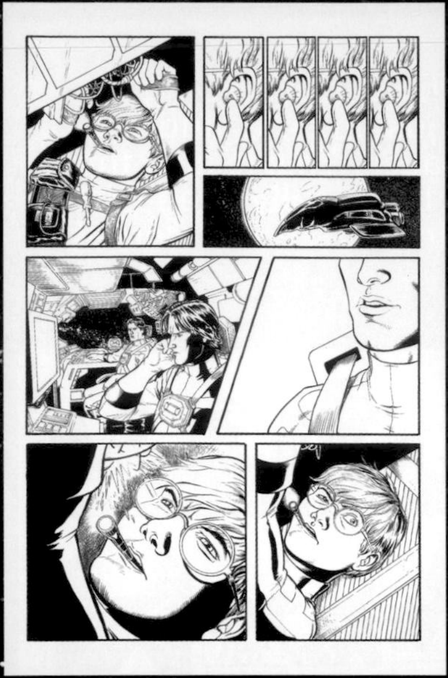

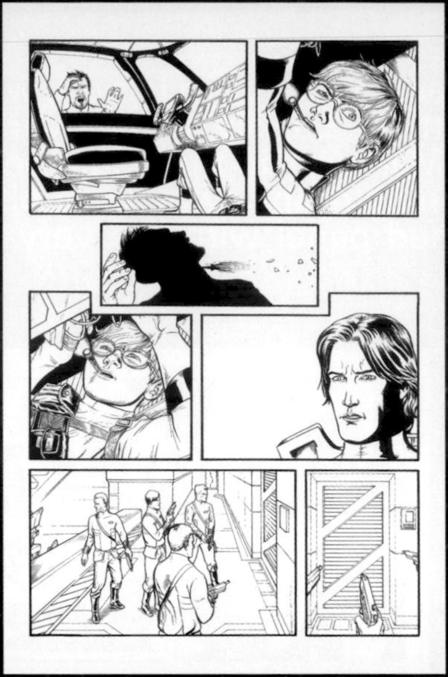

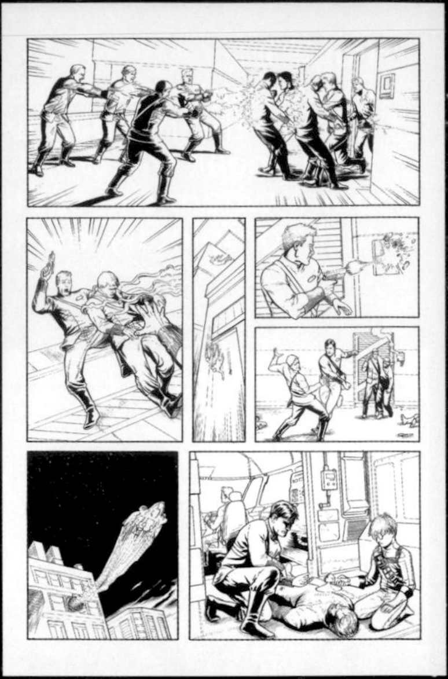

Pages 4 & 5
LOVE everything about Pidge's little sequence here, and it's clear that Craig loves drawing him. Think I described him in an interview as a cross between Damian Wayne, Barry Ween, and my own Jack Warning, which always makes him a lot of fun, cause he has a bit of an attitude and a major chip on his shoulder. It was very important for me to have someone call him "Babyface" or something similar, and that last panel after he tosses the screwdriver into the guy's neck cracks me up every time. Did make a little mistake and didn't move the text bubble far enough off Pidge's chest, so it blunts the gag's impact a bit, but think most people still caught it.

changing perspectives is always a lot of fun to play with, and the ability to cut in and out of scenes in interesting ways is something that really has no conceivable limits. In this instance, cutting the way we did helped me save a ton of space, so that we don't have to actually see the escape shuttle get attacked to get the gist of their situation. And you know, as cool as it would've been to have Craig draw that, the jump cut works a lot better, and it leads into my favorite Lance moment of the entire issue.

Seriously, the more I write him, the more I love him and this bit actually wasn't even in the draft until the last minute. Whole exchange just wasn't coming together and it just hit me that I should have Lance scream this irritated ass recap to Rabins, who awakens suddenly and is filled with a bunch of confused and ultimately unnecessary questions. Makes me laugh a little every time I see it, and think Craig did a fantastic job with the facial expression and body language there.

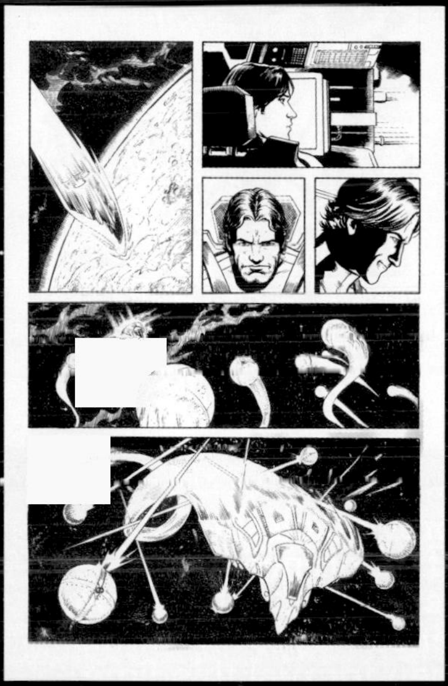

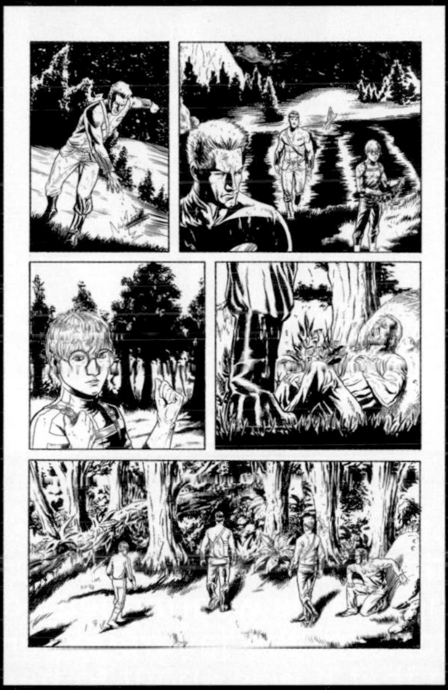

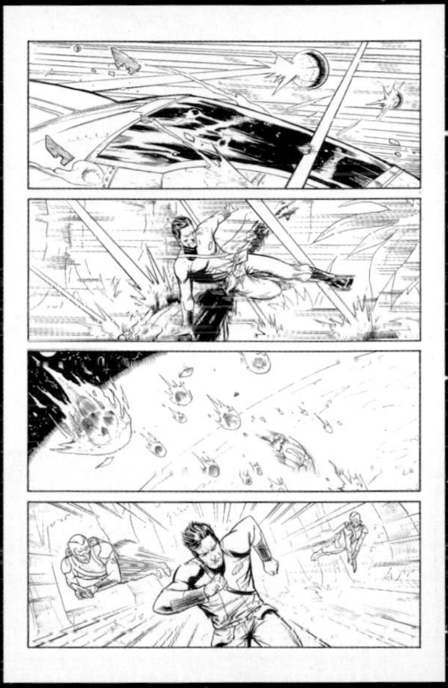

Page 9
This was the first page I wrote for the issue, and this entire middle section with the crash, the jetpack chase sequence, and Rabins' eventual demise came out of me real easy. Every issue is different, sometimes it's the major set pieces, or a real dialogue heavy exchange between two characters, but I've learned not to fight with the initial impulse and start everything by writing what wants to get written first. Here, it was this explosive image of a shuttle plunging into a lake in the middle of a dark forest. The final color work by Adriano Lucas is fantastic, as usual, but I'll probably end up buying the original page from Craig because of the cool "starry night" effect he got from flicking little bits of whiteout (or maybe it was regular paint) across the page.

Oh, and that last panel there? That's Commander Keith Kogane, making a brief appearance from the near future, to give an order with an obvious intensity and a level of self-assuredness that he's not currently capable of bringing on a regular basis. He'll get there though, and this was meant to really foreshadow the direction everything is headed in over the next couple months. There's a confident leader in there somewhere, and the next several weeks are going to slowly draw it out of him, whether he wants it or not.

Pages 12 & 13

Lot of times, I have to make myself shut up and let the actions speak for themselves, but that was pretty easy here. Thought Craig would rock it and he did. Quick note about 13 is that even though I didn't want any actual text on either of these pages, the script called for a couple more panels on the page and one look at Craig's layouts told me that was a really bad idea on my part. Fortunately, we were able [redacted] just and I apologized for it, 'cause in hindsight what I was asking [redacted] was dumb. Funny that even without dialogue, I'm still fully capable of making my artist's job even harder.

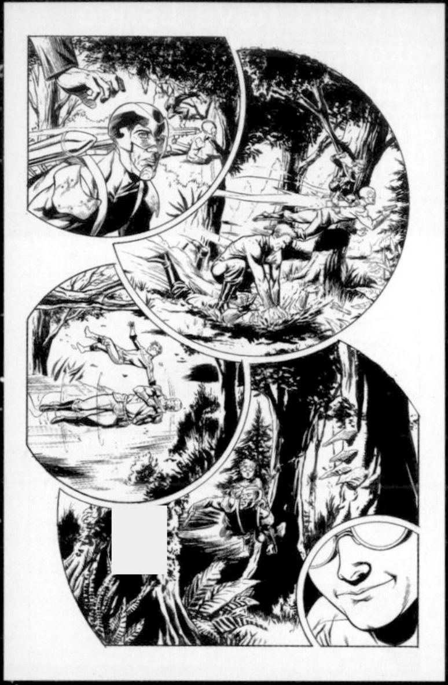

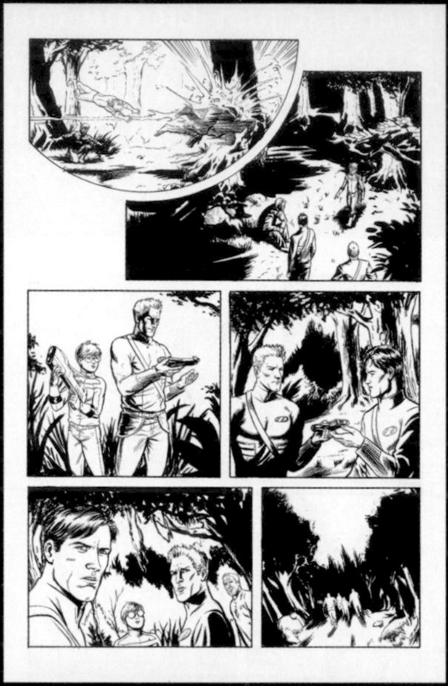

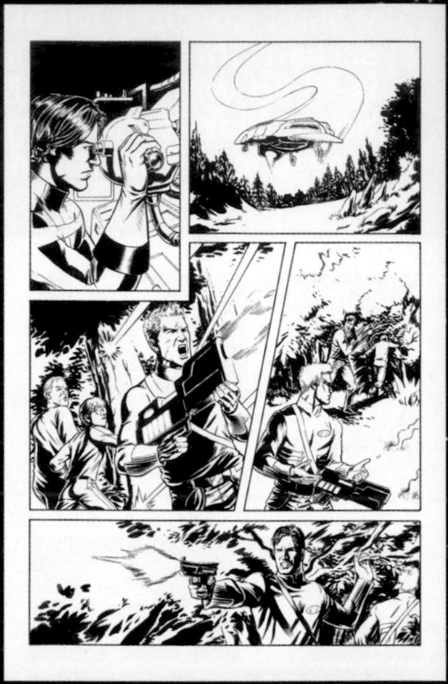

Page 16

This page is a mirror of the first page from the previous issue, with a few background alterations and another couple of differences—-Lance in the place of Keith, the guards wearing jetpacks instead of being on foot, etc. Was meant to echo the failure experienced by Sven in his dream, and clue you in that it was about to happen for real this time. Too bad, the more I write him the more I like him and appreciate what he's dealing with, so I almost feel bad for tipping the first of many dominos leading to his big fall.

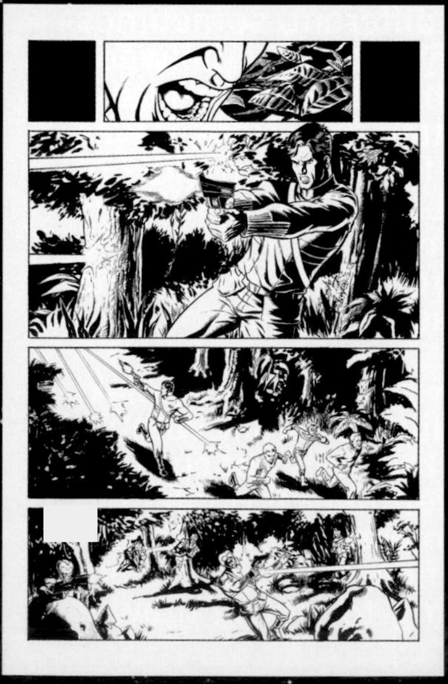

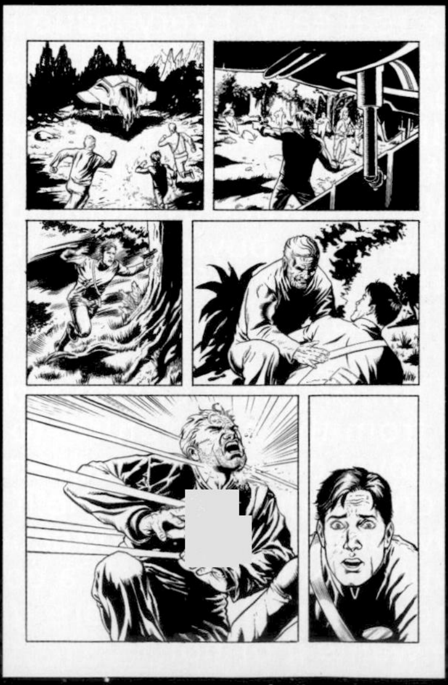

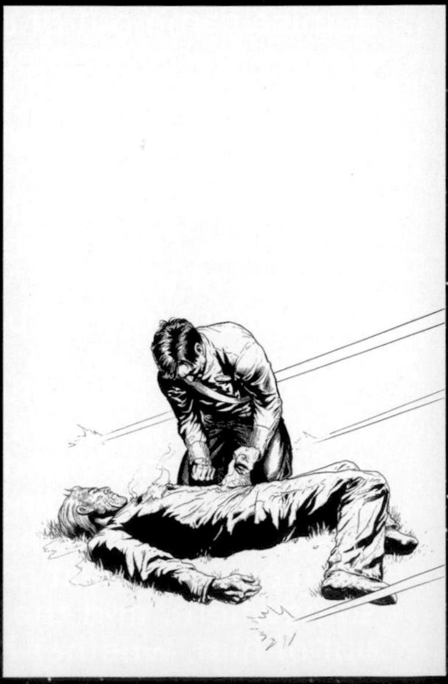

Page 18
Easily my favorite page of the issue, and think Craig did a fantastic job here! Man, just look at it, isn't that awesome!? Know that he wasn't too too happy with the title page from the first issue, so he wanted to really put his foot into this one and he just killed it. Also, Adriano destroyed the colors, and the red accents really give the whole thing an additional weight and heft to everything. Sven just looks crushed here, like the entire world has dropped on his shoulders. Logo and stuff looks great too, props to Simon Bowland. Did I already mention this is my favorite page of the book? Everyone brought that A-game, and it was a moment that really called for it. This is the beginning of the end for Sven...

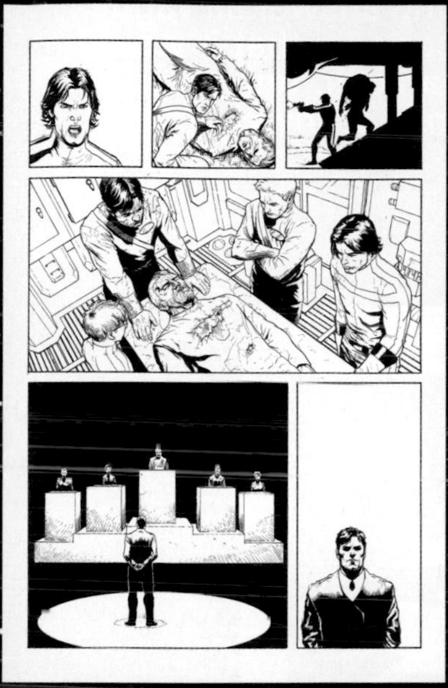

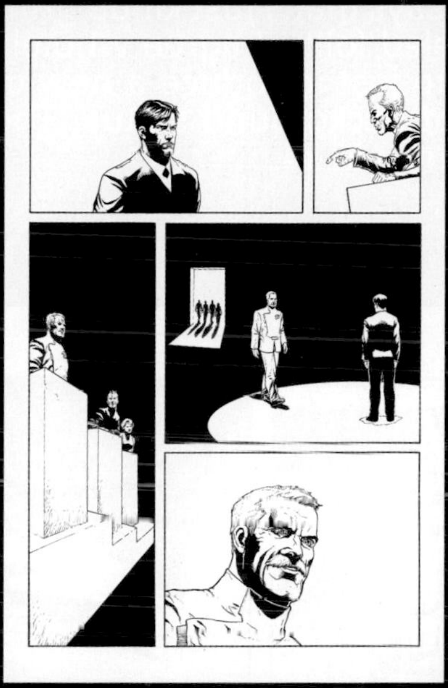

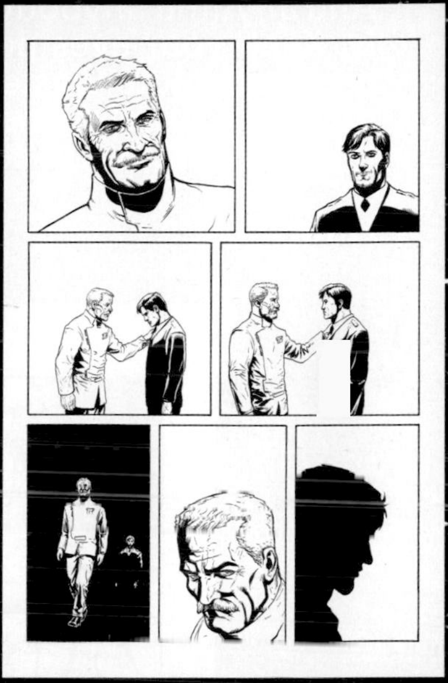

Page 19
I actually wrote a version of this awhile back when Dynamite was still auditioning artists for the main book. It was a little one page scene that had Keith sparring with a general who was none too pleased over something the Voltron Force did, leading into a double page spread that had Voltron dodging missiles or something. But the general idea of the team's commander being questioned in front of this world's version of a military tribunal stayed with me, and given what just happened with Sven, seemed very appropriate to utilize it here. None of the dialogue or anything was usable of course, but some of the imagery described there got shifted over here and tweaked.

Page 21
It's a little overt, but Sven's entire character arc in this story is essentially spelled out in this exchange with his friend and sometimes confidant Dylan. It was important to reveal that someone in a position of command and influence is well aware of Sven's struggles, and that despite them, he still maintains a strong, unwavering belief in him and his abilities. And that's what this entire thing is about—belief. As you'll soon learn in the next few issues, Sven is a more than capable leader, who thinks on his feet and always strives to do the right thing. He's a damn good shot too. Every member of his team trusts him to keep them all safe, no matter the situation, and would gladly walk in front of a bullet for him. The problem of course, the most important thing to consider, is that none of that means anything if Sven doesn't

believe it himself. And he doesn't, no matter the overwhelming evidence presented to the contrary.

Lack of belief is something that affects many of us at some point in our lives, and left unchecked, it can destroy everything we ever have the potential to become. And this is the major problem that Sven will be facing down in the next few issues, and watching him fight against it with everything he has will make for some interesting decisions down the line.

Page 22
People keep asking me, "Man, who is that girl in Sven's bed...? What's up with her? She's not just going to be in bed the whole time is she?" And anytime anybody says that, I just kinda grin and answer all vaguely. Keep your eyes peeled folks; I agree wholeheartedly that it would be an absolute waste to just introduce a new character, only to commit them to permanent background status. There's a tiny clue in #3, then full disclosure comes in #4.

Until then...